Narratives of Individuation

In *Narratives of Individuation*, Raya A. Jones and Leslie Gardner present 12 cutting-edge essays that bridge Jungian and narrative approaches to self-understanding, and offer critical appraisal of both approaches. Exploring the Jungian concept of individuation and the related interest in dreams, as well as the premise of the narrative self and the related interest in life-stories, this innovative volume interprets the topic in unique and unprecedented ways.

An outstanding selection of contributors covers several overarching themes to provide a comprehensive understanding of these two powerful narratives. The contributors explore historical and conceptual issues concerning the narrative self, as well as applying it, including to Jung's autobiography. Chapters also examine how Jung developed his theory of individuation, and engage with contemporary thinking in anthropology, psychology (including the dialogical self) and Jungian psychotherapy, towards refiguring how people arrive at self-understanding. Written by leaders in the field, *Narratives of Individuation* is a valuable interdisciplinary resource that illuminates a multitude of perspectives on individuation and self-realisation.

Owing to its original ideas and breadth of scope, *Narratives of Individuation* will appeal to academics and students of Jungian and post-Jungian studies, anthropology, psychology, literary studies and anyone examining concepts of selfhood and the significance of narrativity. It will also be of great interest to Jungian analysts and psychotherapists, and analytical psychologists.

Raya A. Jones, PhD, is Reader in the School of Social Sciences, Cardiff University, UK. Her academic interests include Jungian, narrative and dialogical perspectives on the self. She has authored, edited and co-edited several books in the field, as well as numerous journal articles.

Leslie Gardner, PhD, is Fellow in the Department of Psychosocial and Psychoanalytic Studies at the University of Essex, UK. She was among the founders of the International Association of Jungian Studies, and its journal, *International Journal of Jungian Studies*. She has authored and co-edited several books in Jungian studies.

Narratives of Individuation

Edited by
Raya A. Jones and
Leslie Gardner

Routledge
Taylor & Francis Group
LONDON AND NEW YORK

First published 2019
by Routledge
2 Park Square, Milton Park, Abingdon, Oxon OX14 4RN

and by Routledge
52 Vanderbilt Avenue, New York, NY 10017

Routledge is an imprint of the Taylor & Francis Group, an informa business

British Library Cataloguing-in-Publication Data
A catalogue record for this book is available from the British Library

Library of Congress Cataloging-in-Publication Data
Names: Jones, Raya A., editor. | Gardner, Leslie, 1949- editor.
Title: Narratives of individuation / [edited by] Raya A. Jones and Leslie Gardner.
Description: Abingdon, Oxon ; New York : Routledge, 2019. | Includes index.
Identifiers: LCCN 2018054429 (print) | LCCN 2018057147 (ebook) | ISBN 9780429202667 (Master eBook) | ISBN 9780815367499 (hardback) | ISBN 9780815367543 (pbk.)
Subjects: LCSH: Individuation (Psychology) | Jungian psychology.
Classification: LCC BF175.5.I53 (ebook) | LCC BF175.5.I53 N37 2019 (print) | DDC 155.2–dc23
LC record available at https://lccn.loc.gov/2018054429

ISBN: 978-0-8153-6749-9 (hbk)
ISBN: 978-0-8153-6754-3 (pbk)
ISBN: 978-0-429-20266-7 (ebk)

Typeset in Times New Roman
by Wearset Ltd, Boldon, Tyne and Wear

Contents

Contributors

Paul Bishop is the William Jacks Chair of Modern Languages, University of Glasgow. His most recent publications include *Ludwig Klages and the Philosophy of Life: A Vitalist Toolkit* (Routledge, 2018) and *On the Blissful Islands: With Nietzsche & Jung in the Shadow of the Superman* (Routledge, 2017). He also edited *The Archaic: The Past in the Present* (Routledge, 2011) and (with Leslie Gardner) *The Ecstatic and the Archaic: An Analytical Psychological Inquiry* (Routledge, 2018).

Terence Dawson spent the larger part of his academic career in Singapore. Now retired, he continues to pursue his interest in the relation of Jungian theory to literature and the other arts. He is the co-editor of *The Cambridge Companion to Jung* (2nd edn, 2008) and the author of *The Effective Protagonist in the Nineteenth-Century British Novel* (2004), as well as wide-ranging articles on English, European and Asian literature.

Fabrice Olivier Dubosc is an intercultural psychoanalyst. He has been active in interdisciplinary and interreligious practices in different countries. As an ethno-clinician he operates in a number of settings, supervising clinical aspects of trauma- and migration-related dynamics for communities and institutions involved in refugee relief. He has been recently supervising psycho-social and anthropological aspects of the 'Bodies Across Borders' project for the European University Institute in Florence. He teaches intercultural therapies at a Postgraduate School in psychotherapy in Rome. The main focus of his present psycho-social research is the dialogue between eco-systemic concerns and postcolonial critical thinking.

Mark Freeman is Distinguished Professor of Ethics and Society in the Department of Psychology at the College of the Holy Cross in Worcester, Massachusetts. His writings include *Rewriting the Self: History, Memory, Narrative*; *Finding the Muse: A Sociopsychological Inquiry into the Conditions of Artistic Creativity*; *Hindsight: The Promise and Peril of Looking Backward*; and *The Priority of the Other: Thinking and Living Beyond the Self*. Winner of the 2010 Theodore R. Sarbin Award in the Society for Theoretical and

Philosophical Psychology, he also serves as editor for the Oxford University Press series 'Explorations in Narrative Psychology'.

Leslie Gardner, PhD, is an Honorary Fellow in the Department of Psychosocial and Psychoanalytic Studies, University of Essex. She has headed an international literary agency based in London since 1986, and convenes conferences on depth psychology. She authored *Rhetorical Investigations: GB Vico and CG Jung* (Routledge 2012) based on her thesis, co-edited several books, the latest, *The Ecstatic and the Archaic* (Routledge 2018), with Paul Bishop, and *Feminist Views from Somewhere* with Frances Gray (Routledge 2017). Recently her chapter on Von Franz and Jean Cocteau's 'Beauty and the Beast' appeared in *The Routledge International Handbook of Jungian Film Studies* (2018). Gardner was a committee member and the treasurer of the International Association for Jungian Studies.

Vincent W. Hevern, S.J., PhD, is Professor of Psychology at Le Moyne College, Syracuse, NY, a Fellow of the American Psychological Association (APA) and a licensed clinical psychologist. His scholarly work has focused upon the theoretical, methodological, and historical foundations of narrative as an ongoing perspective in psychology; emerging internet environments in the construction of the self; and dialogical aspects of identity development and the self. He was the first Internet Editor for the Society for the Teaching of Psychology, Division 2 of APA and served as Managing and Associate Editor of *The International Journal for Dialogical Science* for over a decade.

Raya A. Jones, PhD, is a Reader at the School of Social Sciences, Cardiff University, where she teaches psychology. Her long-term research interests include Jungian, narrative and dialogical approaches to the self, and, more recently, social robotics. Her latest authored book is *Personhood and Social Robotics* (Routledge 2016). Earlier books include *Jung, Psychology, Postmodernity* (Routledge, 2007) and *The Child–School Interface* (Cassell, 1995) and several edited and co-edited volumes in Jungian studies. She has published many journal articles. Jones was a committee member of the International Association for Jungian Studies (2003–2009).

Christian Roesler, Prof. Dr. Dipl.-Psych., is a Professor of Clinical Psychology at the Catholic University of Applied Sciences in Freiburg, a lecturer of Analytical Psychology at the University of Basel, Jungian analyst in private practice in Freiburg, and a member of the faculty of the C.G. Jung Institutes in Stuttgart and Zurich. His specialisations are in work with couples and families, and interpretive research methods. He researches and publishes on analytical psychology and contemporary sciences, couple counselling, postmodern identity construction, narrative research and media psychology.

Mark Saban trained with the Independent Group of Analytical Psychologists, with whom he is a senior analyst, working in London and Oxford. He is also a lecturer in Jungian and post-Jungian studies in the Department of Psycho-social and Psychoanalytic Studies, University of Essex. Saban co-edited *Analysis and Activism: Social and Political Contributions of Jungian Psychology* (Routledge 2016) with Emilija Kiehl and Andrew Samuels. Recent articles include 'Segrete e Bugie. Un'area cieca nella psicologia junghiana' (*Rivista di psicologia analitica* 95, 2017) and 'Outside-In: Jung's myth of interiority ambiguated Or Knowing me, Knowing Jung – aha!' (*Journal of Analytical Psychology* 63, 2018).

Inna Semetsky has a PhD in educational philosophy preceded by an MA in family therapy. She was a postdoctoral fellow at Monash University and research academic in the University of Newcastle (Australia). She has over 150 academic publications including ten books. Her research focuses on semiotics (the study of signs) and her 2015 book *Edusemiotics* (co-authored) received the Award from the Philosophy of Education Society of Australasia. Her new book, *Learning with the Unconscious: Semiotic Subjectivity in Education and Counselling*, is forthcoming with Routledge. She serves as a chief consultant to the recently established Institute for Edusemiotic Studies (IES). She is also a long-time Tarot reader.

Megumi Yama, PhD, is a professor in the faculty of Humanities at Kyoto Gakuen University in Japan. She also engages in psychotherapy, mainly based on Jungian thought. She was educated at Kyoto University under Professor Hayao Kawai. Her interest is in images and words. She deals with these themes by exploring clinical materials, art, myth, literature and Japanese culture. She has written many articles and books both in English and Japanese. She was a visiting researcher at Harvard University in 2015 and a visiting fellow at University of Essex, 2008–2009. She gave seminars in the US, UK, China and Taiwan.

Introduction

Raya A. Jones

Narratives of Individuation brings together two powerful narratives about self-understanding. One narrative originates in depth psychology and pivots on a unique concept of individuation that the Swiss psychiatrist Carl Gustav Jung articulated in the first half of the twentieth century. It remains central in Jungian clinical practice, and various aspects of Jung's analytical psychology have become topics for scholarship in the humanities. The other narrative emerged in the second half of the twentieth century, initially in the humanities and later in the social sciences, and has been articulated by many scholars who locate self-understanding in the unfolding of one's personal narrative. This postmodern 'turn' to narrative has constellated into distinctive research programmes that involve analyses of life stories, written and oral, and cut across disciplines within the academia. Interdisciplinarity characterises both the Jungian and narrative movements; but the two have not merged. They seem separated by a shared terminology, each having a different construal of selfhood, individuation, and the significance of narrativity.

What is 'individuation'? According to the 2018 online edition of the *Oxford English Dictionary (OED)*, individuation is '1. The state or condition of being an individual; separate and continuous existence as a single indivisible entity; individuality, personal identity.' It is also '2. a. The action or process of forming something into an individual entity, or of distinguishing an individual entity from others of the same kind. Also: the process of becoming an individual person or entity, individualization.' *Narratives of Individuation* prompts a critical evaluation of the postmodern attribution of personal identity construction to autobiographical telling. We may concur with Charles Taylor (1989, p. 47) that the fact 'we grasp our lives in a narrative' is an 'inescapable feature of human life … a basic condition of making sense of ourselves', and yet wonder whether there's more to human self-experience than narrativity.

The Jungian framework, with its emphasis of the unconscious, provides an Archimedean vantage point from which to critique the postmodern view. The *OED* informs: '2 d. *Psychology*. In the analytical system of C. G. Jung: the process of establishing the wholeness and autonomy of the individual self by integrating consciousness and the collective unconscious. Also more fully *individuation process.*' Under this entry the dictionary quotes, inter alia, Jung (1921, para. 757): 'Individuation, therefore, is a process of differentiation, having for its goal the development of the individual personality.' When read out of context, however, this quotation fails to convey the extent to which the Jungian concept opposes notions of individualisation. He employs the term 'differentiation' to denote a refinement of psychological functions (thinking, feeling, sensation and intuition) – for instance, 'Undifferentiated thinking is ... continuously mixed up with sensations, feelings, intuitions' (Jung 1921, para. 705). For Jung, the 'goal of the individuation process is the synthesis of the self' (Jung 1940, para. 278). His idea is close to what the *OED* lists under the phrase, *principle of individuation*: 'b. Chiefly *Metaphysics*. The principle by which the constituent parts of something are integrated into a single whole.' *Narratives of Individuation* prompts a critical evaluation of Jung's metaphysics. The narrative framework and other postmodern frames-of-reference (e.g. dialogical, psychosocial), with their emphasis on relational being or the social genesis of selves, provide an Archimedean vantage point from which to critique the Jungian premise.

Three general themes guide the sequence of the chapters, though we resist the division of the book into Parts. The themes overlap, and chapters thematically lead into each other, as follows.

Theme 1: the examined life

In the heyday of postmodernism and specifically in the context of the narrative movement, Socrates' counterfactual, 'the unexamined life is not worth living', became a kind of slogan. It was oft-quoted towards asserting that the worth of one's life unfolds by virtue of examining it, and therefore the examined life is the life worth living. For some, the adage served to justify the analysis of autobiographies. This cluster of chapters includes this element too, but also goes beyond any simplistic application.

In Chapter 1, which may serve as an extended introduction, Raya Jones defends the characterisation of Jungian and narrative psychologies as each other's 'other' through a critical comparison of their respective ontologies and epistemologies. Jones uses a real-life vignette to engage with the question of what each psychology enables us to see (and what it leaves out) regarding the processes whereby people find meaning in their lives.

The historical reflection specifically on the narrative movement that is introduced in Chapter 1 is taken further, in greater depth, by Mark Freeman in Chapter 2. Freeman, himself a major exponent of narrative psychology since the 1990s, provides a critical retrospect, querying some aspects of the original argument for narrative knowing. In a way, he challenges the challenge that decades ago he and others had articulated. The butt of their argument was the traditional conceptualisation of development in psychology; that is, development described as maturation towards a predetermined end-goal. We can find the contested conception of teleological progress also in the Jungian idea of individuation as an optimal end-state of adult development. Nevertheless, Freeman approvingly highlights other aspects of Jung's theory. He also raises important questions of ethics and values. To paraphrase, individuation involves a movement of coming-to-consciousness, but the quality of the resultant insight could vary from a gratifying sense of self-realisation to a horrifying sense of the profound ways in which one has been in the dark. Freeman defines individuation as an interpretive process.

While the narrative framework locates the interpretive process in the unfolding of self-narratives – whether these life stories are explicitly told or implicitly lived by – the Jungian framework attends to a vertical movement, a thrust upward to consciousness. Individuation in the Jungian sense is both an ideal state of being (marked by a balance across conscious and unconscious elements of the self) and personal development towards this state. Jung postulated a regulating principle, whereby the unconscious has its say in dreams, artwork, myths, fairy tales, visions or hallucinations, the themes of which compensate for the one-sidedness of ego-consciousness. It nevertheless involves an interpretive process. The spontaneous thrust would remain ineffective, a dream forgotten soon upon waking, unless it stirred a 'horizontal' movement by entering one's conscious dialogue-with-oneself and with others through engagement with one's images (especially under the guidance of a Jungian analyst). In Chapter 3, Megumi Yama demonstrates this process in practice. She presents a case study concerning a young woman, 'Min', that speaks for itself: the account shows how Min's dreams and self-narrative intertwined over time, and intertwined also with Yama's own narrative about her, all of which progressively led to Min's empowered sense of her personal identity as a third-generation ethnic Korean in Japan.

Issues of identity in cultural contexts became highly topical in the closing decades of the last century. Sociologists and anthropologists noted how globalisation, accelerated change, and the fragmentation of society, led to a dissolution of the 'grand narratives' of politics and science and, instead, the 'small' narratives of real lives became prominent. Auto/biographies became popular, and also attracted scholarly interest. The trend manifested itself in an interest in Jung's autobiography, *Memories, Dreams, Reflections*, in its own right (as opposed to an interest in Jung's theory per se). Fascinated by how a life becomes a text, literary critic James Olney (1972) analysed Jung's autobiography, unperturbed by the extent to which it was edited and partially written by Aneila Jaffé. Yet, Jung (and Jaffé) had an agenda. In Chapter 4, Leslie Gardner interrogates Jung's memoirs alongside Augustine's *Confessions* and Giambattista Vico's *Autobiography*, and underlines autobiographical narratives as agenda-driven.

Theme 2: 'Jung' examined

The chapters clustered here represent a 'stream' within contemporary Jungian studies, which is characterised by critiques of how Jung went about developing his theory. A focus on Jung's *Memories, Dreams, Reflections* is carried into

Chapter 5, but in this chapter Mark Saban challenges us to consider the extent to which the canons of analytical psychology are owed to Jung's personal myth. Saban's analysis of the autobiography highlights Jung's self-reported sense of having two personalities (Personality No. 1 and Personality No. 2) and how these conjointly influenced his life-course choices. This personal myth of 'split' personality may have underpinned not only Jung's interpretation of the particular course that his own life had taken, but also his formation of a model of the psyche as a divided whole.

In Chapter 6, Paul Bishop points to the unfolding of Jung's personal narrative in a different, more existential way. Bishop proposes to view the opus of Jung's *Red Book* (originally a folio manuscript in which Jung gave free rein to his fantasies, musings and visions) as a self-narrative – not in the autobiographical sense, but in the sense that the narration of the fantasies that gushed forth from Jung's unconscious at the time follows a conventional narrative configuration (a crisis-to-resolution plot line).

In Chapter 7, Terence Dawson goes as far as to suggest, provocatively, that the application of analytical psychology in clinical practice is an offshoot of Jung's analysis of texts that caught his imagination; and that his works first and foremost present a narrative or textual theory. Indeed, Jung's later writings seldom provide clinical material and, instead, present analyses of myths, fairy tales, medieval and ancient texts, and (to a lesser extent) literary works. Dawson problematises Jung's assumptions about the spontaneity or 'purity' of written fantasies, using E. T. A. Hoffmann's 'The Golden Pot' to make his own case.

Literary stylistics have long explored many approaches to narrative, but it seems that only in the twentieth century was the language of the psychological interior first assimilated into narratology, insofar as the modern study of texts approaches stylistics as dynamically motivated, revealing personal drives and agendas. Chapter 4 shows how autobiographies may serve their authors' agendas. In Chapter 8, Leslie Gardner contrasts Jung's assumption about the significance of affect in the process of individuation with the role of affect in the rhetorical device of *narratio* as discussed in the classics. She suggests that while the ancients problematised the rhetorical use of affect, Jung might have place too much faith in the authenticity of emotional 'irruptions'.

Theme 3: 'individuation' refigured

Paul Ricoeur (1984) identified three aspects of narratively representing human experience in literary fiction: prefiguration, configuration and refiguration. The same may apply also to how *Narratives of Individuation* presents its topic. In Ricoeur's literary theory, prefiguration refers to the fact that any fiction presupposes some prior understanding of the real world. Likewise, this volume's expositions of theories and practices – and our very project of bringing them together – reflect prior understanding of the fields in which those theories and practices have emerged. For Ricoeur, narrative configuration denotes how events are assembled into a narrative with a plot. Here, our ordering of the chapters 'tells a story'. We arrive at refiguration: 'an endless spiral' that could revisit the same point from different attitudes (Ricoeur 1984, p. 72). The final juxtaposition of chapters samples the 'fluidity' of the topic area that *Narratives of Individuation* seeks to demarcate. Narratives about individuation are in constant flux even within a well-defined frame-of-reference such as the Jungian, let alone the more nebulous narrative-centred. Particular premises are revisited, reformulated, partially or wholly abandoned by some exponents, and at the same time traditional insights continue to inspire, be applied and elaborated, by others. In our journey through the following chapters, we first move away from Jungian and narrative psychologies, and then return afresh to the 'old' concept.

Jung (e.g. 1950) referred to mandala symbolism as intuitive representations of the self as a complex whole, symmetrically differentiated – and closed. In Chapter 9, Fabrice Dubosc challenges that monadic conception. He prompts attention to the 'open' mandala implied in contemporary anthropology and philosophy. His tour-de-force of current trends draws upon Viveiros de Castro's ethno-narrative of disempowered cultures, Gilbert Simondon's philosophy of the transindividual, and more. Dubosc's account underscores ontologies that decentre from the 'I' of individuated human consciousness and reposition the possibility of consciousness in a relational web that also includes nonhumans and ecosystems.

In Chapter 10, Vincent Hevern directs our attention to everyday life as lived in this century – life with the internet and social media. It is perhaps significant that, in this chapter and other recent publications, Hevern (who promoted narrative psychology throughout the late 1990s and 2000s in a website he had created) considers the impact of communication technologies on human experience through the lens of Hubert Hermans' theory of the dialogical self. The move from the narrative metaphor of the self to the dialogical, with its Bakhtinian emphasis on multivoicedness, has been a 'natural' progression for some psychologists (Raya Jones included).

Having moved a considerable distance away from the Jungian tradition in the above two chapters, we conclude the volume with two chapters that represent contemporary work in the spirit of this tradition.

Interestingly but unsurprisingly, the narrative movement that swept across the academia has made little impact in the Jungian world. The late-twentieth century zeitgeist also manifested itself in subtle shifts of emphasis in the Jungian world – shifts that are sometimes presented as if seamlessly continuous with Jung's own thought, sometimes problematising it. While there is no evidence for a 'narrative turn' within the Jungian community, sporadic publications sought to connect Jungian ideas with narratology (e.g. Roesler 2006; Dobson 2008). In his early work, Christian Roesler (2006) drew directly upon narrative psychology (citing Jerome Bruner and Dan McAdams) towards developing a narratological methodology for identifying archetypal story patterns in life stories. Nevertheless, the very quest for archetypal pattern affirmed his commitment to Jungian ontology.

Reinforcing this commitment in Chapter 11, Roesler directs attention to the 'second' author of the self, the unconscious (originally understated or ignored by narrative psychologists), and reports a new index for content analysis of dream series, a Structural Dreams Analysis (SDA), developed by him. As Dawson (Chapter 7) puts it, key to the Jungian concept of individuation is that active confrontation with one's dreams over time could lead to a balanced acceptance of oneself, but Jung realised that it is not easy to measure such change in a person. As seen, Yama (Chapter 3) provides a vivid example of such confrontation; she mostly lets the dreams speak – a narrative of individuation unfolds in the telling – but also reflects on her own subjective responses. This could hardly be more diametrically opposed to Roesler's SDA procedure, whereby patients' dreams are coded by several 'blinded' interpreters who are deliberately not told anything about the dreamer and the case history. Put side by side, Chapters 3 and 11 demonstrate two very different directions in which the 'classic' Jungian premise is translated into clinical practice.

Finally, while the creation of self-narratives through the interpretation of dreams – as well as 'spontaneous' paintings (see Chapter 8) – is staple in Jungian practice, in Chapter 12 Inna Semetsky takes *Narratives of Individuation* along the 'road less travelled' (although extensively explored in her numerous publications): self-understanding by means of reading and interpreting the archetypal images of Tarot cards.

Summing up, the various roads travelled towards self-understanding are sampled here, albeit with particular reference to the Jungian. Jung started to lay the conceptual cornerstones of his analytical psychology in the 1910s. By mid-century, Jung (1954) regarded his own concept of individuation as confirmed, so much so that 'To one familiar with our psychology, it may seem a waste of time to keep harping on the long-established difference between ... the coming-to-be of the self (individuation)' and 'the coming of the ego into consciousness' (Jung 1954, para. 432). Having embarked upon the project of *Narratives of Individuation*, we do not regard it as 'a waste of time' to harp on the difference between the two aspects of self-experiencing. On the contrary, it is important to consider both.

Historically, the Jungian and narrative movements appear like islands within the vast sea of modern discourses about selfhood. For decades, the two of us (Jones and Gardner) navigated the waters between the Jungian and the narrative in our own ways and from our respective backgrounds in the humanities (Gardner) and the social sciences (Jones). Gardner's study of rhetoric and the classics in the context of Jungian studies links to psychoanalytical-psychosocial and feminist theories, whereas Jones' engagement with Jungian studies is grounded in social psychology, in particular dialogical and narrative frameworks. In conceiving the idea for an edited book, we wished to create a space for voices other than only our own, even if particular essays remain in one 'island' or the other. We hope that the juxtaposition of the essays will allow readers who are familiar with one perspective and not with the other to get a glimpse of the other shore.

The promise of the book does not end there. While both the Jungian and narrative movements continue to thrive at the time of writing, following their own trajectories, neither is the 'last word' historically. The present-day zeitgeist – with its discourses of posthumanism and transhumanism, cyberspace, New Materialism, the Age of the Brain, 'turns' to affect, and debates about the Anthropocene – puts the original canons of both Jungian and narrative psychologies under scrutiny within their respective intellectual communities. *Narratives of Individuation* arrives at this arena.

References

Dobson, D. (2008) *Transformative Teaching.* Rotterdam: Sense.

Jung, C. G.: the following are from *The Collected Works of C. G. Jung* (CW). London: Routledge & Kegan Paul/Princeton, NJ: Princeton University Press.

Jung, C. G. (1921) Psychological Types. (CW 6).

Jung, C. G. (1940) The psychology of the child archetype. (CW 9i).

Jung, C. G. (1950) Concerning mandala symbolism. (CW 9i).

Jung, C. G. (1954) On the nature of the psyche. (CW 8).

Olney, J. (1972) *Metaphors of Self.* Princeton, NJ: Princeton University Press.

Ricoeur, P. (1984) *Time and Narrative* (Vol. 1). Chicago, IL: Chicago University Press.

Roesler, C. (2006) A narratological methodology for identifying archetypal story patterns in autobiographical narratives. *Journal of Analytical Psychology* 51, 574–586.

Taylor, C. (1989) *Sources of the Self.* Cambridge: Cambridge University Press.

Chapter 1

Dialogues with a talking skull that refuses to speak

Jungian and narrative psychologies

Raya A. Jones

Coming across a talking skull

A hunter walking in the jungle came across a human skull, and wondered aloud, 'What brought you here?' To his astonishment, the skull replied. 'Talking brought me here,' it said. The hunter ran back to the village to tell the king. The king didn't believe him and sent a guard to verify the hunter's story, with orders to kill him if it wasn't true. All day long the hunter begged the skull to speak but it remained silent. The hunter was killed. As his head rolled next to the skull, the skull asked, 'What brought you here?' The hunter's head replied, 'Talking brought me here.'

This tale is widespread throughout sub-Saharan Africa. The above paraphrases a version collected from the Nupe of Nigeria, reported in Leo Frobenius' *Volksmärchen und Volksdichtungen* in 1924 (translated: Frobenius and Fox 1937/1983, p. 161). Bascom (1977) documented 43 versions gathered by various researchers. I found a few more in folktale anthologies. Often, the message is not to tell lies. Sometimes the skull talks to the executioner, who then realises that the hunter told the truth. As told by the Yoruba of Nigeria (reported in Bascom), the skull speaks to the executioner, who in turn tells the king, who sends another guard to verify the story. Again, the skull refuses to speak, the first guard is killed, and the skull talks to his executioner. The cycle repeats until an appropriate ritual of atonement is performed for the original deceased. In a Somali variant told in 1998, the skull says, 'Beware of divulging secrets, because that is what got me here, dead' (Morgan 2013, p. 181, n. 41). Morgan notes also the appearance of the tale in a novel by the Irish novelist Peter Murphy, in which an African immigrant to Ireland tells another version of the tale.

While the tale's origin is uniquely African, it has made an unexpected impact in a Welsh community. I first heard it from Jack (pseudonym), a middle-aged working-class white Welshman with no African connections. During the 1990s he used to participate in storytelling events, and came across the Frobenius and Fox version reprinted in Yolen (1986, p. 8). Not long afterwards, an acrimonious situation unfolded in his workplace, which involved a conflict with his boss over some project. Jack resorted to telling the tale to his boss in order to communicate his own frustrations. The humour diffused the immediate confrontation but didn't resolve the practical situation. Subsequently among Jack's colleagues, the phrase 'talking skull' became insider-code for situations when opening your mouth to try to improve things, or perhaps volunteering to do something, ends up making matters worse or awkward for you. Ever since he shared that anecdote with me I've been noticing talking-skull situations in my own working life. But we wouldn't be having the current dialogue with the tale if that was all.

The talking skull acquired meaningfulness beyond words for Jack. He started to collect visual reminders, such as a cartoon skull for the background on his phone and laptop, and also showed me a small skull-looking pebble he had found and kept. Why?

Hearing this 'why' as querying Jack's peculiar obsession prefigures the inquiry as a clinical or quasi-clinical case study. Investigating the case would require in-depth interviews with Jack, on the basis of which we may create some story about him (possibly co-constructed with him and likely changing his self-understanding in the process). I was not inclined to pursue the case-study line, however, and did not invite my friend to participate in formal research. His story remains anecdotal because my interest lay in the kind of inquiry where the 'why' raises theoretical issues about general processes of meaning making. The 'Jack and the Talking Skull' vignette became assimilated into my academic narratives in a variety of ways (Jones 2002, 2008, 2010, 2014).

The present return to the vignette aims to bring together Jungian and narrative approaches without losing sight of their differences. What may come into sight when we look at this empirical material through Jungian-tinted glasses? What may come into sight through a narrative-psychological lens? This is my position: the two psychologies are not options for explaining the same phenomenon. It is not a case of some phenomenon becoming an object of study, and therefore can be understood correctly or incorrectly. Instead, Jungian and narrative psychologies are discrete discourses that construct different abstract entities under similar, even identical terms, and consequently identify different phenomena as relevant for their constructs.

The problem of meaning

It's plain to see that the talking skull was meaningful to Jack, and reasonable to assume that there is a psychological explanation. The problem with 'meaning' as a scientific problem starts with the lack of consensus about what exactly is the phenomenon in question, and is exacerbated by the irony of objectively investigating subjectivity. As Jung (1948a) pointed out, modern psychology 'does not exclude the existence of faith, conviction, and experienced certainties of whatever description,' but 'completely lacks the means to prove their validity in the scientific sense' (Jung 1948a, para. 384).

Recently, the editors of a book entitled *The Psychology of Meaning* (Markman, Proulx and Lindberg 2013) announced the emergence of a science of meaning as 'a distinct discipline ... just now beginning to coalesce', commenting that the word *meaning* – formerly 'the province of existential philosophy, existential psychology, and the related clinical literature' – started to appear more frequently in social psychology, cognitive psychology, and neuroscience (Markman *et al.* 2013, p. 4). Nevertheless, as their description implies, a psychology of meaning remains a loose assemblage of ideas and issues that have diverse disciplinary trajectories and gravitate towards a shared interest. The array of contributions to Markman *et al.*'s volume attests to this heterogeneity. It also reveals a bias. While narrative psychology is duly represented in a chapter by Dan McAdams, a leading figure in this field, only three out of the 23 chapters mention Jung in passing, and none engages with what Jung had to say.

The omission of analytical psychology reflects the historical marginalisation of Jung in the academia, a situation that has resulted in ignorance about his ideas. More significantly, however, Jung and his followers approach meaning in a fundamentally different way than do traditions such as existentialist, humanistic and constructivist psychologies. In the non-Jungian contexts, the focus is on meaning-making, that is, how persons negotiate life's challenges through articulating their perceptions, feelings, and evaluations of events and situations. This presupposes a self-aware subject who *makes* meaning, however tacit the construction process might be. In contrast, Jung's analytical psychology describes how meaning *happens* to people. Our dreams, fantasies, projections and affective reactions give expression to lived experiences, and in this way make *us*, our constitution as self-aware subjects. The two psychologies may pertain to different stages in an epistemic process: someone is troubled, has dreams, intrusive thoughts and inexplicable emotions that symbolically represent her anxieties and predispose her subjective orientation (enter analytical psychology). Eventually she finds a 'narrative' that makes sense of it all (enter narrative psychology).

Yet, the two psychologies conflict regarding the origins of psychological interiority. Jungian theorising is committed to the idea of an innate blueprint for the psyche; i.e. pregiven rules or principles. This blueprint (so-called the 'objective psyche' or 'collective unconscious') disposes us towards particular kinds of experiences and governs the expression of experiences, and its constituents, archetypes, are 'the "human quality" of the human being, the specifically human form his activities take. This specific form is hereditary and is already present in the germ-plasm' (Jung 1954a, para. 152). In contrast, the discourse of 'meaning making' that emerged in psychology and psychotherapy during the second half of the last century is grounded in constructivism.

In a nutshell, constructivism holds that the human mind generates tacit rules, 'models' or templates of the world based on one's lived experiences, and these templates serve the person to make sense of past experiences and to anticipate future experiences. Mahoney and Granvold (2005) define constructivism as a meta-perspective according to which much of 'human activity is devoted to *ordering processes* – the organizational patterning of experience' – which are 'fundamentally emotional, tacit, and ... are the essence of meaning-making'

(Mahoney and Granvold 2005, p. 74, emphasis in original). Different constructivist frameworks interpret this premise differently, or bring different themes to the fore. Narrative psychology locates the ordering process in narrativity. Jungian psychology too pertains to the mental organisation of experience but (unlike constructivist theories) assumes a pre-existing biologically given template. The incommensurability of ontologies aside, the question at this juncture is which parts of this proverbial elephant – the problem of meaning – particular premises touch, and what they leave untouched. The following illustrates with concrete examples.

Apropos helping people to cope with loss and grief, constructivist therapists Gillies, Neimeyer and Milman (2014, p. 208) define *meaning-making* as a process of negotiating life's challenges by 'retaining, reaffirming, revising, or replacing elements of their orienting system to develop more nuanced, complex and useful systems'. They distinguish the meaning-making process from its outcomes, the *meanings made*. The cited paper reports the development of a 30-category coding system, the Meaning of Loss Codebook (MLC), for analysing meanings made in the wake of the death of a loved one. Gillies *et al.* propose that the MLC could aid the analysis of personal accounts of bereavement experiences such as in diaries, blogs and clinical interviews. The MLC provides a standard list of meanings-already-made by bereaved adults who could articulate their feelings. Coding the presence of particular references in someone's account, however, cannot shed light on how this person arrived at these meanings. Self-reports of feeling grief, guilt, depression, emptiness, regret about things done or left undone, or missing the deceased (Categories 21–24 of the MLC) are a step removed from the 'raw' emotional experience, which in some cases might be expressed in one's inability to talk about a traumatic loss.

Sarbin (2001), who championed narrative psychology in the 1980s, described his own grief and crying when his wife of 50 years died. He used the personal account towards a theoretical point about emotions, reiterating his ontological position that 'we live in story-shaped worlds' (Sarbin 2001, p. 218). Contending that 'actions traditionally subsumed under the substantive term "emotion," such as anger, fear, pride, joy, shame, guilt, etc., are the names of narrative plots,' he proposes that instead of regarding a grieving widow as 'a passive victim gripped by specific emotions,' we should observe that she 'has agentially gripped a narrative plot' of grief (Sarbin 2001, p. 219). The act is agentic not because one can choose to grieve or not to grieve (for instance) but because that's how human agents engage with events. Sarbin (1986) argued that virtually everything psychologists study is storied or story-like – we 'think, perceive, imagine, and make moral choices according to narrative structures' – opining that suffices it to 'reflect on any slice of life' in order to 'entertain seriously the proposal that the narratory principle guides thought and action' (Sarbin 1986, p. 8). He underlined the real even when considering fiction. Reflecting on historical cases of novels influencing lives, such as the wave of suicides that followed the 1774 publication of Goethe's *The Sorrows of Young Werther* (the protagonist commits suicide due to unrequited love), Sarbin (2004) drew attention to the power of the imagination as necessary for readers' identification with literary fiction. As I have commented elsewhere, thinking oneself 'into' a novel requires imagination, but 'it takes something else *to feel* its message so powerfully that one's own destiny ends up mimicking the fate of non-existent beings in an imaginary world' (Jones 2010, p. 561; emphasis added).

Literary works can also be their author's means of investigating something otherwise inarticulable, ill-understood or too painful (Jones 2014). Carvalho (2008) presents a clinical case study of an elderly woman approaching death. To convey his patient's melancholia, he quotes a poem, 'The Setting of the Moon' by Giacomo Leopardi, who died in his 30s after many years of ill health:

> undiminished is desire, hope extinct
> dry the wells of pleasure, pain
> ever growing, and good withheld
> forever
>
> (Carvalho 2008, 53, p. 7; Carvalho's translation)

As an expression of the poet's own end-of-life melancholia, the poem attests to meaning made through artistic creativity and symbolic representation. It is meaningful – and yet eludes analysis in the manner of reality-centred narrative analysis, let alone the aforementioned Meaning of Loss Codebook. It is knowable through qualities of feeling. Carvalho's citation involves the reader in meaning-making beyond words. If we are moved by the poem, the efficacy of its pathos demonstrates the activation of a psychological process in us. The poem creates a mood that the reader enters through empathy. If we succumb to the mood, we might end up ruminating about our own mortality.

Dialogue and subjectivity in contexts

Ruminating about mortality: the iconic image is of Hamlet holding up Yorick's skull. The Shakespearean skull doesn't talk. Hamlet's dialogue is with himself. But there is a dialogue.

According to the Russian thinker Mikhail Bakhtin, *dialogue* is the very essence of authentic human existence and its expression:

> The dialogic nature of consciousness, the dialogic nature of human life itself.... To live means to participate in dialogue: to ask questions, to heed, to respond, to agree, and so forth. In this dialogue a person participates wholly and throughout his whole life: with his eyes, lips, hands, soul, spirit, with his whole body and deeds.
>
> (Bakhtin 1984, p. 293)

Bakhtin's dialogism provides not only a kind of answer to the problem of meaning – more precisely, a direction – but also an epistemology. The ontological statement encapsulated in the above quotation sets a direction for investigating meaning-making as an emergent property of embodied dialogic participation (consciousness), with the corollary that meanings-made depend on the particular context. Bakhtin coined the term *heteroglossia* to express the fact that the same word can have different meanings when uttered under different sets of conditions. Epistemology-wise, dialogism provides a lens through which to engage with one's subject matter (Jones 2017).

Bakhtin (1986) described scholarship as a 'special kind of dialogue' that consists of complex interrelations between a given text constituting the object of study and the 'framing' context that is created through 'questioning, refuting, and so forth' this text (Bakhtin 1986, pp. 106–107). Bringing Jungian and narrative perspectives together in the course of questioning, refuting, and so forth their respective claims creates a context that frames them in relation to each other, and generates some narrative about them both.

Both Jungian and narrative psychologies frame what is relevant for psychologists to know about meaning in relation to what is important to know about selfhood. Put another way, in both psychologies the scientific problem of meaning is closely linked to the scientific problem of selfhood (in contrast to how semioticians study meaning, for instance). In both, the problem-space shifts in ways that one problem appears as a kind of answer to the other problem. When the problem is meaning-making, what is relevant to know is 'answered' by deference to selfhood; that is, assuming a human subject for whom things are meaningful, and explicating what is meaningful and why. When the problem is selfhood, what is relevant to know is 'answered' by deference to meaning; that is, postulating processes whereby people become aware of their existential meaning.

The oscillation between the two problems is reminiscent of optical illusions in which we see the same picture as alternately showing one of two images (a young/old woman, a duck/rabbit) and cannot hold the two images simultaneously in our gaze. Nevertheless, the cognitive act of to-ing and fro-ing between those two images depends on the constant presence of the physical picture and constancy of a perceiver looking at it. Underlying the to-ing and fro-ing between the twin problems of meaning and selfhood there is a constancy of assuming a self-aware human subject. The history of modern psychology could be told in terms of how the rise and demise of schools of thought reflected different attitudes to the so-called Cartesian subject. It was variously taken for granted, ignored, challenged, rejected, and problematised afresh. The issue of what Jungian versus narrative psychologies identify as important to know about meaning and selfhood is nested within that history. But, in accordance with the principle of heteroglossia, how the history is told can change its meaning.

Back in the day when 'narrative' was talk of the day, Sarbin (1986) made his case for narrative psychology by drawing upon Pepper's (1942) root-metaphor theory of how worldviews evolve. People wishing to understand the world may settle upon some common-sense fact and apply it to other areas. This becomes the basic analogy, and its structural characteristics become the basic conception of explanation and description. Pepper delineated formism, mechanism, contextualism and organicism – in that order – as the four standard metatheories in modern sciences (dismissing animism and mysticism as irrelevant in modernity). Sarbin identified formism, mechanism, organicism and contextualism – in that order – in modern psychology. The order of listing those '-isms' is significant. It performs an act of meaning. Unlike Sarbin, Pepper did not favour any particular worldview, and indeed set forth his root-metaphor theory as challenging dogmatism, wryly concluding his book with the open question, 'Am I not dogmatically undogmatic?' (Pepper 1942, p. 348). Organicism comes last in Pepper's list, perhaps because in the 1940s it was the youngest of metaphysical systems. Jung's worldview readily accords with the organism metaphor (he likened the psyche to the body throughout his works). Sarbin (1986) placed contextualism last, however, as if to say: this is better than anything listed before it.

Sarbin located narrative psychology in contextualism, having rejected the machine and organism metaphors that had dominated psychology. Contextualism is historically associated with the American pragmatists – William James, John Dewey and George Herbert Mead are usually cited as forerunners – and with quests to understand human behaviour in its natural setting. But what exactly is humans' 'natural setting'?

In the 1950s, Roger Barker and associates, based in Oskaloosa, Kansas, believed that it was important to understand the synergy between people's activities and structural features of everyday settings in which the activities take place, and that this scientific goal required charting the kinds of habitats (termed 'behaviour settings') into which children grow up. The researchers meticulously observed streams of behaviour in schools, shops, parks, hospitals and more. In a music lesson, the fly-on-the-wall observer noted that ten-year-old Anne entered the classroom, sat down, picked up the music book, listened to the teacher, watched other pupils, and raised her hand in response to the teacher's questions a few times (Barker 1968, p. 12ff.). Those researchers were not interested in what the music lesson meant to Anne herself, her story, or (to paraphrase Sarbin) the story-shaped world she inhabited. Nor were they interested in how the behaviour setting, its rules and power relations, shaped the child's subjectivity – an issue that postmodern scholars who define *subjectivity* as the 'condition and experience of being a subject, including the process of production of subjects through subjectification or subjection' (Walkerdine 2014, p. 1880) may regard as critical to know.

Furthermore, while the behaviour setting analysts documented mundane behaviours, they were not intrigued by the mundane fact that Anne could make her body walk into the classroom, sit down, and so forth. Countless philosophical theses have grappled with this classic mind–body problem, associated with Descartes; namely, how the mind causes bodily movement, such as raising one's hand at will. In 1748, La Mettrie purported to resolve the problem of Cartesian dualism by regarding all mental faculties as aspects of corporeal or material substance, boldly concluding that Man is a machine. A paradox of modernity was already present in La Mettrie's conclusion (de Vos 2011). There is inevitable subjectivity in *imagining* oneself as machine-like with zero subjectivity. By the 2010s, brain–computer interface technology apparently solved the puzzle of how the conscious mind can make one's body move. Successful demonstrations of a mind-controlled robotic arm that paralysed people can control by thought alone – making it pick up things, wave, and so forth – are already old news. If we inquire what picking up something, waving, etc., mean to the actor, we implicitly assume that the person has intentional states.

From early childhood, it is obvious to all humans (barring neurological impairment such as associated with autism) that they and others have mental states. And yet scholars in certain academic enclaves construe this fact as metaphysically freakish. It is inherent in the paradox of modernity that having to acknowledge our undeniable subjectivity is like coming across a talking skull.

Picking up the talking skull

'Regardless of the goal of the research, the only possible point of departure is the text' (Bakhtin 1986, p. 104). This is technically correct, but the text is also a point of arrival. Scholars arrive there in the middle of a journey that follows a sequence of questions already articulated within particular disciplinary contexts. Bakhtin probably had in mind texts such as literary novels and philosophical treaties. In the social sciences, research questions often lead to the production of texts-to-be-analysed. If social scientists who analyse personal narratives happened to be interested in Jack's case, they would arrive at the specific study in the pursuit of other issues that generate reasons for looking into his case, and likely conduct an interview with him, thus creating the text (the interview transcript) that will serve as the point of departure for their analysis.

For some purposes, the folktale itself may serve as a point of departure. Unlike literary novels, philosophical treatises, and even interview transcripts, an orally transmitted tale often has numerous variants (rather than a single text). Taking some definitive theme as the 'textual' point of departure inevitably entails interpretation – and any interpretation arrives at the given text from the standpoint of the scholar's value-laden judgements, disciplinary-specific criteria and cultural associations. The tale's manifest content is reconstructed through its latent content.

Toward the classification of folklore, Bascom (1977) identified the refusal to speak on demand as the defining feature of this family of folktales, and therefore also included in his documentation of its occurrences African stories of speaking and singing animals refusing to perform. The theme he singled out could be construed as the archetypal trickster (cf. Morgan 2013). While the skull and its mischief are the tale's manifest content, its latent content lies in how it 'speaks' to its audience. For people of Jack's (and my) cultural background, animals that speak and sing connote very different emotionally toned associations than does a human skull. Talking and singing animals conjure Disney cartoon characters in my mind. A skull is a grim reminder of mortality.

Propp (1928/1958) observed that when oral tales migrate in time and place, details change in ways that make the tales relevant for the new context (e.g. the dragon kidnapping the princess becomes a whirlwind, devil, falcon or a sorcerer; the daughter becomes a sister, bride, wife or mother) although the functions of hero, villain, etc., remain constant. Bartlett (1920, 1932) offered a psychological explanation for such transformations. In a classic experiment, his British subjects retold a Native American tale ('War of the Ghosts') after periods ranging from a short while after hearing it to days, weeks, months, and even years later. Distortions in verbatim reproductions typically transformed objects into ones that were culturally more familiar (e.g. the canoe became a boat, a bush-cat became an ordinary cat). Bartlett referred to this finding as the principle of familiarisation, and also delineated principles of rationalisation and omission. Content that was felt to be irrelevant or was distressing was not reproduced. 'The material simply disappeared from the reproduction, leaving the subject entirely unaware that anything dropped out' (Bartlett 1920, p. 36). He concluded that remembering is a process of reconstruction, not playback (Bartlett 1932).

The participants in Bartlett's study, however, retold on demand a tale not of their choosing and which likely had little personal significance for them. In contrast, The Talking Skull 'spoke' to Jack, and he chose when to tell it. Although he first read the tale in a book, in his subsequent telling and retelling it became embedded in conversational flows, acquiring qualities of oral transmission. It evolved in the telling. In his rendition, the skull says, and the hunter's head reiterates, 'Talking *too much* brought me here.' Like Bartlett's participants, Jack was unaware that anything was added. He was surprised when later, after I had a chance to look up his source (Yolen 1986), I pointed out that there's no 'too much' there.

His surprise is understandable, for 'talking too much' is what the tale is all about in his own dialogue with it. The 'too much' might seem like a trivial embellishment, but it does change the subtext. Instead of the skull's mischief or the hunter's transgression as the core element, Jack's reconstruction emphasises the hunter's *power of agency*. It was in the hunter's power to refrain from talking too much, the skull had warned him, but he acted rashly nonetheless. Jack's dialogue with the tale changes the skull's role from that of a trickster whose mischief is fatal for the living, to that of an adviser – an inner voice – whose advice is ignored at a cost.

It is tempting to take the African tale as an allegory for a dialogue with one's unconscious, a process that Jung regarded as crucial for individuation: 'It is exactly as if a dialogue were taking place between two human beings' (Jung 1958, para. 186). If this skull represents the unconscious, its refusal to speak may represent one's inability to let the unconscious have its say, a situation that according to Jung has dire consequences for mental health. Tempting as the allegory might be, however, we should bear in mind that it rests on parallels between the manifest content of the African tale and the manifest content of Jungian theory. Parallels don't meet.

Like an alphabet used to write very different things, similar imagery can communicate a diversity of messages. There is a spurious similarity between the core image of the African tale and the motif of a talking head in Inuit and Siberian tales, in which a young unmarried woman finds a disembodied male head who speaks to her. She takes the head home as a secret partner, and when her parents find out she is banished from the village. This is just the beginning of the story, the start of her shamanic journey. Jung's student Marie-Louise von Franz (1972, 1996) saw the head in the circum-arctic tales as a representation of the animus, the masculine in the female psyche. If we follow her lead and formulaically apply an archetypal interpretation to the African tale, the skull could be taken as representing the shadow, the disowned counterpart of the ego, which appears in dreams as a figure of the same gender as the dreamer. We may want to say that the skull represents the hunter's shadow. According to Jung (e.g. 1951), confrontations with projections of the shadow may initiate the process of individuation.

To be clear, I'm not suggesting that the African folktale is about the shadow. My contention is that the Jungian concept is latent in this tale only if one's dialogue with the tale's manifest content is prefigured both by knowledge of Jungianism and by commitment to its truth-claims. Principles of familiarisation, rationalisation and omission are likely to operate when a tale migrates to the Jungian meaning-world. If we seek only archetypal motifs in traditional tales – attuning ourselves to imagined echoes of a collective unconscious – we are likely to remain deaf to the socialising voices in the here-and-now of telling the tale (Jones 2008).

The Jungian world has its own story about skulls. It begins: *One night in 1909, Jung dreamed of a historically layered house ...* As with oral tales, significant details have changed across Jung's repeated retelling (Jones 2007a, 2007b). Nevertheless, in all versions Jung as the dreamer descends the house until he reaches a cave beneath the basement. Amidst dust, scattered bones and broken pottery, he finds half-disintegrated human skulls – and wakes up realising that he made a great discovery. In Jungian interpretation, the prehistoric skulls represent the collective unconscious, the archaic element of the psyche that is still alive deep beneath our modern consciousness, and finds expression in fantasies. 'In myths and fairy tales, as in dreams, the psyche tells its own story' (Jung 1948b, para. 400).

Whereas Bartlett sought to explain why specific content changes when a tale migrates across cultures, von Franz drew upon Jung's theory towards explaining why certain content remains constant. She acknowledged that fairy tales are 'not quite purified of specific factors' (von Franz 1980, p. 13) – since the setup of the story would be quite different in Native American and European tales, for instance – but assumed a natural process of content purification. To start with, an anecdote of something extraordinary or inexplicable that had happened to someone becomes a local legend. Von Franz (1980) illustrated it with a documented account of tracing a certain folktale to a real family's record of an event. I can add that in Wales, the legend of the Physicians of Myddfai demonstrates a survival of historical facts interwoven with the supernatural.[1] Usually, however, oral tales lose the details that pin them down to a particular time and place. Successive storytellers reconstruct the tale in accordance with what resonates with them and their audiences. In the course of uncountable retellings, the tale is distilled into 'the purest and simplest expression of collective unconscious psychic processes' (von Franz 1996, p. 1).

Content that survives migrations across time and place must have pancultural appeal. The Jungian imagination construes this as evidence for archetypal contents of a collective unconscious. There is a Jungian tendency to ignore distinctions between legends, myths, fables, folktales and fairy tales. Although the boundaries between these genres can be fuzzy, and precise criteria are a matter for debate, stories that fall into different categories may serve different functions and survive for different reasons. The jocular tale of a talking skull could survive – not because it contains an archetype – but because it makes people smile at the irony, perhaps laugh as a defensive reaction to this uncanny reminder of mortality, and because its moral messages reflect universal codes of conduct.

Locating the act of meaning

When psychologists first became enthused by the idea of 'narrative', an emphasis was put on its explanatory function. Bruner's (1990) book *Acts of Meaning* expands his description of the narrative mode as one of two modes of human understanding, the other mode being the paradigmatic mode, or logico-scientific (see also Bruner 1986). Whereas the paradigmatic mode achieves understanding through categorisation, logical relationships, and universal abstractions, the narrative mode organises and evaluates the vicissitudes of human experience. As Polkinghorne (1989, p. 21) put it, 'Narrative explanation does not subsume events under laws. Instead, it explains by clarifying the significance of events that have occurred on the basis of the outcome that has followed.'

The Talking Skull tale consists of a sequence of events, actions and consequences that explain why a certain hunter died. But why should anyone care about the death of a man who never existed in a world that isn't there? While a sequential ordering of events is an obvious criterion for distinguishing narrative from other forms of speech, this might not be the most important factor regarding its meaning. Discussing Aristotle's concept of a plot (*mythos*) in literary fiction, Ricoeur (1984, p. 38) defines it as the 'logical character' of a story when taken as a whole. In tragedies, the turn from good fortune to bad necessarily unfolds in story-time, but the *mythos* is the turn-of-fortune theme, not the particular sequence of events. Likewise, the tale in focus has a logical character, which gives it its power to communicate a moral message (see what happens when you tell lies, divulge secrets, don't bury the departed, talk too much). The tale as a whole, its mythos, serves as a trope or allegory for real-life situations and human foibles. Its very existence, however, owes to psychological processes whereby fantasy images are produced and apperceived, and thereby express human experience. The expression of experience does not necessarily explain it, but nonetheless creates the possibility of meaning.

Whereas Bruner posited a dichotomy of narrative versus paradigmatic modes, Jung (1912, 1952) posited a dichotomy of reality-directed thinking and 'associative' thinking. The former is speech-based, communicative in origin, and may encompass both Bruner's modes. Associative or fantasy thinking is image-based. Whereas Bruner highlights the capacity of the human mind for narrativity, Jung highlights the capacity for what he termed *the symbolic attitude*:

> It is only partially justified by the actual behaviour of things; for the rest, it is the outcome of a definite view of the world which *assigns meaning* to events, whether great or small, and attaches to this meaning a greater value than to bare facts.
>
> (Jung 1921, para. 819, emphasis in original)

Bruner regarded his own position as incompatible with Jung's. Speculating that there is 'some human "readiness" for narrative,' he quickly added, 'By this I do not intend that we "store" specific archetypal stories or myths, as C. G. Jung has proposed' (Bruner 1990, p. 45). The disclaimer perpetuates a common misconception. ('My critics have incorrectly assumed that I am dealing with "inherited representations,"' complained Jung 1964, p. 57.) In my reading, Jung deals with the readiness to form symbolic representations of typical human situations, and these representations become crystallised into motifs found in myths, fairy tales, arts, and more (Jones 2003).

Bruner's point is different; namely, that our stories have certain formal characteristics regardless of the motifs they contain. A narrative gives discrete events and mental states a particular meaning by virtue of their placement in the whole, i.e. their emplotment: 'this unique sequentiality … is indispensable to a story's significance and to the mode of mental organization in terms of which it is grasped' (Bruner 1990, p. 44). Since a meaning emerges from the narrative configuration, the story can be real or imaginary without losing its power – a characteristic that Bruner described in terms of a story's indifference to extralinguistic reality. A story has a 'dual landscape' insofar as 'events and actions in a putative "real world" occur concurrently with mental events in the consciousness of the protagonists' (Bruner 1990, p. 51). Ultimately, Bruner centred on the stories that people tell towards explaining real events and situations. The narrative mode 'specializes in the forging of links between the exceptional and the ordinary' (Bruner 1990, p. 47). When encountering something unexpected or extraordinary people tend to seek its meaning by narrative means – telling what had led to it, what happened next, and evaluating its implications.

Noting that a story is always someone's story, Bruner (1990, pp. 54–55) surmises that stories are 'viable instruments for social negotiation'. As mentioned, Jack used to be involved in storytelling. He had a repertoire of folktales he told when invited into schools. The Talking Skull was not one of them, to my knowledge. He conversationally told it to people by way of making a point. If we could analyse some of those conversations, we would surely see how his impromptu storytelling serves as an instrument for social negotiation. Moreover, when Jack tells how this tale once served him to diffuse conflict, he naturally organises his story-about-a-story in a way that makes sense of telling the folktale to his boss by imparting to his present audience what had led to that action and what happened as a consequence. None of that explains why he felt compelled to collect visual reminders of the talking skull.

To make sense of his obsession with the image, we (and Jack too) would inevitably contrive some narrative about it. But the 'feel' of the image's meaningfulness had happened to him before and apart from any explanation. Indeed, coming across a folktale in an anthology – as Jack did – is like looking at a museum exhibit of an artefact from an alien culture. The reader knows that the printed text originated in something that someone had told someone long ago and far away, but if it moves him (or her) in some way, the immediacy of its impact evinces some projections through which this person's unconscious has its say (to paraphrase Jung). Whereas Bruner seeks to explain how people consciously explain their experiences in reality-directed modes, Jung seeks to explain how embodied experiences find expression in 'spontaneous' fantasy. A recurrent motif expresses a constellation of emotions, motivations and actions. Both Jung and Bruner theorise about meaning, but they are not looking at the same phenomenon.

When Jung refers to 'image' in his writings he usually means a fantasy image. Defined as 'a complex structure made up of the most varied material from the most varied sources,' the meaning of the image can start only from the reciprocal relationship between the conscious and the unconscious, according to Jung (1921, para. 745). The image is not a mental representation of an external object. The psychological significance of the fantasy image lies in the extent to which it expresses 'a *condensed expression of the psychic situation as a whole*, and not merely, nor even predominantly, of unconscious contents pure and simple' (Jung 1921, para. 745, emphasis in original). A fantasy image implies a feeling-toned autonomous complex, relatively or wholly dissociated from the conscious ego. In turn, *complex* is defined as 'the image of a certain psychic situation which is strongly accentuated emotionally ... incompatible with the habitual attitude of the consciousness,' which 'has a powerful inner coherence, ... its own wholeness and, in addition, a relatively high degree of autonomy' (Jung 1934, para. 201). Jung (1912, p. 29) introduced the Latin word *imago* as a technical term apropos young women's 'father-imago'. When revising the monograph four decades later, he added a footnote explaining that his preference of the word 'imago' over 'complex' was meant to underline a psychological factor that 'has a living independence in the psychic hierarchy' (Jung 1952, p. 44, n. 4).

The term 'imago' has been adopted by psychoanalysts, who developed it in tangential directions. It underwent a radical transformation when McAdams used it to denote idealised images of oneself that function as the protagonist in one's life story. McAdams (1985, 1993) identified an array of imagoes in the life stories told by his research participants: oneself as warrior, traveller, caregiver, lover, healer, teacher, and more. He introduced his construct by differentiating it from Jungian archetypes. Unlike archetypes, life stories' imagoes are 'highly personalized, idiosyncratic images defining how a person is different from others as well as similar to them' (McAdams 1985, p. 183). Someone might not realise that she describes herself as a warrior when telling about her life struggles, but this narrative representation (imago) distinguishes her from someone who describes himself as a healer. After McAdams, we may point to a father imago when someone portrays himself as a fatherly figure. This use of the term is clearly incompatible with Jung's (1952, para. 62) postulation of 'disturbances brought about by regressive reactivation of the father-imago' in young women who have difficulties expressing themselves in their first romantic love.

The fantasy image makes its salience felt by the intensity of affect, a non-specific sense of heightened meaningfulness; or, in Jungian parlance, its numinous quality. In ancient Roman religion, *numen* referred to the power of a deity or a spirit present in places and objects. Jung (1938) psychologised it by redefining *numinosum* as an involuntary 'dynamic existence or effect' that 'seizes and controls' the person, and is experienced as external in origin, as 'either a quality of a visible object or the influence of an invisible presence causing a peculiar alteration of consciousness' (Jung 1938, p. 4). Jack was clearly seized by the talking skull. I like the tale (clearly) but it doesn't affect me in the same way. Its numinosity is not caused by any objective elements of the tale since this effect is highly subjective.

A brief digression to Freud can help to tone down the Jungianist fixation on the concrete image. Freud's (1919/1985) essay on aesthetics in literature concerns – not the experience of beauty, pleasures of the imagination, and so forth – but 'the opposite feelings of repulsion and distress' (Freud 1919/1985, p. 340). The German word translated as 'uncanny' is *unheimlich* (unhomely). Freud applied it to 'that class of the frightening which leads back to what is known of old and long familiar' (Freud 1919/1985, p. 340). The revulsion we feel upon confronting 'uncanny' motifs in fiction reveals something about ourselves, a recurrence of something repressed (according to Freud). Freud challenges any assumptions of a causal relationship between specific imagery and specific emotion. He cites one literary fairy tale in which the story of a severed hand has an uncanny effect, and another one – in which a severed hand tries to hold fast to a thief – that does not provoke any uncanniness; the reader's attention is on the thief's cunning. Likewise, the skull that suddenly speaks may spook the hunter in the tale, but it does not have this effect on us as audience (at least not anyone I know). The objective image of a supernatural event alone is not enough to elicit unease because we readily accept the impossible in fiction.

Back to Jung. Throughout his works, he demonstrates phenomena attributed to processes of individuation in clinical case studies as well as his analyses of mythologies, religious symbolism, medieval alchemy, and arts. He excavates those for archetypal images. To appreciate his idea of individuation, however, we ought to decentre from the 'objective' image and instead centre on the possibility of fathoming out its subjective meaning.

In an essay on individuation, Stein (2005) quotes an unnamed analyst who had known Jung personally: '"For me," the elder analyst said, "Jung's greatest contribution to psychology was the discovery of an inner world."' (Stein 2005, p. 1). Stein, himself an elder analyst when imparting the impact that the quoted statement had on him, defines individuation as a personal opus that unfolds in complementary movements of analysis and synthesis. To begin with, it requires analysing and making conscious one's unconscious identification with extraneous figures and psychic contents, with 'the effect of creating a mirror of consciousness' (Stein 2005, p. 2). Synthesis comes into play when some progress has been made in the analysis, and requires 'careful and continuous attention to the emergence of the Self' (Stein 2005, p. 2). If Jack were to embark on this opus when the talking skull had a hold on him, he could have started with analysing his affective responses to this image – a process that may rightly be called *meaning-making*.

Who is talking?

As mentioned, Jung gave the analogy of a dialogue with the unconscious as if with another person. But as a theorist he was concerned with the description of abstract mental organisation. The scientific problem was not 'who' is talking when the unconscious has its say, but *how* unconscious contents self-organise and become accessible to one's consciousness. The implicated 'who' was contested by the behaviourists – who caricatured insinuations of a homunculus inside one's head (we'll skip that chapter in the history of ideas) – and took a postmodern twist when reconstructed as a scientific problem concerning the 'who' of discourse.

A distinction ought to be drawn between postmodernism as a critical theory of knowledge and postmodernity as a historically unique context of research and theorising. The 1980s' zeitgeist legitimated a new form of empirical inquiry in psychology: the description of particular, historical, and local aspects of human life in their oral and written forms (Ryan 1999). Not everyone who engaged in such research subscribed to the postmodernist critique. The 'who' of discourse was problematised as an empirical matter insofar as it became important to know who-tells-what – real people, their real lives and real-life stories. Postmodern psychology performs a 'move from the inside of the psyche to the text of the world' and from the 'archaeology of the psyche to the architecture of cultural landscapes' (Kvale 1992, p. 1).

Half a century earlier, the task of psychology was understood as a move in the opposite direction: 'When we examine the personality process or *private worlds* of individuals, ... we are seeking not the cultural and social norms ... but rather the revelation of just that peculiar, individual way of organizing experience and of feeling' (Frank 1939, p. 392, emphasis in original). Jungian psychology has its roots in this epistemology.

As a doctrine and a box of tools for analysing the psyche, traditional depth psychology is premised on the existence of an inner world that reacts and adapts to the outer world of one's milieu. 'In a distinctly intimate way, psychoanalysis defends the private man against the demands made by both culture and instinct,' commented Rieff (1959, p. 329) in his sociological study of the psychoanalytical movement in the early twentieth century. Jung went a step further in attributing the private world to human evolution. He postulated an abstract structure that evolved in tandem with human physiology. Culture was hardly ignored, but Jung and his followers attribute cultural productions, such as myths and fairy tales, to the biological evolution of the psyche, and treat them as instruments for discovering the psyche's innate structure. This hypothetical structure is often talked about as if it were a causal explanation for the occurrence of archetypal motifs, as if something hardwired in the human brain causes people to generate these motifs. Support for this position could be extracted from Jung's writing; e.g. his aforementioned definition of the archetype as the specifically human form of activities, 'already present in the germ-plasm'.

However, Jung stressed also that only the *readiness* to form certain images, a kind of receptibility, had evolved over countless generations. He was critical of causal-mechanistic explanations, and endorsed an epistemological position inter-changeably termed 'energic' or 'final' (Jung 1928) – better called a functional approach (Jones 2001, 2007a, 2018). A functional approach describes how something functions within the whole of a person's psychological constitution, analogous to the function of a cog in a machine or the function of a fictional character in a novel. Jung (1928) proposed to understand symbol formation by reference to the symbol's function within a system of psychological values – a system whose dynamics are not reducible to specific drives, instincts or desires – and contended that this justified 'at least a provisional view of the psyche as a relatively closed system' (Jung 1928, para. 11).

Conceptualising psychological interiority in terms of a self-organising system was hardly unique to depth psychology. The influential American psychologist Gordon Allport (1961) rejected the psychoanalytical approach but nevertheless asserted the notion of an inner structure in the now-classic definition: 'Personality is the dynamic organization within the individual of those psychosocial systems that determine his characteristic behaviour and thought' (Allport 1961, p. 28). Crit-icising theories that dichotomise the individual and the social, Allport singled out Jung's theory as epitomising the contested viewpoint: 'Jung tells us that we cannot escape the impress of archetypes and social tradition; at the same time each of us has a drive toward individuation, a negativism to tribal ways and a desire to be oneself' (Allport 1961, pp. 192–193). In Allport's view, 'Personality is a system within a matrix of sociocultural systems. It is an "inside structure" embedded within and interacting with "outside structures"' (Allport 1961, p. 194).

Psychology is, above all, an empirical science. Conceptualising personality as a dynamic 'inside' system created the practical problem of how to 'gain insight into that individual's *private world* of meaning, significances, patterns, and feeling' (Frank 1939, p. 402, emphasis in original). This exigency gave rise to the plethora of projective techniques of personality assessment (the Rorschach inkblot tests, Thematic Apperception Test, and many more) that flourished into the 1960s. The methodology was not wedded to any school of thought insofar as it served diverse theoretical perspectives. The projective hypothesis also underpins Jung's (1958) active imagination techniques and derivatives such as sandplay therapy, typically used as means for self-exploration in therapy sessions (rather than personality assessment).

Since the 1970s, however, notions of 'inside/outside' were severely condemned in postmodernist circles. The language of structuralism gradually lost its power even when the old paradigm was not directly challenged. In the idiom of the folktale, the Private Man of the early twentieth century was beheaded by the postmodernists, and then its talking skull ceased to speak to more conservative psychologists who cultivated postmodern sensitivities.

McAdams' brand of narrative psychology, building upon Erik Erikson's psychosocial theory, could be viewed as conservatively psychodynamic. Naming Freud, Jung, Adler and Murray, he commented, 'none of these classic personality theorists from the first half of the 20th century explicitly imagined human beings as storytellers and human lives as stories to be told' (McAdams 2006, p. 13). His own framework does not deny the private world but reconceptualises its dynamic structure in terms of narrative construction: 'A person's life story is an internalized and evolving narrative of the self that selectively reconstructs the past and anticipates the future in such a way as to provide a life with an overall sense of coherence and purpose' (McAdams *et al.* 2006, p. 1372). McAdams and cowriters contrast their position with that of postmodernists (citing Gergen and Shotter) who regard personal narratives as 'momentary performances expressing the exigencies of the interpersonal situation in which they are told' (McAdams *et al.* 2006, p. 1374).

From a Jungian standpoint, narrative psychology pertains to the *persona*, that is, characteristic adaptations to one's sociocultural milieu. Jung (1954b) complained that people tend to confuse the individuation process for 'the coming of the ego into consciousness,' and this results in 'a hopeless conceptual muddle' whereby individuation becomes 'nothing but ego-centredness and autoeroticism' (Jung 1954b, para. 432). He made this complaint long before postmodernity, however, and his criticism might not apply to what psychologists who analyse life stories seek to understand about selfhood. The scientific problem is different.

When McAdams first introduced the study of life stories into personality psychology in the 1980s, imagining human beings as storytellers resonated with timely sensitivities. Issues of personal identity became highly topical during the last century's closing decades. Sociologists and anthropologists noted how globalisation, accelerated change, and the fragmentation of society, had led to a dissolution of the grand narratives of politics and science, and, instead, the 'small' narratives of real lives became prominent (Gullestad 1996). Published auto/ biographies became popular, and soon attracted also scholarly interest (see, for example, Olney 1980). *Narrative* and *story* became buzzwords underpinning an interdisciplinary approach to understanding the self. It was as if the 'self' was simultaneously reinvented by many scholars. They contended that 'making sense of one's life as a story is ... not an optional extra' (Taylor 1989, p. 47) and that self-identity is formed in 'the capacity *to keep a particular narrative going*' (Giddens 1991, p. 54, emphasis in original). It became commonplace to say that we 'live in and through stories' and that we are 'locations where the stories of our place and time become partially tellable' (Mair 1988, p. 127). By the mid-1990s, it was obvious:

> We have now arrived at the self's understanding of itself at the crossroads of discourse and narration as a who of discourse in the guise of a narrating self, a *homo narrans*, a storyteller who both finds herself in stories already told and strives for a self-constitution by emplotting herself in stories in the making.
>
> (Schrag 1997, p. 26)

Even though she authors her own self, her stories-in-the-making assemble the events of her life in accordance with some cultural life script and master narratives of gender, ethnicity, sexuality, and so on. The arrival of *homo narrans* meant a refiguration of psychological interiority. The private world became an enfolding of the public milieu. A different talking skull thus appeared: selves conjured into being by virtue of telling their life stories, and living by those private myths.

Who is talking in the case of Welshman Jack and the African tale? His telling does not reproduce an African voice. The tale is a vessel for Jack's own voice. When Jack conversationally imparts his story, he is not simply telling it for amusement (though there's this element too). He tells how he used this tale in the heat of the moment to communicate his frustrations and to diffuse hostility, and how the phrase 'talking skull' subsequently acquired a life of its own in his workplace. The 'who' that talks is Jack himself. He is the author of his own story. *Homo narrans* survived the battle of the fittest, it might seem. But when we wish to explain why Jack finds himself darkly mirrored in a folktale from a culture alien to him, we encounter ghosts of the Private Man. If it spooks us, we might feel compelled to reduce it to the *res extensa* of either language or brain.

In the era of *homo narrans*, the African tale may serve as an allegory for the narrated self – a talking head, disembodied, 'So much so that what comes first is ... an anonymous murmur in which positions are laid out for possible subjects:

"the great relentless disordered drone of discourse." ' (Deleuze 1988, p. 55, quoting Foucault). By the twenty-first century, its head too rolled next to the Private Man of traditional psychology. Too much *talking* has sealed its fate. The error of locating the self in nothing-but-talk has led to its demise. New intellectual fashions, empowered by advances in neuroscience, emerged in the form of 'turns' to affect, the body and New Materialism.

Postnarrativity

When this chapter was still in the planning stage, I wondered how to pinpoint its direction. The word 'postnarrativity' came to my mind like a flash of inspiration. I invented the neologism on the spot (it felt like). Nevertheless, aware that wheels are often reinvented, I carried out an internet search. Sure enough, the terms 'postnarrativity', 'post-narrativity' and 'post-narrative' occur in a variety of contexts – including McAdams' work, which I read many years ago. McAdams (1996) used 'post-narrative' to denote a mature developmental stage, when one's life story has crystallised. Contrastingly, currently prevalent usages identify the collapse of narrative as a linear form of storytelling, explore the demise of socio-political grand narratives, or critique the narrative movement. None of these meanings parallels what I wanted the chapter to do; namely, to draw attention to an epistemic process whereby a text acquires meaningfulness beyond words.

Before continuing with the exposition, it is worth pausing to reflect on the symbiotic relationship between scholar and software that is performed in the act of scrolling down pages of hyperlinks generated by computer algorithms. In this act, scholarly labour devolves to automated searches, eruditeness rests on a capacity to absorb disconnected occurrences of the search term, and the dialogue with one's material becomes judgements about the relevance of particular items. This gloomy reflection echoes how media theorist Rushkoff (2013) uses the term *postnarrativity*. It denotes the collapse of narrative, a state of affairs that he construes as a consequence of digital technology, and regards as exacerbating the disintegration of the grand narratives of politics and a diminishing sense of purpose or goals in civic life. To Rushkoff, postnarrativity implies forfeiting the capacity to articulate future directions and to imbue both past and present with meaning. In other words, if narrativity is the capacity to create a narrative about the world and about oneself, and narratives have end-goals, then there must be a loss of teleological vision when narrativity and narratives are no more. Nevertheless, to make sense of staring at a computer-generated list of links to occurrences of 'postnarrativity', one must inevitably have an articulable narrative of why the search was initiated, how to appraise the relevance of what appears on the screen, and what is the outcome in terms of useful information. There is a past, present and future. There is a goal, a direction, and thus a 'point' to the activity. This mundane instance evinces the necessity of narrativity for any agentic action.

While postnarrativity or post-narrative could imply the breakdown of the traditional narrative form, the prefix post- can also indicate a standpoint that has emerged as a consequence of the narrative turn, either as a 'strong' critique (like the relation of poststructuralism to structuralism) or as a 'soft' critical stance that seeks to protect the narrative perspective by recognising its shortcomings. In a paper entitled 'Post-narrative – an appeal', Woods (2011, p. 399) articulates the need for 'identifying the limits of narrative and of exploring alternative approaches to interpreting the self and social world' in the context of medical humanities. In psychology, however, it was the turn to narrative that opened up precisely this possibility of investigating real human lives in the real world. Narrative psychology is about 'the living, loving, suffering, dying human being ... human lives, existing in culture and in time' (Freeman 1997, p. 171). Bruner (1986) presented his theory of the narrative mode as an agenda for culture psychology. Gergen (1994, p. 188) defined self-narratives as 'forms of social accounting or public discourse'. McAdams (2006) found that the life stories told by midlife Americans revealed as much about American culture and tradition as about the people who told them, for their stories captured 'cherished, as well as hotly contested, ideas in American cultural history' (McAdams 2006, p. 17). Further quotable examples abound. The upshot is that narrative psychology in any of its variants cannot be accused of neglecting the social world.

Narrative psychology might be remiss in other respects. Efforts to push the boundaries of narrative psychology beyond narratology could be regarded as post-narrative. Hevern (2008) pointed to lingering Cartesianism that threatens the cogency of this perspective, and urged attention to biological psychology as a means to challenging the Cartesian pitfall of viewing human beings as storied selves. Freeman (2002, 2012, 2016) has forwarded the idea of a *narrative unconscious* that comprises aspects of personal history that are rooted in the shared life of one's culture but have not yet been explicitly integrated into one's life story. My own critical angle identified the understatement of fantasy, and in particular situations when fiction acquires meaningfulness beyond words.

Bachelard (1958/1994, p. xxiii) observed that when a literary work moves us, 'we feel a poetic power rising naively within us ... the image has touched the depths before it stirs the surface'. Bakhtin (1986, p. 68) averred that when someone understands the semantic meaning of an utterance, he 'simultaneously takes an active, responsive attitude toward it. He either agrees or disagrees with it'. The term *para*-narrative might be appropriate, but the prefix *post*- reinforces the focus on what happens after hearing or reading something. Postnarrativity in this sense applies also to the 'gut-feeling' one may get upon reading the texts of Jungian and narrative psychologies: neither one provides the complete picture of how human beings make sense of their existence.

' "*Ars totum requirit hominem!*" exclaims an old alchemist. It is just this *homo totus* whom we seek' (Jung 1944, para. 6). In plain English, the alchemist is saying that the art requires the whole person, and Jung says that we seek this whole person. Individuation is the quest for 'that hidden and as yet unmanifested "whole" man' (Jung 1944, para. 6). As scholars, it is *homo totus* whom we may seek to fathom out through Jungian, narrative or some other psychology. It forever eludes us. There is always a crucial moment when this enigmatic talking skull refuses to speak.

Note

1 The physicians of Myddfai were real historical figures, a family of herbalists who lived in the village of Myddfai from at least the thirteenth century until the last one died in 1739. Their knowledge of preparing herbal medicine has survived in Welsh manuscripts. The legend traces the family's origin to a local man who married a mysterious woman who had risen from a nearby lake, bringing cattle with her. She agreed to marry him on condition that he would not hit her three times. They lived happily for years, but on three occasions he did hit her for transgressions such as laughing at a funeral and crying at a wedding. She returned to the lake, taking her cattle with her, but occasionally she came back to help and instruct her sons, who became the first physicians in the line. The groove in the bank where the legendary cattle descended to the lake is still there. I've seen it.

References

Allport, G. W. (1961) *Pattern and Growth in Personality.* New Haven, CT: Yale University Press.

Bachelard, G. (1958/1994) *The Poetics of Space.* Boston, MA: Beacon Press.

Bakhtin, M. M. (1984) *Problems of Dostoevsky's Poetics.* Minneapolis, MN: University of Minneapolis Press.

Bakhtin, M. M. (1986) *Speech Genres and Other Late Essays.* Austin, TX: University of Texas Press.

Barker, R. G. (1968) *Ecological Psychology.* Stanford, CA: Stanford University Press.

Bartlett, F. C. (1920) Some experiments on the reproduction of folk stories. *Folk-Lore* 3, 30–47.

Bartlett, F. C. (1932) *Remembering: A Study in Experimental and Social Psychology.* Cambridge: Cambridge University Press.

Bascom, W. (1977) African folktales in America: I. The talking skull refuses to talk. *Research in African Literatures* 8, 266–291.

Bruner, J. S. (1986) *Actual Minds, Possible Worlds.* Cambridge, MA: Harvard University Press.

Bruner, J. S. (1990) *Acts of Meaning.* Cambridge, MA: Harvard University Press.

Carvalho, R. (2008) The final challenge: ageing, dying, individuation. *Journal of Analytical Psychology* 53, 1–18.

de Vos, J. (2011) From La Mettrie's voluptuous machine man to the perverse core of psychology. *Theory & Psychology* 21, 67–85.

Deleuze, G. (1988) *Foucault.* London: Athlone Press.

Frank, L. K. (1939) Projective methods for the study of personality. *Journal of Psychology* 8, 389–413.

Freeman, M. (1997) Why narrative? Hermeneutics, historical understanding, and the significance of stories. *Journal of Narrative and Life History* 7, 169–176.

Freeman, M. (2002) Charting the narrative unconscious: cultural memory and the challenge of autobiography. *Narrative Inquiry*, 12, 193–211.

Freeman, M. (2012) The Narrative Unconscious. *Contemporary Psychoanalysis*, 48, 344–366.

Freeman, M. (2016) From the collective unconscious to the narrative unconscious: reimagining the sources of selfhood. *Europe's Journal of Psychology* 12, 513–522.

Freud, S. (1919/1985) The Uncanny. *The Pelican Freud Library* (Vol. 14) (pp. 335–376) London: Penguin.

Frobenius, L. and Fox, D. C. (1983) *African Genesis: Folk Tales and Myths of Africa.* New York: Dover.

Gergen, K. J. (1994) *Realities and Relationships.* Cambridge, MA: Harvard University Press.

Giddens, A. (1991) *Modernity and Self-identity.* Cambridge: Polity.

Gillies J., Neimeyer, R. A. and Milman, E. (2014) The meaning of loss codebook: construction of a system for analyzing meanings made in bereavement. *Death Studies* 38, 207–216.

Gullestad, M. (1996) *Everyday Life Philosophers.* Oslo: Scandinavian University Press.

Hevern, V. W. (2008) Dialogicality and the internet. In: H. J. M. Hermans and T. Gieser (Eds), *Handbook of Dialogical Self Theory.* Cambridge: Cambridge University Press.

Jones, R. A. (2001) Psychological value and symbol formation. *Theory & Psychology* 11, 233–254.

Jones, R. A. (2002) Self and Place in 'The White Light' by Amalia Kahana-Carmon. *Textual Practice* 16, 93–110.

Jones, R. A. (2003) Mixed metaphors and narrative shifts: archetypes. *Theory & Psychology* 13, 651–672.

Jones, R. A. (2007a) *Jung, Psychology, Postmodernity.* London: Routledge.

Jones, R. A. (2007b) A discovery of meaning: the case of C. G. Jung's house dream. *Culture & Psychology* 13(2), 203–230.

Jones, R. A. (2008) Storytelling, socialization and individuation. In: R. A. Jones, A. Clarkson, S. Congram and N. Startton (Eds), *Education and Imagination.* London and New York: Routledge.

Jones, R. A. (2010) 'Talking brought me here': affordances of fiction for the narrative self. *Theory & Psychology* 20, 549–567.

Jones, R. A. (2014) Writerly dynamics and culturally situated authentic human existence in Amalia Kahana-Carmon's theory of creative writing. *Culture & Psychology* 20, 118–144.

Jones, R. A. (2017) Towards dialogic epistemology: the problem of the text. *Qualitative Research* 17, 457–472.

Jones, R. A. (2018) The stream of desire and Jung's concept of psychic energy. In: P. Bishop and L. Gardner (Eds), *The Ecstatic and the Archaic.* London: Routledge.

Jung, C. G. Unless otherwise stated, the following are from *The Collected Works of C. G. Jung.* (CW). London: Routledge & Kegan Paul/Princeton, NJ: Princeton University Press.

Jung, C. G. (1912) *Psychology of the Unconscious.* London: Kegan Paul, Trench, Trubner & Co.

Jung, C. G. (1921) *Psychological types.* (CW6).

Jung, C. G. (1928) On psychic energy. (CW8).

Jung, C. G. (1934) A review of the complex theory. (CW8).

Jung, C. G. (1938) *Psychology and religion*. New Haven, CT: Yale University Press.

Jung, C. G. (1944) *Psychology and Alchemy*. (CW 12).

Jung, C. G. (1948a) The phenomenology of the spirit in fairy tales. (CW 9i).

Jung, C. G. (1948b) The psychological foundations of belief in spirits. (CW 8).

Jung, C. G. (1951) *Aion*. (CW 9ii).

Jung, C. G. (1952) *Symbols of transformation*. (CW 5).

Jung, C. G. (1954a) Psychological aspects of the mother archetype. (CW 9i).

Jung, C. G. (1954b) On the nature of the psyche. (CW 8).

Jung, C. G. (1958) The transcendent function. (CW 8).

Jung, C. G. (1964) Approaching the unconscious. In: C. G. Jung and M.-L. von Franz, (Eds), *Man and His Symbols*. London: Picador.

Kvale, S. (1992) Introduction. In: S. Kvale (Ed.), *Psychology and Postmodernism*. London: Sage.

Mahoney, M. J. and Granvold, D. K. (2005) Constructivism and psychotherapy. *World Psychiatry* 4, 74–77.

Mair, M. (1988) Psychology as storytelling. *International Journal of Personal Construct Psychology* 1, 125–137.

Markman, K. D., Proulx, T. and Lindberg, M. J. (Eds). (2013) *The Psychology of Meaning*. Washington, DC: American Psychological Association.

McAdams, D. P. (1985) *Power, Intimacy and the Life Story*. Homewood, IL: The Dorsey Press.

McAdams, D. P. (1993) *The Stories We Live By*. New York: Guilford Press.

McAdams, D. P. (1996) Personality, modernity, and the storied self: a contemporary framework for studying persons. *Psychological Inquiry* 7, 295–321.

McAdams, D. P. (2006) The role of narrative in personality psychology today. *Narrative Inquiry* 16, 11–18.

McAdams, D. P., Bauer, J. J., Sakaeda, A. R. *et al.* (2006) Continuity and change in the life story: a longitudinal study of autobiographical memories in emerging adulthood. *Journal of Personality* 74, 1371–1400.

Morgan, W. (2013) *The Trickster Figure in American Literature*. New York: Palgrave Macmillan US.

Olney, J. (1980) Autobiography and the cultural movement: a thematic, historical and bibliographical introduction. In: J. Olney (Ed.), *Autobiography Essays*. Princeton, NJ: Princeton University Press.

Pepper, S. C. (1942) *World Hypotheses*. Berkeley, CA: University of California Press.

Polkinghorne, D. E. (1989) *Narrative Knowing and the Human Sciences*. Albany, NY: State University of New York Press.

Propp, V. I. (1928/1958) *Morphology of the Folktale*. Bloomington: Indiana University.

Rieff, P. (1959). *Freud*. London: Victor Gollancz.

Ricoeur, P. (1984) *Time and Narrative* (Vol. 1). Chicago, IL: Chicago University Press.

Rushkoff, D. (2013) *Present Shock*. New York: Penguin.

Ryan, B. A. (1999) Does postmodernism mean the end of science in the behavioural sciences, and does it matter anyway? *Theory & Psychology* 9, 483–502.

Sarbin, T. R. (1986) The narrative as a root metaphor for psychology. In: T. R. Sarbin (Ed.), *Narrative Psychology*. Westport, CT: Praeger.

Sarbin, T. R. (2001) Embodiment and the narrative structure of emotional life. *Narrative Inquiry* 11, 217–225.

Sarbin, T. R. (2004) The role of imagination in narrative construction. In C. Daiute and C. Lightfoot (Eds.), *Narrative Analysis*. London, UK: Sage.

Schrag, C. O. (1997) *The Self after Postmodernity*. New Haven, CT: Yale University Press.

Stein, M. (2005) Individuation: inner work. *Journal of Jungian Theory and Practice* 7(2), 1–13.

Taylor, C. (1989) *Sources of the Self*. Cambridge: Cambridge University Press.

von Franz, M.-L. (1972) *Problems of the Feminine in Fairytales*. Dallas, TX: Spring.

von Franz, M.-L. (1980) *The Psychological Meaning of Redemption Motifs in Fairytales*. Toronto: Inner City Books.

von Franz, M.-L. (1996) *The Interpretation of Fairy Tales* (revised edition). Boston: Shambhala.

Walkerdine, V. (2014) Subjectivity, overview. In: T. Teo (Eds), *Encyclopaedia of Critical Psychology*. New York: Springer.

Woods, A. (2011) Post-narrative. An appeal. *Narrative Inquiry* 21, 399–406.

Yolen, J. (1986) *Favourite Folktales from around the World*. New York: Pantheon Books.

Chapter 2

Moments of becoming

Narrative knowing and the ethics of individuation

Mark Freeman

Introduction: the challenge of positing 'development'

In many ways, this chapter harkens back to some thinking and writing I did some three decades ago, when I became transfixed by the challenge of how to think about progressive human change. There was, of course, a sizeable literature about such change in developmental psychology through the work of Piaget, Vygotsky, and others. Much of this literature, however, essentially said that the process of development topped out in adolescence and that, consequently, there was no viable way of conceptualizing the process for the (many) years beyond that. It might have been argued that Erikson's (e.g. 1994) work was a notable exception. But it's a stretch to call his model a developmental one – if, by development, we mean progressive human change. The psychosocial model is a normative charting of stages tied to specific life tasks, especially as manifested in (some notable corridors of) Western culture. For that, it is certainly valuable. But it's not particularly valuable as a way of thinking about development.

I found myself between a rock and hard place. Those whose developmental theorizing ended at adolescence – at the Piagetian stage of formal operations, perhaps – had a point. By all indications, there was nothing quite so teleologically structured and orderly in the adult years. Erikson and company had a point too. For, what else could be done except to chart the culture-specific way in which lives (some at any rate) tended to unfold? There was another set of ideas lurking in the background of all this that complicated matters even further. That had to do with the fact that it was difficult to conceptualize developmental progress without positing some sort of *telos*, some sort of end, some sort of *good*, to which the process moved. And it was not at all clear what this could be. Moreover, the *telos* issue aside, for now, the very idea of developmental *progress* could be held suspect. By what criteria could such progress be posited? Maybe it was all just saccadic change – this, then that, then something else. Wasn't this fundamentally aimless movement really what life was about? Armed with the consolations of narrative, we may convince ourselves otherwise; we may see the movement of our lives, as embodied in the stories we tell about them, as possessing some sort of order and direction. But it could be an illusion. As Roquentin, the protagonist in Sartre's *Nausea* (1964) puts the matter, 'Nothing really happens when you live. The scenery changes, people come in and go out, that's all. There are no beginnings. Days are tacked on to days without rhyme or reason, an interminable monotonous addition' (Sartre 1964, p. 39). All of this changes when one turns to narrating the story of one's life, but 'it's a change no one notices' (Sartre 1964, p. 39). The result is that we tend to mistake the stories we tell about our lives for the decidedly more 'monotonous' movement of our lives themselves.

It is possible. That is, it's possible that narrative knowing entails projecting meaning and significance onto the flux, giving it an order and directionality it doesn't deserve. This is familiar territory: narratives smooth, distort, ultimately *lie* (e.g. Gazzaniga 1998; Sartwell 2000; Strawson 2004). Georges Gusdorf has written:

> The difficulty is insurmountable: no trick of presentation even when assisted by genius can prevent the narrator from always knowing the outcome of the story he tells – he commences, in a manner of speaking, with the problem already solved. Moreover the illusion begins from the moment that the narrative *confers a meaning* on the event which, when it actually occurred, no doubt had several meanings or perhaps none. This postulating of a meaning dictates the choice of the facts to be retained and of the details to bring out or to dismiss according the demands of the preconceived intelligibility.
>
> (Gusdorf 1980, p. 42, emphasis in original)

'It is here that the failures, the gaps, and the deformations of memory find their origin,' according to Gusdorf:

> They are not due to purely physical cause nor to chance, but on the contrary they are the result of an option of the writer who remembers and wants to gain acceptance for this or that revised and corrected version of his past, his private reality.
>
> (Gusdorf 1980, p. 42)

How could it be otherwise?

As for the idea of development, this basic line of thinking might continue, the 'illusion' will have become that much more pernicious. For the story being told is inevitably progressive, elevating, *triumphal*. Not surprisingly, just as there have emerged critiques of narrative, there have emerged critiques of the idea of development as well (e.g. Morss 1995). This too stands to reason. Positing development in childhood and adolescence is challenging enough. What can it possibly mean when it comes to the later course of life? And yet, for all of the force of these critiques, there was little question in my mind but that (1) narratives were not necessarily the fictional illusions they were often made out to be, and (2) development was not necessarily the self-aggrandizing, triumphalist tale some were considering it. For one, while it is in indeed the case that the stories one tells about the personal past can and often do entail fictions and even outright lies, they can also entail moments of insight and self-understanding: what had heretofore been obscure or opaque can be made visible, brought to light (Freeman 1993, 2010). For another, such moments of insight and self-understanding may themselves be moments of *self-realization* – that is, moments of becoming something other than what one was, something a step beyond, something more fully formed, something … *better*. That, at least, is how it appeared to me. How might this perspective be defended?

It was precisely in the face of these ideas and questions that I commenced the task of rethinking the concept of development. One outcome of this project was a piece, written with Rick Robinson, entitled 'The development within: an alternative approach to the study of lives' (Freeman and Robinson 1990). A brief review of that piece may be helpful. In keeping with what has been thus far, we began the piece by acknowledging the challenge of thinking developmentally about the adult years. Especially problematic was 'the very notion that the movement of life in adulthood could be graded and hierarchized', which appeared 'antithetical to everything we know about the multiplicity of ways to live' (Freeman and Robinson 1990, p. 53). A further, related problem was that 'all too often this putatively "natural," "evolutionary" process merely serves as a pretext for advocating … the values and beliefs we (liberal Western individuals, who care about ourselves and others, hopefully striking a decent balance) cherish' (Freeman and Robinson 1990, p. 53). Seen from this angle, 'the concept of development becomes little more than an unreflecting, ethnocentric reification of our own essentially arbitrary hierarchy of values' (Freeman and Robinson 1990, pp. 53–54).

Coming at the problem from a more empirical standpoint, it had also been argued that another roadblock to thinking developmentally about the adult years was the preponderance of factors affecting the movement of the life course and the sheer complexity of the process, with the result that that 'the sort of epistemic "containment" that is the hallmark of most extant models of development may no longer be possible' and that, consequently, 'it has become difficult to construct a model of adult development with the ability to encompass adequately as large a portion of the relevant information as those models concerned with the early course of development seem able to do' (Freeman and Robinson 1990, p. 54). In a related vein, there had also been the dawning conviction that theorists of the life course had perhaps focused too much on continuity at the expense of discontinuity (Neugarten 1969), constancy at the expense of change (Brim and Kagan 1980), order at the expense of chance (Gergen 1977). In short, perhaps life was rather more like the one depicted by Sartre than the teleological march to the future posited by much extant developmental theorizing – and, one might add, some theorizing about the process of individuation. Appealing though some of these critiques were in their efforts both to decentre the self and to acknowledge more adequately the pervasive impact of culture on the movement of human lives (Bruner 1986, 1990), they also left some of us feeling that it wasn't quite right. In the end, everything 'is equivalent to everything else', it seemed; 'there is no higher and lower, no better and worse, no more and less; there is no grid of values and beliefs with which the flux might be ordered' (Freeman and Robinson 1990, p. 54). Indeed, instead of 'attesting to and avowing the multiplicity of ways of life – a kind of psychological pluralism, as it were', it could be argued that this critical movement, we ventured, might instead attest to 'the loss of meanings, especially shared meanings, in the modern world' (Freeman and Robinson 1990, p. 54).

For some of us, there also remained the stubborn conviction that there were in fact moments in lives, throughout the entirety of the life course, that deserved to be called developmental: moments of insight, growth, *becoming*. As opposed to those who posited some sort of 'ceiling' to the process of development, such that the rhyme and reason of the earlier years gave way to the free verse of history, in other words, we held to the idea that these moments of becoming could occur as long as there was sentient life. Whether such moments could be charted in the 'grid'-like fashion referred to above was questionable; that is, it wasn't at all clear whether it was possible to fashion some normatively-structured model able to capture the movement of this becoming. Nor were we inclined to posit some form of developmental individuation – if by that is meant a teleological unfolding of what is essentially there from the beginning, *in nuce*. What *had* become clear was that we did 'not yet have an adequate way of speaking about the process of development in adulthood', with the result that all of the 'twists and turns people go through are levelled out onto a plateau of fundamentally directionless change, ... an asymptotic levelling of experience' (Freeman and Robinson 1990, p. 55). Again, maybe this was what life was actually like for many. Maybe the aforementioned 'loss of meanings' endemic to much of modern culture had, in effect, been hypostatized into this new, essentially anti-developmental, perspective. A theory for our time, as it were.

Whatever the source of this perspective may have been, we found ourselves wanting to move in a different direction by devising a way of conceptualizing development in adulthood. And what we knew was that, somehow or other, we would need

> to split the difference between the prevailing conception of development, which continues to seek to establish some sort of hierarchically constructed grid upon which any and all individuals may be placed ... and that point of view which negates the concept of development entirely, in the name of 'pure history'.
>
> (Freeman and Robinson 1990, p. 55)

As above, we also sought to steer clear of the kind of teleological thinking that characterized more extreme forms of developmental theorizing, including those seen in some versions of individuation theory. We therefore found ourselves committed to conceptualizing the process of development 'not "across" individuals, as is most often done, but "within" them' (Freeman and Robinson 1990, p. 55). Moreover, we were interested in speaking about development

> not in terms of some discrete end or "telos" to which all life processes must point, but in terms of the continually revised ends that pull us from what we come to realize is an inferior state of being to one that is arguably or demonstrably a better one.
>
> (Freeman and Robinson 1990, pp. 55–56)

From the perspective being advanced, the developmental process was intrinsically 'differential', such that 'the superiority of any given end can only be predicated in relation to that end which is being superseded', and also intrinsically 'narrational', such that 'the meaning of one's past and present experience becomes reconstructed with every new figuring of what it means to live optimally' (Freeman and Robinson 1990, pp. 55–56). I didn't know much about Jung's (e.g. 1934) idea of individuation at the time. And if truth be told, I am hardly an expert now. Looking back, however, I can discern some significant affinities between what I, along with Robinson and others, was seeking and some of the concerns Jung had pursued beforehand. Finding an adequate space for something akin to developmental self-realization was part of the challenge. What exactly was meant by 'superiority'? What made it so? Also, how was it possible to reconcile the idea of developmental self-realization, with its connotations of moving forward in time, with the idea of narrative, with its connotations of looking backward?

Justifying development

The story continues. By moving from a normative model of development to an 'ipsative' one – that is, by moving from a model positing development *across* individuals to one positing development *within* them – we had also called for a 'relativization' of the concept and avowed that 'we will no longer be operating in the context of an ordered hierarchy within which placement is made' (Freeman and Robinson 1990, p. 60). This was, and remains, risky territory. For, in the absence of shared ends and endpoints, what else could the process be but the subjective, hyper-individualized form of triumphal storytelling referred to earlier? Somehow, we had to justify continuing to rely on the concept of development, and we had to do so in a way that avoided the wholesale subjectivization of the process. We thus undertook a couple of fancy conceptual manoeuvres that now strike me as interesting, still, but highly questionable, not least because we couched these manoeuvres in the language of 'optimal experience.' If we couldn't posit agreed-upon optimal developmental ends, might we not be able to posit agreed-upon modes of optimal experience? We proposed to locate development in 'the space between "goals" or absolute developmental end-points, on the one hand, and the complete absence of ends, on the other.' The process of development, in short, must be based on those forms of experience that 'avow the fundamental multiplicity of ways of living by refusing to adhere slavishly to preconceived discrete ends and, at the same time, avow the necessity of creating new ends despite this very multiplicity'. Moreover, by 'being predicated neither upon preconceived ends nor the absence of ends, but upon the *revision* of ends, it is a process that sows the seeds of its own per-petuation'. Hence the 'differential' dimension referred to earlier: 'there are no final ends, only differences, but what is important is that this condition of difference somehow makes a difference in the experiential world of the indi-vidual' (Freeman and Robinson 1990, p. 61).

Why do I now find some of this 'highly questionable'? For one, it seems pre-sumptuous to exclude from view those who adhere to preconceived ends, from which they don't swerve. Why should people perpetually be unsettled, 'on the move'? For another, and more generally, why should experience be oriented toward 'better' ways of living? Maybe one's best way of living is to continue living the life one lives. Actually, maybe the ideas of better, best, and so on are unnecessary. Indeed, maybe ideas such as development and individuation are unnecessary too. Maybe, in the end, it's narrative, all the way down. After all, the only way to *posit* development or individuation is by telling a story, after the fact, of how they came to be. Maybe, therefore, ideas such as development and individuation are little more than modern myths, storytellings transmuted into quasi-teleological evolutions, retrospects transmuted into prospects.

But maybe not. So, let us set aside these larger concerns for the moment and see whether, within the fabric of the perspective being offered, there may remain something of value for thinking about these processes. 'Alongside the revision of ends,' we went on to say,

> it follows that development entails a process of reconstructing one's past and the self in which it has culminated. This is simply because for every new end that is figured in the course of one's life, old ends are superseded, which in a more general sense can be taken to mean that the 'text' of one's life, one's narrative, is being rewritten.
>
> (Freeman and Robinson 1990, p. 61)

The process being described is thus an *interpretive* process, and 'always requires the reflective mediation of the experiencing individual, who is engaged in the task of taking a portion of the self as other and simultaneously identifying both its limitations and its possibilities' (Freeman and Robinson 1990, pp. 61–62). It is also a process entailing an *ethical* dimension; it is about how one ought to live, what one ought to be or do, if only for the time being. I will address this issue in greater detail shortly. For now, what I want to highlight is the idea is that the 'narrative of individuation' that is the main focus of the present volume bears an element of *narrativity* within its very fabric. We can tell a story about the movement of individuation because the movement of individuation itself is a storying – or *re-storying* – process (Kenyon and Randall 1997; Randall 2017).

In view of the interpretive dimension referred to above, Robinson and I went on to consider a distinction that had been made in the context of hermeneutics – the theory of interpretation: that between *explication* and *demystification* (e.g. Palmer 1969; Ricoeur 1981; see also Josselson's 2004 consideration of 'the hermeneutics of faith' and 'the hermeneutics of suspicion'). The former generally refers to the kinds of interpretive processes that involves conscious discernment – in this case, of some aspect of one's experience that warrants being revisited, such that there emerges some new measure of meaning or significance. With the distance conferred by time, a wider interpretive context is formed, and the experience in question comes to play a new and different role in the evolving story of one's life (Freeman 1993, 2010). Demystification, by contrast, generally refers to those kinds of interpretive processes that seek to decipher and decode some aspect of one's experience (or character or relationships, etc.) that appear opaque and impenetrable and that thereby warrant a 'special' hermeneutic strategy for breaking through the opacity. We are therefore considering here the kinds of processes frequently associated with Nietzsche, Marx and, especially, Freud, ones that dig beneath the surface of things with the aim of unearthing meanings that may be all but invisible to the untutored – or analysed – eye. Most important for present purposes, in any case, is that in both versions of the interpretive process there is a movement of coming-to-light and coming-to-consciousness: what had heretofore been inchoate or opaque is being seen anew, bringing the person in question one step farther in the movement of individuation. It should be noted that nothing is being said here about the quality of the resultant insight; it could be a deep and gratifying sense of self-realization, and it could be a quite horrifying sense of the profound ways in which one has been kept in, or has kept oneself in, the dark. Either way, there is, arguably, progressive movement – 'enlightenment', one might say; for better or for worse, one's inner world has been illumined.

Terms such as 'better', therefore, are emphatically not to be equated with contentment or happiness or some other ostensibly desirable state of experience. One may have been quite content basking in the illusory comfort of one's defences or delusions; one's 'happiness' may have been utterly superficial and meaningless, a crude means of stopping oneself in one's developmental tracks. As for the term 'ethical', it is not, in this context at least, to be equated with some pre-identified and prescribed way of life presumed to be a better one. Generally speaking, being attentively present to the needs and wishes of others is surely a good thing – better, indeed, than being inattentive, disrespectful, and narcissistically encased in one's own needs and wishes. Nevertheless, it remains conceivable from the perspective presented thus far that the movement of development will at times lead to ends that may consensually be regarded as unethical if not positively abhorrent. Hurting someone that one has been terribly hurt by may be a developmental achievement. Behaving irresponsibly in the wake of a too-responsible life may be one as well. We may of course hope that the 'larger' goods that tend to be associated with ethical and moral behaviour – kindness, compassion, and so on – will ultimately gain the upper hand. But it may be some time before this is possible, and until that time, there may well be instances of developmental movement that lead one to a 'better' place even while being ethically problematic.

Can the same be said of the process of individuation, as conceptualized by Jung and others? Is it conceivable that the movement of individuation can culminate in comparably problematic ethical places and positions? More to the point still: in speaking of the 'ethics of individuation', are we considering the 'smaller' ethics involved in developmental transformation or the 'larger' ethics involved in living a good and worthwhile life? That there is an aspect of ethics involved in the process of individuation seems unassailable. The question is what sort of ethics it is. I will address this issue by the chapter's end. Before doing so, it is important to gain a clear sense of the different moments comprising the developmental process.

Charting the process of development

In our initial formulation of the process of development, we posited four fundamental 'moments' of the process – that is, hierarchically ordered phases that could be said to characterize any and all instances of development (Freeman and Robinson 1990). We called these *recognition, distanciation, articulation* and *appropriation.*

By *recognition*, we referred to 'some semblance of a disjunction or contradiction between what exists and what is posited as representing a more ideal state of knowing or being, even if it is the case that this ideal state is not yet fully known' (Freeman and Robinson 1990, p. 64). More simply put, in this initial phase of the process, one is 'at odds' with oneself in some way; one recognizes, however inarticulately, that something is amiss in one's life, that it is less than what it might be or ought to be; and it is precisely this state of disjunction, this 'rift', as we called it, that serves as the motor for the process to follow, 'a provocation to restore, to move beyond' (Freeman and Robinson 1990, p. 64).

Once there is some measure of recognition that all is not well in one's life, one needs to both get clearer what the source(s) of one's unease may be and begin to extricate oneself from the provoking situation. Inspired by the hermeneutical efforts of Paul Ricoeur (1981), we spoke of *distanciation* as a moment wherein one begins to 'divest' oneself of current modes of experiencing so as to pave the way for newer ones. As Ricoeur (1981, p. 106) had put the matter, 'I find myself only be losing myself'. Looking back, a number of related ideas come to mind in this context. One is Iris Murdoch's (1970) idea of 'unselfing'. 'We are anxiety-ridden animals,' Murdoch writes. 'Our minds are continually active, fabricating an anxious, usually self-preoccupied, often falsifying veil which partially conceals the world' (Murdoch 1970, p. 84). Because of this, we need to take measures to get beyond or 'out' of ourselves; we need to resist our own egocentric fantasies and preoccupations so as to behold what is really there (see also Freeman 2014a, 2015). One might also consider this moment of the developmental process a kind of hermeneutical mindfulness, wherein, through distancing, through noticing attentively what is going on in one's world, one may see more clearly why it is problematic.

This moment of the process is potentially fraught. One reason is implicit in what has been said already: 'for every instance of self-gain, there must necessarily be an instance of self-loss' (Freeman and Robinson 1990, p. 65), a giving-up of some facet of who and what one has been. This may be difficult in its own right. One may wish to remain within the confines of the familiar, the secure. One may hold on doggedly to one's ways, dysfunctional or even destructive though they may be, and fear the grief that would ensue were one to give them up. And of course one's defences and unconscious machinations may prevent one from seeing 'what is really there'. These defences and machinations need to be exposed and, ultimately, dismantled before further progress is made. This sort of breaking-down is bound to be painful. The main point for now, in any case, is that 'development must be seen not merely as the addition of the new, but ... the supersession and displacement of the old' (Freeman and Robinson 1990, p. 65).

Necessary though this moment of the developmental process is, there is much more to be done. Now that one may have gathered some preliminary sense of what is 'wrong', one needs to gain a clearer sense of what might be 'right' – or at least more right than the mode being superseded. 'After distanciation, this separation of self from self,' therefore, 'there needs to be a further moment of definition or *articulation*' (Freeman and Robinson 1990, p. 65), such that the contours of the self-to-be come into view. This moment too is potentially fraught, not least because one may well have a clearer sense of what *not* to be than what *to* be. Consequently, one may find oneself in a kind of developmental limbo, a betwixt and between state of existential liminality (to paraphrase Turner 1967). One may, for instance, come to the realization that the kind of work one is doing, or the kind of relationship one is in, or the very life one is leading is no longer adequate, but without having a clear sense of either what exactly the problem is or how to move forward, to a more optimal state.

We might think of the therapeutic process in this context as well: before one is ready to establish new patterns for living one's life, ones that are more consonant with one's innermost being, one must identify, as clearly as possible, the problematic nature of the patterns left behind; only then will the movement toward the future proceed authentically. These patterns are *narrative* patterns; they are 'the stories we live by' (McAdams 1997). The moment of articulation, therefore, entails both the reconstruction or 'rewriting' of the past self and, at the same time, the creation of the self-to-be. As has been suggested already, this newly articulated vision of the self-to-be is, on some level, tied to the *good* – that is, to a state of being or knowing that is arguably, or demonstrably, better than the one left behind. And 'this sense of the good', Charles Taylor has written,

> has to be woven into my life as an unfolding story ... making sense of my present action, when we are not dealing with such trivial questions as where I shall go in the next five minutes but with the issue of my place relative to the good, requires a narrative understanding of my life, a sense of what I have become which can only be given in a story. And as I project my life forward and endorse the existing direction or give it a new one, I project a future story, not just a state of the momentary future but a bent for my whole life to come.
>
> (Taylor 1989, p. 48)

One's convictions about the permanence of this future story notwithstanding, the kind of narrative transformation Taylor is describing here inevitably entails 'a change which is qualified as "growth," or "sanctification," or "higher consciousness,"' and also 'involves our repudiating earlier goods' (Taylor 1989, p. 70). In this respect, the process of development is a process of 'reasoning in transitions.... It aims to establish, not that some position is correct but rather that some position is superior to some other. It is concerned, covertly or openly, implicitly or explicitly, with comparative propositions' (Taylor 1989, p. 72). This 'superiority' might be considered as what I have elsewhere referred to as 'narrative gain', such that, through narrative, one articulates 'a view of one's existence that is demonstrably more adequate, capacious, truthful, and/or ethically sound than the one it has superseded' (Freeman 2014b, p. 19).

For reasons to be considered in greater detail later on, I have come to question some aspects of Taylor's perspective. As important as 'reasoning in transitions' may sometimes be, it is not at all clear that developmental transformation always entails reasoning. Indeed, it is not all clear that such transformation finds its source in the experiencing person him- or herself. Rather, it may be that the source of one's transformation is the *Other* – for instance, another person, in need, who calls me out of myself, in responsibility (Levinas 1994, 1999; also Freeman 2014a). In a related vein, the basic perspective we have been considering has come to seem too individualistic, too bound up with the particular interests and proclivities of individual persons, seeking their own self-realization. I suppose this may be a liability of any perspective that highlights 'individuation' and that refuses a priori pronouncements of what this means. Yes; my path may well be unlike any other. And yes; it is my challenge to find it. But is there anything to be said about the nature and quality and 'validity' of this path?

For now, let us consider the final moment of the developmental process, which we called, following Ricoeur (1981) once again, *appropriation*. Articulating the direction of the future, while necessary, is not sufficient; the fact is, one may know precisely where one needs to go in order to move forward but be unable, or unwilling, to actually do it. One classic case of just this sort of resistance is that of Saint Augustine, as described in his *Confessions*, written in AD 397 (see also Freeman 1993). He knows full well that it is time to leave behind his lustful, self-indulgent ways and devote himself to God; the proverbial writing is on the wall. But he's not quite ready. As he put the matter,

> I could no longer claim that I had no clear perception of the truth – the excuse which I used to make for myself for postponing my renunciation of the world and my entry into your service – for by now I was quite certain of it.
>
> (Augustine 1980, p. 165)

Nevertheless, 'Instead of fearing, as I ought, to be held back by all that encumbered me, I was frightened to be free of it.... "Soon,"' he would say. '"Presently", "Let me wait a little while longer"' (Augustine 1980, p. 165). '"Give me chastity and continence, but not yet"' (Augustine 1980, p. 169). So it was that he had remained mired in what he knew to be his wrongful ways. And so it was that, eventually, he would strike out in rage against himself, for his pitiful refusal to live the life he knew he must. Somehow, he would need to make the truth his own by truly embracing and living it.

It should be noted here that the process of leaving one's previous 'patterns' behind may never be brought to completion. While Augustine surely had to mend his evil ways, he could not fully disavow the operative forces. Nor, of course, could he fully disavow his past and the self he had been. There is no way to fully cut the cord of one's history and story. On the contrary, as a general rule, one must remain cognizant of the patterns one has sought to leave behind; otherwise, we may see the 'return of the repressed' and, in turn, the resurgence of the very self one may have assumed, erroneously, had been deposed.

A further qualification is in order as well. Calling appropriation the 'final' moment of the developmental process does not mean that the process is now halted. As Robinson and I put the matter,

> this final moment of development, far from being an end in itself, sealed off from the future, from the continued revisioning of ends, is instead best seen as a new beginning. No problem area can ever be totally reconciled with the fabric of the self; there will always be residues, vestiges that remain to be dealt with. In addition to the difference between the old and the new, therefore, there ideally arises a further tension: between the new, already in the process of being relegated to the old, and those future ends, however ill-defined, that will eventually serve to pull us into yet another cycle of development.
>
> (Freeman and Robinson 1990, p. 66)

Bearing this last set of ideas in mind, one may plausibly say that development is a *never-ending* process – an ongoing story, as it were, ever to be rewritten. The same has been said of individuation: 'as an event proceeding throughout life, [it] is *never completed*. It is a continual unending approach to a distant goal, death being the ultimate boundary' (Jacobi 1967, p. 96, emphasis in original).

To refer briefly to another classic example, that of Lev Tolstoy's *The Death of Ivan Ilych*, first published in 1886 (see also Freeman 2010): it was not until shortly before his death that the protagonist achieved a developmental break-through. Inconceivable though the thought would once have been, given how 'proper' his life had appeared, he is brought to wonder: 'Maybe I did not live as I ought to have done' (Tolstoy 1886/1960, p. 145). No, he had initially con-cluded; it can't be. So, as Tolstoy tells it,

> whenever the thought occurred to him, as it often did, that it all resulted from his not having lived as he ought to have done, he at once recalled the correctness of his whole life and dismissed so strange an idea.
>
> (Tolstoy 1886/1960, p. 145)

In any case, and to make a long story short, Ivan Ilych eventually arrives at the realization that he had been mistaken. '"Yes, it was all not the right thing," he admitted' (Tolstoy 1886/1960, p. 151). Distanciation, par excellence. '"But what *is* the right thing?"' The answer appeared in the form of his son, standing by the side of his bed, crying. 'At that very moment Ivan Ilych fell through and caught sight of the light, and it was revealed to him that though his life had not been what it should have been, this could still be rectified' (Tolstoy 1886/1960, p. 151). It should be noted that there is no 'reasoning' happening in this scene; rather, the 'light' that finally emerges issues from his son and then his wife, now visible. Before, they had been veiled; they had been mere objects, mere instru-ments of his own relentless self-aggrandizement. Now, he can finally see them for what they are. '"Yes, I am making them wretched," he thought' (Tolstoy 1886/1960, p. 151). What, then? Perhaps he can say something to them, some-thing that might serve to diminish their pain? But that can't possibly be enough. '"Besides, why speak? I must act."' As for how, 'he must act so as not to hurt them: release them and free himself from these sufferings' (Tolstoy 1886/1960, p. 152). All's well that ends well (though he does die some two hours later). Was there anything to distinguish this later framing of the developmental process from the earlier one?

The ethics of individuation

My 2010 treatment of the developmental process that Ilych had gone through was much the same as the one Robinson and I had identified and that which I saw played out in St. Augustine's *Confessions*. In this more recent work (Freeman 2010), I was especially concerned to demonstrate the connection between the developmental process and *hindsight*, the ability to discern the errors of one's ways and to thereby move beyond them. In addition, however,

I had begun to entertain what I (cautiously) referred to as the 'transcendent horizon' of the life story and also to reflect further on the idea that the process of development is 'as much about the *Other* as it is about the self'. By 'transcendent horizon,' I was referring to 'those dimensions of the life story that are, finally, about the state and destiny of one's very soul' (Freeman 2010, p. 94). As for the increasingly prominent place of the Other in the story of the self, I was exploring the related idea that some larger sphere of *goodness* had to be brought into the developmental picture.

This brought me back to Taylor (1989). In addition to his having posited the replacement of an 'inferior' mode with a 'superior' one, he had introduced the idea of 'hypergoods' – that is, those 'higher-order goods [that] not only are incomparably more important than others but provide the standpoint from which these must be weighed, judged, decided about' (Taylor 1989, p. 63). As he explained, 'If hypergoods arise through supersessions, the conviction they carry comes from our reading of the transitions to them, from a certain understanding of moral growth' (Taylor 1989, p. 72). I have already confessed my uncertainty about certain aspects of Taylor's perspective. His language of that which is 'weighed, judged, decided about' confirms this uncertainty. More substantively, I went on to suggest that, 'rather than hypergoods arising through supersessions, it is just the opposite: supersessions arise through hypergoods, through some sphere of goodness – some Other, outside the perimeter of the self – that draws the developmental process forward' (Freeman 2010, p. 214).

In the case of Ivan Ilych, as we saw, the living presence of his son and his wife was what awakened him and drew him beyond himself. It is not only the human Other, however, that 'inspires' in this way; it can be art, nature, God – whatever it is that draws the self beyond its own borders. 'What is key is the idea of *relatedness* to some Other, whether human or nonhuman, that can serve as a point of orientation and direction for the process of discerning the direction of one's life' (Freeman 2010, p. 216).

It is precisely at this juncture that the process of development, as we have been considering it in the preceding pages, may be related to Jung's idea of individuation. I will not pretend mastery of this idea in the few remaining pages of this chapter. Rather, I am proceeding largely on an intuition that, although the languages employed differ in significant ways, there is some fertile ground to be cultivated in exploring this relationship. I first caught a glimpse of this in reading *Modern Man in Search of Soul* (Jung 1933) – specifically, the chapter on 'Problems of modern psychotherapy', when he introduces his own four-stage process, involving 'confession, explanation, education, and transformation' (Jung 1933, p. 31). The overlap between the four moments we have been considering and Jung's four stages is both substantial and inexact. By *confession*, Jung is making a direct reference to its 'prototype', the confessional, the supposition here being that some form or other of 'concealment' – the hiding of a 'secret' – is foundational. If by 'secret' is meant some sort of already-articulated disturbing 'object', locked away in the unconscious, I am not sure I concur. If, however, he is referring to some unarticulated strand of the past, bringing forth the kind of 'unease' referred to earlier, I am with him. I am certainly not disputing the possible existence of bona fide secrets, unconsciously held; all I am saying is that unarticulated experience may be as likely, if not more, to be the inaugural moment of the process. Jung (1933) says as much when he writes:

> unconscious contents are by no means exclusively such as were once conscious and, by being repressed, have later grown into unconscious complexes. Quite otherwise, the unconscious has contents peculiar to itself which, slowly growing upward from the depths, at last come into consciousness.
>
> (Jung 1933, p. 32)

These may leave us with just the sort of unease discussed above. One way or the other, the 'motto' Jung highlights in this context – 'Give up what thou hast, and then thou wilt received' (Jung 1933, p. 35) – is surely an important one. Whatever it may be that is being concealed, or withheld, or that is serving as a vague disturbance, must be 'given up', for 'it is only with the help of confession that I am able to throw myself into the arms of humanity freed at last from the burden of moral exile' (Jung 1933, p. 35).

This leads us to Jung's second stage, that of *explanation*. Cathartic though it may be to confess one's 'sins', it is not enough. In addition, there must be a moment wherein the origins, or likely origins, of one's sins is disclosed. As Jung points out, this is the moment that is most readily associated with Freud. He writes:

> The end-product of the Freudian method of explanation is a detailed elaboration of man's shadow-side such as had never been carried out before. It is the most effective antidote imaginable to all idealistic illusions about the nature of man; and it is therefore no wonder that there arose on all sides the most violent opposition to Freud and his school.
>
> (Jung 1933, p. 40)

As Jung goes on to argue, 'Freud's method of interpretation rests on "reductive" explanations which unfailingly lead backward and downward, and it has a destructive effect if it is used in an exaggerated and one-sided way' (Jung 1933, p. 41). The rug is pulled out from beneath one, distanciation-style, and if the process rests there, there will be nowhere to stand.

What is ultimately required is some form of *education*, 'which makes us realize that no confession and no amount of explaining will make the ill-formed tree grow straight, but that it must be trained with the gardener's art upon the trellis before normal adaptation can be attained' (Jung 1933, p. 46). By education, I take Jung to mean a process not only of training or moulding (tied to the Latin *educare*) but also of 'leading forth' or 'bringing out' (tied to the Latin *educere*). It would thus appear to be related to the aforementioned idea of articulation.

As for the fourth stage of the process being considered, that of *transformation*,

> we must … take account of those psychic needs of man which were not given a place in the other stages. In other words, we must ascertain what could seem more desirable or lead further than the claim to be a normally adapted, social being.
>
> (Jung 1933, p. 47)

What, for Jung, is the problem with such normality? Along with the idea of adaptation, 'it suggests a restriction to the average' (Jung 1933, p. 47) and thus essentially obviates whatever might lead the individual beyond the norm. This may be fine for some, especially those whose 'abnormality' has left them outside of the kinds of human relations they seek. In other cases, however, the challenge is that of 'developing the creative possibilities that lie within the patient himself' (Jung 1933, p. 61). Along these lines, Jung writes, 'What I have to say begins with the point where treatment ceases and development sets in' (Jung 1933, p. 61). Such development entails work, to be sure. But it also entails play, an ability 'to experiment with [one's] own nature – a state of fluidity, change, and growth, in which there is no longer anything eternally fixed and hopelessly petrified' (Jung 1933, p. 66).

The four stages we have just considered, too briefly, are less about individuation per se and more about the therapeutic process. However, the two are not unrelated. For the therapeutic process – especially insofar as it moves beyond treatment, toward development – is itself a kind of individuation, replete with its own ethics. Is there a way to specify the nature of this ethics without it appearing either absolutist, on the one hand, or hyper-individualistic, on the other? Let us translate this question into the terms of narrative. We can assume that, whether the context is therapy or the life beyond it, the narrative that has characterized the movement of one's life has been found wanting. We can also assume that, by virtue of this being-wanting, there is a need for, or a desire for, a new narrative, one that brings one farther along the path of individuation than the one that has been travelled thus far. Is there a way to specify the nature of this narrative transformation and the 'gain' it is thought to entail? An additional question is in order here as well, one that brings us back to the relationship between development and individuation. One feature of the developmental framework that has been presented in these pages is that it is meant to apply to any and all instances of progressive change, from small to large. This means that it is more about the 'form' of development than the 'content'. For present purposes, I suggest that all of the different cycles of development that occur throughout the course of one's life comprise the process of individuation, and that all of the smaller stories we live and tell along the way comprise the larger story of our lives. The question, then, is: is there a way to specify this larger constellation of meaning and developmental movement? And if so, what sort of ethics does it bring in tow?

In Jung's (1934) reflections on individuation, he is careful to differentiate individualism from individuation. 'Individualism,' he writes, 'means deliberately stressing and giving prominence to some supposed peculiarity rather than to collective considerations and obligations' (Jung 1934, para. 267). Individuation, by contrast, 'means precisely the better and more complete fulfilment of the collective qualities of the human being' (Jung 1934, para. 267). As such, it 'can only mean a process of psychological development that fulfils the individual qualities given; in other words, it is a process by which a man becomes the definite, unique being he in fact is' (Jung 1934, para. 267). I take this to mean that individuation is a process that involves not only my uniqueness, in the sense of characterological peculiarities, but also my distinctive modes of responsiveness and responsibility to what is *other* than me. On my reading, Jung emphasizes the former more than the latter: individuation is largely about recognizing and respecting who I truly am, and cultivating myself accordingly. In my own recent musings on these issues (Freeman 2012, 2014a), I emphasize the latter more than the former: it is the Other that has priority and that is constitutive of the unique constellation that is 'me'. This does not mean the denial of personal agency. Nor is it to suggest that we are mere 'effects' of external sources. What it means is that what nourishes and inspires us derives from outside ourselves, as do our care and compassion. They are drawn forth by what is Other, both human and nonhuman, and the particular way in which they come together and constellate comprises the unique beings we are. Individuation, from this perspective, therefore, may be characterized by a kind of 'excentricity', such that there may emerge 'a larger, unbounded Self, one that knows, and feels, its kinship with the world' (Freeman 2014a, p. 2). Along these lines, one might say that individuation, paradoxically, entails an element of *de*-individuation – or what Murdoch (1970), referred to earlier, has called 'unselfing', the letting-go of the ego-driven self and its replacement by this larger, more capacious Self, spread ex-centrically into the world.

Are these two versions of individuation compatible with one another? It would appear so. For instance, Jung writes of how, in the progressive movement of self-knowledge,

> there arises a consciousness which is no longer imprisoned in the petty, oversensitive, personal world of the ego, but participates freely in the wider world of objective interests. This widened consciousness is no longer that touchy, egotistical bundle of personal wishes, fears, hopes, and ambitions which always has to be compensated or corrected by unconscious counter-tendencies; instead, it is a function of relationship to the world of objects, bringing the individual into absolute, binding, and indissoluble communion with the world at large.
>
> (Jung 1934, para. 275)

As Jung goes on to note, 'The complications arising at this stage are no longer egotistic wish-conflicts, but difficulties that concern others as much as oneself'

(Jung 1934, para. 275). Alongside the necessity of integrating unconscious and conscious processes, there is, for Jung too, the necessity of moving beyond the 'petty', 'touchy' self-enclosure of the hungry, wish-full ego, into the wider world. With this ex-centric movement comes responsibility, to and for others as well as the nonhuman world. In keeping with a point raised earlier, this may be not so much a commitment one makes, as a function of some sort of 'reasoning' process, as it is a direct and spontaneous outgrowth of the Other's claim upon me. 'My' story thus comes to be inseparable from the human story, its transcendent horizon ultimately pointing toward those 'hypergoods' – or gods – that orient and direct the course of life. As Jung (1933), among others, has pointed out, these goods and gods are frequently less visible to us moderns. But they may be no less present, either in the world of experience or in the stories we tell about it. The ethics of individuation would seem to have something to do not only with making the unconscious conscious but also with making the invisible visible and thereby highlighting the sacred wellsprings of personal life.

Coda: thinking otherwise about individuation

What has been presented in the preceding pages may be understood as a narrative version of the process of individuation, one that sees the process less as a teleological unfolding of what is there from the beginning and more as an ongoing process of rewriting the self, such that it is brought to a higher plane. There is no ceiling to this process, no moment of arrival, no final 'peak' of self-realization; there are only movements forward, sometimes through reasoning, sometimes through being drawn forth, ex-centrically, by what is Other. There is always a difference involved in these movements, between a less ideal state and a more, between what has been, in the past, and what is now emerging, in the present, on the way to the future; 'it is always a matter of something obsolete that must be left behind to die in order that the new may be born' (Jacobi 1967, p. 99). These movements cannot be predicted ahead of time. For this reason especially, narrative is the most natural form for describing them.

In closing, one final idea, also tied to the ethics of individuation, seems appropriate to consider. In speaking above about 'making the unconscious conscious', I refer not only to the Freudian view of the process or the more 'collective' view proposed by Jung, but what I have come to call the *narrative* unconscious (Freeman 2002), which has to do with 'those culturally rooted aspects of one's history that have not yet become part of one's story' (Freeman 2002, p. 193) and that we encounter 'precisely during those moments when our own historical and cultural situatedness comes into view' (Freeman 2002, p. 201). As Jung well knew, one's history comprises substantially more than what one can consciously know and tell. Moreover, it cannot be restricted to the swath of time between birth and the moment of telling; rather, we are *born* into a history – a specific world whose contours are provided prior to our entry – and we carry this history with us throughout the course of our lives, often in ways largely unbeknownst to us. In a distinct and important sense, this 'deep' history is another facet of the 'undiscovered self' (Jung 1957/2010) and embodies another way in which what is *other* permeates our lives and narratives. But it is not the history or archetypal 'memory' that Jung posits when discussing the collective unconscious. Rather, it is the history found in our families, communities, and cultures and that remains alive in us, serving as the cultural-memorial 'backdrop,' one might say, for our being in the world.

In a recent piece in which I discussed the relationship between the collective unconscious and the narrative unconscious (Freeman 2016), I also suggested that our way of belonging to this deep history into which we are born often bears within it 'strong valuations regarding what is right and good – and wrong and evil' (Freeman 2016, p. 520). As I went on to acknowledge, these valuations are, in part, products of history themselves and are thus largely conventional in nature. But in view of the sheer weight of this deep history – I am thinking especially of the weight of events such as the Holocaust on those born in its aftermath (see Frie 2014, 2017; Hoffman 2004) – I have come to wonder whether these valuations sometimes transcend conventions and thus bespeak 'something that comes with the realities of being human and feeling the pull – and the priority – of the Other' (Freeman 2016, p. 520). One might think of them as belonging to the *ethical* unconscious. This need not be seen as some wholly different register of the unconscious. Indeed,

> it may be that the narrative unconscious, the ethical unconscious, the 'classical' unconscious of psychoanalysis, and ... the collective unconscious are all of a piece, differentially distributed in accordance with our life circumstances and our varying degrees of awareness of what, in us, may be operative behind the scenes.
>
> (Freeman 2016, p. 520)

Jacobi (1967) offers a similar point of view when she writes,

> As a process of *psychological development*, [individuation] represents the step-by-step maturation of the human psyche to the point where all its potentialities are unfolded, and the conscious and unconscious realms are united by integrating its historical roots with present-day consciousness.
>
> (Jacobi 1967, p. 132)

I don't know that 'all' our potentialities are ever unfolded; the open-ended, step-by-step nature of the process militates against it. This process requires a narrative account, a story. It cannot be foretold, only told. To tell the story of individuation thus turns out to be an extremely complicated narrative task, one that takes us well beyond the confines of consciousness, into those multiple spheres of otherness, both within and outside the psyche, constitutive of our lives.

References

Augustine, St. (1980) *Confessions*. New York: Penguin.

Brim, O. G. and Kagan, J. (1980) Constancy and change: a view of the issues. In: O. G. Brim and J. Kagan (Eds), *Constancy and Change in Human Development*. Cambridge, MA: Harvard University Press.

Bruner, J. (1986) *Actual Minds, Possible Worlds*. Cambridge, MA: Harvard University Press.

Bruner, J. (1990) *Acts of Meaning*. Cambridge, MA: Harvard University Press.

Erikson, E. H. (1994) *Identity and the Life Cycle*. New York: W. W. Norton.

Freeman, M. (1993) *Rewriting the Self: History, Memory, Narrative*. London: Routledge.

Freeman, M. (2002) Charting the narrative unconscious: cultural memory and the challenge of autobiography. *Narrative Inquiry* 12, 193–211.

Freeman, M. (2010) *Hindsight: The Promise and Peril of Looking Backward*. New York: Oxford University Press.

Freeman, M. (2012) Thinking and being Otherwise: aesthetics, ethics, erotics. *Journal of Theoretical and Philosophical Psychology* 32, 196–208.

Freeman, M. (2014a) *The Priority of the Other: Thinking and Living Beyond the Self*. New York: Oxford University Press.

Freeman, M. (2014b) Narrative, ethics, and the development of identity. *Narrative Works* 4, 8–27.

Freeman, M. (2015) Beholding and being beheld: Simone Weil, Iris Murdoch, and the ethics of attention. *The Humanistic Psychologist* 43, 160–172.

Freeman, M. (2016) From the collective unconscious to the narrative unconscious: re-imagining the sources of selfhood. *Europe's Journal of Psychology* 12, 513–522.

Freeman, M. and Robinson, R. (1990) The development within: an alternative approach to the study of lives. *New Ideas in Psychology* 8, 53–72.

Frie, R. (2014) Limits of understanding: psychological experience, German memory and the Holocaust. *Psychoanalysis, Culture & Society* 19, 255–271.

Frie, R. (2017) *Not in my Family: German Memory and Responsibility after the Holocaust*. New York: Oxford University Press.

Gazzaniga, M. (1998) *The Mind's Past*. Berkeley, CA: University of California Press.

Gergen, K. J. (1977) Stability, change and chance in understanding human development. In: N. Datan and H. W. Reese (Eds), *Life-span Developmental Psychology: Dialectical Perspectives in Experimental Research*. New York: Academic Press.

Gusdorf, G. (1980) Conditions and limits of autobiography. In J. Olney (Ed.), *Autobiography: Essays Theoretical and Critical*. Princeton, NJ: Princeton University Press.

Hoffman, E. (2004) *After such Knowledge: Memory, History, and the Legacy of the Holocaust*. New York: Public Affairs.

Jacobi, J. (1967) *The Way of Individuation*. London, UK: Hodder and Stoughton.

Josselson, R. (2004) The hermeneutics of faith and the hermeneutics of suspicion. *Narrative Inquiry* 14, 1–28.

Jung, C. G. (1933) *Modern Man in Search of a Soul*. San Diego, CA: Harcourt Brace Jovanovich.

Jung, C. G. (1934) The relations between the ego and the unconscious. *The Collected Works of C. G. Jung* (Vol. 7). Princeton, NJ: Princeton University Press.

Jung, C. G. (1957/2010) *The Undiscovered Self*. Princeton, NJ: Princeton University Press.

Kenyon, G. M. and Randall, W. L. (1997) *Restorying Our Lives: Personal Growth through Autobiographical Reflection*. Westport, CT: Praeger.

Levinas, E. (1994) *Outside the Subject*. Palo Alto, CA: Stanford University Press.

Levinas, E. (1999) *Alterity and Transcendence*. New York: Columbia University Press.

McAdams, D. P. (1997) *The Stories we Live By: Personal Myths and the Making of the Self*. New York: Guilford.

Morss, J. (1995) *Growing Critical: Alternatives to Developmental Psychology*. London: Routledge.

Murdoch, I. (1970) *The Sovereignty of Good*. London: Routledge.

Neugarten, B. L. (1969) Continuities and discontinuities of psychological issues into adult life. *Human Development* 12, 121–130.

Palmer, R. (1969) *Hermeneutics*. Evanston, IL: Northwestern University Press.

Randall, W. L. (2017) *The Narrative Complexity of Ordinary Life: Tales from the Coffee Shop*. New York: Oxford University Press.

Ricoeur, P. (1981) *Hermeneutics and the Human Sciences*. Cambridge, UK: Cambridge University Press.

Sartre, J.-P. (1964) *Nausea*. Norfolk, CT: New Directions.

Sartwell, C. (2000) *End of Story: Toward an Annihilation of Language and History*. Albany, NY: SUNY Press.

Strawson, G. (2004) Against narrativity. *Ratio XVII*, 428–452.

Taylor, C. (1989) *Sources of the Self*. Cambridge, MA: Harvard University Press.

Tolstoy, L. (1886/1960) *The Death of Ivan Ilych and Other Stories*. New York: New American Library.

Turner, V. (1967) *The Forest of Symbols: Aspects of Ndembu Ritual*. Ithaca, NY: Cornell University Press.

Chapter 3

Listening to a dream-narrative
A language for narrating boundaries

Megumi Yama

The self-healing tendency of the psyche

When we value a dream's images with respect, without trying to interpret or understand them too quickly, sometimes the dream begins to narrate spontaneously and this process itself may bring about healing in a deep sense. In this chapter, I would like to present a clinical case study, first presented in Yama (2001), to show how rich imaginative narratives may emerge if protected with appropriate care.

The client I would like to introduce is a young woman in her early 20s, whom I shall call Min. She was suffering from anthropophobia, anxiety and a sense of inferiority. She was the third generation of a permanent ethnic Korean resident of Japan. Before going any further, some information about the sad history between Korea and Japan is necessary. During the Second World War, many Koreans were forcibly brought to Japan. Although the situation has been changing recently, the Koreans have suffered from discrimination over the years. In order to sustain their family, Min's parents had to work so hard that she was not adequately taken care of as a small child. Her relationship with her family has not been necessarily good, which made her uncomfortable at home. She devoted herself to painting as a university art student.

In a quiet room, which had a calm atmosphere although moderately tense, I gave free rein to my imagination and listened to her as she reported her dreams. They became animated and embodied within myself as I let these images go through my body. We tasted the images of the dreams with a few words and tried to keep holding them together just as they were. We did that for about a year. In the meantime, I tried to look for a model in the custom of 'incubation' in ancient times, when people used to sleep in a temple in order to receive a dream. It used to be very popular in medieval Japan, too. Even in *Kojiki*, the oldest myth narrative in Japan (compiled in the early eighth century), we find descriptions where dreams are taken as something that were sent from the divine power. Meier (1989), who realized the similarity between materials produced by psychotic clients and symbols and motifs in ancient literature, was convinced of the necessity to study incubation in the ancient world. While engaging in that study, he found that there was 'a factor at work that we may call today, rather inadequately, the "self-healing tendency of the psyche," which is also observed in Jung's analytical psychology' (Meier 1989, p. i). He comments, regarding the Jungian method, 'This is possible, however, only if the observer adopts a waiting attitude, letting the process happen, listening to it, as it were, and following it in all humility' (Meier 1989, p. i).

As I found these remarks very helpful for this case, I tried to use my energy to make each session to be a sacred space and time, set apart from daily life, in order to let the unconscious develop its autonomous process. Needless to say, I tried to be as prudent as possible as it proceeded, examining whether we were at risk of being overwhelmed by the unconscious and making sure her ego was working well.

Although Min was mostly quiet with few words during the sessions, she brought more than 60 imaginative dreams and paintings (which unfortunately I cannot show here). I had the impression that her inner journey progressed as if dreams and paintings were interweaving with each other. She selected half of these dreams as significant ones. These are too many to present here, although if I omit some of them I am afraid the narrative would be compromised because images in the dreams are closely connected by invisible threads. Moreover, as the Japanese language generally prefers ambiguous expression, it might be boring to read all the dream-texts. Nevertheless, I would like to convey the original atmosphere as much as possible.

I will show the process of the case mainly by presenting dream-texts as an axis that goes through the session, and which I would like to take as a narrative that was spun between the two of us. Although it was she who actually had these dreams, the images are considered to have emerged from between both of us. I would like to argue that everything occurred as she and I met at that time of our lives.

Before dreams begin to narrate

Min came to visit me at my office on the campus several months after attending my lectures for two years. I should add that having sessions with my students in my university office was an exceptional experience for me. I would like to understand her narratives in the early sessions as a prologue before the dreams begin to narrate.

She said, 'I have been writing about what I remember since I was born. I know that I still cannot write about some parts because I cannot accept them.' I thought that she came to me to do this painful work with me. She said,

I know more or less people suffer from anthropophobia, but mine is tremendous.... I am a Korean resident of Japan. My grandparents have been living as Korean in Japan. Although I don't have particular anti-Japanese feeling, I think about the meaning of the fact that I am here now. My grandmother was learning Japanese language when I was a child. Recently, I have started learning Hangul language.

Her narrative (1)

Min said in, a faint voice, 'Originally I am from the [Eurasian] Continent but I am here [in Japan] and speak Japanese language. We were as if uprooted once and brought to Japan and then put in a plant pot.' And she complained about the innocence and indifference of her friends to the history of Korean residents of Japan. She said that she had two names: one is Korean and the other is Japanese. Although she was using the latter officially at that time, she was wavering between changing to the Korean name and keeping using her Japanese one.

My unspoken narrative within me (1)

As a Japanese, I could not help but have a sense of guilt and feeling of bitterness. However, it felt to me that this was not merely a so-called guilty feeling, in general, but something that touches the basis of human existence. When I heard her narrative, especially when she uttered the word 'uprooted', I even felt a pain as if I myself were uprooted from the ground. I thought that I should look straight at this fact, even if it is tough.

Her narrative (2)

Min said,

> I went to India to see dead bodies last summer. I thought I might be able to change if I meet with 'death'. I saw cremations on the banks of River Ganges. Bodies were exposed to the elements along the bank. I was just absent-minded and couldn't feel anything. There were Buddhist priests. People in the tour group were taking photos of them. I wanted to but I couldn't.... I saw an old man with one leg standing up straight on the platform. Everybody was taking his photo, but I was so scared that I couldn't. He stood more firmly with one leg than I, who have two legs.

My unspoken narrative (2)

Listening to her story about her trip to India, I thought that she intuitively knew that she had to face the idea of death if she really wanted to work on her existential problem. However, just looking at the exposed dead bodies, which was a too direct and simplistic way of meeting 'death', could never have been a profound experience for her. It seemed that she hesitated taking photos of priests because she felt some kind of awe. In contrast, people in her tour group did not care for anything and freely took their photos without hesitation. This experience made her realize that she had different sensitivities from the others, which brought her a deep feeling of isolation. Unfortunately, the travel did not seem to have brought anything she had expected. However, the fact that I sympathized deeply with her way of responding to the Buddhist priests and one-legged old man was important, and made me certain that I was prepared to go through the work with her.

Our conversation

Min said 'I have been wondering if I should start a session. I have been afraid that if I overcome my problem, I might not be able to paint anymore.' As I knew that we have to be careful when meeting an artist as a client, I was wondering how I should meet her. I asked her what kind of pictures she painted. She said, 'Now I paint as if I'm wandering around here but I want to paint more surrealistic pictures. I want to paint as if I'm looking down from a higher place.' I thought we would be able to go through the process together until she acquires a viewpoint from a height. Although I am a psychotherapist, not an artist, writing and expressing myself were matters of great anguish in those days, both personally and professionally. After we had two sessions, she brought a dream for the first time.

Dreams' narrative (1): world of the dead and world of the living

Various therapist-like figures appear one after another

> Dream 1: A friendly person appears, who offers to help me. I depend on his/ her kindness.

Min said that she had the same dream three times in a week. She said, 'This person was neither male nor female. It was a type of person I had never met before.' Listening to her comments, I thought this therapist-like person might have appeared from somewhere beyond the dichotomy.

> Dream 2: It is after a session. I am with Prof. Yama [the author] in her office. There are two puddles or ocean. The colour of the water is deep emerald green. People are going to dive under the water to the bottom. Yama says, 'Let's dive', and she dives. I'm trying to but I'm afraid that I might have difficulty in breathing in the water. I'm bewildered. Yama comes back and asks me why I don't dive. 'I can't because I put in my contact lenses.' I'm making an excuse. Yama says, 'Now go to Rudolph Steiner's office for analysis.' Although I have a map to his office, I'm lost. I enter a wrong room. There are some men who are painting only nude women. I'm wondering if there was such a room in our university and I'm still looking for Steiner's room. In the next room, there are some artist-like people, who are making something with ceramics or fabrics.… Finally I can meet Steiner and a session begins with him. I keep speaking with downcast eyes. I think I

said something like,' I am going to be swallowed by my dark side.' Steiner washes my body with a sponge over my clothes.... A girl with long hair is sitting on a chair at the table.

Min said, 'I am reading Rudolf Steiner's book.' Regarding the girl, she said, 'I think it's me,' definitely. Two different therapist-like figures seem to have appeared; one is Yama, who invites her into the depth and the other is Steiner, who tries to wash her clothed body carefully with a sponge. After the session with Yama, Min was told to visit Steiner's office. It is interesting that although Min was in the studios on campus, with which she was very familiar, it felt to her unfamiliar and strange.

Hayao Kawai (1982/1996, p. 2) states, 'Reality's multifariousness corresponds to that of human consciousness, or ... it corresponds to the human psyche which contains conscious and unconscious layers.' And then he refers to *the Bush Warbler's Home*, a Japanese fairy tale in which one day a young woodcutter went into the familiar forest and came across a splendid mansion and a beautiful lady he had never seen before. Taking this fairy tale, Kawai understands the mansion and the lady as 'manifestations of something existing in deep layer in the psyche' (Kawai 1982/1996, p. 2).

Returning to the case, these artists, Steiner and a girl are all considered to be manifestations of those who exist in a deep layer of Min's psyche. At first, she was reluctant to dive into the water, but somehow she seemed to have descended into the depth and finally, after wandering around the campus, she reached Steiner's office, which means that she had gone down into the depths of her psyche where Steiner seems to have been waiting for her. He never invites her into the depths as Yama did but tries to treat Min more attentively and gently. It seems that two different types of therapist-figures began to work, compensating each other.

The beginning of the journey

Dream 3: I'm traveling with my girlfriend. There is a suspicious pilot. A taxi driver helps us and says, 'When you look for a pilot you have to be careful. You can tell if he is suspicious or not by the way he speaks and his attitude. You have to prepare a pail and a ladle to scoop water.' I'm satisfied and relieved with his words.

Her/our journey seems to have just started. The accompanying girlfriend may be another figure of therapist. A reliable and excellent guide is essential for such a journey of descending into the inner depth. Fortunately, the taxi driver in the dream is wise enough to distinguish a suspicious pilot from a reliable one, and he seems to be kind and helpful. From this dream, I realized that she had ambivalent feelings toward me as well as toward dealing with dreams. Based on my experience as a psychotherapist in Japan, I knew that we should be discreet about dealing with images with those who tend to jump at mysterious things without any hesitation or scepticism. In such cases, occasionally, their ego strength is so weak that they cannot go through the tough inner work without being swallowed up by the unconscious. Min's careful attitude toward Yama in Dream 2 and the suspicious pilot in Dream 3 made me trust her more. In addition, a sign of a meaningful motif of 'searching for water' is found, which appears repeatedly afterwards.

> Dream 4: I go to Tibet with my sister. There is a gentle and mysterious atmosphere. At the first gate of Tibet, there is an exotic emerald green building and something impressive like a coat of arms is on it. There is an island in the northernmost part of the sea, where a river flows and the landscape is beautiful. I want to bring back water from the river to Japan and I'm preparing a water bottle. Although the mountains are quite high and rising into the sky, we can climb up there. Houses are located regularly. They look like caverns that were dug in the mountain. They merge into the mountain and seem to be integrated. I'm climbing there with my sister. We gain the summit. I don't remember what was there on the other side. It's dim. The snow accumulated on the ground. It is the area where no one has stepped in before. It might be the first time for a human being to enter.

Talking about China, Min said, with reserved gestures, 'There is Korea, then there stretches China. Beyond China there is Tibet. China is a multi-ethnic country, where various kinds of languages are spoken. There should be confusion but I think it is good that nationalism is quite strong.' Regarding emerald green, 'It is my favourite colour, which is neither blue nor green.'

As this dream is full of imaginative picturesque descriptions, while listening to her I closed my eyes to visualize and taste every detail as if I myself were in the scene. In this dream, she goes to China and then to Tibet with her sister, which means that their journey is heading to the west, as they started from Japan. The motifs of 'going to the west' and 'going to the north' appear; these also turn out to be important later. According to de Vries (1974), in folklore the north is the territory where death dominates. And according to Harva (1938/2013), in Yakut legend the residence of spirits is in the deep north; the north is the direction of night as well as the country where the dead reside. 'This is the area where no one has stepped in before' (Harva 1938/2013, p. 30), which implies that Min went into the deep layer of the psyche where she had never entered before.

The colour of emerald green appears both in Dreams 2 and 4, and which, as she mentioned, is her favourite colour. I imagined emerald green might be the colour she is looking for, which is neither green nor blue. It resonated with the idea that she might be searching for her identity, as neither merely Korean nor merely Japanese.

Deepening the experience of facing 'death'

Dream 5: A blonde special lecturer is leading us in rich green woods. There is a building. Although she had been making her works of art in the basement of the building secretly, they were finally discovered and unveiled. There were so many works that the building was preserved as a gallery, which was named 'Corpse Art Gallery'. We go down into the room underground. The light comes from above. It stinks. There are corpses of frogs and snakes, and skeletons. They are almost decomposed. All of them are the lecturer's art works. I'm too scared to go any further and decide to go out. Other people are going into further admiring her works. I go out and sit on a bench at the entrance and wait for them to come out.... The exit is like an automatic ticket checker at a station. [After they come out from the basement] we keep walking in the wood in a group. There is a building which is made of concrete with stairs and a stage. There is a big water pool in the centre of the building. We have to soak our face in the water many times, which is like a ritual.

Min said, 'It was a grotesque dream'. In this dream, being led by a special lecturer, she descends to the underground, where she meets many decayed animals and skeletons. As mentioned above, she went to India to meet 'death' in the expectation that some change may occur in herself. However, as it turned out it was a superficial experience, and she felt nothing but a sense of isolation. In this dream, although she is the only one who cannot go further in the basement and she goes outside – which overlaps with her self-experience in India – the difference in the dream is that she senses fear. What is more, she reported a smell, to which I would like to pay special attention. Phylogenetically, a sense of smell is the oldest of the five senses and ontogenetically develops in the earliest stage. As the sense of smell is instinctive and primitive, reporting the experience of smell is considered to imply that the image of the dream emerged from the deep layer of the psyche. I would like to argue that her experience to face 'death' seems to have deepened through this dream. When they return to the ground from the basement, that is to say the underworld, they are forced to dip their faces in water. It reminds me of a ritual of purification, which is essential when we return from the underworld.

Something unordinary happens

Dream 6: I am at the Nachi Falls [one of the best-known waterfalls in Japan]. Something like a tower rises high above in the sky. I see the Second Falls and the Third Falls. At the top of the falls there is a statue of Kongo Rikishi Zou [a Guardian Deity in Buddhism] who begins to move. His eyes meet my eyes. He begins to get angry and he is looking at me. I'm scared and hide myself behind someone next to me.

Min said,

> Recently, I went to see the Nachi Falls. Unfortunately, it was not permitted
> to see the Second and the Third Falls because they are objects of worship. In
> the dream, I saw these three falls which were all connected into one. From
> the rising tower, I felt sexual as well as sacred.

This dream shows two important things. One is the violation of ban; that is,
seeing something sacred. The other is that something that cannot possibly
happen is taking place; three separate falls are integrated into one and the
Guardian Deity begins to move. It seems that something mysterious beyond
human power has been activated.

Helping a drowning woman

> Dream 7: In the northern part of Japan. I'm on the ice with a woman. I write
> something like, 'I came here' on the ice in memory of visiting here. After a
> while, the ice begins to shake and break. The woman falls into a chasm of
> ice. I try very hard to help her and bring her up to the safer place. She is not
> breathing and she is dying. I keep on pushing her stomach in order to make
> her vomit water. After a while the water comes out from her mouth. She
> wakes up. I'm deeply impressed that if I don't leave her alone, and if I try
> hard, she can revive.

Min said, 'This woman is the girl [in Dream 3] as well as myself. I helped her.'
Min animated a nearly drowned woman/herself. I would like to understand it as
an impressive and moving dream where she saved anima/soul. I believe that
anima is also in the female psyche.

Peeking into a cave

> Dream 8: We are going down the river along the cliff. Our view is as if we are
> on a helicopter. Finally, we come to the ocean. We are trying to peek into a
> cave through a crevice between rocks to find ancient remains of girls….

The cave seems to lead to the underground, into which she is peeking.

The gate between the opposite opens

> Dream 9: A funeral for someone who seems to be a famous musician or
> revolutionist is being held in Berlin…. A reporter's voice is saying, 'Now
> Berlin is going to separate into the East and the West again.' It seems that
> the gate between East Berlin and West Berlin has been opened and that they
> became one only during the funeral.

The important person seems to have died and the gate between East and West Berlin opens, which is the gate that separates the opposite. As Min associated East Berlin and West Berlin with Korea and Japan, the boundary between them might have been removed, that means the integration took place within a limited time, only during the funeral.

Something new develops

Dream 10: I'm giving directions to the people who are building a house.

Dream 11: I'm going somewhere to get something important that Grandmother has left but it's not easy.

It seems that Min is looking for something that has been transmitted over generations through the female line.

Dream 12: Four girls are digging for water under the white cement with a scoop....

A motif of 'seeking water' appears in this dream, too.

Looking for clothes

Dream 13: I am going somewhere by bus. It'll be difficult to get there when it snows in winter. It's dim ... I'm in a boutique, in which there are some women with their children.... I am a woman and at the same time a child. I'm looking at children's clothes which are boys' as well as girls'. I like them. There is a kind of a dress I have never seen before, which is like a Chinese dress but it is not. It is ethnic fashion and too traditional for modern clothing. I'm looking at them wondering how mysterious they are.

Min said, 'I felt clothes and names mean the same for me'. She seems to be looking for her 'persona', which is a new motif. She has been wondering if she should use her Korean name officially instead of the Japanese one, which required courage on her part.

Going north

Dream 14: I don't know why but I think I have to go north. I have to decipher some important code, which seems to have something to do with water spilled on the table.

Min said that it should have been an important message, which she could not remember. The motifs of 'going to the north' and the 'water' appear in this dream, too. Additionally, a motif of 'deciphering some important code' appeared.

I do not have to hide my 'Korean-ness'

Dream 15: I'm looking for something on a back street at night. I go into a barn or a ruined house. There is a baby white unicorn with a horn on its head, whose wings are showing various different shapes every minute. Beside him there is a horse of ordinary appearance who looks like his mother. I think he doesn't have to conceal himself. I and these two horses go out to eat in the well-lit city.

Min said, 'I thought I don't have to hide "the Korean-ness" in me. I think I'm looking for my roots.' Needless to say that she knew what Unicorn and Pegasus looked like, however, the baby horse in this dream seems to have a mixed appearance of these two imaginary horses. Both Pegasus and Unicorn are special horses that are different from ordinary ones. I was pleased from the bottom of my heart to hear that she seemed to come to realize that she did not have to hide the Korean-ness any more. Their movement from the house on the dark back-street to the well-lit city suggests that something that had been hidden in the darkness/unconscious is now being brought to the light/conscious.

Looking down into the crater

Dream 16: I plan to travel around East Iran and Islamic countries in a group. We are to climb up a mountain covered with snow and look into a crater....

Min said, 'Steiner's book helped me a lot. It was something about alchemy. I thought about transformation of myself and my past.' She was heading to the west and reached Middle East. When I heard this dream, I had an intuition that she was looking down into the crater on the mountain where the West and the East meets, which I would like to understood as looking down on the boundary where the opposite meets.

Min said, 'My father said that he wanted to hand down the Korean culture to me' (to which she used to be rather negative). 'We held a memorial service for the dead for the first time.' She talked about her nameless anxiety that she had had for a long time. She said, 'I used to be attacked by an indescribable disquiet but it's much better now. When I become mentally unstable, I try to think about my roots, which brings me peace.'

Dream 17: I'm appealing to my parents that I want to go to the Islamic countries [in the Middle East]. My mother says, 'Wasn't it Tibet [where you wanted to go]?' 'Definitely, I want to go to the Middle East!' I am appealing to the people around. There is a man wearing a turban, who seems to be from the Middle East. I am approaching to him to listen his story … A TV personality who went to the Middle East to gather materials for a TV programme is complaining about something. Contrary to her intentions, she was forced to report about a fashion show which was held in Milan or Paris. She is insisting that she wanted to report the people's everyday life in the Middle East and that she should have done it.

A new type of woman appears, who has a strong will and insists on her opinion against the powerful. I am not sure what kind of impressions she had of Islamic countries, which may be the unknown mysterious countries that lie between Europe and Asia.

Separating the worlds between the dead and the living

Dream 18: I go down on the earth. The dark brown ground stretches far and wide, where a lot of dead bodies covered with white bandages lie. Some of them are missing their hands and legs. An infectious disease seems to have broken out. There is a Japanese woman who is in her forties or fifties. We walk through these corpses. She leads me to a small house. The outside and inside of the house are separated by the *fusuma* [traditional Japanese-style sliding door]. Entering the small house, she shuts the *fusuma* in order to defend against infections. There is an old-style kitchen and she cooks something for me. I am standing beside her. It is interesting and strange that there is a kitchen in such a place.... A group of tourists come in opening the *fusuma*. I can see the scenery outside. They come here to see the dead bodies. I want them to shut the *fusuma* quickly for fear that we might be infected.

Min said that she remembered the trip to India the previous year. As for the Japanese woman, she said, 'She might have resembled my mother'. The dream begins with a scene where she came down from above and landed on the ground. She seems to have visited the world of the dead again, where she meets a woman who resembles her mother. It is considered that the woman is her personal mother as well as the collective mother, the Great Mother who resides in the world of dead. In Dream 5, she went down to the underworld being led by a female lecturer. At that time, Min was so scared to see these collapsed animals that she left there alone. In contrast, in this dream, being protected by the mother-like figure, she walks through the ground covered with dead bodies until they reach a small house. The woman shows maternal care by cooking and serving a meal to Min The experience of facing 'death' seems to have deepened step by step; first, the actual trip to India, and second through Dream 5 and third through this dream. It seems to have been a shocking experience for her to see the insensitivity of the people in the tour group.

Finally, the worlds of the dead and of the living are separated by a *fusuma*. I find it interesting that the door that separated these two worlds was not a solid door, such as an iron door, but a *fusuma*. As both sides of a *fusuma* are covered with thick paper or cloth, there is permeability between the outside and the inside, which means that the world of the dead is not completely excluded from the living world. I would like to take it positively that the world of the dead is not totally shut out of her cosmology.

Conversation

Min said, 'I had an anxiety of losing the urge to paint for a couple of days', and asked me about what motivates me to do my research and psychotherapy. As mentioned earlier, how to articulate and express images and ideas that arose within me used to be my primary concern as well as a source of anguish, both professionally and personally, in those days. I thought I should answer her question as honestly as I could, even though it has something to do with my personal matters. Needless to say, I do not usually speak about my personal matters with my clients. I said, 'I think your painting has the same meaning as my writing, reading, doing research and engaging in psychotherapy. They are not a purpose in itself but they are indispensable and I cannot cut them off from my life.' Although she said nothing, she was listening to me very seriously.

Min said, 'My mother says that recently she has nightmares.' Then she reported one of them: 'A road is made by connecting arms and legs, which were cut off from the people one after another. At the moment when my turn came, I woke up with the desire to go to the restroom.' I heard from Min that her parents had kept working very hard, using their anti-Japanese feelings as a source of energy. Listening to her mother's dream, I thought of these Korean residents in Japan who have lived their lives as if by symbolically cutting off parts of their bodies. At the same time, I noticed some resonance with Min's dream, where bodies without arms and legs covered the ground. I thought that Min's change might have triggered some changes in her mother's psyche, too.

Moreover, I also had a very impactful dream. In my dream, after a long story (which I don't remember), I'm going through a very large and long tunnel at a tremendously high speed. I hear a phrase 'In her case~' which was repeated both in English and Japanese (Kanojo no baai~) one after the other very quickly. Gradually they (English and Japanese) intermingle and the speed increases. Finally, they become one as if they were merged. I woke up in terror. When I woke up, somehow I was convinced that 'her' in this dream meant Min. I do not remember why I was in such a terror, but it was absolutely different from the terror I had in previous dreams. While I would like to keep mention of my personal matters to the minimum, I should explain that, having lived in America in my adolescence, I had the experience of living with both a Western 'I' and a Japanese 'I' within me; hence, what the English and Japanese languages symbolize used to be (and still is), without exaggeration, a matter of life or death. As already mentioned, engaging in psychotherapy and research of depth psychology have not merely been my job, but activities through which I have been exploring my life. Dream 16, in which Min was looking down into the crater on the mountain where the West and the East meet, felt to me as meaningful as well as valuable.

Dreams' narratives (2): reunion with ancestors

Something new develops

> Dream 19: The store that had been closed for a long time opens. There are dresses in styles from the late seventies.... My mother is making my dress.

> Dream 20: I find a cute abandoned baby. I can sense her smell, and she is so soft. I think I shouldn't leave her here.... Finally, she seems to be left in some rich person's care.

> Dream 21: My family begins to carry on a new business. We make foods, furniture and everything out of faeces. At first, I'm reluctant to. We are to make a drama on the theme of faeces. I'm to play an unimportant role. It won't be a hit, I first thought. While I'm looking at them making a film, I begin to think it might become the talk of the people.

These dreams suggest that a new development is taking place. It seems that her family possibly succeeds in carrying a new business using something that is usually taken to be worthless. Some important change of a sense of value seems to have taken place within her.

> Dream 22: A girl died. I ask my mother where she is. There is a box in which she is contained.... I feel like drawing wings on her back in her photo. I begin drawing wings praying for her to go to Heaven. The girl emitted a brilliant light when she died.

Min said, 'Although the girl died, I felt she was rewarded.' The girl may have been the one who was sitting at the table while Min and Steiner was having a session in Dream 2.

Reaching a height

> Dream 23: It seems to be after the war.... I'm walking along the shore with children.... I am climbing up the slope alone. There is a park on the left-hand side. I stop at the entrance and turn around. There is a small bay and the sea stretches beyond. Suddenly I have an intuition that I know it!

Min said, 'I was deeply moved that I finally could reach up here and stand on a height.' She used to say, 'I am painting pictures as if I am wandering around here, where it is thick and muddy. I want to paint as if standing on a height.' She tried to paint the scenery in the dream, but she said it did not ring a bell. Although it seems to be still difficult to express it in painting, I was glad to hear that at least in the dream she reached where she did and had an intuition that she knew it.

Getting shoes soon

Dream 24: I found shoes just as I have been imagining for a long time at a department store. They are narrow Chinese style and modern ones. There are subtle variations in colours and designs.... I'll be able to get them two days later.... I buy a favourite CD and listen to it.

Shoes are considered to represent the basis or foundation. Along with clothes, they could also imply the persona. She seems to be able to get them before long.

Music, song, poem and dance

Dream 25: On campus. Many students are singing or reciting at a landing place in front of a spiral staircase. It is a mysterious and attractive song that I've never heard, which reminds me of the recital of poem.

Dream 26: It is not in Japan. Mother and two sisters live there, who belong to a minority ethnic group somewhere in Southeast Asia. I seem to be the elder sister. I am wearing ethnic clothes, which are simple and oriental in style. The colour is calm reddish brown. Grandmother is in front of the house. Mother or the elder sister pairs up with a man and they dance a traditional folkdance. A man dances first then a woman joins him. He dances with a big kite in his hands.

Music and dance appear in Dreams 24, 25 and 26. Music in general has the power to evoke emotion. As we have been traveling across China to the Middle East in her dream, we could encounter many ethnic minorities who live there. Min heard a mysterious and attractive song or poem she has never heard, which made me feel as if I myself were listening to the songs of these ethnic groups, too. I know that they have their unique folk melodies. In folkdance, especially in traditional dance with music we can sense their delight and sorrow in their history, which shows their vivid life.

Reunion with ancestors: healing

Dream 27: Sister has many clothes handed down from the ancestors. We look at them and try them on. I envy her. Someday I want to borrow them from her. Sister says that she wanted to be a 'therapist' [Yama's note: I do not know if Min knew what it meant] which has something to do with Pegasus. When she graduated from high school, her school records were so good that she was advised to be a 'therapist'. A 'therapist' seems to mean Unicorn which is a horse with wings. The blood of the Unicorn runs in my family. Some of my ancestors were 'therapists'.

It's a foreign world, different from this world. The Unicorn is running inside the earth. Pegasus is running on the green ground inside the earth.

I'm looking from above from a distance. Suddenly hands come out from the earth and I was almost caught and grasped by them. I wanted to be a 'therapist'. I did not know that we were the family of the Unicorn, the Pegasus. I really wanted to be one. Why not?

My mother seems to have died soon after I was born. She already knew that she was going to die very soon when she was pregnant. She tried very hard to leave something for me. She is somewhere in a farming village. It looks like before the Meiji era [1864–1912]. She is wearing a cherry pink kimono with her long hair bound. She digs the ground around a tree. There is a hollow under the roots. She is trying to put something in it, which is probably her last will.

Now I'm with a man of about my age. My consciousness is both his and mine. We are likely to have found the last will which was hidden in a water-melon. There are some messages. I feel that I might be able to solve riddles about 'therapist', Pegasus and my mother.

Min said, 'I thought, I might be going to live what mother and grandmother had repressed.' She seems to have her clothes handed down from ancestors. The blood of the Unicorn, Pegasus and the 'therapist' have been in her family for generations. Pegasus is running inside the earth. I find a similar image in the cosmology of the people of the Altaic languages. According to Harva (1938/2013), there are some examples showing that they believe everything in this world and the next world to be completely opposite to each other. He points out, 'the next world is a reflected mirror image of this earthy world' (Harva 1938/2013, p. 33). The 'death' seems to have been thus settled in her cosmology. Then Mother leaves a last will. It takes over the motif of 'something important that Grandmother left' in Dream 11. Min said,

I might be going to live what Mother and Grandmother had repressed, which is wonderful. What is handed down from Grandmother to Mother and from Mother to Daughter; this would be handed down through the female line. I would like to argue that she realized its existence in herself, which is considered to be a deep experience of reunion with ancestors.

As Meier (1989, p. 66) states, 'It is well known that reunion with the ancestors means healing'.

Min said,

When I spent my time on practical things, I have fewer dreams … I come to feel stable being X [her Korean name]. I come to be able to accept it, what's more, not forcibly but naturally. I can live as X. Somehow I overcame what happened in the past and I feel like having completed one chapter.

Changing names

Dream 28: I have a session with Professor Hayao Kawai. There are my sisters, too. Kawai says, 'When something that has been churning inside of you makes its way to the surface, it often causes friction. You cannot help it, just accept it. Everybody has one's own whirl. When it comes up in reality, there is no way to avoid the differences to occur. You were born here. It is very natural that there are cultural differences and therefore the whirl of different culture occurs. Treasure your own whirl.'

Dream 29: My Japanese name on the roll has been changed to the Korean one. I thought that Prof. Yama already knew that I had changed my name.

Min decided to use her Korean name officially, and went to the administration office to register her Korean name. She said she had four dreams about it that night. The dreams shown above are two of them. In Dream 28, Kawai – who was very famous in Japan – appears. Min possibly knew that he was my supervisor throughout undergraduate and graduate school. His figure in this dream reminds me of the Old Wise Man. His words are just wonderful. When and where two different things meet, it may cause friction and suffering; however, creativity may also be generated there.

Min said, 'I happen to know that my friends are talking about me as Chinese-Japanese behind my back. The wrong information seems to have gotten around. It is my fault, too, as I haven't made an effort to communicate about myself.'

Discovering her colour

Dream 30: I go into the dark cavern with my sister. There is a large stone which was made by human beings 500,000,000 years ago. Some mysterious stones of light emerald green are embedded in the stone.... When water runs down from the above, they get wet and glitter. They are so beautiful and marvellous that I am impressed and moved very much.

Believe in yourself

Dream 31: A six- or seven-years-old white boy with blond hair is in the classroom. I seem to be him. When I have to give my opinion, I am influenced by a boy who sits next to me. I almost lean to his opinion. Then a male teacher says, 'Write your own opinion. Believe in yourself. Ignore others and write as you believe,' strongly. I couldn't quite believe him at first but I give my opinion dubiously. Unexpectedly, there are some students who agree with me. I'll try to value beliefs that come from within me.

Min said, 'As I read a book about a child abuse in America, this boy reminded me of the child who was abused.' Kawai's words in Dream 28 seem to be succeeded by the teacher's words, 'Write your own opinion. Believe in yourself,' which is more practical than the former.

> Dream 32: There is a socially vulnerable girl in her late teens in a dark room. She is in a large box surrounded by black boards. People are looking at her through an opening.... Many Islamic people are walking outside very lively.

Min said, 'Although she cannot live bringing her social vulnerability to the forefront, she has to live with it. I thought this girl was not shut up but protected in a safe place.'

Epilogue to the dreams' narratives

Min said,

> I think I have overcome a lot of my personal problems. I feel like I'm suffering from collective problems now. When I write about myself in the notebook, I come to be able to use 'I' instead of 'she', which I used previously. I feel I could accept my past. When I become anxious, I can pick up something from the depth, which can be turned into an impelling force toward painting.... Now I can use the right name in the right place and at the right time; sometimes the Korean one and sometimes the Japanese one. There is some part that never changes in me and there is also other part that turned out to be clear in me. I can't put them in a word. I think I'll express them by painting.... I used to see everything from the dead side, dark side, but I began to think that at least I'm not dead and I'm alive. This brought me peace. When I wake up in the morning, at first I feel a bit remote from myself and my surroundings. I have to make sure gradually that I'm physically here. This seems positive, and it may be a so-called healing.... My family has changed a little, too. They often became hysterical but they are more settled than before. I find it more comfortable at home. I used to dislike anything that is not explainable by causality, like fortune-telling and the occult. But a very strange thing happened to me. I found that the unconscious is something that is absolutely important for me. It felt me as if ten years have passed since I met you.

It was the end of our sessions. After a year, she came to tell me an impressive dream she had.

> Dream 33: A blue and white light or star approached me and said something in English. I'm very satisfied to hear it.

Silence: not to hinder the autonomy of the unconscious

As shown above, the deep healing process seems to have taken place over time. It is no exaggeration to say that all I tried was to devote my energy to not hindering the autonomous flow of the unconscious and to exploring what I could convey to Min, not with my words but with my 'being' there. First of all, I would like to emphasize that silence and waiting are essential for images to emerge from the vague chaotic unconscious. Generally, it is not with rational words but through images that the unconscious tells its story. Images have a tendency to connect with each other and, as a result, they make complex nets. What is more, they tend to change their structures as they like, which are usually impossible to understand according to rational thinking. Too quick verbalization about images including interpretation may prevent these images from amplification and may even cut their interrelated linkages. Consequently, it might bring about a destruction of the life in the images.

Oda (1990), a Jungian psychiatrist, understands psychotherapy as helping to encourage the process for someone who is confronted with a crisis and has to reconstruct his/her inner world. Regarding this case, I would like to know that I accompanied Min in her process of constructing a cosmology.

After deepening the experience of facing 'death' step by step, she seemed to have been connected with her ancestors. As Min said about her future, 'I might be going to live what Mother and Grandmother repressed', it could be considered that a vertical movement in time – past, present, future – was completed. A vertical spatial movement from the upper world to the earth and down to the underworld was also observed. There is also a journey to the west, which starts from Japan, Korea, China and Tibet, and then reaches Iran and Islamic countries in the Middle East. This is also a journey to meet the West and to experience a fusion of West and East. And there is a journey to the north, where she reached the place no one had entered before. This is a journey to the north on the Earth as well as a vertical journey down to the underground. In Dream 33, a messenger from the other world came to her to tell something in English. After experiencing a grand spatial movement and following a temporal stream, we can see the completion of a cosmology of time and space.

A language beyond dichotomy

To tell the truth, at the very beginning when taking the case, I was thinking of a theme such as 'how Min establishes her identity as a third generation Korean resident in Japan' or 'how I can support her to integrate the Korean and the Japanese within herself'. However, as time went by, her dreams began to narrate the large-scale unique story beyond dichotomy.

In our daily lives, we tend to assume all that exists is what we can perceive. Behind it, however, there stretches an unknown invisible ambiguous world that can never be grasped by logical dichotomy. We can catch a glimpse of the depths only when we try to look between the two and go down.

If we lower the level of the consciousness, the boundary between 'A' and 'B' becomes vaguer, which can be compared to the experience at deepening dusk, when the outline of the things gradually becomes unclear. Needless to say, the distinction between two different things is essential in daily life for not falling into disorder; however, the boundary in the dreams is often vague.

As mentioned above, Min's dreams began to speak of a world beyond dichotomies, such as Korea/Japan, adult/child, man/woman, life/death, sacred/sexual, and more. In her dreams, the following characteristic expressions were observed, which may suggest the vagueness of the boundary, 'This person was neither male nor female' (Dream 1); emerald green is 'neither blue nor green' (Dreams 2 and 4); 'I felt sexual as well as sacred' (Dream 6); 'clothes which are boys' as well as girls'' (Dream 13); 'Chinese, not modern and ethnic clothes and shoes' (Dreams 13 and 24); 'My consciousness is both the man's and mine' (Dream 27); and more. The motif of the fusion of opposites appeared in the following: 'A gate between East Berlin and West Berlin opens and they became one' (Dream 9); 'When something that has been churning inside of you makes its way to the surface [outside]' (Dream 28). 'Looking down into the crater where the West and the East meet' (Dream 16) could be understood as looking down from where the opposites meet. It is from where the opposites meet that something creative may arise; however, it is also true that where there is difference, there is pain.

When the two different persons, Min and I, met and shared something in the depth of the psyche, dreams began to narrate themselves spontaneously. All we had to do was just be silent so as not to interrupt them. We worked on a theme of containing the opposites as well as the theme that touches a fundamental question of existence, 'Who am I?' Kawai (1989) noted that dreams are the language of the soul, a language for narrating boundaries.

References

de Vries, A. (1974) *Dictionary of Symbols and Imagery.* Amsterdam: Elsevier.

Harva, U. (1938/2013) *Shamanizumu 2.* Tokyo: Heibonsha. (Originally published in German in 1938.)

Kawai, H. (1982/1996) *The Japanese Psyche: Major Motifs in the Fairy Tales of Japan.* Dallas, TX: Spring.

Kawai, H. (1989) *Sei to shi no setten [Interface between Life and Death].* Tokyo: Iwanami Shoten.

Meier, C. A. (1989) *Healing Dream and Ritual.* Einsiedeln: Daimon Verlag.

Oda, T. (1990) *Oken no shinrigaku [Psychology of Kingship].* Tokyo: Daisanbunmeisha.

Yama, M. (2001) Yume no imeji no naka ni iyashi o motomete [Searching for healing in the images of dreams]. *Journal of Japanese Clinical Psychology* 19, 97–108.

Chapter 4

Autobiographical narrative
Augustine, Vico and Jung

Leslie Gardner

In this chapter, I contend that autobiography is a primal form of narrative, generating the familiar patterns of fiction and non-fiction. I am also proposing that self-narratives are written for a purpose other than simply setting out the chronology of a life. This purpose is specific to that author and impacts on that narrative. As Mathien says in the introduction to *Autobiography as Philosophy*, autobiography is often written to expound a moral cause, to justify behaviour, to apologize, to console or to present philosophical ideas (Mathien and Wright 2006). The three autobiographies I focus on in this chapter, Augustine's *Confessions*, Giambattista Vico's *Autobiography* and Carl Gustav Jung's *Memories, Dreams, Reflections*, clearly establish themselves in this tradition. As this is part of a longer work on self-presentation, I can tackle only a part of the discussion of these works here.

Augustine's investigation of narrative and time in his *Confessions* is the crux of Ricoeur's (1984–1988) important work *Time and Narrative*. He maintains that Augustine's ideas are fundamental to any discussion of narrative. Vico (1744/1944 and (1740/1968) seeks to correlate axioms about individual development with the laws of history (and narrative) to pick up another stream of associations in autobiography that are related to the neo-Platonic ideas of Augustine. These theories form a backdrop to a lengthier discussion here of Jung's (1963) *Memories, Dreams, Reflections*. Augustine's and Vico's theoretical decisions are useful in exploring Jung's controversial and contemporary autobiography, revealing that it is part of the long tradition of polemical autobiography too.

Autobiography as narrative

In his essay 'The Storyteller', Walter Benjamin (1969) claims that death as a natural function is a primal coordinate of 'storytelling'. Stories participate in an oral tradition predating written narrative. Scripted narratives are frozen outside personal and place contexts. Narrative in this essay, which uses written work as illustration, is about the utterly familiar narratives of lives. In Benjamin's essay, a story is an *exempla* and/or a means of transmitting information. Benjamin shows the links of contextual, multi-perspective narratives to time, and especially as essential to stories of self:

It is, however, characteristic that not only a man's knowledge or wisdom, but above all his real life – and this is the stuff that stories are made of – first assumes transmissible form at the moment of his death. Just as a sequence of images is set in motion inside a man as his life comes to an end – unfolding the views of himself under which he has encountered himself without being aware of it – suddenly in his expressions and looks the unforgettable emerges and imparts to everything that concerned him [an] authority which … the dying possess for the living around him. This authority is the very source of the story.

(W. Benjamin 1969, p. 94)

Particularity is an 'interruption' and, in fact, Walter Benjamin says, a series of 'interruptions' define what 'time' is because 'time' is marked in that way. This notion is commensurate with Augustine and Vico's ideas of time and narrative as we will see. As Andrew Benjamin points out, the way in which events cohere in a self-narrative reflects on what that life amounts to, which concerns Augustine. And, additionally, this reflection of the era in which that person has lived is one of Vico's themes.

Standing aside to contemplate the era and a man's accretion of personal data into a certain sequence in time reveals an *intention* in that life (sometimes secret or 'suppressed'), enabling its transmissibility (to use Benjamin's word). This transmissibility is what stories are for and what they do. If we cannot handle this attitude, and if we do not appreciate this drive, we will not be able to make appropriate judgements. As Benjamin says in another essay ('Theses on the Philosophy of History'), 'There is a secret agreement between past generations and the present one. Our coming was expected on earth. Like every generation that preceded us, we have been endowed with … a power to which the past has a claim' (W. Benjamin 1969, p. 254).

That underlying agreement applies equally to an older narrator's investigation of a younger self. Augustine (1992) fashions his life as a step toward achieving prayer, moving outside time into the eternal plane of his Lord, while Vico (1744/1944) in his Autobiography constructs his life as a demonstration of his epistemology (see an expansion of the idea in Verene 1991). In *Memories, Dreams, Reflections*, Jung (1963) creates a fable of his life to demonstrate the unfolding of individuation in the human psyche.

To pursue this exploration in an 'amplified' context (in Jung's sense of amplification), I will relate the argumentative strategies of the three autobiographies to the idea of the *rhetorical space*. The rhetorical space is definable as a place of communicative disruption or interruption. In the rhetorical space, arguments operate as both propositions and as assumptions in the formula of discourse. Resolutions of a kind are proposed. A rhetorical approach assumes a common expressive technique that reflects and participates in empirical and symbolic exchange.

Autobiographical narrative in contexts

Autobiographical narrative has a relatively short history, as many comment-ators have suggested (e.g. Olney 1980; Mathien and Wright 2006; Colling-wood 1939/1944; Fisch in his Introduction to Vico 1944); and, further, when individuals did write about themselves, they did not always think it was 'auto-biography' as we know it. The 'self-presented' life in rhetorical terminology is an epideictic form, allowing the writer the opportunity to show the con-sequences of either mistakes or virtuosities along the way. Perelman (1982) insists also on the basic involvement with community values of this form: 'Epideictic discourses must include a process of self-fashioning ... simultan-eously and coincidentally with the figurative audience as an ethical subject' (Perelman 1982, p. 20). In conforming to its vital part in the community, *nar-ratio* in Vico's (1740/1996) handbook on rhetoric is presented as a device in support of a legal case. A woman accused of murdering her husband is por-trayed as the long-suffering abandoned mother of starving children; the advo-cate presents a full scenario to the jury as evidence in her support (Vico 1740/1996, p. 121). In this instance, a specific narrative is aligned with the laws of the community.

These life-stories are also designed to provide entertainment which naturally figures into stories of the saints' lives prevalent from medieval days. Saints were pious role models but their stories of martyrdom or conversion were embellished to hold the attention of readers. These techniques were used later in works also purporting to be autobiography: Carlo Goldoni's *Memoirs*, Casanova's *The Story of my Life* or Tristan L'Hérmite's *Memoirs*. These were bestsellers in their day. It was not expected that they were wholly 'truthful' accounts, since they embroi-dered stories of the escapades in a colourful rogue's life, making grand escapes from prison, from women's beds, committing murders, etc. (like many of the saints' lives also did) for sheer diversion. Indeed, commentators note that fiction mimicked underlying forms based on life stories. We might, therefore, go so far as to categorize these autobiographies as an early form of fiction, fulfilling readers' hunger for stories. Early fictions were often presented as autobiography or as biography: Thackeray's *Vanity Fair*, Fielding's *Tom Jones*, or Laurence Sterne's *Life and Opinions of Tristram Shandy* or Richardson's *Clarissa* and Defoe's *Robinson Crusoe*, to name only a few in the English language, rely on the autobiographical genre, except that autobiography is reputed to be 'true'. Primary patterns of expectation were already in place however, and merged with the particulars of the narrator's story.

Paul Ricoeur and Frank Kermode wrote extensively about narrative, and both argued that emplotment and agency are inextricably intertwined, based on expec-tation. In this case, our expectation is of how a life would play out. Our intention as storytellers mingles with an expectation we seek to fulfil. In fact, Ricoeur (1984, p. 74) argues, we base our quotidian expectations on 'as-yet untold stories': 'To characterize these situations I shall not hesitate to speak of a pre-narrative quality of the experience.' Juri Lottman (1979) explores two primeval kinds of plot: (1) the 'mythic' plot that has no 'excesses or anomalies', and which operates in a motionless, timeless state; and (2) a narrative plot that is a linear tale of incident, gossip or news – which streams along in time. Lottman demonstrates these exist in 'dialectical interaction'. We will see below that this division correlates to Vico's binary analysis of narrative.

Common ('archetypal') narrative patterns derive from character type, which not unnaturally generates plot. Although I do not have space to comment further here, the agent's role in plot is central to various theorists on narrative: Brémond's (1980) 'semiotic square' and, later, Greimas's analysis of narrative (cited in Ricoeur 1986), focus on the agent instead of formal story patterns. Narrative derives from the agent's intentions, which Greimas refines in order to demonstrate that predication is integral. But Ricoeur disputes these structuralist analyses, pointing out that both analyses rest on already assumed narrative expectations. We see this also in Jung's (1921) discussion of 'types' in Chapter 10 of *Psychological Types*, when the variety of 'types' is explained by telling stories to define them. Lottman's (1979) analysis describes the patterns, but like other structuralist studies fails to recognize the 'primal' symbolic drive. Centuries earlier, Vico's (1740/1968) discussion in his *The New Science* proposed what I would suggest is an advance on that view. As summarized succinctly by Tristram (1988), Vico explores two levels of narrative: (1) the ideal eternal sequence and (2) the empirical level (common tales of the populace akin to gossip and 'old wives' tales') which exist in a state of 'metaphysical' (as Vico puts it) interaction. While the empirical sphere is mostly subsumed to the ideal eternal sphere, it is the close mingling of the two that is the standard. This classification of narrative levels circumvents the formal outlines of narrative. These forays seek the sources of the interpretive formations of story rather than its 'logic'.

Autobiography has another variable: the reliability of the narrator and the relationship to a younger self. Irregularity or inconsistency in the narrator's report calls 'external fact' into question. But are there ever reliable narrators? An investigation of these issues opens up the underlying significance of narrative rather than focusing on description of patterns. Reliability and agency, action and location form constraints on self-narrative and are the stuff of 'interruptions'. Autobiography provides a site of conflicting interpretations – and these interpretations, Kermode (1979) says, form what narrative is, and demand its reception, recognition or rejection by witnesses, without whom the narrative is not complete.

Autobiography as argumentation

To analyse the argumentative forms of these autobiographies, it will be useful to use Lionel Bitzer's rhetorical observations. Bitzer (1968) sets out three components of the 'deviant' or rhetorical event:

(1) *Exigency*: imperfection marked by urgency, a controlling incongruity that functions as an organizational principle: it specifies the audience to be addressed and the change to be effected;

(2) *Audience*: people mediating change, even when a person engages himself or the 'ideal' mind as audience;

(3) *Constraint(s)* made up of persons, objects, and relations which are part of the situation because they have the power to constrain decision and action needed. When the rhetor enters the situation, his/her discourse not only harnesses constraints given by situation but provides additional important constraints; for example, his/her personal character, his/her logical proofs, and style.

To start, I assume that each of the three autobiographies is a site of rhetorical exchange. And, as it is the principal argument of my paper, I will focus on the efforts of the autobiographers to establish exigency. They have a wider aim than straightforwardly recounting a sequence of events that make up their lives. Following this discussion of each, I will concentrate on the constraints and audience, as Jung's *Memories, Dreams, Reflections* demonstrates, since there is not enough space to explore the others in such detail here. I will, however, include some material from Augustine and Vico's works.

Exigency

Each of these self-narratives presents purposeful *exigency* as its self-reflexive goal. The different aspects of autobiography are exploited for this purpose. Like all self-narrative, Augustine's *Confessions*, Vico's *Autobiography* and Jung's *Memories, Dreams, Reflections* are samples of epideictic rhetoric. But these volumes are more developed forms than the standard epideictic, which offers praise and blame for actions of a personage. Epideictic relies on shared values of the community. Yet, these volumes affirm what their authors believe to be authentic community values but which they know are not apparent to the community. In asserting these new values, they create exigency, a vital call on the occasion of the attention of a reader.

Augustine

Augustine (1992) raises the question:

> Lord, eternity is yours, so you cannot be ignorant of what I tell you. Your vision of occurrences in time is not temporally conditioned. Why then do I set before you an ordered account of so many things? ... I am stirring up love for you in myself and in those who read this, so that we may all say 'Great is the Lord and worthy of our high praise' ... I tell my story for love of your love.... And if I have the capacity to proclaim this in an ordered narrative, yet the drops of time are too precious for me.
>
> (Augustine 1992, Book XI ii, para. 2)

In other words, he asks, in the final quarter of the volume: why am I bothering to set my life out, when you know it all anyway? And so in the sequence of *Confessions*, after the *encomium* for his mother, he stops relating his life. He makes transition to prayer in the narrative then by way of an exegesis of time (cf. Vance 1978).

Through intense questioning, Augustine comes to recognize what the Lord's eternal time is, speculating on mortal, sinful man's experience of time as he is caught in a world of dissimilarities and change. Like Benjamin's (1969) 'interruptions' in time and Hauser's (1986) 'disruptions', it is those differences that reveal time to us and thereby eternity. Interpretations of causality and meanings create narrative sequence from these markers. But, at bottom, there is an expectation of narrative sequence already in place in human time.

Augustine's conjectures about the 'threefold present' offer an interplay among various times (memory, the past as we remember it now), attentive present, expectation (the future as we anticipate it now), that frustrate the saint, but also open up possibilities and potentialities for new development:

> To whom shall we cry? 'The day is yours and the night is yours' (Ps 73:16). At your nod the moments fly by. From them grant us space for our meditations on the secret recesses of your law, and do not close the gate to us as we knock.
>
> (Augustine 1992, Book XI. ii, para. 3)

Realizing that beseeching God is a metaphysical plea, outside time, Augustine offers his reader an analysis of his own particular occupancy of time, as a demonstration of the abiding backdrop of the Lord's eternal time.

Ongoing time is measured by subjective standards of common sense; it feels long or short. A mutable stream of time that is particular and mortal is in the foreground for sinful humankind. But he addresses the extensions of time that the soul perceives.

> Nevertheless we speak of 'a long time' and 'a short time,' and it is only of the past or the future we say this ... but how can something be long or short that does not exist? This time past which was long, was it long when it was past or when it was still present? ... Human soul, let us see whether present time can be long. To you the power is granted to be aware of intervals in time and to measure them.
>
> (Augustine 1992, Book XI. ii, para. 19)

Augustine contrasts this to eternal time, by imagining the soul's capacity to understand. Eternal beings do not mark time – for example, the angels (like his teacher Anselm who read silently and who he felt had achieved a high holiness) do not speak aloud because making a sound is to mark time, and they are outside time. It is against these anomalies of time, that he invites us to witness the eternal time of God:

You, Lord, are my consolation. You are my eternal Father, but I am scattered in times whose order I do not understand. The storms of incoherent events tear to pieces my thought ... until that day when, purified and molten by the fire of your love, I flow together to merge with you.... A person singing or listening to a song he knows well suffers a distension or stretching in feeling and in sense – perception from the expectation of future sounds and the memory of past sounds. With you it is otherwise. You are unchangeably eternal.

(Augustine 1992, Book XI: xxvi, para. 33)

This is what Augustine calls *distentio*: 'a shift in, the non-coincidence of the three modalities of action' (Ricoeur 1984, p. 20). It is the passive reverse side of the 'attentive' mind focused on and engaged with the present.

Ricoeur (1984) explains that Augustine associates the *distensions* of the past and the future to the *distension* of the soul: Augustine ties

this *distension* to the slippage [or shift], that which never ceases to find its way to the heart of the threefold present ... and he sees discordance emerge again and again out of the very concordance of the intentions of expectation, attention and memory.

(Ricoeur 1984, p. 21)

By the recurrence of the paradigm of the shifts of time in memory, expectation and present, Augustine has noted a 'story' of time, and an analogy to other actions (Ricoeur 1984, p. 20). By halting the self-narrative to move to prayer, Augustine shifts his *Confessions* outside chronology (Vance 1978). And, Ricoeur (1984) suggests that by 'de-chronologizing' narrative he 'deepens its temporality'; in other words, 'de-chronologizing' in fact goes toward asserting the particularity of time: a pattern-less-ness (chaos) oscillating with 'laws' of expectation (Ricoeur 1984, pp. 23–24). The organization of particularities are therefore cumulative, and organized into bundles of significance, representing manoeuvres of 'given' models. This is the definition of 'topics' which is Vico's favoured argumentative pattern.

Vico

Augustine's *Confessions* influenced Vico to create a self-narrative that was a systematic construct and a microcosm of the world. Vico's intentions were both epistemological and educational. Vico's ideas of history corroborated his intuitions about his personal intellectual presence in this era against the laws of universal history. He 'discovered' the three eras of human development from Egyptian histories, finding the principles of history. He discovered that they were replicated in the individual. Vico saw himself as a hero in ironic and rebarbative times, history brought into reverse by Cartesian de-humanization of knowledge. Students were taught to analyse matters with extreme critical scepticism before they had experienced the world, whose universal laws Vico discovered deep under the layers of civilization. In the *Autobiography*, Vico gains philosophical distance by referring to himself in the third person (he is copying Plato's Socratic dialogues). But, additionally, there are two approaches to counter the critical and logical style of learning for students: show partiality towards imagination, and engage with 'topics'.

Imagination. The primary human faculty of 'ingenuity' (or 'discernment') allows cultivation of a natural, primordial, figural awareness; appreciation of metaphor brings the world more readily to us as 'given'. Like Aristotle, Vico felt the most important faculty is the capacity to see similarities. Poetry is historically the first mode of communication. *Vera narrativa*, or 'true speaking' (poetry) in Vico's *schema* was communally expressive and merged with the mythic state humans lived through in the age of the divine. This *vera narrativa* is metaphoric, poetic speech or, otherwise 'indicative' – no verbs, no predicates, as children speak, there is:

> immediately a 'showing' – and for this reason 'figurative' or 'imaginative' and thus in the original sense 'theoretical' [*theorin*; i.e. to see]. It is metaphorical, i.e., it shows something which has a sense, and this means that to the future, to that which is shown, the speech transfers [*metaphorein*] a signification; in this way the speech which realizes this showing 'leads before the eyes' [*phainesthai*] a significance.
>
> (Grassi 1980, p. 74)

(See also Verene 1981, Chapter 4, on 'Rhetoric', and Shotter 1993 on 'indicative speech' in his chapter on Vico.) A critical analysis by a mind fettered with logic cannot unravel a pre-narrative expectation embedded in human imagination (Verene 1981, Chapter 3). But Vico does not replicate this language in his autobiography (Vico 1744/1944); he refers to it as the first language in summarising his ground-breaking work, *The New Science* (Vico 1740/1968). Each era has its own stylistic: the 'dumb language of hieroglyphics or sacred characters in the age of the divine; symbolic language of metaphor as the heroic language; the epistolographic [demotic] consisting of expressions agreed on from everyday use' (Vico 1744/1944, p. 139).

Topics. We come to realize in Vico's biography of himself how ideas are discovered; a *topical* logic infiltrates 'reality'; that is, a 'logic' based on bundles of significance ('monads' or, as above, collections of interrelated meaningful bundles). Shotter (1993) describes Vico's idea in *Conversational Realities*:

> Already set events – in which we are not involved ... are presented within a single framework, [functioning as a] 'structured container' for all such events [thereby offering a] stable order created [according to] what our compulsion is: ... single coherent order – we must doubt this though [in order]

to grasp the nature of our third, sensuous, involved kind of knowing. But how might we provoke such a doubt within ourselves, let alone the task of giving it intelligible expression?

(Shotter 1993, pp. 57–58)

To illustrate in one simple example: Vico changed his birth date so that it was celestially marked to underscore his association to the god of genius Saturn (more on this below). And he underplays his experiences as a tutor in Vatolla early in his career to demonstrate that he was an outsider, misunderstood by those around him and the greater for it. For these reasons Vico lived in his native city not only a stranger but quite unknown. His solitary tastes and habits did not prevent his venerating from afar, as sages, the older men who were recognized for their knowledge of letters (Vico 1744/1944, p. 134).

To explain his ideas of pedagogy and the necessity of aligning the right form of learning with the right age of the student – the main purpose of his auto-biography – he gives us many instances of such misalliance in his own intellec-tual life. His book is also a counter-argument to Descartes' 'logic' as it had permeated educational institutions in Europe (not to speak of Vico's patriotic aims as a Neapolitan). Unlike Descartes, who had feigned the method of his studies to aggrandise his own philosophy,

with the candour proper to a historian, we shall narrate plainly and step by step the entire series of Vico's studies, in order that the proper and natural causes of his particular development as a man of letters may be known.

(Vico 1744/1944, p. 113)

Throughout his education, Vico stumbles across teachers or books that he is not ready for. Reception of knowledge is closely correlated to bodily development. He falls on his head as a boy and the ensuing melancholia indicates that he is a genius, and inspires him to intense study. A doctor predicts either idiocy or death from his fall as a boy:

By God's grace neither part of the prediction came true, but as a result this mischance he grew up with a melancholy and irritable temperament such as belongs to men of ingenuity and depth, who thanks to the one, are quick as lightning, and thanks to the other, take no pleasure in verbal cleverness or falsehood.

(Vico 1744/1944, p. 111)

It was commonly known that melancholia and irritability were signs of genius. And Vico was famous from his adolescence for his autodidactic habits. In fact, a misalliance could have disastrous results: having learned from his teacher (a Jesuit imbued with nominalism) that

Venetus was the most acute of all the summulists, he began also to study him, with a view to further advancement. But his mind, still too weak to stand that kind of Chrysippean logic, was almost lost on it, so that to his great sorrow, he had to give it up. His despair made him desert his studies (so dangerous it is to put youths to the study of sciences that are beyond their age!) and he strayed from them for a year and a half.

(Vico 1744/1944, p. 113)

Vico tells his father that he cannot learn and that he is wasting his time. He digresses to read Lucretius whose poetry is potentially corrupting (not to speak of his ideas) but recommends nevertheless that young men study poetry while their imaginations are receptive so that they may know how to take chances in their thinking, and not to adhere too closely to the maxims and abstractions of law until later.

However, living up to his reputation as a famous autodidact even at this early age, and in a story reminiscent of Plato's chariot in *Symposium*, he gets back on track:

Just as a high-spirited horse, long and well trained in war and long afterwards let out to pasture at will in the fields, if he happens to hear the sound of a trumpet feels again the martial appetite rise in him and is eager to be mounted by the cavalryman and led into battle; so Vico, though he had wandered from the straight course of a well-disciplined early youth, was soon spurred by his genius to take up again the abandoned path, and set off again on his way.

(Vico 1744/1944, pp. 113–114)

Vico suggested that ideal eternal narrative was a sequence of history that had elements which were repeated in all nations. But each particular nation also had its own history and its own maxims and commonplaces, an empirical style used every day: 'This eternal history is traversed in time by all the particular histories of the nation each with its rise, development, acme, decline and fall' (Vico 1744/1944, p. 169). Knowing this, we can better sift 'truth from the popular tradition of nations' (Vico 1744/1944, p. 139).

Jung

Jung's (1963) memoir also serves a philosophical (or psychological) agenda. It is an anomalous autobiography for many reasons: written in collaboration, it jettisons dates and (most) places, and organises its narrative sequences by metaphoric association and not by sequential chronology (except that individuation takes place as a sequence of development of the psyche over time). Places are emblematic, such as Africa or the habitations of the Pueblo Indians in America. They are not geographical locations but rather serve Jung's theme as spiritual-geographical zones. Written while many of the participants were still alive, there was much controversy. The memoir is designed to enact individuation, and that is its core meaning and organization.

As in Vico's work, these strategies work alongside a philological approach to sequence and meaning. Philological derivations of words supersede logical, 'objective' causal chronologies. Narrative moves by links of meanings embedded in the history of a word (as its significance is shaded by its placement within a sentence, surrounded by predicates – adjectives, or nouns and verbs). Topics function this way, as bundles of significance, like the categories appearance/ reality or opposition/agreement. It is not that elements of event or of his personality or others' traits *cause* things to happen to him – although Kermode (1979, p. 90) would say that we require this background 'connexity' as readers to make sense of a narrative, i.e. we may impute that there is a 'positivistic' drive. Concepts and meanings are traced back to a repository of interconnected images buried in the collective unconscious within the individual. Like Vico and Augustine, Jung exploits the ambiguities of allusion in words and in event to make new associations and significance.

Jung incorporates what he expects will be the reader's response. He expects that his choice to privilege internal experience in what is supposed to be a 'memoir' will meet with resistance. Accordingly, by not meeting expectation, it will seem that he is overturning community values. But, he wants us to realize, that although we may not immediately recognize it, the values he proposes are authentic values. And further, we will discover in ourselves that we have always known this. The exploration of the psyche is the focus for a rhetorical space at its inception: 'The psyche appears as the *disturbance* of a probable mode of behaviour postulated by one or other of these methods. This procedure is, *cum grano salis*, that of natural science in general' (Jung 1963, p. 93, emphasis in original; see also Jung 1934). Things run along unnoticed until the psyche, in this case, the collective 'complex', intervenes with its own independent 'deviant' purpose. The psyche is an anomalous organization of elements that invites narrative.

Later in *Memories, Dreams, Reflections*, in a chapter entitled 'On Life after Death', Jung explains that the psyche is the site of constructive contention. Fragments of figure and image collide to influence personal meanings:

> The inner images keep me from getting lost in personal retrospection ...
> [You can remain] imprisoned in these memories. But if it is reflective and is
> translated into images, retrospection can be a *reculer pour mieux sauter*. I
> try to see the line which leads through my life into the world, and out of the
> world again.
>
> (Jung 1963, p. 320)

Jung warns us that he will eschew externals and prioritize internal experience. Revelations unravel gradually. Occasional incidents at home and at school, in the psychiatric hospital or on his travels, and dream narratives are included when they impinge on an undisclosed (and therefore 'secret') *schema*. The reader discovers at the conclusion of *Memories, Dreams, Reflections* that the schema is the process of individuation, and it manifests itself in this narrative's unique shape.

Jung's secret manikin is one example of how he accomplishes this 'showing forth' that is characteristic of the volume. This 'indicative technique' has many similarities to Vico's *vera narrativa*, which I don't have the space to develop here. The manikin is a symbol of a secret, and it is also the secret itself, with its scrolls of writings whose content Jung can no longer remember. It both *is* and is *representative of* a quality of eternity in his childhood. Jung is frightened when he thinks of it even as an older man, returning to his early home. He is nearly sucked back into the fears still attached to what were other emblems of secrecy for him as a child, like the site of a fire he tended. These symbols have maintained their potency (Jung 1963, pp. 20–22). Certain mysteries need to be resolved, perhaps by incorporation in a world view that seeks to argue creatively with 'deviance'.

Regarding the other phases of Bitzer's suggestions of a rhetorical space, I will focus on Jung's *Memories, Dreams, Reflections* so as to discuss the constraints and audience of a polemical autobiography. A full discussion of constraints in Augustine's and Vico's self-narratives is found in Gardner (2013); but many of the issues are shared by each of those writers. (I will indicate these common themes briefly below as I investigate constraints in Jung's text.)

Constraints: literary device

One of the major constraints on *Memories, Dreams, Reflections* is the hidden polemic of the genre. In fact, Augustine works 'acutely' within this covert framework to startle us when he departs from it. Formal genre constraints are among the most important, as we have discussed: the sequence in order of birth, childhood, development, illness and death. But weighing in with these to shape the narrative are ethical constraints, such as (in Jung's instance) a family objecting to the inclusion of mistresses, or a desire to play down unpopular political affiliations. In Vico's case, he alters dates and locations to highlight his isolation as a genius.

A constraint in Jung's endeavour is also his agenda to provide opportunities for revelation of a personal myth. The common intention of autobiography to tell us about private and public matters is well-known and Jung can rely on our expectations as experienced readers of memoirs. As readers, for example, we will permit a biased selection of events.

Starobinski (1980) argues that autobiographical narration is 'discursive narrative' rather than 'portraiture'. We sense strains on the material whenever Jung reaches back to gloss earlier activities. (Clearly also, recalling the past, we note Augustine's manipulation of event, such as for example his story of his friend's conversion by a random selection of a passage in the Old Testament.) Our sense of the truth of the account is disturbed; these glosses on the text are a 'kind of obstacle to the fidelity of the exact happening' (Starobinski 1980, p. 76). A perfect stylistic and theoretical fit as the boy grows to be a man, creates a sense of contrivance, or manipulation. We are reading transparent 'fable'. But, actually, this is what Jung promised us and, as in examples above of Vico's stories (and Augustine's), it is what we come to expect from these autobiographies. We are reoriented as we read.

An important genre feature is the identification of the older narrator with the younger man, which is constantly affirmed. By adding a theoretical curve to this – i.e. in Jung's case that the individual emerging from unconsciousness into consciousness and then integrating into an awareness of the larger, collective unconscious – another fabulist dimension is added. In Augustine's narrative, the young man's increasing awareness and receptivity of his Lord is an ongoing theme; in Vico, the older man recognizes the younger man's pattern of gaining knowledge. But, I would argue, this is what a life story always is. Starobinski explains:

> It is the internal transformation of the individual, and the exemplary character of this transformation – that furnishes a subject for narrative discourse in which 'I' is both subject and object … the discursive character of the narrative is justified anew by content not by addressee.… [It is about] retracing the genesis of present situation … antecedents of the moment from which the present discourse stems.
>
> (Starobinski 1980, p. 79)

The theme of Jung's memoir is embedded in its retrieval of past events to exemplify a present revelation of hidden meaning. The particular is impregnated with the universal for Vico, Augustine and Jung with their shared neo-Platonic inclinations. They seek to recreate the particular in all its uniqueness as it mirrors and embodies the universal.

When narrators omit events that they have deemed irrelevant or contradictory, they deliberately hide them. This leads us to an important theme of narrative, and *Memories, Dreams, Reflections* most explicitly: secrets. (Augustine's attitude to exegesis depends on his belief that texts are veils hiding true meanings; see Book XII in *Confessions* in which he explores the hidden meanings of *Genesis*.)

Constraints: secrets

Creating secrets is a personal and/or collective drive to create the ordering of a narrative. The formation of secrets is motivated by a desire to cover over discrepancies or else to make an interpretation coherent (Kermode 1979). Secrets shape personalities, motivating action. For Kermode, secrets are the cornerstone of narrative which is a series of interpretations that foreground some matters, and thereby hide others, sometimes deliberately. Since Jung argues that underlying personality is covert, to tell one's life story may well uncover that secret schema. The integrity of the personality is bound up by hidden patterns. Thinking of our narrative issue, secrets are 'at odds with sequence, which is considered as an aspect of propriety ("refined common sense"); and a passion for sequence may result in the suppression of the secret' (Kermode 1980, pp. 87–88). In fact, our suspect narrator 'breaks down the conventional relationship between sequential narrative and history-likeness, with its arbitrary imposition of truth' (Kermode 1980, p. 89).

During the first three chapters of *Memories, Dreams, Reflections*, and later when describing interactions with people in his travels, his encounters with Freud (to whom, he discloses here, he had lied), with his patients in treatment, and finally in his arduous tussles with another layer of (what are) involuntary 'secret' repositories of meaning – the unconscious – we grasp that secrets are pervasive in Jung's psychic life. The boy Jung hides his frightening dreams, his illicit associations of meaning – the black-skirted fearful Catholic priests who swallow little children – his manikin and scroll with secret writings. He tends a sacred fire and engages others to help him maintain the ritual fire. These were 'inviolable secret(s) which must never be betrayed, for the safety of my life depended on it. Why that was so I did not ask myself. It was simply so' (Jung 1963, p. 22). The child, Jung, constructs 'givens' in this way, underlying motivations for behaviour, aroused by fear. These private 'myths' or 'fables' which he discovers (and manipulates) in his patients for therapeutic purposes, are the unconscious 'complex'. These motivating underlying clusters of significance impact on our every act. Cognition and conatus are filtered through these underground elements; Jung's *Memories, Dreams, Reflections* reflects this conviction.

> In many cases … the patient who comes to us has a story that is not told, and which as a rule no one knows of. To my mind therapy only really begins after the investigation of that wholly personal story. It is the patient's secret, the rock against which he is shattered. If I know his secret story, I have a key to the treatment.
>
> (Jung 1963, p. 117)

Secrets are fearful 'premonitions of things unknown' (Jung 1963, p. 356) and that is because they 'fill life with something impersonal':

> [Man] must sense that he lives in a world which in some respects is mysterious; that things happen and can be experienced which remain inexplicable; that not everything which happens can be anticipated. The unexpected and the incredible belong in this world. Only then is life whole.
>
> (Jung 1963, p. 356)

Differentiation is the first move toward consciousness for ancient men. The individual takes the same path. Jung tells us about the river near him where dead bodies are often found along its banks. He nearly becomes one of those bodies later, still a boy, when he nearly trips off a dangerous high bridge. The older Jung concurs with his mother that his act was suicidal. (Were there other such events in his life?)

By defining the near-slip as showing suicidal potential, Jung presages the ritual of dismemberment, self-destruction followed by self-recollection in the individuation process. Individuation requires differentiation of the self, first from the comprehensive collective unconscious Self as a step towards self-knowledge. This hidden impulse throws up images which are 'impersonal' and from independent sources since they are not part of the young boy's personal repertoire of known imagery. These unconscious, archetypal images, present themselves in response to his seeking resolution of a fear.

In 'Transformation symbolism in the Mass', Jung (1954) asks if we can explain where the collective images come from in any other way but from an impersonal source?

> It is necessary that the transubstantiation should be a cause of wonder and a miracle which man can in no wise comprehend. It is a *mysterium* in the sense of a ... secret that is acted and displayed. The ordinary man is not conscious of anything in himself that would cause him to perform a 'mystery'.
>
> (Jung 1954, para. 379)

Whatever the source, the dream of the cathedral, when he reflects on it, leads Jung to realize astonishing and new things about God and about grace; and his manikin comes to seem a kind of repository of the boy's intuition of the collective unconscious. Jung confirms this in his last chapters of *Memories, Dreams, Reflections*:

> The individual on his lonely path needs a secret that for various reasons he may not or cannot reveal. Such a secret reinforces him in the isolation of his individual aims.... The need for such a secret is so compelling that the individual finds himself involved in ideas and actions for which he is no longer responsible.... [He becomes] deviant from the collective. Internal oppositions are battled with in secret....
>
> (Jung 1963, pp. 342–345)

In fact, the more things are hidden, from his mother's concealed second personality and illnesses, to his father's unravelling faith, the more certain he is that realities are the opposite of what they appear to be. In the same way, Augustine uncovers hidden meanings as he pursues the quest to find meanings in his life story: meeting Anselm by his mother's friendship; her discovery of Christianity – where was it all leading to? As a child he is jealous of other children's occupation of his mother's time – he develops, thereby, as a social being away from the being-ness of the child in original communion with the Lord. He steals a fruit and he discovers that he does this as a gratuitous, guilty act of rebellion – all as steps in what is his unknowing development away from a pagan conscience but also away from communion with the Lord. Like Jung, the saint recollects his own fable, differentiating himself in the flux of sensation, to discover the idealized human soul he can become. For both Augustine and Jung, recollection is an act of the imagination. Jung specifically comes to recognize that he is constituted as a 'psychic process' (Jung 1963, p. 4).

Constraints: associations

Lifetime associations are formed based on early sensations, like fixed sequences. The warmth of the sun and milk, sparkling water, the security of a closed home, the strange odour and look of a fascinating nanny, and, a little older, seeing the exhibits in a natural history museum: these are this child's first meanings formed into an underlying narrative of his life. Apart from the personal dimension, associations are also embedded in the culture and in our natural surroundings.

In *Memories, Dreams, Reflections* we find the same pivotal associations and fascinations cropping up beginning early on with discussions of the sun, bridges, water, secret compulsions themselves, and secret myths, occurring again and again. Jung's search for resolution to his terrors inspired creative meanings. We trace the stages of differentiation in the baby by following how Jung constructs the story of his infantile associations. The baby, Jung, separates himself out from his surroundings, and begins the early moves toward individuation in this story. The voice of the older Jung calls attention to and thereby fashions recollections of 'crucial' moments. From primary and wholly bodily sensation, the baby soon evolves reflective responses. Associations are thereby forged or else they are discovered, remembered. After his experience of well-being in the pram in the sunny warmth, he recalls spooning up warm milk and bread: 'The milk has a pleasant taste and a characteristic smell. This was the first time I became aware of the smell of milk. It was the moment when, so to speak, I became conscious of smelling' (Jung 1963, p. 6). Emotions, concepts, self are awakened as he interacts with the life around him. He 'recognizes' these sensations because they were already there, dormant in him.

Ambiguities are inevitably embedded in association. These anomalies enable the narrator to lead us in directions responding to the older narrator's purposes. Motivations show a personal and a collective dimension. Vico's exploitation of 'copiousness' in which associations of words are explored is an important part of the argumentative style of his autobiography. He describes the importance of looking at the Latin language to find earliest associations to date concepts and so to construct past times that later came into the Italian language (see Vico 1744/1944, p. 205).

In his book, Jung is constrained to engage us, overturning reader expectation with newly discovered contrary, yet incontrovertible, links, which he has just constructed. But there are pitfalls. If we don't 'buy' the association, Jung is on thin ice. The psyche accounts for incompatible realities along its path of integration, just as Vico chartered inappropriate directions in his intellectual path.

Constraints: mythic formulae

An important collective (and often unconscious) constraint is collective myth. As we noted above, Vico exploited some of the elements of the myth of Saturn. Jung's chronicle of individuation is also tainted by this figure who embodies the *topos* of passing Time, burnished harvests, and destructive fathers whose powers paradoxically generate new life. This is the figure of 'Saturn' (or 'Chronos') and he underlies the fable of the personality of Carl Gustav Jung. Vico (1740/1968) investigates Saturn in *The New Science*, the age of Saturn appears in his timeline in the opening chronology. The time of Saturn is the moment of the inception of time itself. And, then, the mythic figure, Saturn, is the backdrop to philosophic autobiography. Aristotle opens his essay on genius with the question: 'Why is it that all men who have become outstanding in philosophy, statesmanship, poetry or the arts are melancholic?' (Aristotle 1937, p. 155). Aristotle is referring to Saturn here. Any important intellectual's life invites comparison to this figure. There is a long history to this personality type. And its history comes down to the present day in image and literature. We can pick up the references from many sources, but I will use Vico's discussion. He tells us that, later in Roman times, the name 'Saturn' derived from 'sati' (Vico 1740/1968, para. 73): 'sown fields' – the golden harvest is in. Reference to the agricultural cycle is the beginning of marking time. 'Two-harvests-ago' signifies two years ago; so 'sati' comes to mean Time (Vico 1740/1968, para. 73). The black bile associated with Saturn had the accompanying personality and physical difficulties of the melancholic humour. In fact, the chronic maladjusted physical state – overheated brains – affects the saturnine personality's dreams (Aristotle 1937, p. 181). Dreams were more disturbing and powerful. Jung claimed to have those attributes. In fact, while a heroic backdrop is the pattern for every memoir, the saturnine hero is rather distinct in some of his attributes. Vico shares this with Jung.

Overcoming difficulties, working through to successful life from uneasy beginnings, is a pattern we expect in autobiography. However, the saturnine figure also has destructive elements. These personality types are often cold, rational beings seeking neat conclusions. Repeated chaotic, dark and disturbed events punctuate the story that need the resolution this figure achieves. In the end, the rationalized scenarios overcome destruction. The melancholy quest moves ever further inward and toward isolation. In his darkest moments, Jung suffered the negative side of Saturn. Jung points out his own early signs of self-destruction, which emerged again when he plunged headlong into his unconscious. To salvage time past, Saturn figures typically search for the beginnings of genius in their own childhood.

In an introduction to an exhibition catalogue for Goya's drawings of Saturn at the Prada, Malraux (1957, p. 4) puts it specifically that the saturnine 'genius rescues his childhood by reinventing it in the shadow of what is to come, and the self-presentation the self-proclaimed genius posits'. Jung's 'creative illness' traces a fall and a rise against overwhelming odds. He tells us of his long period of sinking into his psyche: talking aloud to Philemon, the anima, and other figures inside himself – the 'frenzy' from which he was born anew, giving him the tools to empathize with and analyse his patients' psychoses. Not only, in retrospect, does he position this event in his life as having had creative outcome, but it also serves as a bid for validation in the community. It contributes to his mythologizing himself. He claims it was a 'creative illness'. This paradoxical claim enabled him to salvage this period of his life. He doesn't want us to feel that he was ill, but that he was creative.

As I noted Vico did too, Jung instinctively alters events in his life to coincide with the shape of the melancholic hero's life. This obfuscation serves to high-light characteristics of his personality that correspond to the hero's quest. After all, it is the revelation of his mythic personality that is the important point of his self-narratives. In Jung's case, it is how the individuation process took him on this quest that coincides with the formula of the heroic journey. We know within ourselves the heroic narrative structure of a life story. We constantly tell it to ourselves about our self.

Audiences

The anticipated response of an audience is fully integrated into the product. The anticipated response imposes both constraints on the message and on its exigen-cies. As Bakhtin (1986, p. 79) pointed out, 'We learn to cast our speech into generic forms, and when hearing others' speech, we guess its genre from the very first words'. Bakhtin's super-addressee, the audience for whom arguments are formulated, participates in formulating the proposition, in the same way. Individuation is the process by which the Self interacts creatively with the per-sonal self. In those respects, I will explore briefly, the impersonal 'Self' is the 'super-addressee' in Jung's *Memories, Dreams, Reflections*. The 'Self' is differ-entiated from the personal self, and also coexistent and intermingling. Meanings oscillate between them. The resulting revelation is of a pre-conceptual ubiquitous Self: substantiation already in mind, already given, responsive to the personal self and a mythic, generic self. We learn this upon reading *Memories, Dreams, Reflections.*

Vico's audience is the rational, learned educators of Europe for the most part. The constraints he suffered – fears of the Inquisition, 'old boy' networks he could not join in Naples, patriotism and an aristocratic patronage system – were navigated to sustain the universal and trained minds he aimed at who were his audience. He wrote *The New Science* in both Latin and in the vernacular, but his *Autobiography* was written only in Latin in response to an invitation by an aristocrat in Venice. Augustine's audiences are a population of high and low, educated and ignorant, but Christian or those inclined to convert. He also wrote in both Latin and in the vernacular, and was a powerful preacher. In his *De doctrina cristiana* he writes a long section on the appropriate levels of rhetoric for high and low audiences depending on the nature of the material. He marvelled at the new appropriateness Christ created in telling parables aimed at ordinary people which talked of sublime sacred principles (see Book IV of *De doctrina cristiana*). His autobiography sought to demonstrate in the ordinary events of his life how true spirituality is found. Jung projects an audience he assumes are reasonable people, persuaded by cogent and objective presentation of fact. Perelman and Olbrechts-Tyteca (1969) call this impersonal construction, the 'universal audience'.

Jung's projection of reasonableness persuades his readers that they are reasonable. As rational people, accustomed to real fact, he expects his audience will resist his description of autobiography as a fable. Believing, as a matter of cultural convention, that incontrovertible fact does exist, and that it needs no disguising, they would feel 'fable' is the wrong word to describe the facts of a man's life. Defining *fact* as 'myth' or 'fable' undermines what the word means in common parlance. To argue this point, Jung takes a two-pronged approach. First, he redefines fact, confirming that his readers' psychic experiences correspond to external reality despite the prevailing conviction that external reality is most often thought to have autonomous existence. Jung points out that external reality is utterly dependent on internal processes. In fact, reality is a psychic phenomenon. Einstein (1949/1979) makes a related point in his *Autobiographical Notes*. He places realism among the pre-rational springs of human behaviour, 'those springs that we often conceive of not just as the source of creativity, but also as the source of deep satisfaction in creative endeavours' (Einstein 1949/1979, p. 54). Arthur Fine (1986) explores what he calls Einstein's 'motivational realism': it is a faith in the access of reason to reality. In a letter, Einstein explains:

> I have no better expression than the term 'religious' for this trust [*Vertrauen*] in the rational character of reality and in its being accessible, at least to some extent, to human reason. Where this feeling is absent, science degenerates into senseless [*gestlose*] empiricism.
>
> (Quoted in Fine 1986, p. 110)

Second, Jung uses teleological tactics that recall Vico's co-mingling of the ideal eternal history and the empirical history into a new form: the expectation sensed in the fable is fundamental. The fable shapes the 'facts' of the narrative, and transfers to facts a *feeling* of cohesion. And then, Jung transforms psychic fact into the realm of rational discourse where a 'universal audience' accesses it. Perelman and Olbrechts-Tyteca (1969) tell us more about the 'universal audience': it is 'always a more or less systematized construction'; 'Everyone constitutes the universal audience from what he knows of his fellow men, in such a way as to transcend the few oppositions he is aware of' (Perelman and Olbrechts-Tyteca 1969, p. 31).

Conclusion

The argumentative narratives I have discussed in this chapter demonstrate well that autobiography mostly has a purpose apart from its most obvious one of listing events. Lives are unique and they interrupt the flow of time by their very nature. Narrators shape the details of events into significant sequence to fit a theme, and conform to constructing the feeling we require from narratives that they are coherent and plausible. Examining rhetorical strictures as well as genre constraints, 'real world' contexts and a personal sense of how a life warrants attention are necessary tools if we are to be truly present in time as readers and writers of autobiography. Further investigation of aspects of Jung's idea of individuation is required to find its close reflection of self-narrative as I have discussed it here.

References

Aristotle (1937) Problems connected with Thought, Intelligence and Wisdom. *Problems II*, Book XXX, 1. Cambridge, MA: Harvard University Press.
Augustine (1992) *Confessions*. London: Oxford University Press.
Augustine (1465/1995) *De doctrina cristiana*. Oxford: Clarendon Press.
Bakhtin, M. M. (1986) *Speech Genres*. Austin, TX: University of Texas Press.
Benjamin, A. (2006) *Style and Time: essays on the politics of appearance*. Northwestern University Press.
Benjamin, W. (1969) *Illuminations*. New York: Schocken Press.
Brémond, C. (1980) The logic of narrative possibilities. *New Literary History* 11, 387–411.
Bitzer, L. (1968) The Rhetorical Situation. *Philosophy and Rhetoric* 1, 1–14.
Collingwood, R. G. (1939/1944) *An Autobiography*. London: Oxford University Press.
Einstein, A. (1949/1979) *Autobiographical Notes*. La Salle: Open Court.
Fine, A. (1986) *The Shaky Game*. Chicago: University of Chicago Press.
Gardner, L. (2013). *Rhetorical Investigations: G. B. Vico and C. G. Jung*. London: Routledge.
Grassi, E. (1980) *Rhetoric as Philosophy*. Philadelphia: Penn State University.
Hauser, G. A. (1986) *Introduction to Rhetorical Theory*. New York: Harper and Row.
Jung, C. G.: Unless otherwise stated, the following are from. *The Collected Works of C. G. Jung*. (CW) London: Routledge & Kegan Paul/Princeton, NJ: Princeton University Press:
Jung, C. G. (1921) *Psychological Types*. (CW 6).
Jung, C. G. (1934) A review of the complex theory. (CW 8).
Jung, C. G. (1954) Transformation symbolism in the mass. (CW 11).
Jung, C. G. (1963) *Memories, Dreams, Reflections*. Fontana, London.
Kermode, F. (1979) *The Genesis of Secrecy*. Cambridge, MA: Harvard University Press.
Kermode, F. (1980) Secrets and narrative sequence. *Critical Inquiry* 7, 83–101.
Lottman, J. (1979) Origin of Plot in light of typology. *Poetics Today* 1, 161–184.
Malraux, A. (1950/1957) *Saturn*. London: Phaidon.
Mathien, T. and Wright, D. (2006) *Autobiography as Philosophy*. London: Abingdon/Routledge.

Olney, J. (1980) *Autobiography, Essays Theoretical and Critical*. Princeton, NJ: Princeton University Press.

Perelman, C. (1982) *The Realm of Rhetoric*. London: University of Notre Dame Press.

Perelman, C. and Olbrechts-Tyteca, L. (1969) *The New Rhetoric*. London: University of Notre Dame.

Ricoeur, P. (1984) *Time and Narrative* (Vol. 1). Chicago: University of Chicago Press.

Ricoeur, P. (1986) *Time and Narrative* (Vol. 2). Chicago: University of Chicago Press.

Ricoeur, P. (1988) *Time and Narrative* (Vol. 3). Chicago: University of Chicago Press.

Shotter, J. (1993) *Conversational Realities*. London: Sage.

Starobinski, J. (1980) The Style of autobiography. In: J. Olney (Ed.) *Autobiography: Essays Theoretical and Critical*. Princeton: Princeton University Press.

Tristram, R. J. (1988) Vico on the production and assessment of knowledge. *Philosophy and Phenomenological Research* 48, 355–388.

Vance, E. (1978) Augustine's *Confessions* and the Poetics of the Law. *Modern Language Notes* 93, 618–634.

Vance, E. (1984) The functions and limits of autobiography in Augustine's 'Confessions'. *Poetics Today* 5, 399–409.

Verene, D. P. (1981) *Vico's Science of the Imagination*. Ithaca: Cornell University Press.

Verene, D. P. (1991) *The New Art of Autobiography*. Oxford, UK: Oxford University Press.

Vico, G. (1744/1944) *Autobiography of Giambattista Vico*. Ithaca: Cornell University Press.

Vico, G. (1740/1968) *The New Science*. Ithaca: Cornell University Press.

Vico, G. (1740/1996) *The Art of Rhetoric*. Amsterdam: Rodopi.

Chapter 5

Jung's 'personal myth' and the two personalities

Mark Saban

When Jung came, at the end of his life, to write his 'so-called autobiography', *Memories, Dreams, Reflections* (henceforth MDR), his intention was not only to offer a chronological itemisation of significant experiences and memories, but also to reveal to the reader those events in which, as he put it, 'the imperishable world irrupted into this one' (Jung 1989, p. 4), and thereby throw new light upon his psychology. The subjective and personal experiences he describes in MDR lay behind and informed the articulation of many of the fundamental concepts that constituted analytical psychology.

We are told, for example, that the contrasexual anima archetype developed not from an abstract idea or concept but from an experience of Jung's: she was heard by him as an inner voice (the voice of an actual woman known to Jung) which engaged Jung in conversation (Jung 1989, p. 185). With this example, and many others, MDR revealed to the general public what had hitherto been understood only by Jung's inner circle:[1] that the psychology to be found in conceptualised and universalized form in the 20 volumes of Jung's *Collected Works* was the intellectual crystallisation of an intimate, personal and subjective core. The dimension of that core that I am going to address in this chapter is Jung's account of what he calls his two personalities, a theme that dominates the first three chapters of MDR.

In a previous paper I drew attention to what I saw as the critical importance of Jung's treatment of his two personalities in MDR (Saban 2013). It seemed to me that Jung's account of his experience of the two personalities offered a red thread that, if followed, led to the heart of Jung's central concept of individuation. Moreover, if we examine the ways in which Jung engaged with this problem we can shed new light upon some of the persistent difficulties that have emerged in and around analytical psychology in the hundred years since Jung's foundational 'confrontation with the unconscious'. In this way, we can dream forward the individuation of Jung's psychology.

My research since then has only reinforced my intuition that this dimension of Jung's life and work provides us with a crucial lens through which to re-vision the ideas of analytical psychology. Here I aim to extend this project by re-encountering the two personalities in the specific context of Jung's 'personal myth'.

Jung's personal myth

When Jung overcame his initial resistance to the idea of an autobiography and finally started writing an account of his early years he told Aniela Jaffé that he had become enthused by the unexpected turn which the project had taken:

> This 'autobiography' is now taking a direction quite different from what I had imagined at the beginning ... it has become a necessity for me to write down my early memories. If I neglect to do so for a single day, unpleasant physical symptoms immediately follow. As soon as I set to work they vanish and my head feels perfectly clear.
>
> (Jung 1989, p. vi)

For Jung, this new direction was to open up a fresh perspective onto his whole psychological life. As Jung became caught up in his memoir, Jaffé wrote excitedly to the publisher, Kurt Wolff,

> something so wonderful and meaningful happened ... Jung himself is writing his autobiography all over again ... so much had become clear to [Jung] and especially the meaning of his life which he had apparently not seen to its full extent.
>
> (Bair 2004, p. 595)

Jung's exhilaration would seem linked to a burgeoning awareness that the story he was telling not only threw new light upon both his life and his work, but also illuminated a dynamic link between the two that might offer a new way to understand both. When he came to write the prologue to his memoir, he chose to articulate this insight in a characteristically Jungian way by telling us that what he was about to narrate was his 'personal myth' (Jung 1989, p. 3) or *den Mythus meines Lebens* (the myth of my life).[2]

This coinage, 'personal myth', is particularly striking because it places together (in what is, as Lucy Huskinson 2008, p. 4, has observed, 'strictly speaking ... a category error'), two different worlds of meaning: a subjective/individual dimension that concerns individual human experience and an objective/universal dimension that takes mythic (archetypal) form.[3] Moreover, the term 'personal myth' performs what it signifies, bringing together precisely the two ingredients that the narrative in question insists upon putting into tension. As we enter the early chapters of MDR, we meet these two dimensions again, though in a new guise: the two personalities.

For Jung, the tale of the two personalities functions as personal myth because the dynamic revealed within it brings into play the tension that dominates Jung's mature psychology. Although Jung describes, under the broad headings of 'personality no. 1' and 'personality no. 2', a whole range of different motifs, ideas and images, the central problem he addresses through the telling of this narrative myth can be expressed in the one question which Jung's psychology never ceases to circumambulate: how can a human being function day-to-day as an individual person in the world, without losing touch with the dynamic, numinous timeless aspects of existence that are essential for a meaningful life?

But before we look more closely at Jung's struggles with this issue and before we see how Jung shaped his own psychology as a way of engaging with this problem, we need to begin with a more immediate question: what does Jung mean by emphasising in MDR the *mythic* importance of his *personal* experiences?

Jung and the personal

In Jung's 1952 Forward to the fourth Swiss edition of *Symbols of Transformation*, he tells us that when, in 1912, he had finished writing *Wandlungen und Symbole der Libido* (Jung 1912), a work that had involved him in a wide-ranging psychological amplification of world mythology, he found himself beset by inner turmoil. The question that presented itself to him at that time was, 'What is the myth you are living?' (Jung 1952, p. xxiv). Looking back, at 65, Jung reflected, 'I did not know that I was living a myth, and even if I had known it, I would not have known what sort of myth was ordering my life without my knowledge' (Jung 1952, p. xxv). In that moment, he says, he set himself a 'task of tasks ... I took it upon myself to get to know "my" myth' (Jung 1952, p. xxv). After all, Jung asked himself, how could he make 'due allowance for the personal factor, for my personal equation, which is yet so necessary for a knowledge of the other person, if I was unconscious of it?' (Jung 1952, p. xxv). This 'task of tasks' was to become a lifetime's work for Jung, since even in his 83rd year, as he set about writing his autobiography, the nature of that myth was, it seems, still in question.

As Jung emphasised again and again throughout the *Collected Works*, the 'personal equation' is a psychological factor that has the capacity to warp not only personal and therapeutic relations, but also, should it remain unrecognised, the entire project of psychology as a scientific endeavour. Under these circumstances, the best that any psychological researcher can achieve is to make the requisite allowance for what are inevitable and ineradicable subjective biases. As Jung puts it, 'The demand that [the psychologist] should see only objectively is quite out of the question, for it is impossible. We must be satisfied if he does not see too subjectively' (Jung 1921, para. 10).

Jung makes it clear that unconsciousness of one's own personal equation or personal myth has the potential (a) to play havoc with interpersonal relationships (and especially that between analyst and patient), and (b) to fatally distort the psychologist's would-be objective conclusions about his science. We might then expect Jung, as psychologist, to be urgently concerned with finding ways to minimise the potential of his personal myth to distort his psychology's claim to objectivity and universality. After all, Jung begins *Psychological Types* by telling us that it was the distortions caused by the respective personal equations of Freud and Adler (in Freud's case that of one-sided extraversion and in Adler's that of one-sided introversion) that made him aware of the necessity of a universal system of types that could transcend precisely this problem (Jung 1921, para. 91).

In contrast, what we learn from MDR is that, far from seeing his personal myth as a factor that might distort his psychology, Jung in fact regarded it as a red thread running through every aspect of both his life and his psychology, ineradicable from any understanding of either. Since writing the foreword to *Symbols* in 1950, Jung seems to have shifted his ground: understanding the personal myth is important, not because it has the potential to obscure our 'knowledge of the other person' (Jung 1952, p. xxiv), but because *this* myth, Jung's myth, is to be understood as, in some sense, *relevant to us all*.

This idea brings into sharp focus the curious tension within which Jung's psychology is situated: on the one hand it is a kind of 'personal confession' while on the other it claims to be an objective and universally applicable body of ideas. What Jung requires us to accept, implicitly or explicitly, is not only that his personal experiences are in some sense exemplars of human experience as a whole, but also that by paying attention to the myth that conveys the essence of these experiences we can all gain insight into our own lives.

But how can this be? How can a factor that Jung himself has repeatedly trumpeted as the source of considerable and profound distortion also be the very factor that provides us with the central meaning to our lives?

Ultimately, the answer to this question will depend upon our ability to discern which aspects of Jung's personal equation and personal myth are, as it were, peculiar to Jung alone, and therefore the source of potential distortion, and which aspects are indeed universally human. Our difficulty is that we cannot necessarily rely upon Jung himself to be our best guide to this discernment, since we are dealing with precisely those areas that are likely to be in his blind spots. By looking closely at the narrative of the two personalities in MDR, I hope to shed some light on this problem.

Two personalities

As a child, Jung tells us, he suffered a disturbing sense of inner division. 'Somewhere deep in the background I always knew that I was two persons.' (Jung 1989, p. 44). In MDR, Jung expresses himself, as a rule, in non-technical language, and avoids utilising the jargon of analytical psychology. In this passage he not only refuses to use diagnostic language to describe this duality of personality but, more importantly, he refuses to retrospectively pathologise himself. The conflict between the personalities, he tells us, 'has nothing to do with a 'split' or dissociation in the ordinary medical sense. On the contrary, it is played out in every individual' (Jung 1989, p. 45).

With this claim, Jung makes a striking bid for exemplarity. The division between two inner personalities was not, he insists, a mere contingent detail of his childhood, but rather a psychological given for the psyche. To put the point in a different way, Jung seems to be suggesting that the dynamic encounter of personality no. 1 and personality no. 2 functions psychologically (or perhaps existentially) as an essential and universal tension within human life.

The key question is, of course, how we should understand this extraordinary claim. Jung verges on the enigmatic here, because his insight about inner division never gets spelled out or developed into a full-fledged theory. Presumably his intention is that the narrative of the two personalities will itself somehow make his meaning evident, providing the meaning which he 'had not seen to its full extent' but which the hindsight of old age has now revealed to him, and which he will in turn reveal to us through his personal myth. If so, it is a dynamic that, it seems to me, takes shape first as a division between two personalities but later, after repeatedly recurring in various different forms, eventually shows up in the form of what Jung describes in his mature psychology as the 'problem of the opposites'.

As is often the case with Jung, and particularly when it comes to the apparently pathological, he uses a teleological perspective. The significance of his early experience of the two personalities does not, for Jung, derive from its source in early life; rather it looks forward to what will be in time revealed as that goal which is central to his life and work.

In order to evaluate this important claim of Jung's we need to pay close attention to the way in which his inner division manifests itself. The prime importance of the mythic narrative of the two personalities and their vicissitudes does not derive from the specific values, motifs and images Jung associates with them; these are mostly local to Jung and his time. Far more important is the nature of the dynamic process whereby their engagement with Jung reveals itself within his life. It is nonetheless worth summarising the key aspects of each personality.

Personality no. 1

Jung's personality no. 1 is described as being associated with the 'bright daylight world' of ordinary life (Jung 1989, p. 19). It combines much that we would expect in an ordinary little boy, and then later in a conventional adolescent and young adult. Jung associates it with the familiar, the everyday, and the reliable. Relative to personality no. 2 it is portrayed as limited and superficial, concerned with the time-bound phenomena of ordinary life. It also shows up in the very mundane shadow qualities of meanness, vanity, mendacity and egotism (Jung

1989, p. 45). As personality no. 1, Jung was merely the grubby, naughty and lazy little 'schoolboy who … deserved his punishment, and who had to behave to his age' (Jung 1989, p. 35). At a later point, he tells us, personality no. 1 became associated with the systematic investigation of 'consciously framed' questions (Jung 1989, p. 68), and was drawn to facts, 'concrete things' and empirical science (Jung 1989, p. 82). Personality no. 1 was also the dimension that involved Jung in the world of outer relationships, in the context of family school and work.

Personality no. 2

As Renos Papadopoulos (1991) has delineated, in MDR personality no. 2 is foreshadowed in the shape of various treasured secret and meaningful events of Jung's early years, such as the giant phallus dream, the stone on which Jung sits, wondering if he is sitter or stone, and the secret manikin and its soul-stone. In this context, Jung repeatedly utilises the word 'secret', although he nonetheless makes it clear that this is not the kind of secret that could be revealed. It is more a question of impenetrable mystery and unanswerable questions.

Later Jung relates personality no. 2 to the idea of what he calls 'God's world' (Jung 1989, p. 67): nature in wild and cosmic form; earth, sun, moon, weather, the night and dreams (Jung 1989, pp. 44–45). It brings with it a sense of timelessness, infinity, and the imperishable, or as Jung puts it, 'superhuman dazzling light, the darkness of the abyss, the cold passivity of infinite space and time, the uncanny grotesqueness of the irrational world of chance' (Jung 1989, p. 72). Personality no. 2 is sometimes experienced in the form of 'intuitive premonitions' (Jung 1989, p. 68), is often drawn to 'meaning' and seems associated with a romantic nostalgic sense of history, philosophy (especially Eckhart, Schopenhauer, Kant and Nietzsche), Greco-Roman, Egyptian and prehistoric archaeology, and comparative religion.

In contrast with personality no. 1, the inward-facing personality no. 2 is very much concerned with solitude and, as we have seen, with secrets. Jung tells us that no. 2 'knew God as a hidden, personal, and at the same time suprapersonal secret' (Jung 1989, p. 45). It therefore possessed an emphatically non-relational character.

The interactional process

When we contrast the two personalities by supplying an inventory of their respective domains we risk missing a crucial aspect of Jung's narrative: the alternating and shifting ways in which Jung (1989), especially in the early chapters, is subject to, and even possessed by the two personalities in turn. Later he becomes more consciously aware of the difference between them and is able to reflect upon them, to take up a more active approach toward them, and eventually to negotiate a difficult path between them. He remains nonetheless powerfully affected by their gravitational pull and especially the pull toward personality no. 2. This continues even into later life (e.g. Jung 1989, p. 20).

In his early years, Jung seems to primarily regard personality no. 2 as 'self' and personality no. 1 as 'other'. In its earlier stages, personality no. 2 seems to manifest itself as a secure place to which Jung can retreat in the comforting knowledge that he alone knows its secret: 'This possession of a secret had a very powerful formative influence on my character; I consider it the essential factor of my boyhood' (Jung 1989, p. 22). In contrast, personality no. 1, which overtook him when, for example, playing with his schoolmates, had the effect on him of 'alienat[ing] me from myself' (Jung 1989, p. 19), and it seemed to him dubious, suspect and even hostile.

However, Jung's tendency to shelter in personality no. 2 also manifested itself as an unconscious avoidance of school and personality no. 1, an avoidance that was eventually enacted in a series of fainting fits that overtook him for six months. Allowed to stay away from school, Jung became completely absorbed in the 'mysterious realm' (Jung 1989, p. 22) of personality no. 2 (i.e. whiling away the hours dreaming, drawing and reading, deep in nature). Although he relished this opportunity to dwell in the realm of personality no. 2 he 'had the obscure feeling that [he] was fleeing from [him]self' (Jung 1989, p. 31). This period ended with what Jung calls a 'collision with reality' (Jung 1989, p. 31) whereby he suddenly understood (through, significantly, overhearing the voice of the father) the crippling effect on his family of this 'illness' that enabled him to avoid work, and the consequent necessity for him to re-enter the world as an active person.

At this point, Jung's sense of self made a significant shift in the direction of personality no. 1. Shortly afterwards he describes an experience of 'having just emerged from a dense cloud' – 'I knew all at once: now I am myself! ... Previously I had existed too, but everything had happened to me. Now I happened to myself. Now I knew: I am myself now, now I exist' (Jung 1989, p. 32). The way in which Jung hammers the word 'I' in this passage speaks volumes with regard to the stage of ego-development he has reached. Indeed, this conscious possession of and identification with ego-hood seems to have enabled him to achieve differentiations hitherto impossible, as we witness in the subsequent episode in which Jung first became fully conscious of the two personalities as separate persons – a process that brought him to the 'disappointing realisation that now, at any rate, I was nothing but the little schoolboy who had deserved his punishment, and who had to behave according to his age. The other person must be sheer nonsense' (Jung 1989, p. 35).

Jung here seems to describe a shift of psychic centre of gravity towards a conscious identification with personality no. 1. As he points out, the sphere of the 'old man,' who 'belonged to the centuries,' for all its enticing profundity, was simply not enough (Jung 1989, p. 48); what Jung needed was an 'active and comprehending ego' (Jung 1989, p. 68). Later still, Jung describes how the 'No. 2 personality became more and more doubtful and distasteful to me, and I could no longer hide this fact from myself. I tried to extinguish No. 2, but could not succeed in that either' (Jung 1989, p. 74). Increasingly, Jung felt the need to live 'in the here and now' and specifically he needed make a choice of profession (Jung 1989, p. 75). He rebelled against what he experienced as the 'passivity' of personality no. 2, which although it 'lifted [him] beyond the here and now' left him 'incapable of moving so much as a pebble upon the earth'. Now there was nothing for it but to 'wait and see what would happen'. For the moment he was 'caught in an insoluble conflict' (Jung 1989, p. 75).

In his essay, 'The Stages of Life', Jung (1931) offers a description in more technical language of the 'inner division within oneself' that can occur in the psyche of a young person, which

> arises when, side by side with the series of ego-contents, a second series of equal intensity comes into being. This second series, because of its energy value, has a functional significance equal to that of the ego-complex; we might call it another, second ego which can on occasion even wrest the leadership from the first. This produces the division with oneself, the state that betokens a problem.
>
> (Jung 1931, para. 757)

Jung goes on to point out that the apparently practical solution to the problem would be to identify with one of the two ego-states and reject the other. However, Jung continues,

> Whoever protects himself against what is new and strange and regresses to the past falls into the same neurotic condition as the man who identifies himself with the new and runs away from the past. The only difference is that the one has estranged himself from the past and the other from the future. In principle both are doing the same thing: they are reinforcing their narrow range of consciousness instead of shattering it in the tension of opposites and building up a state of wider and higher consciousness.
>
> (Jung 1931, para. 767)

Jung's emphasis here is upon the broadening of consciousness, a process that can occur only when there is neither a chronic alternation of the two ego-perspectives (as Jung experienced earlier in his childhood) nor a one-sided repression of one by the other. Each needs to be brought into contact with the other in consciousness – a process that will inevitably constellate an experience of tension and conflict but which, Jung implies, is the only way to further the process of individuation.

Something very similar is detailed in Jung's MDR account of his attempts to settle his identity within the domain of each of the two personalities in alternation, and his ultimate realisation that he needed to accept that he owes allegiance to both personalities, even though this also meant accepting the need to negotiate the conflicts that will inevitably arise between the two.

The rare occasions on which the two personalities seemed to coexist in harmony were significant. Here, for example, Jung describes the feeling that accompanied his important decision to pursue a career in psychiatry:

> It was as though two rivers had united and in one grand torrent were bearing me inexorably toward distant goals. This confident feeling that I was a 'united double nature' carried me as if on a magical wave through the examination, in which I came out at the top.
>
> (Jung 1989, p. 109)

An earlier example is perhaps more revealing. Faced with the problem of what direction his academic studies should follow, Jung was at first in doubt, but eventually decided 'overwhelmingly in favour of science'. This resolution was taken after two dreams, which Jung tells us, at one stroke 'removed all my doubts' (Jung 1989, p. 85). We can see how both personalities contributed to this decision since, on the one hand, as Jung puts it elsewhere, 'there was no doubt in my mind that No. 2 had something to do with the creation of dreams' (Jung 1989, p. 89), while on the other, 'Science met, to a very large extent, the needs of No. 1 personality' (Jung 1989, p. 72). By utilising insights gained from personality no. 2 to guide his path toward goals framed by personality no. 1, Jung is implicitly revealing to himself and to us the creative workings of the dynamic between them.

These dreams and Jung's reception of them indicate also that at this point he is beginning to develop the ability to use a kind of *binocular* vision: nature is perceived not only through the lens of personality no. 2 as the numinous 'God's world' but simultaneously through the personality no. 1 lens of scientific curiosity. Jung's stated determination to 'get to know nature, the world in which we live, and the things around us' (Jung 1989, p. 85) involves, on one level, the extraverted use of instrumental reason and the objectification of nature, but on another level, it engages the deeper and darker kind of understanding that for Jung was always constellated by a movement toward subjective interiority.

The crucial point is that the conjunction of these two opposing tendencies in Jung added up to considerably more than either could offer in isolation. It was another dream that was to finally clarify for Jung the roles that personalities no. 1 and no. 2 needed to play within his life: the so-called Storm lantern dream:

> It was night in some unknown place, and I was making slow and painful headway against a mighty wind. Dense fog was flying along everywhere. I had my hands cupped around a tiny light which threatened to go out at any moment. Everything depended on my keeping this little light alive. Suddenly I had the feeling that something was coming up behind me. I looked back, and saw a gigantic black figure following me. But at the same moment

I was conscious, in spite of my terror, that I must keep my little light going through night and wind, regardless of all dangers. When I awoke I realized at once that the figure was a 'spectre of the Brocken,' my own shadow on the swirling mists, brought into being by the little light I was carrying. I knew, too, that this little light was my consciousness, the only light I have. My own understanding is the sole treasure I possess, and the greatest. Though infinitely small and fragile in comparison with the powers of darkness, it is still a light, my only light.

(Jung 1989, pp. 87–88)

Jung comments:

Now I knew that No. 1 was the bearer of the light, and that No. 2 followed him like a shadow.... In the role of No. 1, I had to go forward into study, moneymaking, responsibilities, entanglements, confusions, errors, submissions, defeats ... I recognized clearly that my path led irrevocably outward, into the limitations and darkness of three-dimensionality.

(Jung 1989, p. 88)

One of the striking aspects of this dream is that, although it so clearly performs the kind of compensatory work that, according to Jung, dreams invariably perform, the conjured image inverts the symbolic universe we generally expect to find in Jung. The one-sidedness that seeks correction here is one that favours personality no. 2, which sees interiority alone as a source of insight, and so in the dream 'the inner realm of light appears as a gigantic shadow'. Because Jung's conscious experience of the realm of personality no. 2 is that it brings deep illumination to his life, the dream offers the compensatory image of personality no. 1 as candle and personality no. 2 as deep shadow. This is why Jung describes the dream as providing an insight that 'was not something I would have hit on of my own accord' (Jung 1989, p. 89).

At this point in his life, the path of individuation required Jung to submit to 'study, moneymaking, responsibilities, entanglements, confusions, errors, submissions, defeats' (Jung 1989, p. 88), all of which he found consciously antipathetic. But this difficult path was not required merely because of a developmental need to tick off a series of first-half-of-life achievements. More importantly, the alchemy of Jung's soul-work required him to bring the personal world of work and relationships into conscious relation with the mythic/archetypal world of personality no. 2, a dimension hitherto maintained as a radically separate compartment within Jung's psyche.

The dream also implies that it is inaccurate to depict individuation simply as a shift by the ego in the direction of the numinous riches of personality no. 2. This dream points to a context in which the deeper necessities of the soul require a shift away from 'God's world' toward man's world (personality no. 1). Because one-sidedness can occur in either direction, what matters is not the intrinsic value of either personality in itself, but the nature of the relationship between them. This is why personality no. 2 is represented in the dream as the shadow of personality no. 1, an image that evokes a relationship of fundamental interdependence and complementarity.

In MDR, Jung says to himself at this point, 'I must leave No. 2 behind me, that was clear. But under no circumstances ought I to deny him to myself or declare him invalid. That would have been a self-mutilation' (Jung 1989, p. 88). Important though this insight was, the dream points to deeper realisation: neither personality *could* really be 'denied', since each only exists as the shadow of the other. One of the things this points to is, to paraphrase Mary Williams' (1963) title, 'the indivisibility of the personal and collective unconscious', the personal is meaningless in the absence of the archetypal, and conversely, the archetypal is meaningless when cut off from the personal.

In Marie Louise von Franz's (1997, p. 38) discussion of the storm lantern dream she directly maps personality no. 1 onto Jung's 'own human ego' and personality no. 2 onto 'the activated, and therefore, perceptible, unconscious'. By narrowing down the dynamic of the two personalities to a relationship between ego and unconscious von Franz reveals an immunity to the depth, richness and novelty of what Jung is actually describing. No doubt the relationship Jung is seeking to sketch out in MDR can be conceptualised within the discourse of ego and unconscious, but ultimately this reductive articulation seems both doctrinaire and underpowered.

The richness and complexity of what I am describing becomes evident in Jung's description of the sudden illumination he received from his reading of a psychiatric textbook by Kraft-Ebbing. With great excitement he realises that psychiatry might provide the place in which 'the two currents of my interest could flow together and in a united stream dig their own bed,' an image clearly referring us back to the two personalities. It appears that Jung's excitement derived from the powerful insight that psychiatry could provide an arena in which he might empirically explore both 'biological and spiritual facts': 'Here at last was the place where the collision of nature and spirit became a reality' (Jung 1989, p. 118).

Jung's subsequent comment further deepens our understanding of this important event. He points out that Kraft-Ebbing's textbook stimulated this insight because it is

> in part the subjective confession of the author. With his specific prejudice, with the totality of his being, he stands behind the objectivity of his experiences and responds to the 'disease of the personality' with the whole of his own personality.
>
> (Jung 1989, p. 119)

In other words, the psychiatrist's 'specific prejudice' (i.e. his 'personal equation', the limits intrinsic to any subjective approach) is put into dynamic relation with 'the objectivity of his experiences' (i.e. his scientific perspective, the limits that are intrinsic to any objective approach) and it is precisely the conjunction of the two that offers the possibility of a response 'with the whole ... personality'.

Whether or not the aged Jung is here retroactively imposing later concerns upon his youthful self, what he points to is the extent to which these dynamic tensions – precisely the tensions we find between personality no. 1 and personality no. 2 – constitute the primary motor within every dimension of his psychology. In this passage Jung brings together two quite different oppositional pairings – that between the biological and the spiritual and that between the subjective and the objective, and does so not because he wants us to regard them as identical or even similar, and not because one is primary and the other secondary, but in order to emphasise, first, the particular nature of the relationship between the opposites that constitutes these syzygies, and, second, the psychologically crucial requirement within individuation to find ways to live these opposites together in order that a third position may be achieved which transcends both.

Jung's point is that, whether we are dealing with nature/spirit, or subjective/objective or any of the numerous oppositional pairings that recur throughout Jung's writings, one of these opposite ideas or qualities will tend to dominate and one will be marginal, one will tend to be the candle and one the shadow. Under these circumstances, the psychological work consists of bringing what is shadowy, hidden and marginal into awareness and thus into tension with the dominant quality or idea. In differing contexts, nature or spirit might be either dominant or hidden, and the same goes for objective or subjective perspectives.

This psychological process is far from merely theoretical, Jung suggests, since it involves the whole person. As he remarks later in MDR,

> The opposites and the contradictions between them do not vanish ... even when for a moment they yield before the impulse to action. They constantly threaten the unity of the personality, and entangle life again and again in their dichotomies.
>
> (Jung 1989, p. 346)

Return to the personal myth ...

We are now in a position to see that Jung's tale of the two personalities is also the account of a difficult negotiation between the claims of two mutually conflicting teloi, each of which seeks to find its place in the emergent unfolding of Jung's psychological life. Jung dwells in detail upon the twists and turns of the two personalities because he understands these experiences as tracing out the first version of a process to which he will later give the name of individuation.

We can now return to the question of whether Jung's personal myth can be convincingly considered to be exemplary, or whether we should be taking account of it as a potentially distorting factor within his psychology. If the theme of the two personalities is indeed central to, or at least representative of, Jung's personal myth, then a good case can be made for that myth as exemplary. Within his mature psychology Jung develops and broadens this theme in various ways. First, the development of complex theory (1903–1908) provides him with a psychological model that allows for non-pathological multiplicity and hence a normal level of inner friction and even conflict. The development of active imagination (1913–1916) offers the setting for dialogical relationships between the conscious ego (qua personality no. 1) and any number of inner others (qua personality no. 2). The concept of the transcendent function (originally formulated in 1916) provides us with a dynamic explication of the creative and developmental process by which any meeting between conscious ego (personality no. 1) and inner (unconscious) other (personality no. 2) enables psychological movement (i.e. individuation).

The theory of types (Jung 1921) provides us with a powerful example of this process in action: in order to avoid psychic stasis and enable psychic movement, the dominant conscious typological identification (whatever it may be) (personality no. 1) needs to be brought into tension with the so-called inferior function (whatever it may be) (personality no. 2), so that the transcendent function may enable the (individuation) process to occur. Generally, neurosis gets defined by Jung as psychological one-sidedness, and this becomes generalised outward and applied to the wider culture, such that a narrowly rationalistic, positivistic or materialistic culture is perceived as requiring a creative tension with energies, images and forces that are (for example) irrational and spiritual. By contrast, in the case of a Christianity seen as one-sidedly spiritual, the factors that require to be introduced include the material. The point is that this approach apportions no particular a priori values to either side of any binary: what is valuable can never be decided in advance because it always depends upon what quality or dimension is missing in the particular situation. Finally, all of Jung's late alchemical works revolve around this same question, which finds its fullest expression in his chef d'oeuvre, *Mysterium Coniunctionis* the subtitle of which speaks for itself: *An Inquiry into the Separation and Synthesis of Psychic Opposites in Alchemy* (Jung 1955). However esoteric such a project may appear, on the psychological level which remains always Jung's primary concern, it is clearly intimately linked to the problem described in personal mythic form as that of the two personalities.

... And its problems

Nonetheless it seems to me necessary to acknowledge the serious potential problems that will inevitably arise in the context of any psychology that is so closely identified with one person's personal myth. Of course, many will find the whole idea of a psychology so intimately bound to the inner world of its creator nonsensical and will turn away with a shrug or will join Winnicott in using it as a stick with which to pathologise Jung and his ideas (Saban 2016). However, for those of us who share an intuition that there is something of great value in Jung's psychology, the responsibility to 'dream the myth onward' means a particular need for vigilance with regard to the problems that a psychology grounded in the personal myth of its creator will uniquely provoke.

As is well known, Jung (like Freud) never underwent a thorough analysis. However impressive Jung's insight into his own psyche may appear to the outsider, it would be dangerously naive to assume that there exist no blind spots in his self-understanding. As Jung himself puts it, 'In respect of one's own personality one's judgment is as a rule extraordinarily clouded' (Jung 1921, para. 2). If we are to consider the objective claims of Jung's psychology to be co-extensive with his subjective understanding of his personal myth, then our ability to question or critique the quality or extent of that understanding becomes vitally important.

This is a big question that requires considerably more attention than I can offer here. However, I would like to make a few suggestions as to where we might expect the problem to manifest. As we have seen, the correction of psychological one-sidedness is closely bound up with Jung's concept of individuation, and that dynamic can be easily traced back to Jung's own struggle with the two personalities. However, the fact that the struggle to avoid one-sidedness is primary does not mean that the particular *character* of that struggle as it showed up in Jung's life is equally significant. Jung's personal equation involved him in wrestling with a psychic undertow that drew him repeatedly toward the numinosity of personality no. 2 (the archetypal); as a result, Jung needed again and again to strenuously reassert the claims of personality no. 1 (the personal). The particular colouring of this dynamic within Jung's life should not be allowed to obscure the important fact that the underlying dynamic itself is fundamentally neutral. As Jung himself says, 'Hence it is essential for progression … that impulse and counter-impulse, positive and negative, should reach a state of regular interaction and mutual influence' (Jung 1928, para. 61). This neutrality is an expression of Jung's conviction that the personal and the mythic coinhere, a conviction articulated in his psychology in a repeated emphasis (on a theoretical level) that both realms need to be brought together and kept together, and indeed on a fundamental level *are* together.

There is, however, a problematic tension between these facts and the contrasting fact that Jung's persistent pull toward personality no. 2 tends to show up again and again – throughout his psychology – in a strongly reductive tendency to separate out and prioritise those images and experiences that align with personality no. 2 over the dimension of life that is identified with personality no. 1.

Freud and Jung

A violent turn in this direction seems to have occurred in the wake of the Jung/ Freud split. It is well known that Jung found the loss of his personal and professional connection with Freud to be highly traumatic. It seems unlikely that the wound caused by this violent separation ever really healed, for either Freud or

Jung. The circumstances of this event are far too complex to enter into here, but I would suggest that its unresolved nature had serious implications for Jung's psychology and the playing out of his personal myth within it.

If we review this question through the lens of the two personalities and the assumption that individuation requires both to be fully present to each other, I would suggest that the excitement with which Jung first entered into his relationship with Freud marks out the event as a clear parallel to those events in MDR (such as the decision for psychiatry) in which important shifts within individuation are perceived as stemming from the encounter of oppositional energies in creative tension.

The relationship with Freud was ground-breaking for Jung in two interrelated ways. As Jung himself acknowledged to Freud in 1907, transference was the 'alpha and omega' of psychoanalysis (Jung 1946, para. 358). It was Jung's liaison with Freud and psychoanalysis that first made available to him a therapeutic dimension whereby unconscious processes could become visible as relational dynamics inside the analytic vessel itself. It thus brought personality no. 2's concerns – numinosity, meaning and purpose – into simultaneous play with a personality no. 1 dimension, relational engagement with the outer other.

This theoretical and methodological leap forward was a direct result of Jung's professional engagement with Freud. The personal relationship with Freud also, and perhaps more importantly, offered the possibility of a safe container within which Jung might reveal some of his long-held secrets and divulge something of that intimate realm of meaning that had hitherto been kept carefully compartmentalised as personality no. 2. We can see an example of this in Jung's admission, in a letter of 28 October 1907, that as a child he had been sexually assaulted by an older man, and that this fact was colouring his relationship with Freud (Freud and Jung 1977, p. 95).

In short, this new relationship created *in the meeting of inner and outer worlds* was a vessel sufficiently secure to allow personality no. 1 and personality no. 2 to be brought into tension in ways that had not hitherto seemed possible. Jung's experiences of personality no. 2 had until now been wholly intrapsychic; outer-relational contact with the world had been limited to the realm of personality no. 1. Jung had experienced his most authentic sense of self while alone and his most extreme sense of alienation while with others. As a child (and indeed throughout his life) he displayed a distinct preference for the inner world over the outer, prioritising solitude and the untellable secret over a relational and communicable life. For a particularly powerful amplification of this theme see Jung (1989, pp. 342–345; for the importance of secrets in Jung's life and work, see Saban 2017a). In short, to invoke Jung's own theory of types, it is clear that as a child Jung showed all the signs of extreme introversion.

Given this, the logic of individuation (and of the two personalities) clearly indicates that in order to maintain psychological health, Jung needed to find a way to bring his dominant introversion into tension with the extraverted realm.

However, it also follows from this logic that a shift of this sort, into the realm of relationship to the outer other, would be accompanied by feelings of inferiority that would probably be experienced by Jung as dangerously threatening to his psychic integrity. The relationship with Freud had instigated a new development that was simultaneously promising and yet problematic.

Perhaps inevitably, this relationship, impossibly burdened as it was beneath a crushing weight of conscious investments and unconscious projections, ended in bitterness and recrimination. The consequences for Jung were devastating but also creative in terms of both his biography and his psychology. Residual aspects of it remained however dangerously unprocessed. For example, Jung seems to have been left with a strong tendency, especially during the 1930s, to project what he experienced as the negative qualities of personality no. 1 onto Freud and his 'Jewish' science of psychoanalysis, while identifying his own 'Aryan' psychology closely with qualities associated with personality no. 2. (See Saban 2012, for this question apropos enchantment/disenchantment; and Saban 2017b, apropos wider political concerns). This egregious example of pathological splitting, occurring when it did, was to be all but catastrophic for Jung's psychology.

Jung's evident blindness toward the logic of his own psychology in these cases seems to point to some kind of complex. Given that personality no. 1 was for Jung an area of perpetual weakness and inferiority, whereas personality no. 2 had always functioned as a place of strength and allure, the logic of individuation dictated (as indicated by the storm lantern dream) that both be brought into a conscious dialogical relationship, despite the sense of conflict and discord that would inevitably result. Instead, what occurred was the rejection and banishment of personality no. 1 and the glorification of and identification with personality no. 2. This, I would suggest is what we find in Jung's problematic attacks on the 'Jewish' science of psychoanalysis.

Moreover, the woundedness that lay behind Jung's reaction to what he saw as Freud's betrayal contributed, both in his personal life and in his psychology, to a tendency toward defensive retreat from the outer world of the relational in favour of one-sided prioritisation of the personality no. 2 dimensions of interiority, secrecy and mystery, and it is these latter dimensions that have become closely identified with Jungian psychology ever since. Examples are too numerous to mention. However, this passage from the introduction to MDR will serve as a representative instance:

> Fate will have it and this has always been the case with me – that all the 'outer' aspects of my life should be accidental. Only what is interior has proved to have substance and a determining value. As a result, all memory of 'outer' events has faded, and perhaps these 'outer' experiences were never so very essential anyhow, or were so in that they coincided with phases of my inner development.
>
> (Jung 1989, pp. vii–ix)

Conclusion

As a child, Jung experienced the inner secret world of personality no. 2 as possessing a reality that far exceeded that of the ordinary world of personality no. 1. Despite what Jung tells us about the non-pathological nature of his experience of the two personalities, the compartmentalisation of this inner secret dimension of Jung's life and his experience of it as radically separate from his 'ordinary' life created a situation that might easily have led to a severe neurotic split, had the struggles he delineated in the early chapters of MDR not resolved in the way they did. For Jung to have maintained this level of compartmentalisation and to have identified with personality no. 2 would have meant a life cut off from any meaningful relationship with others. On the other hand, a schizoid/solipsistic threat of this kind might have led to an enantiodromic inversion of the problem, whereby the realm of personality no. 2 would be declared to be unreal and that of personality no. 1 alone to possess reality, but this 'solution' would have led only to neurosis and psychic sterility.

Remarkably, the way Jung solved the problem enabled him not only to survive his childhood split, but ultimately to create a new psychological paradigm. His vow, in the wake of the storm lantern dream, never to perform the 'self-mutilation' of denying the reality of personality no. 2, led him directly to the model of analytical psychology, whereby the realm of personality no. 2 is not only real, but exists as a transcendent and universally shared reality: the realm of the archetypes. At one stroke, Jung transfigured what was most intensely personal – the privately meaningful experiences of personality no. 2 – into psychic realities that are *universally* meaningful. From this perspective, the exemplarity of Jung's personal myth expresses that perennial theme in his psychology that what is personal is always also mythic. The idea that the psychological could be *only* personal, is for Jung as incoherent as, for Wittgenstein, the idea of a private language.

My suggestion here has been that the myth of the two personalities exemplifies a certain logic that unfolds in the process of individuation. This logic, both flexible and dynamic, offers the potential for psychological movement precisely because it has not pre-emptively decided where one-sidedness occurs or where compensation is required. However, because the literature of analytical psychology, whether that of Jung or his followers, frequently by-passes this logic by reproducing Jung's biases and blind-spots, it is too often characterised by the hypostasisation and reification of a whole set of personality no. 2 shibboleths. Above all, what is assumed is the self-evident superiority of inner over outer, and individual solitude over social engagement.

In this chapter, I have chosen to highlight the related tendency to prioritise the archetypal/mythic over the personal. When this occurs it directly undoes what the phrase 'personal myth' attempts in its insistence upon the *equal importance* of both of its constituent terms, which it brings together in creative tension.

Out of this highly concentrated point of origin, as we find it in MDR, Jung articulates that very personal and yet universal mythic logic that runs through his life and his thinking. Paradoxically, Jung's achievement in creating this personal myth is to have provided us with the very tool with which we can begin the work of re-vision and critique required for analytical psychology to flourish.

Notes

1 Much of the information of this sort, to be found in MDR, had been available to Jung's inner circle since the 1925 seminar (Jung 1990). Those who were acquainted only with Jung's published writings were unaware of the importance of the personal dimension until the posthumous publication of MDR.
2 The term occurs in this sentence of the English translation: 'Thus it is that I have now undertaken, in my eighty-third year, to tell my personal myth.' It is a rendering by the English translators, Richard and Clara Winston, of this German passage: 'So habe ich es heute, in meinem dreiundachtzigsten Lebensjahr, unternommen, den Mythus meines Lebens zu erzählen.' The German phrase, *den Mythus meines Lebens* (the myth of my life) conveys something subtly different from the phrase 'my personal myth' although precisely where the difference lies is hard to discern. Presumably the translators chose to use the phrase 'personal myth' because they wanted to particularly emphasise the personal dimension apparent in Jung's statement that this is 'den Mythus meines Lebens' an emphasis he reiterates a little later: it is, he says, '*my* fable, *my* truth' (*mein* Märchen, *meine* Wahrheit). What we are to read is not just the *myth* of Jung's life, it is the myth of *Jung's* life. Hence it is a myth, but it is also Jung's myth – his 'personal myth'.
3 Kris (1956) introduced the term to psychoanalytic literature. However, Kris means by it something quite different from Jung. Kris refers to the pathological phenomenon of a patient turning their personal history into 'a treasured possession to which the patient is attached with a peculiar devotion'. There may be a sense in which this is true of Jung but it is not what Jung means by it. The term crops up, not surprisingly, in post-Jungian literature, and especially in the writings of Susan Rowland. In various works over a ten-year period Rowland has put repeated emphasis upon the importance of the 'personal myth' in Jung's writings (see Rowland 2002, 2003, 2005, 2011). As Pietikäinen (1999) has pointed out, the term 'personal myth' possesses a paradoxical quality which resides in the fact that 'it is one of the few basic characteristics of myth that it is an anonymous text, without a known author and therefore irreducible to an individual' (Pietikäinen 1999, p. 237). For Rowland its critical importance resides in this dual or ambiguous dimension; this is because, 'personal myth' possesses, for her, a crucial function as a bridging term between understanding that derives from individual experience and understanding that relates to the conceptual, and particularly, in Jung's case, the universalising tendency toward Grand Narrative. In this paper I stay with what I see as the richness of this paradoxical concept, although my arguments and my intentions differ from those of Rowland, without I hope being in conflict with them.

References

Bair, D. (2004) *Jung: A Biography.* London: Little, Brown.
Freud, S. and Jung, C. G. (1977) *The Freud-Jung Letters.* Princeton, NJ: Princeton University Press.
Huskinson, L. (2008) Introduction: ordinary mythical. In: L. Huskinson (Ed.), *Dreaming the Myth Onwards.* London; New York: Routledge.

Jung, C. G. (1912) *Wandlungen und Symbole der Libido: Beiträge zur Entwicklungsgeschichte des Denkens*. Leipzig & Vienna: F. Deuticke (in German).

Jung, C. G.: the following are from *The Collected Works of C. G. Jung* (CW) London: Routledge & Kegan Paul/Princeton, NJ: Princeton University Press:

Jung, C. G. (1921) *Psychological Types*. *(*CW 6).

Jung, C. G. (1928) On psychic energy. (CW 8).

Jung, C. G. (1931) The stages of life. (CW 8).

Jung, C. G. (1946) The psychology of the transference. (CW 16).

Jung, C. G. (1952) Symbols of transformation. (CW 5).

Jung, C. G. (1955) *Mysterium Conjunctionis*. (CW 14).

Jung, C. G. (1989) *Memories, Dreams, Reflections*. New York: Vintage Books.

Jung, C. G. (1990) *Analytical Psychology: Notes of the Seminar given in 1925 by C. G. Jung*. London: Routledge.

Kris, E. (1956) The personal myth; a problem in psychoanalytic technique. *Journal of the American Psychoanalytic Association* 4, 653–81.

Papadopoulos, R. K. (1991) Jung and the concept of the other. In: G. S. Saayman and R. K. Papadopoulos (Eds), *Jung in Modern Perspective*. Bridport: Prism.

Pietikäinen, P. (1999) Jung's psychology in the light of his 'personal myth'. *Psychoanalysis and History* 1, 237–251.

Rowland, S. (2002) *Jung: A Feminist Revision*. Cambridge: Polity Press.

Rowland, S. (2003) Jung, myth, and biography. *Harvest*, 49, 22–39.

Rowland, S. (2005) *Jung as a Writer*. New York: Routledge.

Rowland, S. (2011) *The Ecocritical Psyche*. New York: Routledge.

Saban, M. (2012) The dis/enchantment of C. G. Jung. *International Journal of Jungian Studies* 4, 21–33.

Saban, M. (2013) Ambiguating Jung. In: J. Kirsch and M. Stein (Eds), *How and Why We Still Read Jung*. New York: Routledge.

Saban, M. (2016) Jung, Winnicott and the divided psyche. *Journal of Analytical Psychology* 61, 329–349.

Saban, M. (2017a) Segrete e Bugie. Un'area Cieca Nella Psicologia Junghiana. *Rivista Di Psicologia Analitica* 95(3), 39–76 (in Italian).

Saban, M. (2017b) The dissociated psyche and its politics. In: S. Carta, A. Adornisio and R. Mercurio (Eds), *The Analyst in the Polis Vol. 1*. Rome: Streetlib.

von Franz, M.-L. (1997) *C. G. Jung: His Myth in Our Time*. Toronto: Inner City Books.

Williams, M. (1963) The indivisibility of the personal and collective unconscious. *Journal of Analytical Psychology* 8, 45–50.

Chapter 6

Telling stories

Jung's *Red Book* as an exercise in narrative

Paul Bishop

Narrative theory plays a key role in different kinds of literary theory – a discipline that used to be described as '*modern* literary theory' but nowadays has become so commonplace that it can simply be referred to as 'theory'. In Formalist theory, for instance, a distinction is made between *fabula* and *syzuhet*, i.e. between events and narrative construction, or in other words between the 'story' or the chronological sequence of events, and the 'plot' or the manner in which the narrative presents them (Jefferson and Robey 1986, p. 39). A classic example of this approach to narrative is Victor Shklovsky's (1965) famous essay on *Tristram Shandy*, first published in Russian in 1921.

Then again, narratology is a central part in structuralist literary theory, based on the structuralist principle of the distinction between *langue* and *parole* (Jefferson and Robey 1986, p. 99). Two examples of the narratological approach would be Tzvetan Todorov's (1969) *Grammaire du Décaméron*, an analysis of the fourteenth-century collection of novellas by the Renaissance humanist, Giovanni Boccaccio; and Gérard Genette's (1980) *Narrative Discourse*, in which he defines the subject of his study as 'narrative discourse' (Genette 1980, p. 29).

Finally, there is an important parallel between literature and psychoanalysis, inasmuch as both are concerned with narrative. As Jefferson and Robey (1986, p. 150) put it, the task of psychoanalysis is to read the past in order to be able to make sense of the present. In this respect, Freud's case histories have been compared to detective stories (Loewenstein 1992). And such theorists as Peter Brooks and Jonathan Culler have discovered an analogy between the Russian Formalist distinction of *fabula* and *syzuhet* and the narrative that arises in the psychoanalytic situation (Jefferson and Robey 1986; Brooks 1979; Culler 1980).

Now it would be possible to take one or all of these theoretical positions and apply it or them to Jung's *Red Book* (originally a red-leather bound folio manuscript in which, during 1915–1930, Jung recorded and elaborated his thoughts and visions in a sequence of chapters and paintings, first published in 2009). However, in this chapter I wish to approach narrative in a rather different, and more existential, sense. In the prooemium to *Ecce Homo*, the short epitaph-like text that stands between the foreword and the first chapter of this quasi-autobiographical work of 1888, Nietzsche writes:

> On this perfect day, when everything is ripening, and not only the grapes are getting brown, a ray of sunshine has fallen on my life: I looked behind me, I looked before me, and never have I seen so many good things all at once. Not in vain have I buried my four-and-fortieth year to-day; I had the right to bury it – that in it which still had life, has been saved and is immortal. The first book of the *Transvaluation of all Values, The Songs of Zarathustra, The Twilight of the Idols*, my attempts to philosophize with the hammer – all these things are the gift of this year, and even of its last quarter. How could I help being thankful to the whole of my life? That is why I am now going to tell myself the story of my life.
>
> (Nietzsche 1911, p. 7)

As this prooemium makes clear, *Ecce Homo* presents itself as an exercise in self-narration, even as an exercise in self-construction. And I would like to argue in what follows that the same can be said for Jung's *Red Book*.

After all, at the age of 38 when Jung began his so-called 'confrontation with the unconscious', he was not far off the age of 44 mentioned by Nietzsche in his prooemium. According to the German mystic Johannes Tauler in one of his sermons on the Ascension:

> Until a man has reached his fortieth year, he will never attain lasting peace, never be truly formed into God, try as he may. Up to that time he is occupied by so many things, driven this way and that by his own natural impulses; he is governed by them although he may imagine that he is governed by God. Before the proper time has arrived, he cannot achieve true and perfect peace, nor can he enter into a God-seeing life.
>
> (Tauler 1985, pp. 72–73)

Yet Tauler also goes on to argue that the crucial age in the life of the individual is 50, for 'if the soul has reached this point' – i.e. one's fiftieth year when one may 'receive the Holy Spirit in the loftiest and most sublime manner' – 'it will turn into itself to sink down and be immersed and melted into the pure, divine, simple, and innermost core, where *the sublime spark of the soul* flows back to the source from which it sprang' (Tauler 1985, p. 73; emphasis added). When Nietzsche turned 50, he was insane; when Jung turned 50, he was embarking on his safari to Kenya, Mount Elgon, and the Nile, returning from Africa via Egypt (1925–1926). But arguably the sublime spark of Jung's soul had already flowed back to the source in the time leading to the creation of the *Red Book*.

In the *Red Book*, Jung draws attention to the time of his life when he composed the work. In 'Refinding the Soul', Jung writes that his vision of the flood in October 1913 happened at a time that was 'significant for me as a man [*als Menschen*]' (Jung 2009, p. 231). For in the 40th year of his life, Jung had achieved 'everything' that he had wished for himself – 'honour, power, wealth, knowledge, and every human happiness' (Jung 2009, p. 231). But then something happened:

> Then my desire for the increase of these trappings ceased, the desire ebbed from me and horror came over me. The vision of the flood seized me and I felt the spirit of the depths, but I did not understand him. Yet he drove me on with unbearable inner longing and I said …

And so the text moves on to another of those discourses which Jung addresses to his soul (Jung 2009, pp. 231–232).

The circumstances in which Jung began to experience the dreams and the visions that gave him the impetus to create the *Red Book* are well-known from the account in Jung's own semi-autobiographical work, *Memories, Dreams, Reflections*, albeit ultimately unverifiable. (Likewise, the influence of the 'cultural moment' in which Jung began his work on the *Red Book* has been foregrounded by Sonu Shamdasani, in Jung 2009, p. 194.) Because of the unverifiability of these experiences, they must remain forever closed to us; in this respect, it would be wrong to view the *Red Book* as a kind of 'new revelation', because ultimately the *Red Book* does not refer to anything outside of itself, even if it includes all kinds of textual (and, it has also been argued, visual-artistic) quotations and allusions. (For an opposing view, see Kingsley 2018, vol. 2, p. 509.) Rather, the meaning of the *Red Book* resides, at least in part, in its structure – and this includes its narrative structure.

From the outset, the *Red Book* is insistent on its textual and visual – and, in this respect, whatever Jung might say, *artistic* – aspects (Thackrey 2014). To begin with, there is the disposition of text and image on the page: the medieval-style capital letter, the calligraphic script, and the series of quotations from the Old and New Testaments that constitute the opening of 'The Way of What is to Come'. And in the first sentence that is neither a quotation or the note of the date of composition, the *Red Book* gestures towards its essential act of enunciation: 'If I *speak* in the spirit of the time, I must *say*: no one and nothing can justify what I must *proclaim* to you' (Jung 2009, p. 229, emphasis added). *Reden, sagen, verkünden* – all these verbs highlight the communicative act that constitutes the essence of the *Red Book*. And this turns out to be the work's crucial aspect. This is because the response to the conflict between the spirit of this time and the spirit of the depths is an eminently linguistic one.

While the spirit of this time wants to 'hear' of 'use and value' (*Nutzen und Wert*), the spirit of the depths forces Jung to speak (*reden*) – 'to speak beyond justification, use, and meaning' (Jung 2009, p. 229). Yet this speaking is no ordinary speech, because the spirit of the depths takes Jung's understanding and his knowledge, placing them at the service of 'the inexplicable and the nonsensical' (Jung 2009, p. 229; translation modified). In so doing, the spirit of the depths interferes with the speech associated with the spirit of this time: 'It robbed me of speech and writing for everything that was not in the service of this one thing, namely the melting-together of sense and nonsense' (Jung 2009, p. 229; translation modified).

In 'The Way of What is to Come', Jung is forced to make the strategic decision to exchange verbal discourse for another medium – the image (*Bild*). Jung admits that his speech (*Sprache*) is 'imperfect', but this imperfection is a strategic one: 'Not because I want to shine with words', he writes, 'but out of the impossibility of finding those words, I speak in images' – *rede ich in Bildern* (Jung 2009, p. 230). For 'in no other way', he concludes, could he 'express the words from the depths' (*die Worte der Tiefe auszusprechen*) (Jung 2009, p. 230; translation modified). This 'supreme meaning' (*Übersinn*) is something that is at once linguistic and non-linguistic: it is linguistic, inasmuch as it contains or conveys meaning (*Sinn*), it is non-linguistic, inasmuch as it is not a word but an image (*ein Bild*). On the one hand, this image acquires a theological dimension, because it is the image of the god that is yet to come (Giegerich 2010, pp. 383–384). On the other, it is extremely important that it is an image, since this informs an important shift operated by Jung in the *Red Book* – a shift away from the Judeo-Christian God and away from the psychoanalytic god that was Freud (Hogenson 2014).

The shift away from the Judeo-Christian God takes place, inasmuch as Jesus in the Gospel of John tells the Samaritan woman, 'God is a spirit; and they that adore him, must adore him in spirit and in truth' (John 4: 24); by contrast, Jung in the *Red Book* declares that 'God is an image, and those who worship him must worship him in the images of the supreme meaning' (Jung 2009, p. 229). And the shift away from Freud takes place, inasmuch as Jung places an emphasis on the visual, rather than the linguistic. For, as becomes clear in Chapter 6 of *The Interpretation of Dreams*, Freud regards the dream as a rebus or picture-puzzle:

> The dream-thoughts and the dream-content are presented to us like two versions of the same subject-matter in two different languages. Or, more properly, the dream-content seems like a transcript of the dream-thoughts into another mode of experience, whose characters and syntactic laws it is our business to discover by comparing the original and the translation. The dream-thoughts are immediately comprehensible, as soon as we have learnt them. The dream-content, on the other hand, is expressed as it were in a pictographic script, the characters of which have to be transposed individually into the language of the dream-thoughts. If we attempted to read these characters according to their pictorial value instead of according to their symbolic relation, we should clearly be led into error.
>
> (Freud 1998, pp. 311–312)

After considering an example (a house with a boat on its roof, a single letter of the alphabet, and the figure of a running man whose head is missing), Freud comes to the following conclusion: 'A dream is a picture-puzzle of this sort and our predecessors in the field of dream-interpretation have made the mistake of treating the rebus as a pictorial composition: and as such it has seemed to them nonsensical and worthless' (Freud 1998, p. 312).

This conception of the dream explains why, for Freud, the *linguistic* element of the dream is so important – an aspect which was later developed further by Jacques Lacan (and in such a way that the dream – indeed, the unconscious itself – disappears into language …). As becomes clear in a footnote added to the 1911 edition of *Interpretation of Dreams*, in this respect Freud saw himself as part of a tradition that reaches back to Artemidorus of Daldis or Ephesus, a professional diviner who lived in the second century and the author of the five-volume work, the *Oneirocritica* or *Oneirokritikon*. In this work (Book 4, Chapter 24), Artemidorus recounted the following episode (as Freud reminds us):

> I think too that Aristander [of Telmsessos] gave a most happy interpretation to Alexander of Macedon when he had surround Tyre [Τύρος] and was besieging it but was feeling uneasy and disturbed because of the length of time the siege was taking. Alexander dreamt he saw a satyr [σάτυρος] dancing on his shield. Aristander happened to be in the neighborhood of Tyre, in attendance on the king during his Syrian campaign. By dividing the word for satyr into in σά und τυρος he encouraged the king to press home the siege so that he became master of the city [Σά–Τύρος = yours is Tyre].
>
> (Freud 1998, pp. 131–132)

To a certain extent, Jung followed Freud in the application of this theoretical approach to the interpretation of dreams, but only to a certain extent. For at the beginning of his scientific career, Jung was relatively uninterested in dreams, concentrating instead on word-association tests; later, he became more interested in visions and *sequences* of visions.

In fact, if one looks more closely, one can see that Jung – especially after his break with Freud – was much more inclined toward another tradition, which is completely different from the one on which Freud drew. At the same time, this tradition is also a kind of *theory*, understood in its etymological sense. For, etymologically, 'theory' is derived from the Greek θεωρεῖν or *theorein*, which means 'to observe' or 'to contemplate'. (See Aristotle's account of *theoria* in his Nicomachean Ethics, book 10, §7–§8; Roochnik 2009.) Correspondingly, θεορία or *theoria* means 'observation', 'contemplation', 'intuitive vision' or 'insight', especially in the context of contemplating Beauty. One of the most important sources of this tradition is Neoplatonism in general and the thought of Plotinus (205–270) in particular.

In his philosophy, Plotinus posits the One as something absolute and transcendent, beyond conceptuality; indeed, even beyond being. Thanks to the hypostases – the *nous* (or Mind), the Ideas, and the Soul – we can attain to knowledge of at least some aspects of the One, and we do so through *theoria* or contemplation (Jacob 2011, pp. 15–18; Böhm 1996, pp. 70–72). The classic text in which Plotinus expounds his understanding of contemplative *theoria* is the

Ennead (III. 8) entitled 'On Nature and Contemplation and the One', which opens with the following arresting argument:

> Suppose we said, playing at first before we set out to be serious, that all things aspire to contemplation, and direct their gaze to this end – not only rational but irrational living things, and the power of growth in plants, and the earth which brings them forth – and that all attain to it as far as possible for them in their natural state, but different things contemplate and attain their end in different ways, some truly, and some only having an imitation and image of this true end – could anyone endure the oddity of this line of thought? Well, as this discussion has arisen among ourselves, there will be no risk in playing with our own ideas. Then are we contemplating as we play?
>
> (Plotinus 1967, p. 361)

In the case of Plotinus and in this tradition it is important that *theoria* or contemplation is accompanied by the counterpart of contemplation, i.e. by a certain kind of productivity. For his part, Goethe – for all his anti-Platonic polemic elsewhere – appears to appeal to this tradition when, in his preface to the first edition of his *Theory of Colours* (1810), he says: 'Every act of seeing leads to consideration, consideration to reflection, reflection to combination, and thus it may be said that in every attentive look on nature we already theorize' (Goethe 1970, p. xl). Into this theoretical tradition whose main currency is not just concepts but also *Anschauungen* or images, Jung introduces the principle of sequentiality. Or in other words, he is interested in narrative; the *Red Book*, contrary to what one might expect, has a plot.

This plot involves a narrative structure that might be described as a structure of crisis and (near) resolution, and it means that there is a linear movement in the narrative that accompanies the sequentiality of the images. The first book, or *Liber Primus*, begins with a reworking of that sequence of visions experienced by Jung in the run-up to the First World War (including a period when he was visiting Scotland, beginning in October 1913 and continuing up to 25 December of that year). Entering into dialogue with his soul, Jung travels to the desert of his self, and undertakes a 'descent into hell in the future' (Jung 2009, p. 237). Here we find the vision of the murdered youth, the black scarab, and the rising sun, followed by the fantasy of the slaying of Siegfried, familiar from *Memories, Dreams, Reflections* (Jung 1989a, pp. 180–181) and his 1925 seminar on analytical psychology (Jung 1991, pp. 48, 56–57, 61–62). Subsequently, he meets the quasi-biblical figures of Elijah and Salome, an encounter which teaches Jung that 'to live oneself means: to be one's own task'; that one should 'never say that it is a pleasure to live oneself'; and that 'it will be no joy but a long suffering, since you must become your own creator' (Jung 2009, p. 249). Following his transformation into the 'deus leontocephalus', an episode recounted in the 1925 seminar and the centrepiece of Richard Noll's scathing critique in *The Jung Cult* (Noll 1994), Jung learns that 'Man doesn't only grow from within himself, he is also creative from within himself', and so 'the god becomes revealed in him' (Jung 2009, p. 253). In a vision on Christmas day of 1925, Jung sees how 'in the mystery Man himself becomes the two principles, the lion and the serpent', and realizes that he himself must 'become a Christ' and be 'made into Christ' (Jung 2009, p. 255).

In 'Liber Secundus', containing 'The Images of the Erring' (otherwise known as 'The Adventures of the Wandering'), we find Jung's visions from 26 December 1913 to the end of February 1914, with a final section dating to 19 April 1914. This book opens, not with Isaiah, but with Jeremiah, the great prophet of the Exile. After the door of the Mysterium in 'Liber Primus' had closed on the vision of a giant crushing a city amid terrible destruction (Jung 2009, pp. 252–254), Jung now finds himself standing on the tower of a castle, watching a red horseman approach: not just the devil, but Jung's own devil. Next, Jung wanders through a dark forest at night, and in a castle discovers a lonely scholar and his beautiful daughter – the 'beauty of the soul' (Jung 2009, p. 262). Then he meets a tramp with a liking for the cinema (a medium that informs the highly imagistic nature of the *Red Book*), who coughs up blood and dies in the room next to his in a tavern. The following night, Jung is taken into a vast desert, where he meets Ammonius, a Libyan anchorite, newly converted to Christianity. The next morning, Jung admires the sunrise, watches a small scarab-beetle at work, and questions Ammonius's beliefs. In the next chapter, Jung wanders along by the sea, until he meets a man in a black, wrinkled coat: death himself, and the sea turns to blood. In a chapter entitled 'The Remains of Earlier Temples', Jung encounters an old monk and a tall thin man, who turn out to be Ammonius and the Red One, while Jung himself is transformed into a Green Man, 'a laughing being of the forest, a leaf green daimon, a forest goblin and prankster, who lived alone in the forest and was itself a greening tree' (Jung 2009, p. 276).

The next chapter introduces the figure of Izdubar (otherwise known as Gilgamesh), strikingly described (and illustrated) as having 'two bull horns ris[ing] from his great head' and 'a black beard', wearing 'a rattling suit of armour', and carrying a 'sparkling double axe' (Jung 2009, p. 278). Yet Izdubar, 'the mighty, the bull-man', has been lamed by the 'magical poison' of 'science' (Jung 2009, p. 278), so Jung undertakes to cure him, shrinking the god to the size of an egg. Following a sequence of incantations, Jung opens the egg, and the healed and transformed figure of the god rises, like the sun. But the counterpart to his creation of his god is Jung's return to hell, symbolized by the struggle of a maiden with three demons. In 'The Sacrificial Murder', Jung is told by his own soul to eat the raw liver of a murdered child – a 'great and dark mystery', representing Man's 'complicity in the act of evil' (Jung 2009, p. 290). A sequence of mandalas separates this episode from the following ones, where Jung discusses Thomas à Kempis's *Imitation of Christ* with a librarian in a large library, then with a cook in a kitchen, into which, 'like a horde of large birds – with frenzied flapping of wings', a crowd of shades suddenly burst (Jung 2009,

p. 294). These are, as 'a bearded man with tousled hair and dark shining eyes' tells Jung, the dead wandering towards Jerusalem (Jung 2009, p. 294), of whom more later. Pushed into a van, Jung is taken to the madhouse, where he discusses Thomas à Kempis's work with two doctors, for Jung's imitation of Christ, it turns out, will be a quite literal one. After a conversation with another patient, who identifies himself with Nietzsche and Christ, Jung contemplates the crucifixion and sees the image of the divine child, Phanes. Wondering whether he is alive or dead, Jung awakes to find himself back in the kitchen, or maybe it is 'the realm of the mothers' (Jung 2009, p. 302). Returning to the library, he pushes aside green curtains to witness a scene from *Parzival*, and prepares for his subsequent experiences: the awakening of 'the son of the earth', and 'the Good Friday when we complete the Christ in us and we descend to hell ourselves' (Jung 2009, p. 304).

On 22 January 1914, after Jung's soul has shown him three 'ancient things that point to the future', namely 'the misery of war, the darkness of magic, and the gift of religion' (Jung 2009, p. 306), a 'magical rod' enables Jung to witness the crucifixion as an external event – 'I saw the black serpent, as it … crept into the body of the crucified and emerged again transformed from his mouth', and 'wound itself around the head of the dead one like a diadem'; 'a light gleamed above his head, and the sun rose shining in the east' (Jung 2009, pp. 309–310). But is Jung a magician, or is Philemon, the figure introduced in the final chapter, and to whom Jung ultimately came to ascribe the responsibility for his visions (cf. Jung 2009, p. 339)?

Lengthy dialogues between Jung and Philemon ponder the nature of magic, the transition from the age of Pisces to the age of Aquarius, and introduce the theme of midday. The throne of God ascends into empty space, followed by the Holy Trinity together with Satan, but nothing results of this union of opposites, so Satan crawls back into his hole. The Cabiri, dwarf-like deities (familiar from Creuzer's *Symbolism and Mythology*, Schelling's *The Gods of Samothrace*, and Goethe's *Faust*), emerge to build Jung a tower (in 1920, the construction of Jung's real 'tower' in Bollingen was begun). Rejecting their invitation to become the executioner of his own brain, Jung turns the sword on the Cabiri themselves, and subsequently engages in a dialogue with a man condemned to death by hanging – an image of himself. Following the return of Elijah and Salome, Jung actually becomes Christ/Odin hanging on the cross/tree of life, suspended above the earth for three days and three nights. Alternating between her form as a black serpent and a white bird, Jung's soul talks to him, before she gives birth to a monstrous son, 'a frightful miscreant, a stammerer, a newt's brain, a primordial lizard … a lazy bug-eyed frog' (Jung 2009, p. 327). Has Philemon deceived Jung? Has he laid 'a puny basilisk in the nest of the dove', turning his soul into an 'adulterous whore' and him, Jung, into the 'laughable father of the Antichrist' (Jung 2009, p. 327)? Subjecting himself to the dominion of his son, 'the unnaturally born, the son of the frogs', one day Jung watches him emerge from the water, with the mane of a lion and the shimmering skin of a serpent, transform himself into a god, and fly away, leaving Jung alone – alone with himself (Jung 2009, p. 330).

As this overview of the 'plot' of the *Red Book* shows, there are considerable correspondences and parallels between Books 1 and 2, but the third section, 'Scrutinies', does not explore them, instead constituting a third, and incomplete, act of its own. Based on material dating from April, May and 1 June 1914, it consists of transcriptions of dialogues between Jung and his soul, between Jung and Philemon, and between Jung and the shade of a dead woman, who brings him the symbolic figure of Hap. A series of lengthy speeches by Philemon leads up to seven sermons which he delivers to the dead – the *Septem Sermones ad mortuos* published in 1916 by Jung in a private edition. When the sermons are over, Jung speaks to 'a dark form with golden eyes' (Jung 2009, p. 354), 'a man wearing a long coat and a turban' (Jung 2009, p. 355), and (for a third time) Elijah and Salome. The final scene, set in a garden at midday, involves a conversation between Philemon and a 'blue shade' or Christ, whose words – 'I bring you the beauty of suffering. That is what is needed by whoever hosts the worm' (Jung 2009, p. 359) – brings the text to an abrupt close.

Thus, the *Red Book* exhibits a narrative structure of crisis and (near) resolution, conforming to a pattern found in many other works, including Wolfram von Eschenbach's *Parzival*, Dante's *Divine Comedy*, Goethe's *Faust* and Nietzsche's *Thus Spoke Zarathustra*. All these epics can be read in a psychological sense, much as the Neoplatonists read *The Iliad* or *The Odyssey* as allegories (Lamberton 1986). In the remainder of this chapter, I shall focus on the narrative structure of the *Red Book* in relation to *Parzival*, *Faust* and *Zarathustra*.

Parzival

Wolfram von Eschenbach's medieval German romance, written in the early thirteenth century, has at its focus the Arthurian hero figure Parzival (or, in English, Percival), and his quest for the Holy Grail. *Parzival* can be read as a work of fiction constructed by Wolfram as a response to his predecessor, Chrétien de Troyes (Stevens 1999), and it features a variety of modes of narrative presentation (Thomas 1999). For Joseph Campbell (1968), Wolfram's *Parzival* represents 'the first example in the history of world literature of a *consciously developed secular Christian myth*' (Campbell 1968, p. 476, emphasis in original) – a description which, *mutatis mutandis*, one might also apply to the *Red Book*.

According to one critic, the 'bow metaphor' (see Book 5, §241) used by Wolfram is emblematic of his narrative technique in this work (Groos 1972; cf. Parshall 1981). At the same time, *Parzival* can be seen as an exemplar of what Jung (1930/1950), in 'Psychology and literature', termed a 'visionary' work of art, i.e. one based on 'primordial experiences' that 'rend from top to bottom the curtain upon which is painted the picture of an ordered world, and allow a glimpse into the unfathomable abyss of the unborn and things yet to be' (Jung

1930/1950, para. 141), as Winder McConnell (1999, p. 204) has suggested. Wolfram's recounting of the Grail legend evidently informed Wagner's opera, *Parsifal*; however, it is the Eschenbachian spelling of the hero's name that Jung uses in the *Red Book* when he explicitly engages with this figure, even if the scenario is reminiscent of Wagner's reworking of the legend.

In 'Nox Quarta' Jung pushes aside the curtain after talking to the librarian in the library who has lent him Thomas à Kempis's *The Imitation of Christ* and suddenly finds himself in a high-ceilinged hall with, in the background, a magnificent garden. Immediately, Jung identifies this garden as the 'magical garden' belonging to Klingsor, the evil magician in Wolfram's epic and Wagner's opera – and thereby finds himself on a stage on which, so it seems, the legend is being re-enacted, for 'Parzival enters from the left' (Jung 2009, p. 302). This Parzival, however, is uncannily familiar to him, as is Klingsor: 'How closely Klingsor resembles me! ... How strange, [Parzival] also looks like me' (Jung 2009, p. 302). Indeed Jung identifies with, participates in, and receives the redemptive power of the legendary Grail, creating his own version of the Grail myth:

> The scene changes. It appears that the audience, in this case me, joins in during the last act. One must kneel down as the Good Friday service begins. Parzival enters – slowly, his head covered with a black helmet. The lionskin of Hercules adorns his shoulders and he holds the club in his hand; he is also wearing modern black trousers in honour of the Church holiday. I bristle and stretch out my hand avertingly, but the play goes on. Parzival takes off his helmet. Yet there is no Gurnemanz to atone for and consecrate him. Kundry stands in the distance, covering her head and laughing. The audience is enraptured and recognizes itself in Parzival. He is I. I take off my armour layered with history and my chimerical decoration and go to the spring wearing a white penitent's shirt, where I wash my feet and hands without the help of a stranger. Then I also take off my penitent's shirt and put on my civilian clothes. I walk out of the scene and approach myself – I who am still kneeling down in prayer as the audience. I rise and become one with myself.
>
> (Jung 2009, pp. 302–303)

Yet this is by no means the sole echo of Wolfram's *Parzival* in the *Red Book*. After the door to the Mysterium – the climactic scene of *Liber primus* – has closed behind him, Jung finds himself standing on the highest tower of a castle, looking out over the countryside. From this vantage-point, Jung espies the figure of the Red One, a figure whom he suspects of being the devil.

This figure appears to allude to the figure of the Red Knight as one finds it in Wolfram, and which has been described as 'the most bafflingly ambiguous of Wolfram's figures' (Richey 1931, p. 316). (Incidentally, Jung is not alone in being intrigued by this figure: the Swiss novelist Adolf Muschg published his own version of the Parzival saga focusing on the Red Knight in 1993.) On his way the court of King Arthur in Book 3 of Wolfram's account, Parzival meets Ither of Gaheviez, the king of Cucumerlant and a knight of the Round Table who is also (as it turns out) distantly related to Parzival. Because of the colour of his red armour – even his horse is dressed in red – Ither is known as the 'Red Knight':

> His name was Ither of Gaheviez and he was otherwise called 'The Red Knight', for his gear was so red that it infected the eye with its redness! His charger was a swift sorrel, its crinière red all over, its trappers were of red samite, his shield redder than fire. His surcoat, well and amply cut to his figure, was all red. Lance-headed and shaft were both of them red. The warrior's sword was all red as he had wished it, but well hardened at its edges. And the finely chased goblet which this King of Cucumerlant had standing had standing in his hand, having seized it from the Round Table, was entirely of red gold.
>
> (§145; von Eschenbach 1980, p. 84)

When he meets Ither for a second time, Parzival kills him with a blow of his spear, which pierces Ither's armour; having slain his kinsman, Parzival himself assumes the title of the Red Knight. How are we supposed to interpret this episode and what might its meaning be? The usual view is that by killing his kinsman Ither, who is a member of the Grail dynasty, Parzival sins both against ordinary mortality and against the Grail itself (Barber 2006, p. xxii). Interpreting the work as a 'threefold wisdom' or a way of perceiving the 'three worlds' of being and experience, i.e. the realm of society, the realm of love, and the realm of the Grail, David R. Fideler suggests that Parzival's defeat of the Red Knight represents 'an act of self-initiation into the realm of knighthood, even if accomplished in an unorthodox fashion' (Fideler 1991, p. 193). In her study of the Grail legend, which Emma Jung (1882–1955) researched for over 30 years and Marie-Louise von Franz (1915–1988) completed as volume 12 of the series *Studien aus dem C. G. Jung Institut Zürich* (1960), the Red Knight is interpreted as Perceval's (i.e. Parzival's) 'double or *shadow*' (Jung and von Franz 1986, p. 56). Outside the Jungian tradition, the founder of anthroposophy, Rudolf Steiner (1861–1925), refers to Arthurian legend in general and the *Parzival* saga in particular on numerous occasions in his writings (Steiner 2010), and in 1928 the Austrian anthroposophist Walter Johannes Stein (1891–1957) offered an account of the entire ninth century with reference to the Grail legend, reading Wolfram's *Parzival* as representing the individual's inner development and insisting on the work's 'educational' as well as 'historical' importance (Stein 1991, p. 91). More recently, Matthew Barton has argued that the Grail path of the Parzival story represents a 'modern initiation in the midst of everyday life' (Steiner 2010, p. 179), and within the tradition of anthroposophical thought initiated by Steiner, the story of Parzival is read as representing different stages of growing up, and the episode of the Red Knight can be interpreted as follows:

Just as Parzival has a high ideal – to become a knight – but acts thought-lessly and recklessly in killing the Red Knight for his armour, the ninth grader may find his impulsiveness overcoming his idealism. Parzival giving his horse free rein and allowing it to take him where it will is a picture of the adolescent unconsciously allowing his destiny to unfold.

(Wulsin 2007, p. 10)

Consequently, one of the key stages of the 12 years of education in Waldorf schools is the 'Parzival' block in Class 11, in which Wolfram's epic is retold, re-enacted and contemplated in a variety of different artistic ways in order to inspire 17-year-old students in their personal growth and self-discovery – and even to promote intercultural, inter-religious tolerance (Caris 2007). To the extent that Wolfram's *Parzival* draws on a number of Hermetic sources (Kahane and Kahane 1965; Fideler 1991), connects the Grail with the psychologically important realm of alchemical symbolism (Jung and von Franz 1986, p. 34) and instantiates 'a journey toward speaking that heals and transforms' (Sussman 1995), *Parzival* embodies a number of common themes with Jung's *Red Book*, over and above the structural similarities of their respective narrative arcs.

Faust

At the opening of Part One of Goethe's dramatic poem or poetic drama, Faust finds himself right in the middle of a full-blown mid-life crisis:

I have studied, alas! Philosophy,
And Jurisprudence, and Medicine too,
And saddest of all, Theology,
With ardent, labour, through and through!
And here I stick, as wise, poor fool,
As when my steps first turned to school.
Master they style me, nay, Doctor, forsooth,
And nigh ten years, o'er rough and smooth,
And up and down, and acrook and across,
I lead my pupils by the nose,
And know that in truth we can know naught!
My heart is turned to coal at the thought.
I am wiser, true, than your coxcomb-tribe,
Your Doctor and Master, your Parson and Scribe;
To no idol of scruple or doubt do I grovel,
I know no fear of Hell or of Devil.
But joy is a stranger to my seclusion.
I hug to my heart no fond illusion,
As that I know aught worth the knowing,
Or men could better, my wisdom showing.

(*Faust I*, ll. 354–373; Goethe 1908, p. 25)

While Faust's turn to *magic* is repeated by Jung in the *Red Book*, and Goethe's *Faust* inspires aspects of Jung's *Red Book* in myriad other ways, not least in its reference to 'the spirit of the times' (*Faust I*, ll. 577–579; cf. Bishop 2014; Woolger 2015), there is a clear affinity between these two works in terms of their narrative structure as well. This structure helps explain Jung's comments on *Faust* in 'On the psychology of the unconscious' (Jung 1943) and *Symbols of Transformation* (Jung 1952).

In the first of these works, Jung (1943) draws a distinction between Parts One and Two of *Faust*, writing: 'In the first part of *Faust* Goethe has shown us what it means to accept instinct and in the second part what it means to accept the ego and its weird unconscious world [*seines unheimlichen Hintergrundes*]' (para. 43). In other words, Part Two shows us the essential 'otherness' of the individual self:

All that is insignificant, paltry, and cowardly in us cowers and shrinks from this acceptance – and there is an excellent pretext for this: we discover that the 'other' in us is indeed 'another' [*daß das "andere'" n uns ein "anderer" ist*], a real man, who actually thinks, does, feels, and desires all the things that are despicable and odious.

(Jung 1943, para. 43)

Elsewhere, in *Symbols of Transformation*, Jung (1952, para. 615) offers the following gloss on a line from *Faust*, Part One, where Faust tells Wagner: 'One only passion is thy bosom's guide', adding: 'Seek not to know the other yearning!' (*Faust I*, l. 1110–11; Goethe 1908, p. 55). Jung extracts this line from its immediate context in *Faust* and places it into two further contexts – the fantasies of Miss Miller (and the discourse of their heroic figure, Chiwantopel); and the broader intellectual context of post-Enlightenment culture. Jung considers – in a way that recalls the introductory words to the *Red Book* in 'The Way of What is to Come' – the possibility of a moment when 'it is as if a new instinct were aroused, and the soul were seized by a hitherto unknown longing' (Jung 1952, para. 615). In this moment, the image of earthly love 'pales' before the image of heavenly love, turning the heart and mind 'away from their "natural" destination' (Jung 1952, para. 615). Somewhat acerbically, Jung adds that he is using the word *natural* 'in the sense given it by the French Enlightenment', yet in reality 'the world-spurning passion of the "spirit" is just as natural as the marriage-flight of insects' (Jung 1952, para. 615). Expressed in Judeo-Christian terms, this instinct is love for the 'heavenly bride' (cf. Revelation 19: 7). A variant of this motif is found in a popular religious text of 1751, *The Bride Who Hurries from the Earthly to the Heavenly Bridegroom*, where one reads that 'the well-formed body lies in dust and ashes; but the spirit has passed from the earthly to the heavenly bridegroom' (Woldershausen 1751, p. 20), and is taken up by Georg Trakl in his poem, 'De Profundis': 'Past the hamlet/The gentle orphan girl still garners frugal ears of corn./Her eyes feast round and golden in the twilight/And her womb awaits the heavenly bridegroom' (Trakl 2005, p. 15).

And expressed in Gnostic terms it is love for Sophia, but expressed in the most general possible terms it is 'the "other", equally natural instinct to cleave to the realities of the soul' (Jung 1952, para. 615).

For these 'realities of the soul' are, Jung insists, not 'makeshift inventions' – 'as certain theories would have us believe' – but 'facts and figures which can seize, deceive, and delight with just as much passion as the creatures of this world' (Jung 1952, para. 615; translation modified). In terms of the mythical system as confected by Miss Miller, the hero Chiwantopel 'personifies [her] otherworldliness'; or to use the imagery found in her visions (as well as in E.T.A. Hoffmann's *The Golden Pot*, as a footnote points out), he 'falls foul' of the green snake (Jung 1952, para. 615). In terms of the *Red Book*, this is a highly suggestive and resonant image, given the topos of the Green Man and the numerous snakes that inhabit the imaginary of the *Red Book*. In *Symbols of Transformation* Jung tells us that green is the colour of 'the vegetation numen', citing another line from Goethe's *Faust* in the form of a reference to 'green is life's tree' (Jung 1952, para. 615; cf. *Faust I*, ll. 2038–2039). And the snake is the representative of 'the world of instinct, especially of those vital processes which are psychologically the least accessible of all' (Jung 1952, para. 615). Snake dreams, Jung adds, are always an indication of 'a discrepancy between the attitude of the conscious mind and instinct', since the snake serves to personify the 'threatening aspect' of that conflict (Jung 1952, para. 615). In short, Jung presents us with the following stark choice:

> Whoever loves the earth and its glory, and forgets the 'dark realm', or confuses the two (which is mostly what happens), has spirit for his enemy; and whoever flees from the earth and falls into the 'eternal arms' has life for an enemy.
>
> (Jung 1952, para. 615)

In this passage, Jung mixes allusions to German classical and biblical texts: the 'dark realm' echoes the words of Oreste to Iphigenia in *Iphigenia in Tauris*, Act 3, Scene 1, 'Thee let me counsel/To view too fondly neither sun nor stars./Come, follow to the gloomy realms below!' (ll. 1232–1234) (cf. the title of Seiling 1919), while 'eternal arms' echoes the words of Moses in his blessing to the tribes of Israel,

> There is no other God like the God of the rightest: he that is mounted upon the heaven is thy helper. By his magnificence the clouds run hither and thither. His dwelling is above, and underneath are the everlasting arms.
>
> (Deuteronomy 33: 26–27)

At the same time, the very structure of *Faust* underpins the central transformative message of Goethe's work, inasmuch as it consists of a sequence of crises (Jantz 1987; Anderegg 2011).

In fact, the entirety of *Faust* Part One very clearly consists of a sequence of crises, including the existential crisis of the opening scene (see above) and Faust's near suicide on Easter morning, which find a resolution in the Pact Scene where Faust signs the agreement with Mephistopheles, 'When to the moment fleeting past me,/Tarry! I cry, so fair thou art!/Then into fetters mayst thou cast me,/Then let come doom, with all my heart!' (*Faust I*, ll. 1699–1702; Goethe 1908, p. 78), which in turn sets into the motion the narrative dynamic of the rest of the work, encapsulated in Mephisto's words, 'The little world and the great we'll see' (*Faust I*, l. 2052; Goethe 1908, p. 92). That narrative dynamic proves to be equally crisis-ridden: the farce that nearly ends in disaster in Auerbach's Cellar, the emotional turmoil of the scene 'Wood and Cave' in the midst of the seduction of Gretchen, and the total personal crisis of the concluding scene where Faust is confronted with Gretchen, imprisoned for killing her love-child, and is whisked away by Mephistopheles.

If the sequence of crises in *Faust* Part Two is less evident at first glance, this is less to do with the profound nature of those crises and more to do with the monumentality of the work as a whole. Indeed, the virtual unperformability of *Faust* as a piece of theatre has, in part, obscured the underlying narrative structure, and turned it instead into a quarry for quotable (and often much quoted) material. Nevertheless, each of the five acts of Part Two can be seen to culminate in a crisis: at the end of Act 1, after Faust has conjured up the figures of Paris and Helena, an explosion knocks Faust unconscious to the floor, and the scene comes to an end in darkness and tumult; at the end of Act 2, the Classical Walpurgisnacht reaches its stunning conclusion in the scene 'Rocky Inlets of the Aegean Sea' and the smashing of the retort containing Homunculus amid the roaring of the waves and the triumph of the four elements (water, fire, earth and air); at the end of Act 3, the pagan world of classicism evoked by the iambic trimeters of the opening scene (and echoed in the stychomythic exchanges between Helen and Faust) ends in the trochaic tetrameters that mark the transformation of the Chorus into elemental nymphs and the Bacchantic whirl that brings the 'Shady Grove' scene to an end in collapse and chaos; at the end of Act 4, the military, religious, and political intrigue and corruption reaches a climax in the construction of a Gothic cathedral – but also the bestowal of land on Faust for his reclamation scheme that will prove fatal for Philemon and Baucis; and at the end of Act 5, Goethe attempts a complex resolution of this vast work, in which Faust dies and his soul is taken up, accompanied by cherubs, into a parodic, pastiche, pseudo-Dantesque heaven and the Chorus Mysticus sings the praises of the Eternal Feminine.

In terms of narrative structure, but also in terms of the significance the work had for its author, it is no exaggeration to describe the *Red Book* as Jung's *Faust*, albeit with this crucial difference: *Faust* has an ending, whereas the *Red Book* doesn't, the transcription breaking off in 1928 when Jung turned his attention to alchemy, prompted by the receipt of a translation of *The Secret of the Golden Flower* by Richard Wilhelm, himself an enthusiastic reader of Goethe (see Wilhelm 1931).

Zarathustra

Nietzsche's *Thus Spoke Zarathustra* begins with a midlife crisis of sorts. At the beginning of the Prologue, the narrator tells us that, when Zarathustra was 30 years old, he had abandoned his home and the lake of his home, and set off for the mountains. Here, Zarathustra enjoys 'his spirit and his solitude' and for ten years 'he did not tire of them' (Nietzsche 2005, p. 9). Jung himself appears to allude to this opening when, in his seminar on *Zarathustra*, he explained (on 21 November 1934) his work on the *Red Book* coincided with his re-engagement with Nietzsche:

> I read *Zarathustra* for the first time with consciousness in the first year of the war, in November 1914, twenty years ago; then suddenly the spirit seized me and carried me to a desert country in which I read *Zarathustra*.
>
> (Jung 1989b, vol. 1, p. 259)

Once again, it is the experientially and psychologically significant age of 40 that marks the moment of a turning-point or *metanoia*, described in the narrative text as 'a change of heart' (*sein Herz verwandelte sich*), and indicated in Zarathustra's discourse addressed to the sun as a 'going-down' or an emptying-out:

> I must, like you, *go under*, as human beings call it, to whom I would go down.
> [...]
> Behold! This cup wants to become empty again, and Zarathustra wants to become human again.
>
> (Nietzsche 2005, p. 9, emphasis in original)

This language recalls the theological notion of *kenosis*, or the 'self-emptying' by means of which Christ, in the incarnation, divested himself of his divine nature (cf. Philippians 2: 7) and by means of which the believer 'empties' himself or herself of his or her individual will and embraces instead the divine will of God.

This decision provides the motivation for the action in the rest of the Prologue, in Part 1, and indeed in the second, third, and eventually fourth Parts that Nietzsche added. It is important to appreciate that, like the *Red Book*, *Zarathustra* has a simple, if somewhat diffused, plot and hence a clearly discernible narrative structure. In Part 1, Zarathustra leaves his mountain and goes to the town known as the Colourful Cow; by Part 2, he has returned to his mountain but he descends again and visits the Blissful Islands; in Part 3, he sails from the Blissful Islands and travels cross-country via the Great City and the Colourful Cow back to his mountain; and in Part 4, he wanders through the mountains and forests, encountering the various Higher Men whom he invites back to his cave. The final chapter of Part 4, 'The Sign', closes the narrative circle by restaging the moment at the beginning of the Prologue, as Zarathustra again addresses the sun, calls on the Great Midday to 'rise up' and commences his own final descent. This time, however, Zarathustra himself is identified with the sun, for he leaves his cave 'glowing and strong, like a morning sun coming out of dark mountains' (Nietzsche 2005, p. 287).

So there is a clear narrative structure of descent, ascent, and descent again, onto which Nietzsche maps a narrative of crisis and resolution. The following episodes form the critical moments in this narrative structure: the decision at the end of Part 1 in 'On the Bestowing Virtue' to leave his disciples, bidding them 'Lose me and find yourselves; and only when you have all denied me will I return to you' and proclaiming the Great Midday, the moment when 'the human stands in the middle of its path between beast and Overhuman and celebrates its way to evening as its highest hope: for it is the way to a new morning' (Nietzsche 2005, p. 68); his flight to the fire-mountain (i.e., volcano) and his descent through the gate to the underworld where he converses with the firehound, followed by his subsequent return five days later ('On Great Events'); the terrifying moment when he hears the voice of his 'terrible mistress' speaking to him in 'The Stillest Hour'; the intuition of the eternal recurrence recounted to his fellow-travellers in 'On the Vision and the Riddle' and the exposition of the thought of eternal recurrence to his animals in 'The Convalescent'; and the deep calm and tranquillity of Zarathustra's vision in 'At Midday' when the world 'becomes perfect' (Nietzsche 2005, pp. 241–242).

In addition to explicit echoes of *Thus Spoke Zarathustra* – most obviously the verbal echo of Nietzsche's philological symbolism in such expressions as *Übermensch, Überwindung*, etc., and the neologism coined by Jung, *Übersinn* (Schmitt 2011) – there is thus a deep affinity between Nietzsche's *Zarathustra* and Jung's *Red Book* in terms of narrative structure. In both texts, the episodic structuring of crisis and resolution drives the movement of transformation forward, engaging with dreams, visions, and intuitive experiences as a way of achieving closer integration of the various elements of the self and an exalted, even ecstatic, sense of wholeness. While Nietzsche's *Zarathustra* – like Goethe's *Faust* – conveys a sense of closure which is absent from Jung's *Red Book*, all three texts are pervaded by an ironic, even parodic, tone that subverts the epic dimension of the narrative structure.

Conclusion

According to Aristotle, every tragedy has six constituent parts, namely plot, character, diction, thought, spectacle, and melody; and the most important of these is plot (or narrative), defined by Aristotle as 'the arrangement of the incidents of the story' (*Poetics* 1450a; Aristotle 1984, vol. 2, p. 2320).

In everything that is beautiful, whether it be a living creature or any organism composed of parts, these parts must not only be orderly arranged but must also have a certain magnitude of their own; for beauty consists in magnitude and ordered arrangement,

Aristotle argues; accordingly, 'as then creatures and other organic structures must have a certain magnitude and yet be easily taken in by the eye, so too with plots: they must have length but must be easily taken in by the memory' (1451b-1452a; Aristotle 1984 vol. 2, pp. 2321–2322). And then Aristotle goes on to make a point that is crucial in relation to the works discussed in this paper. 'A plot does not have unity, as some people think, simply because it deals with a single hero', and 'many and indeed innumerable things happen to an individual, some of which do not go to make up any unity' (1451a; Aristotle 1984, p. 2320). Rather, as

> in the other arts of representation a single representation means a representation of a single object, so too the plot being a representation of a piece of action must represent a single piece of action and the whole of it; and the component incidents must be so arranged that if one of them be transposed or removed, the unity of the whole is dislocated and destroyed.
>
> (1451a; Aristotle 1984, p. 2320)

In other words, the unity must arise from the combination of various aspects of the narrative, much as the Self arises from the combination of the various components of consciousness and the unconscious, or as Jung puts it: 'The self is not only the centre but it is the whole circumference which embraces both consciousness and unconscious; it is the centre of this totality, just as the ego is the centre of consciousness' (Jung 1944, para. 44). In this sense, 'the self is our life's goal, for it is the complete expression of that fateful combination we call individuality' (Jung 1928, para. 404); the process of individuation might, then, be described as way of *narrating the Self into being*.

While Jung's works lend themselves to cherry-picking – a recent anthology calls itself *The Quotable Jung* (Harris 2016) – it is important not to overlook the structure of his argumentation (which often takes the form of a binary synthesis) or, in the case of the *Red Book*, its plot. The sequencing of the episodes that make up its storyline is as important as the textual (and visual) shape given to those episodes themselves. And there is a wider lesson here. The Jung-inspired tagline for the internet radio show *Aeon Byte Gnostic Radio*, 'write your own gospel and live your own myth', has to be understood to mean that it is only if we *write* our own gospel that we shall be able to *live* our own myth. In this respect, what the *Red Book* enacts is a search for a style – albeit one that is 'new and unaccustomed' to Jung (2009, p. 391) – which is also a search for a myth: a search for that moment when 'the myth commences, the one that need only be lived, not sung, the one that sings itself' (Jung 2009, p. 328).

References

Anderegg, J. (2011) Transformationen: Über Himmlisches und Teuflisches in Goethes Faust. Bielefeld: Aisthesis (in German).

Aristotle. (1984) *The Complete Works*. (Ed. J. Barnes. 2 vols). Princeton, NJ: Princeton University Press.

Barber, R. (2006) Introduction. In: W. von Eschenbach, *Parzival and Titurel*. Oxford and New York: Oxford's World Classics.

Bishop, P. (2014) Jung and the quest for beauty: the *Red Book* in relation to German classicism. In: T. Kirsch and Hogenson (Eds), *The Red Book: Reflections on C. G. Jung's 'Liber Novus'*. London and New York: Routledge.

Böhm, T. (1996) *Theoria – Unendlichkeit – Aufstieg: Philosophische Implikationen zu "De Vita Mosis" von Gregor von Nyssa*. Leiden: Brill.

Brooks, P. (1979) Fictions of the Wolfman. *Diacritics* 9, 72–83.

Campbell, J. (1968) *The Masks of God: Creative Mythology*. New York: Viking.

Caris, A. (2007) Bridging the gap between Muslim and Christian: reflections on Parzival and its medieval background. *Journal for Waldorf/Rudolf Steiner Education* 9, 13–21.

Culler, J. (1980) Fabula and syuzhet in the analysis of narrative. *Poetics Today*, 1, 27–37.

Fideler, D. R. (1991) The path toward the Grail: The hermetic sources and structure of Wolfam von Eschenbach's *Parzival*. *Alexandria: The Journal of the Western Cosmological Traditions* 1, 187–227.

Freud, S. (1998) *The Interpretation of Dreams*. New York: Avon Books.

Genette, G. (1980) *Narrative Discourse: An Essay in Method*. Ithaca, NY: Cornell University Press.

Giegerich, W. (2010) Liber Novus, that is, the New Bible: a first analysis of C. G. Jung's Red Book. *Spring: A Journal of Archetype and Culture* 83, 361–411.

Goethe, J. W. (1908) *Faust, Parts I and II*. London; New York: Dent; Dutton.

Goethe, J. W. (1970) *Theory of Colours*. Trans. C. L. Eastlake. Cambridge, MA, and London: MIT Press.

Groos, A.B. (1972) Wolfram von Eschenbach's 'Bow Metaphor' and the narrative technique of Parzival. *Modern Languages Notes* 87(3), 391–408.

Harris, J. (Ed.) (2016) *The Quotable Jung*. Princeton, NJ: Princeton University Press.

Hogenson, G. (2014) 'The wealth of the soul exists in images': From medieval icons to modern science. In T. Kirsch and G. Hogenson (eds), *The Red Book: Reflections on C.G. Jung's 'Liber Novus'* (pp. 94–107). London and New York: Routledge.

Jacob, A. (1991) *De Naturae Natura: A Study of Idealistic Conceptions of Nature and the Unconscious*. Stuttgart: F. Steiner.

Jantz, H. (1987) *The Form of Faust: The Work of Art and its Intrinsic Structures*. Baltimore: Johns Hopkins University Press.

Jefferson, A. and Robey, D. (1986) *Modern Literary Theory: A Comparative Introduction* (2nd edn). London: Batsford.

Jung, C. G.: Unless otherwise stated, the following are from *The Collected Works of C. G. Jung* (CW) London: Routledge & Kegan Paul/Princeton, NJ: Princeton University Press:

Jung, C. G. (1928) The relations between the ego and the unconscious. (CW 7).

Jung, C. G. (1930/1950) Psychology and literature. (CW 15).

Jung, C. G. (1943) On the psychology of the unconscious. (CW 7).

Jung, C. G. (1944) *Psychology and alchemy*. (CW 12).

Jung, C. G. (1952) *Symbols of transformation.* (CW 5).

Jung, C. G. (1989a) *Memories, Dreams, Reflections.* New York: Vintage Books.

Jung, C. G. (1989b) *Nietzsche's 'Zarathustra': Notes of the Seminar given in 1934–1939.* London: Routledge.

Jung, C. G. (1991) *Analytical Psychology: Notes of the Seminar given in 1925.* Princeton, NJ: Princeton University Press.

Jung, C. G. (2009) *The Red Book: Liber Novus.* New York and London: Norton.

Jung, E. and von Franz, M.-L. (1986) *The Grail Legend* (2nd edn). Boston: Sigo Press.

Kahane, H. and Kahane, R. (1965) *The Krater and the Grail: Hermetic Sources of the Parzival.* Urbana: University of Illinois Press.

Kingsley, P. (2018) *Catafalque: Carl Jung and the End of Humanity.* London: Catafalque Press.

Lamberton, R. (1986) *Homer the Theologian: Neoplatonist Allegorical Reading and the Growth of the Epic Tradition.* Berkeley, CA: University of California Press.

Loewenstein, E. (1992) The Freudian case history: a detective story or a dialectical progression? Reflections on psychoanalytic narratives from a Lacanian perspective. *Psychoanalytic Psychology* 9, 49–59.

McConnell, W. (1999) Otherworlds, alchemy, Pythagoras, and Jung: symbols of transformation in Parzival. In: W. Hasty (Ed.), *A Companion to Wolfram's 'Parzival'.* Rochester, NY: Camden House.

Muschg, A. (1993) *Der Rote Ritter: Eine Geschichte von Parzival.* Frankfurt am Main: Suhrkamp.

Nietzsche, F. (1911) *Ecce Homo: Nietzsche's Autobiography.* New York: Macmillan.

Nietzsche, F. (2005) *Thus Spoke Zarathustra: A Book for Everyone and Nobody.* Oxford and New York: Oxford University Press.

Noll, R. (1994) *The Jung Cult: Origins of a Charismatic Movement.* Princeton, NJ: Princeton University Press.

Parshall, L. B. (1981) *The Art of Narration in Wolfram's 'Parzival' and Albrecht's 'Jüngerer Titurel'.* London and New York: Cambridge University Press.

Plotinus (1967) *Ennead III.* Cambridge, MA: Harvard University Press.

Richey, M. F. (1931) Ither von Gaheviez. *The Modern Language Review* 26, 315–329.

Roochnik, D. (2009) What is theoria? Nicomachean Ethics Book 10.7–8. *Classical Philology* 104, 69–82.

Schmitt, G. (2011) Vom Übermensch und Übersinn: Nietzsches Metaphorik im Roten Buch. *Recherches germaniques: Art, sciences et psychologie: Autour du "Livre rouge" de Carl Gustav Jung (1914–1930)* [hors série, no. 8], 117–133.

Seiling, M. (1919) *Goethe als Okkultist: Komme, folge mir ins dunkle Reich hinab!* Berlin: J. Baum.

Shklovsky, V. (1965) Sterne's Tristram Shandy: stylistic commentary. In L. T. Lemon and M. J. Reis (Eds), *Russian Formalist Criticism: Four Essays* (2nd edn). Lincoln, Nebraska: University of Nebraska Press.

Stein, J. W. (1991) *The Ninth Century and the Holy Grail.* Forest Row: Temple Lodge Publishing.

Steiner, R. (2010) *The Mysteries of the Holy Grail: From Arthur and Parzival to Modern Initiation.* Forest Row: Rudolf Steiner Press.

Stevens, A. (1999) Fiction, plot and discourse: Wolfram's *Parzival* and its narrative sources. In: W. Hasty (Ed.), *A Companion to Wolfram's 'Parzival'.* Rochester, NY: Camden House.

Sussman, L. (1995) *The Speech of the Grail: A Journey Toward Speaking That Heals and Transforms*. Great Barrington, MA: Lindisfarne Books.

Tauler, J. (1985) *Sermons*. New York and Mahwah: Paulist Press.

Thackrey, S. (2014) Manifesting the Vision: C. G. Jung's Paintings for *The Red Book*. In: T. Kirsch and G. Hogenson (Eds), *The Red Book: Reflections on C. G. Jung's 'Liber Novus'*. London and New York: Routledge.

Thomas, N. (1999) Wolfram von Eschenbach: modes of narrative presentation. In: W. Hasty (Ed.), *A Companion to Wolfram's 'Parzival'*. Rochester, NY: Camden House.

Todorov, T. (1969) *Grammaire du Décaméron*. The Hague: Mouton.

Trakl, G. (2005) *Poems and Prose: A Bilingual Edition*. Illinois: Northwestern University Press.

von Eschenbach, W. (1980) *Parzival*. Trans. A. T. Hatto. Harmondsworth; Penguin.

Wilhelm, R. (1931) Goethe und Lau Dsï. In: *Der Mensch und das Sein*. Jena: Diederichs.

Woldershausen, O. A. (Ed.) (1751) *Die von dem Irdischen zu dem himmlischen Bräutigam eilende Braut*. Wittenberg: J. F. Schlomach.

Woolger, R. (2015) C. G. Jung, mystic or psychologist? Reflections on the *Red Book*. Available on: http://stonemountaincenter.com/site/wp-content/uploads/2015/08/redbook.pdf (accessed 30 June 2018).

Wulsin, J. (2007) Parzival – the journey of adolescence. *Journal for Waldorf/Rudolf Steiner Education* 9, 9–13.

Chapter 7

Between two worlds

The narrative and psychological implications of Hoffmann's 'The Golden Pot'

Terence Dawson

As he grew older, Jung came to realise that his theory about individuation was far more problematic than he had previously thought. In a letter written in September 1956 he conceded that 'all criteria of individuation are subjective and outside the purpose of science' and then, somewhat irritably, as if his use of the word were self-evident, continued: 'The criterion is consciousness' (Jung 1973/1976, II, pp. 323–324). In other words, he candidly admitted that the kind of consciousness to which he refers cannot be measured objectively; and yet he saw no need to specify his definition of 'consciousness' further. There are, however, many different kinds of consciousness. For example, in *Elective Affinities*, Goethe identifies one kind: 'We are willing to acknowledge our shortcomings, we are willing to be punished for them, we will patiently suffer much on their account, but we become impatient if we are required to overcome them' (Goethe 1809/1971, p. 181). Willingness to acknowledge our shortcomings, willingness to be punished for them, and a willingness to suffer much on their account all imply consciousness of a kind – a passive awareness of how things are, without *any* determination to do very much to change them. But if we become impatient whenever someone touches upon one of our shortcomings, it can only be because we have never really sought to bring it under any form of control. A merely passive consciousness of one's shortcomings leaves the door open for self-indulgence: it does not provide a criterion for individuation.

Jung was of course referring to the kind of consciousness brought about by a sustained engagement with the content of one's dreams. He referred to this process as an *Auseinandersetzung*, an untranslatable German word that suggests an active confrontation with the contents of one's dreams, 'having it out with, discussing, [and] analysing' them, with a view to 'an eventual coming to terms' with their underlying implications (Hannah 1981, p. 22). Sustaining a 'dialogue' with the implications of one's dreams over a period of time, Jung argued, can lead to a more balanced acceptance of oneself as the specific person one is. The change in one's attitudes that can result from this provides an altogether more satisfactory definition of individuation. But, as Jung realised, such change is not easy to measure.

A worrying by-product of this definition is the temptation to see all change – sometimes even wildly inappropriate change – as indicative of individuation. This was a besetting problem with Jungian readings of literary texts in the 1950s and 1960s. They often approached texts as if they were allegories waiting to be decoded, i.e. they assumed that they were accounts of one or other of the underlying conflicts identified by Jungian theory, whether confrontation with the shadow, or the anima/animus, or the trickster archetype, or the *puer aeternus*, or the self, or whatever. In Aristotelian terms, this is to treat the details of the text as *accidentals* and to locate its *substance* in an issue that has less to do with the unique properties of the specific text examined than with the ideas underlying the assumptions one takes to its exploration. If the purpose of one's analysis is only to uncover the way in which the text gives expression to an issue that exists independently of the text, one is in effect reading allegorically. And allegory is *always* circular: only by accepting its assumptions (whether those of the *Divine Comedy* or those of *Animal Farm*) can one appreciate the nature of its central concerns. In similar fashion, if one reads a novel *as if* it were an allegory of psychological processes one locks oneself in similar circularity.

In these pages I want to consider the issue of individuation in the light of a text whose classic analysis by Aniela Jaffé envisaged it as the beginning of a process of individuation – an argument that was often praised by Jung. Her analysis is a substantial work. Here there is space only to comment on those features of it that relate to the question of interpreting the text as an illustration of a stage in the process of individuation. My argument is in three parts. The first part begins with the reminder that Jungian psychology *is* textual criticism. The second questions Jung's definition of 'The Golden Pot' as a 'visionary work'. And the third proposes caution when approaching a text that belongs to the fantastic. My principal aim is to argue that 'consciousness' is too ambivalent a term to provide a useful definition of individuation; and to suggest that a more useful definition might be whether the interactions of a text suggest that its author was not only 'engaging' with its possible psychological implications but also 'working on' his or her attitudes in the light of this dialogue.

Textual criticism

As I have written elsewhere (Dawson 2008), beginning in 1907, Freud and his followers produced a succession of imaginative applications of his theories to literary and other cultural products. They include Freud's (1907) own analysis of a novel, *Delusions and Dreams in Jensen's 'Gradiva'*, two studies by Otto Rank, *The Artist* (1907/1989) and *The Myth of the Birth of the Hero* (1909/1914), Franz Riklin's (1908/1915) essay on 'Wish fulfilment and Symbolism in Fairy Tales', and 'The Oedipus Complex as an Explanation of Hamlet's Mystery' by Ernest Jones (1910). These works, the product of a few short years, set the ground for the transformation of psychoanalysis from a controversial but negligible clinical practice into one of the most influential cultural theories of the twentieth century.

Ironically, they also helped to change the course of Jung's dominant interest. Up until this time, Jung had been an earnest experimental psychiatrist. The decisive moment in his break with Freud may have been brought about by the publication of the second part of *Psychology of the Unconscious* (Jung 1912). But the decisive moment in his own development came earlier, for by the time he had written the first part he had already ceased to be either an experimental or a clinical psychologist. He had become a textual critic.

Psychology of the Unconscious is an extended analysis of the fantasies of Miss Frank Miller as they were recorded in a professional journal (Jung 1952a, pp. 445–462). A large part of *Psychological Types* (Jung 1921) is based on his interpretation of either philosophical or literary works. Jung's writings on the East and on Christianity (e.g. 1938, 1939, 1952b) and extensive studies of Western alchemy (1944, 1955a, and works spanning 1929–1954, collated in 1967) are entirely derived from his interpretation of texts. *Answer to Job* (Jung 1952c) is based on the biblical text. Remarkably few of his mature publications are based on case studies, and some of those that are (e.g. 'A study in the process of individuation', Jung 1934) might be regarded, and equally accurately, as 'textual'. Almost all the evidence for his major ideas came from his reading. According to Joseph Henderson, by 1934 'his seminars no longer contained case material' (quoted in Bair 2003, p. 395). Analytical psychology emerged from his attempt to understand the psychological implications of the texts that caught his imagination.

Analytical psychology is fundamentally different in kind from psychoanalysis. Freud's theories were derived from an analysis of his patients and their dreams. Jung did not formulate his ideas from a considered analysis of his patients' dreams; he developed them through engaging with his wide-ranging but very selective reading. Because he read these texts from a psychological perspective, inevitably he found in them evidence for views about psychological processes – views upon which he built his therapeutic practice. Jung spent most of every working day in his private practice, and he continued to see patients long after he might have found a good reason to stop doing so. He always assumed that his theories belonged to the domain of psychology. But as he described his practice not long after his break with Freud, the theories that underlie analytical psychology belong to a 'hermeneutic method' (Jung 1916, para. 501). They represent a narrative, a textual and a cultural theory. Their application in clinical practice is a secondary phenomenon.

All his life Jung claimed to be an empiricist (Jung 1973/1976, I, p. 195; 1952b, paras. 1507–1511). Certainly, he had a profound respect for the psyche. He was genuinely fascinated by dream-images to which his peers were either reluctant to attribute any great importance or interpreted in the light of a personal psychology. He was firmly convinced that such images could best be understood in relation to analogous images found in world mythology. But he always confused the *fact* of their experience with his own *interpretation* of their significance. His ideas are the expression not of any kind of empiricism, but of theories

devised from his study of a broad but eclectic range of cultural texts. And hermeneutics is not an empirical science. Readers approaching a text from significantly
different critical perspectives are astonishingly reluctant to negotiate with views
that come from approaches different from their own. There is nothing 'scientific'
about textual studies.

Although Jung repeatedly denied that his ideas constitute a theory (e.g. Jung
1929, para. 86; 1952b, para. 1507), this is precisely what they are: a *theory* – a
word derived from the Greek θεωρία, 'a looking at, viewing, contemplation'
(*OED*). They are the expression of his long 'contemplation' about the nature and
possible significance of a great many kinds of experience and interaction – from
the personal, through the domestic, to the spiritual – derived, very often, from
his reading. The value of analytical psychology is not that it uncovers the 'truth'
of experience, but that it offers a persuasive and intriguing aid to further reflection on the phenomenology of experience (cf. Brooke 1991, 1999).

That Jung was unbelievably slow to think of applying his essentially textual
theory to works of literature is revealing. When he did, he explains why. He
did not believe that analytical psychology had much to contribute to the discussion of most literary texts. He believed in the separation of disciplines. He
distinguished between two modes of artistic creation: between 'psychological'
works, whose psychological implications are fully explained by the author,
and 'visionary' works that are not under the author's conscious control, but
have been dictated by an 'alien' will (Jung 1922, para. 113) and thus, somewhat confusingly, 'demand' a psychological commentary (Jung 1930, para.
143). He had no interest in the former. He was only interested in what he
called 'visionary' works, which arise from the 'timeless depths' of the psyche
and '[burst] asunder our human standards of value and aesthetic form' (Jung
1930, para. 141). His category of 'visionary works' was remarkably wide-
ranging. It includes Dante's *Divine Comedy*, Colonna's *Hypnerotomachia*,
Blake's poetry and paintings, Hoffmann's 'Golden Pot', Melville's *Moby
Dick*, Wagner's great operas, Nietzsche's *Zarathustra*, and Conan Doyle's
Sherlock Holmes stories – in other words, works so radically different that one
cannot help but suspect that the only thing they have in common is that they
happened to interest Jung.

The assertion that his ideas are only useful for analysing a certain kind of
experience suggests that he was caught in his own circular thinking. Jung would
only explore texts that dealt with a certain kind of experience, he assumed his
methodology provided an empirical explanation for this experience, and then
insisted that even though his ideas weren't useful for looking at texts that didn't
interest him his psychology was nonetheless universally valid.

In contrast with most of his other ideas, Jung devised his theory of individuation not from his reading, but from his clinical practice. The term refers, in the
first instance, to a maturation of a specific individual over an extended period of
time. It is not clear why it should ever have been applied to literary texts, for it is
doubtful whether it can ever be a sufficiently specific term to identify an aspect

of a text that other approaches might overlook. Moreover, the purpose of textual criticism is not to uncover evidence of the author's possible growth of personality, but to explore possible patterns of significance in the text(s) in which it is interested.

The Kunstnovelle

That Jungian psychology is deeply indebted to German Romantic philosophy and to the figures of Goethe and Schiller in particular has been well established (Ellenberger 1970, pp. 728–731; Bishop 2008). But, although widely acknowledged in Germany, the debt to other German literature of the long Romantic period is far less widely recognised within the Anglo-Saxon nations – especially the debt to two of the most characteristic genres of German literature, which arose at the end of the eighteenth century and contrast a more or less credible reality with a wholly imaginal one. Interestingly, they are so very 'other' to the Anglo-Saxon reader that neither has yet been given a satisfactory name in English translation. The first is the *Märchen*, usually translated as 'fairy tale', but which might be better rendered as 'imaginal tale' (i.e. a story 'of or pertaining to the imagination' *OED*). Novalis, Tieck, and Brentano all published sophisticated *Märchen* before the appearance of the first great collection of *Hausmärchen* by the Grimm brothers in 1812. The other is the *Novelle*, a kind of long short-story which differs from the *Märchen* in that it is usually set in a recognisable location and it often involves a marked tension between this credible social reality and a purely imaginal reality. Perhaps inevitably, the two genres frequently overlapped. Not even the Gothic, which was almost contemporary and has aroused such interest in the last 30 years, offers a more profound and diverse exploration of the range and variety of possible connections between the outer and the inner world than these two genres. Even so, they have never won much enthusiasm from the broader Anglo-Saxon reader: to date only a handful of tales are readily available in English translation (e.g. Grimm and Grimm 1812–1815/1975; Tully 2000; works by Hoffmann and by Kleist); one has to look hard to find English translations of the tales of Jean Paul, Novalis, Schlegel, Bonaventura, Bettina von Arnim, Achim von Arnim, Eichendorff or Chamisso, to mention only some of the other prominent exponents of these genres.

'The Golden Pot: A *Märchen* for the New Times' (Hoffmann 1814/1992) is one of E. T. A. Hoffmann's best-known tales. It is set in early nineteenth-century Dresden (and thus has one of the main characteristics of the *Novelle*) and yet many, some might say all of its events belong to the dream-like world of the *Märchen*. What is curious about it is that the events in the credible social reality do not constitute a plot in any ordinary sense of this word: they present only an *outline* for a plot. Anselmus is an unusually awkward student who meets Veronica but is only intermittently conscious of his interest in her. His friend Heerbrand secures him a job working for an archivist (Lindhorst) as a copyist of old manuscripts. Meanwhile Veronica falls in love with Anselmus, a feeling largely incited by her being told that he might one day become a *Hofrat* (councillor, a grade in the civil service). When it becomes evident that he is unlikely to obtain such a post soon, and she learns that his friend Heerbrand has been made a *Hofrat*, she accepts the latter's proposal and marries him. None of these events, however, is elaborated upon. The events that give the tale its interest mostly concern Anselmus – and they belong to an entirely imaginal reality. They are set in motion the day that he sinks into a waking dream in which he 'sees' a small snake in a tree with which he falls head-over-heels in love, and in which he feels 'some unknown force stirring within him and causing that blissful pain, that yearning, which assures humanity of another and higher existence' (Hoffmann 1814/1992, p. 21). The Archivist Lindhorst (in a social reality) tells him that the snake in question is his (Lindhorst's) daughter Serpentina (who exists only in the imaginal reality). As in a fairy tale, the copying that he does for the Archivist seems to be a test. One day he spills the ink on an original document, which results in a battle between an old woman, who is identified as an evil power, and Lindhorst who, in the imaginal reality, is a salamander and is identified as a good power. Lindhorst defeats the old woman; Anselmus marries Serpentina and they settle happily in Atlantis. 'The Golden Pot' draws heavily from a great many texts, including *Heinrich von Ofterdingen*, the Witch's Kitchen scene from *Faust*, and *The Count of Gabalis*, the same work as provided Alexander Pope (1714/2006) with material for his deliciously witty 'The Rape of the Lock', Novalis (1802/1964), Goethe (1808/1987) and Montfaucon (1670/1922). It is the only one of Hoffmann's works to have an apparently happy ending. It has often been contrasted with 'The Sandman', written a year later, which ends tragically.

As we have seen, Jung referred to it as one of his examples of 'visionary' literature. The classic Jungian reading of it is amongst the small handful of works by his disciples that he allowed to appear in one of his own publications. *Gestaltungen des Unbewussten* (Jung 1950a) is a collection of revised versions of three of his earlier essays with one new one (1930, 1934, 1940 and 1950b). And yet more than half the volume is given over to Aniela Jaffé's extended analysis of '*Images and Symbols in E. T. A. Hoffmann's Fairytale "The Golden Pot"*' (1950a, pp. 239–616; see also Jaffé 1950/1978). Jung often referred to it approvingly (e.g. 1955b, para. 931*n*.; 1952a, para. 615*n*4). Jaffé turned to this tale to demonstrate how this example of 'visionary' literature illustrates a stage in the process of individuation. Between the two world wars, Hoffmann had enjoyed a brief period when he was regarded as 'a guiding spirit full of knowledge, faith, and beneficent clarity' (Reddick 1976, p. 577). Jaffé's claims for him were very much in keeping with the critical spirit of these years. She attributed the process to which the tale gives expression to the author and she closely, perhaps too closely, examined the story's possible archetypal implications. But, as McGlathery (1981, p. 92) has pointed out, she paid too little attention to the story's irony.

Hoffmann, like many of the German writers of his generation, took considerable interest in the inner world: he very probably intended the reader to do likewise. For all his irony, Hoffmann clearly believed that first-hand experience of one's own imagination was of vital importance to one's personality. Albeit in his somewhat droll language, he expresses this clearly at the beginning of Chapter 4 of 'Princess Brambilla':

> You must not be surprised, beloved reader, if something that may call itself a capriccio, but in fact resembles a fairy-tale as closely as though it were one, contains a great deal of weird goings on and dream-like delusions, such as the human spirit nurtures; or rather, if the action of the story is at times transferred to the inner lives of its characters. May not that indeed be the right place for it? Perhaps, O my reader, you agree with me that the human spirit is itself the most wondrous fairy-tale imaginable. What a magnificent world lies locked up in our bosoms! No horizon sets bounds to it, and its treasures outweigh the incalculable riches of the entire visible creation!
>
> (Hoffmann 1814/1992, p. 170)

Jung was later to make almost equally bombastic claims about the 'treasure hard to attain'. It is no surprise that he included Hoffmann as one of his 'visionary' writers.

Something about Hoffmann's intensely imagined scenes lends the best of his imaginative fictions a startling immediacy that reminds one of what he wrote about one of the characters from his later collection of stories, *The Serapion Brethren*: 'When Sylvester sits down and fixes some inner images into words, there is sure to be some irresistible impulse constraining him to do so. He never writes anything that he has not most vividly felt, and seen' (Hoffman 1886/1892, I, p. 277). 'The Golden Pot' gives the impression that its author has both 'vividly felt, and seen' every episode of his tale. And every episode – not just the different sections of the Archivist's creation myth but each of the equally topsy-turvy social scenes – has a dream-like logic. For these reasons, it might seem as if the text came into being through a process akin to active imagination. Jaffé worked from this assumption. She sees the text as marking the beginning of Hoffmann's individuation. But on what grounds? Even such explicit assertions as the two we have quoted do not imply that Hoffmann was reproducing the content of his own authentic imagination in any his tales.

Scholars of German literature have always recognised the artistry of the *Novelle*: they refer to the more obviously self-conscious examples of the genre as *Kunstnovellen* (lit., art short stories) or, in the case of *Märchen*, as *Kunst-märchen* (art-fairy tales). When approached to write a preface for the collection of stories in which 'The Golden Pot' was to appear, Jean Paul (a well-known writer at the time) suggested that Hoffmann use the generic title *Kunstnovellen* instead of his preferred, and eventual title: *Fantasy Pieces in the Manner of Callot* (Hoffmann 1967, p. 207). As Jean Paul recognised, 'The Golden Pot' is a very cleverly articulated work of literature. It plays with the idea of a spontaneous and autonomous fantasy; it is not a transcription of such a process.

The *Kunstnovelle* begins with Anselmus running out of the Black Gate on Ascension Day on his way to Linke's café-restaurant, where he hopes to have an enjoyable holiday evening and, perhaps, get to impress some local girls. Instead, he clumsily knocks over an old woman's basketful of apples and cakes, and she foretells a fearful doom for him, shrieking after him: 'into glass you'll soon pass – into glass!' (Hoffmann 1814/1992, p. 1). The tale hinges on what this might mean. Following his accident, Anselmus ponders his misfortune and begins to imagine what he would have done had he not felt obliged to surrender his purse to the old woman. He would have sat next to 'a group of beautiful girls in magnificent finery' and started up a conversation with them. He is an adolescent dreamer, and as soon as he sits down beneath the elder-tree, he begins to hear 'a strange rushing, swishing sound' from its branches. Listening intently, he gradually discerns 'faint words' which turn out to be spoken by three little snakes that are coiled around the branches above his head, 'stretching their heads towards the evening sun' (Hoffmann 1814/1992, p. 5). This opening may have a dreamlike logic, but there is nothing spontaneous about it. Hoffmann has considered his material carefully. He chooses Ascension Day (40 days after Easter, when Christ ascended into Heaven, see Acts 1: 1–11) in order to contrast humorously with the more modest delights that Anselmus hopes to find at 'Linke's paradise' (Hoffmann 1814/1992, p. 2). And as dozens of critics have observed, the opening material reproduces the three key images from the story of the Fall: apples, a tree, and a snake. This is not fortuitous: Hoffmann wants the reader to enjoy the contrast between hoped-for paradise and the fall.

Anselmus is shaken from his waking-fantasy by his friend Paulmann calling to him. The latter, his two daughters, and their mutual friend Heerbrand are about to take a boat across the Elbe to enjoy the evening in Pirna. It is while crossing the river that Anselmus

> notices for the first time what beautiful dark-blue eyes Veronica seemed to have, never giving a thought to those wondrous eyes that he had seen in the elder-tree. In fact, the incident under the elder-tree had suddenly vanished from Anselmus's mind.
>
> (Hoffmann 1814/1992, pp. 10–11)

The link on which the *Novelle* hinges is established: Veronica and Serpentina are two related but contrasted figures. The former belongs to a social world: she has a father who works as a Sub-Rector (schoolmaster) and she has other friends from the social world (the Miss Osters; Hoffmann 1814/1992, pp. 29–31). In contrast, Serpentina belongs to an imaginal realm: her father is a Salamander and whilst she may have two sisters, she has no friends from a social world. Most of Hoffmann's stories contrast a social and an imaginal reality, and many (e.g. 'The Sandman') also contrast a young girl from a social reality with another whose qualities are experienced only by the young hero (whether Anselmus or, in 'The Sandman', Nathanael).

As the narrative of 'The Golden Pot' develops, it is clear that Veronica is head-over-heels in love with Anselmus and that he is happiest when he is with her. In the 'Ninth Vigil', he has just agreed to marry her when Heerbrand produces the ingredients for a punch from his pockets. A moment later Anselmus is drunk – and he takes hold of Veronica's hand while uncontrollably sighing for Serpentina (Hoffmann 1814/1992, p. 62). In the ensuing confusion, he is called away to the Archivist's home, where he blots his copy and is confined to a bottle, exactly as the old woman had predicted at the outset (but see Nygaard 1983). In other words, his confinement in 'glass' corresponds to his inability to free himself from his fascination with Serpentina: it represents a psychic impasse. At the end, he is living in Atlantis, happily 'married' to Serpentina – and it is Heerbrand who marries Veronica. That is, Anselmus has been unable to prevent his psychic energy from being given over to an adolescent-like fantasy-life and consequently he *loses* his girl. This is a tale about a 'fall': 'The Golden Pot' does *not* end as happily as many critics still assume it does (e.g. Robertson's Introduction in Hoffmann 1814/1992, pp. xi–xvi).

The witty contrast between paradise and fall continues with Lindhorst's story about his origins. The latter's story – a would-be creation myth – is not experiential; it is transparently conceptual. And it is as interesting for its assumptions as it is for its implications. Spirit is masculine; the sun (as it is in German) is feminine, a nurturing mother. The black hill represents male torpor (melancholy) stirred to desire by the sun; masculine spirit tries to block the sun, but the sun resists, the black hill gives birth to a fiery lily, who falls in love with Phosphorus as soon as he appears. Phosphorus warns the lily that the consequence of leaving her parents will be terrible, that if he casts a spark of thought into her, she will be racked by a despair in which she will perish. This is neither a philosophical tale nor an expression of active imagination. Its events clearly mirror those of the main tale, albeit obliquely. Veronica has no problem with her father; it is Anselmus who has difficulty freeing himself from the power of his own nurturing, sun-like (and thus maternal) fantasy. Some of this 'fairy tale' may well have come from Hoffmann's own dreams or waking fantasies – but we can be sure that he carefully moulded it to his own purposes.

Anselmus associates everything about the old woman with 'evil', and believes that Lindhorst is the principle of good. As has been suggested, however, might the opposite not be the case? We know that Hoffmann conducted Mozart's *Magic Flute* four times in the weeks immediately prior to beginning 'The Golden Pot' and that he may even have conducted it 'on the very day ... on which he started writing the tale' (Reddick 1976, p. 587, n. 1). One might be tempted to equate the old woman with the 'evil' Queen of the Night and Lindhorst, with the 'good' Sarastro. But this may be to miss the point. At the outset of *The Magic Flute*, Tamino, the hero, assumes that the Queen of the Night is the principle of *good*; it is not until half way through the opera that he is undeceived and that he learns that Sarastro, whom the Queen hates, is the real principle of good. Might the same not be the case in 'The Golden Pot'? Hoffmann teases us into believing that the old woman is evil. But her evil consists of little more than giving Anselmus an over-sharp warning not to lose himself in his fantasy world and in her trying to steer him away from Serpentina, who is not a partner for anyone belonging to a social reality. In spite of thinking that 'The Golden Pot' is 'visionary' literature, Jung would have given *any* young student consulting him exactly the same warning and exactly the same advice. In similar fashion, how 'good' is Lindhorst? Is he really a magus figure, as Jaffé would have us believe? Or is he something altogether more sinister? Might he not be an aspect of the shadow (rather than the self) drawing Anselmus into a world of inconsequential fantasy? In other words, Hoffmann would seem to have wittily reversed the roles from *The Magic Flute*. His hero mistakes Lindhorst for a principle of 'good', and doesn't even begin to understand that the old woman is trying to help him get together with Veronica – which, in psychological terms, would have provided an altogether more appropriate ending.

A carefully elaborated literary work is not a spontaneous fantasy. And every aspect of 'The Golden Pot' – and, indeed, of most other *Novellen* too – suggests that it has been carefully thought through. It is not until the beginning of the 'Fourth Vigil' that the reader is given an explanation of why the chapter headings are called vigils: because the story is being told by an unnamed narrator who is writing late at night (as did Hoffmann). This narrator intermittently addresses the reader directly, for example in order to ask whether he or she has ever felt a 'yearning for something unknown' that has caused them to lose all interest in their surroundings' (Hoffmann 1814/1992, p. 20). This appeal to the reader's experience is of course partly serious – but it is also deeply ironic, as he makes clear a moment later when he refers to 'the impish humour that teases us with the bewilderment of magic' (Hoffmann 1814/1992, p. 21). Hoffmann may be interested in the world of the imagination, but his ever-present self-conscious irony reminds us that he is not transcribing an experience so much as playing with the elements of a hypothetical experience. He enjoys playing with uncertainty; as, for example, not allowing the reader to decide whether Veronica went out on the night of 23 September or whether she only had a vivid dream. Such ploys, which include the repeated use of bathos, the playfulness of the social satire, and the evident borrowings from other works of literature, all indicate that this is a highly self-conscious text.

When he wrote 'The Golden Pot' Hoffmann was not, as was his hero, an awkward young student: he was a 37-year-old multi-talented workaholic, the energetic musical director of an opera company, a competent composer, an extraordinarily sharp music critic, and he had trained as a lawyer, a profession to which he returned with considerable success soon after the publication of 'The Golden Pot'. As has often been asserted, his tales may well examine tendencies of his own character, but one should be wary of making too close a connection between him and any of his various protagonists. Novalis treats his own hero with high seriousness; Hoffmann, in contrast, pokes constant and merciless fun at Anselmus, as he does at Nathanael in 'The Sandman'.

These are not the usual conditions for a narrative that mirrors an author's unmediated inner world, let alone one about individuation. Which raises the question: what can a *Jungian* approach contribute to its understanding?

The fantastic

Hoffmann never allows his reader to grasp one possible interpretation of an event before presenting another, very different, reading. For example, as Anselmus is crossing the Elbe, a display of fireworks is released from the opposite bank (social reality). A moment later, he notices 'the sparkling, crackling flames reflected in the water', and fancies that 'the little golden snakes [are] swimming through the waves' (Hoffmann 1814/1992, p. 9; imaginal reality). He cries out with delight and lunges forward, imperilling not only himself but all his friends. The boatman catches him by the coat-tails; Anselmus is close to fainting. But as he comes round, he realises that 'what he had taken for the sparkling of the golden snakes was only the reflection of the firework display in Anton's Garden' (Hoffmann 1814/1992, p. 9; social reality). But even *after* admitting this possibility, he continues to hear the voices of the snakes calling to him, begging him to 'believe' in them (imaginal reality). Anselmus – and later Veronica – is constantly torn between 'a natural and a supernatural explanation of the events described' (Robertson, in Hoffmann 1814/1992, p. x). And Hoffmann goes to almost excessive length to ensure that his readers experience the same hesitation themselves. In a very real sense, this is one of the work's themes.

'The Golden Pot' thus fulfils the first two of Todorov's (1970/1975) three criteria for the fantastic:

> The fantastic requires the fulfilment of three conditions. First, the text must oblige the reader to consider the world of the characters as a world of living persons and to hesitate between a natural and a supernatural explanation of the events described. Second, this hesitation may also be experienced by a character; thus the reader's role is so to speak entrusted to a character, and at the same time the hesitation is represented, it becomes one of the themes of the work – in the case of naive reading, the actual reader identifies himself with the character. Third, the reader must adopt a certain attitude with regard to the text: he will reject allegorical as well as 'poetic' interpretations.
>
> (Todorov 1970/1975, p. 33)

But Todorov's insistence that the fantastic also requires readers to 'reject allegorical as well as "poetic" interpretations' is more problematic for most approaches, for criticism of all persuasions – and not just hermeneutic theories – is marked by an itch to interpret.

All critical approaches recognise that 'The Golden Pot' hinges on a tension between two levels of reality. This is not in dispute. It is a sign of our times, however, that very few of the more fashionable critical approaches are able to shed useful light on the relation between them. They have other, mostly ideological concerns. They recognise only one reality: that of the material or physical world. They are not concerned with literature as a reflection of imaginal processes. As a result, they have no other recourse than to reproduce the terms used by Hoffmann. For example, Horst Daemmrich, picking up from the ending of Hoffmann's tale (which identifies Atlantis with 'life in poetry'; Hoffmann 1814/1992, p. 83), argues that 'Serpentina symbolises poetic inspiration' (Daemmrich 1973, p. 29). But does she? As was pointed out in an anonymous review published soon after the tale first appeared, 'Nothing about the student Anselmus, except at most his awkwardness, testifies to his poetic sensitivity, which indeed he does not possess' (Woltmann 1815, col. 422, quoted in McGlathery 1997, p. 21). It is hard enough to imagine the hero of 'The Sandman', Nathanael, writing *good* poetry, it is well-nigh impossible to imagine Anselmus writing poetry at all. There is nothing poetic about Anselmus or his imagination – and the happiness that he gets to enjoy with Serpentina on the Lindhorst estate in Atlantis is a parody of 'life in poetry' rather than any kind of representation of it. This may be a story about the poetic imagination, but it is not about poetic character. Anselmus is not a poet, and there is no obvious reason why a little green snake in a tree should symbolise any kind of connection with poetic inspiration.

Jungian criticism recognises not only the reality of the imaginal world, but also, and no less importantly, the conditions for accessing it. Jung is often associated with mystification. But interestingly, one of the chief merits of his theories is that they allow one to elaborate upon common-sense distinctions. Literature was one of Jung's blind spots: he may have regarded Hoffmann as a 'visionary' writer, but, thankfully, he also had very strong views on the need to keep one's feet firmly planted on the ground when one accesses the imaginal (i.e. the unconscious). It is of course possible (perhaps even likely) that Hoffmann encountered some of the material for his tales in his dreams. But if he did, before making use of it, he shook it about as if it were in a kaleidoscope and the tales that emerged from his pen have very little left of any authentic experience. And the reason why he did this is given in the tales themselves.

The clearest example of this is found in *The Serapion Brethren*, where he contrasts the interests of the happy few who seek 'the higher regions' of the mind with the multitude of those who are suspicious of any kind of inner experience. But, he insists, one needs a very firm foothold in reality before one can explore the inner world. As Theodore says:

> 'What I think, and mean, is, that the foot of the heavenly ladder, which we have got to mount in order to reach the higher regions, has to be fixed firmly in every-day life, so that everybody may be able to climb up it along with

us. When people then find that they have ... climbed up higher and higher
into a marvellous, magical world, they will feel that that realm, too, belongs
to their ordinary, every-day life....'

'Don't forget, though, Theodore, my friend,' said Ottmar, 'that there are
qualities of people who won't go up the ladder at all, because it isn't
"proper" or "becoming". And many turn giddy by the time they get to the
third rung of it. Many never see the ladder at all, though it is facing them in
the broad, daily path of their lives, and they pass by it every day.'

(Hoffmann 1886/1892, II, pp. 94–95)

Jung may have decried the fact that the vast majority 'won't go up the ladder at
all', that a large number 'turn giddy by the time they get to the third rung', and
that only a handful of people seek to explore the possible significance of their
inner world (and, in his day, most of these belonged in what he called the
second half of life, i.e. they had already fulfilled their professional, family and
other social obligations). But he too always insisted that one must have one's
feet firmly planted in reality before exploring one's inner world. Sub-Rector
Paulmann may illustrate the majority 'who won't go up the ladder at all'. Reg-
istrar Heerbrand may belong to either the category who keep their feet 'fixed
firmly in every-day life' or those who 'turn giddy by the time they get to the
third rung' (there isn't enough evidence to be certain in which of these to place
him; but see Crisman 1994). The hero, in contrast, does not belong in any of
these three categories: Anselmus may have climbed the ladder, but he is not
firmly anchored 'in every-day life'. He has been carried away by the images he
has encountered in the reality of his own imagination. Jung described this condition as possession.

Hoffmann repeatedly underlines this point. At the outset of the 'Second
Vigil', a passer-by remarks about Anselmus: 'That gentleman doesn't seem right
in the head' (Hoffmann 1814/1992, p. 7) – which, given that Anselmus is
hugging a tree as she speaks, is a delightful example of understatement. A short
while later, he sinks into 'a dreamy, brooding state which made him insensible
to all contact with ordinary life' (Hoffmann 1814/1992, p. 21). And, as he begins
to settle into his job as copyist, 'the wonders and marvels which Anselmus met
with every day ... altogether estranged him from ordinary life. He no longer saw
any of his friends, and each morning he waited impatiently for twelve o'clock,
which admitted him to his paradise' (Hoffmann 1814/1992, p. 59). His paradise
consists of chatting with a little green snake with dark-blue eyes. Anselmus has
lost all contact with his immediate social reality. He has become a 'tiresome
fellow' (Hoffmann 1814/1992, p. 77) who has lost his way in life.

One doesn't need Jung to interpret the tale. If one can resist being misled by
Hoffmann's irony, it interprets itself: indeed, in Jung's own terms, it is self-
evidently 'psychological literature'; all the Jungian could do is throw some
jargon (e.g. shadow, anima, self, *puer aeternus*) around the obviously intended
reading – without adding a great deal to it. Jung is always being accused of

mystification. But aren't those who have seen the final Vigil as Hoffmann's only happy ending (and countless critics have insisted on this) equally, and perhaps even more guilty of mystification?

Todorov very sensibly reminds us that we sometimes have to control our compulsion to interpret. Hoffmann tempts his readers into believing that there is a physical cause for what Anselmus experiences. Many critics cling to these explanations, as they seem to explain the inexplicable. But they are missing the point. Hoffmann goes to inordinate lengths to insist that readers hold incompatible possibilities in balance. In other words, that they both *note* the parallels established between the social and imaginal realms, and yet also *accept* the existence of magnificent blue-eyed snakes that talk to one from the branches of a tree. He does not want the reader to read allegorically. If all one can take away from the tale is that Anselmus is something of a *puer aeternus*, then one might as well not have read it.

The point of the tale lies in the ceaselessly witty instability of the narrative. Hoffmann was writing 15 years after Novalis. He was clearly both attracted by and also uncomfortable with the somewhat precious seriousness of Novalis. He parodied it in 'The Golden Pot', not because he believed the inner world was any less valuable than Novalis thought it was, but because he had his feet more firmly planted in reality. He realised instinctively that one cannot renounce life, as Anselmus does, and drift away in one's imagination to 'Atlantis'. The value of the Novelle, the Märchen, and the fantastic is that they explore an element that burst into European literature at the end of the eighteenth century: the tension between the real and the imaginal. As soon as we fix on what Todorov called either an allegorical or a poetic interpretation, we lose this tension – and, with it, the pleasure that comes from being able to 'contemplate' – i.e. explore – the significance of this tension for ourselves and so further reflect on the phenomenology of experience.

Conclusion

The critical temper has changed since the 1950s. Hoffmann is no longer regarded as 'a guiding spirit full of knowledge, faith, and beneficent clarity'; he is valued, to borrow from Reddick (1969, 1976), for the range and variety of his irony. 'The Golden Pot' is infused with a dark and restless, but also playful, imagination. It is difficult to understand how Jung could have regarded such a consistently ironic narrative about a student pining for a little snake as 'visionary' literature. Not every salamander belongs to the unmediated inner world and not every text with a happy ending is about individuation. It all depends on the nature of the interactions and the tone. In Hoffmann's first draft, 'the golden pot' was 'a golden chamber pot' and when the hero 'pisses into it the first time he turns into a long-tailed monkey' (Hoffmann 1967, p. 203): this should have sufficed to warn Jaffé that her author had not only a wacky and mischievous sense of humour, but also the good sense to keep it under firm control. Precisely because the author considerably revised his initial conception, it neither pertains to the 'visionary' mode nor does it illustrate an initial stage in the process of individuation. It is a prime example of what Todorov defined as the fantastic.

Writers work in different ways and at different speeds, but very few texts span the same number of years as one needs to produce the kind of change at issue in individuation. And 'consciousness' may not be the best measure of its occurrence. Whether individuation has been achieved is possibly more easily established by assessing the nature of the main protagonist's engagement with his experience. Anselmus does not engage with his. He merely surrenders to his experience. He swoons, he goes into ecstasies, but he never wonders why he might be falling in love with a creature from an imaginal world, i.e. a projection of his own inner world. He makes no connection between his interest in Veronica and Serpentina, and thus he cannot even begin to reflect on, let alone work toward correcting his wrong-headedness. And there can be no individuation without such sustained engagement – in other words, without persuasive evidence that the author has struggled with his or her inappropriate tendencies and come to new terms with them.

References

Bair, D. (2003) *Jung: A Biography*. Boston: Little, Brown & Co.

Bishop, P. (2008) *Analytical Psychology and German Classical Aesthetics: Goethe, Schiller, and Jung*. London: Routledge.

Brooke, R. (1991) *Jung and Phenomenology*. London: Routledge.

Brooke, R. (1999) *Pathways into the Jungian World*. London: Routledge.

Crisman, W. (1994) Registrator Heerbrand, Fantasy broker and forgotten figure in Hoffmann's *Goldner Topf*. *Germanic Notes and Reviews* 25(2), 8–11.

Daemmrich, H. (1973) *The Shattered Self: E. T. A. Hoffmann's Tragic Vision*. Detroit: Wayne State University Press.

Dawson, T. (2008) Literary Criticism and Analytical Psychology. In: P. Young-Eisendrath and T. Dawson (Eds), *The Cambridge Companion to Jung* (2nd edition). Cambridge: Cambridge University Press.

Ellenberger, H. F. (1970) *The Discovery of the Unconscious: The History and Evolution of Dynamic Psychiatry*. New York: Basic Books.

Freud, S. (1907) Delusions and dreams in Jensen's *Gradiva. The Standard Edition of the Complete Works of Sigmund Freud* (Vol. IX). Hogarth Press and the Institute of Psychoanalysis, 1953–1974.

Goethe, J. W. (1808/1987) *Faust: The First Part of the Tragedy*. Oxford: Oxford University Press.

Goethe, J. W. (1809/1971) *Elective Affinities*. Harmondsworth: Penguin.

Grimm, J. and Grimm, W. (1812–1815/1975) *Grimm's Fairy Tales*. London: Routledge & Kegan Paul.

Hannah, B. (1981) *Encounters with the Soul: Active Imagination as Developed by C. G. Jung*. Santa Monica CA: Sigo.

Hoffmann, E. T. A. (1886/1892) *The Serapion Brethren* (Vol. 1 & 2) London: George Bell.

Hoffmann, E. T. A. (1967) *Selected Letters*. Chicago: University of Chicago Press.

Hoffmann, E. T. A. (1814/1992) *The Golden Pot and Other Tales*. Oxford: Oxford University Press.

Jaffé, A. (1950/1978) *Bilder und Symbole aus E. T. A. Hoffmanns Märchen, Der goldne Topf zweite, veränderte Auflage*. Hildesheim: Gerstenberg.

Jones, E. (1910) The Oedipus-Complex as an explanation of Hamlet's mystery: a study in motive. *The American Journal of Psychology* 21, 72–113.

Jung, C. G.: Unless otherwise stated, the following are from *The Collected Works of C. G. Jung*. (CW). London: Routledge & Kegan Paul/Princeton, NJ: Princeton University Press:

Jung, C. G. (1912) *Psychology of the Unconscious*. (CW 8).

Jung, C. G. (1916) The structure of the unconscious. (CW 7).

Jung, C. G. (1921) *Psychological Types*. (CW 6).

Jung, C. G. (1922) On the relation of analytical psychology to poetry. (CW 15).

Jung, C. G. (1929) The aims of psychotherapy. (CW 16).

Jung, C. G. (1930) Psychology and literature. (CW 15).

Jung, C. G. (1934) A study in the process of individuation. (CW 9i).

Jung, C. G. (1938) Psychology and religion. (CW 11).

Jung, C. G. (1939) Psychological commentary on *The Tibetan Book of the Great Liberation*. (CW 11).

Jung, C. G. (1940) Concerning rebirth. (CW 9i).

Jung, C. G. (1944) *Psychology and Alchemy*. (CW 12).

Jung, C. G. (1950a) *Gestaltungen des Unbewussten. Psychologische Abhandlungen* 7 (with a contribution by Aniela Jaffé). Zurich: Rascher.

Jung, C. G. (1950b) Concerning Mandala symbolism. (CW5).

Jung, C. G. (1952a) Symbols of transformation. (CW5).

Jung, C. G. (1952b) 'Reply to Martin Buber'. (CW18).

Jung, C. G. (1952c) *Answer to Job*. (CW11).

Jung, C. G. (1955a) *Mysterium Conjunctionis*. (CW14).

Jung, C. G. (1955b) Synchronicity: an acausal connecting principle. (CW8).

Jung, C. G. (1967) *Alchemical Studies*. (CW13).

Jung, C. G. (1973/1976) *Letters* (Vol. I & II). London: Routledge & Kegan Paul.

McGlathery, J. (1981) *Mysticism and Sexuality: E. T. A. Hoffmann: Part I, Hoffmann and His Sources*. New York: Peter Lang.

McGlathery, J. (1997) *E. T. A. Hoffmann*. New York: Twayne.

Montfaucon, Villars de (1670/1922) *Comte de Gabalis*. London: Macoy & Masonic Supply Co.

Novalis (1802/1964) *Henry von Ofterdingen*. New York: Ungar.

Nygaard, L. C. (1983) Anselmus as amanuensis: the motif of copying in Hoffmann's *Der goldne Topf*. *Seminar: A Journal of Germanic Studies* 19, 79–104.

Pope, A. (1714/2006) The rape of the lock. In: P. Rogers (Ed.), *The Major Works*. Oxford: Oxford University Press.

Rank, O. (1909/1914) *The Myth of the Birth of the Hero*. New York: Nervous & Mental Disease Publishing Co.

Rank, O. (1907/1989) *The Artist*. New York: W. W. Norton.

Reddick, J. (1969) E. T. A. Hoffmann. In: A. Natan (Ed.), *German Men of Letters* (Vol. 5). London: Oswald Wolff.

Reddick, J. (1976) E. T. A. Hoffmann's *Der goldne Topf* and its *Durchgehaltene Ironie*. *Modern Language Review* 71, 577–594.

Riklin, F. (1908/1915) *Wish Fulfilment and Symbolism in Fairy Tales*. New York: Nervous & Mental Disease.

Todorov, T. (1970/1975) *The Fantastic: A Structural Approach to a Literary Genre*. Cornell: Cornell University Press.

Tully, C. (Ed.) (2000) *Romantic Fairy Tales: Goethe, Tieck, Fouqué, and Brentano*. Harmondsworth: Penguin.

von Kleist, H. (1978) *The Marquise von O – and Other Stories*. Harmondsworth: Penguin.

Woltmann, K. L. (1815) *Jenaische Allgemeine Literatur-Zeitung* 12, no. 232.

Chapter 8

Affectivity in *narratio* and individuation

Leslie Gardner

This chapter focuses on affectivity and its problematic use in the Jungian process of individuation, using correlative struggles engaged in by ancient rhetoricians in considering the forensic technique of *narratio*. The ancients were well aware of the difficulties, ethical and instrumental, of using affect as a marker or signifier, and particularly as a component of *narratio* in a courtroom case. *Narratio* provides the rhetor the opportunity to present a narrative account of what happened, in a particular and persuasive way, thereby setting out and influencing the nature of the case.

Jung's individuation process relies on spontaneous and transformative encounters with the unconscious marked and revealed by the emotion at the moment of its occurrence. Guided by an analyst, the individual's rational, conscious self encounters elements of the unconscious on its way toward becoming an integrated personality. Jung based this opinion on his empirical observations. He talks about his theory multiple times in his writings, but this chapter will draw on 'Part II: Individuation' of 'The Relations Between the Ego and the Unconscious' (Jung 1928) and on his narration of a sequence of developments in 'A Study in the Process of Individuation' (Jung 1934/1950, hereinafter 'the Study'), focusing on the 'irruptions' of emotion.

Emotion in an individuation process guided by an analyst resembles a courtroom case guided by the rhetor insofar as it is either undermined by the emotion – due to the distortions that emotion could create (as a critic may see it) – or benefits by it. A rhetor can use emotion to assert persuasion. Is it unfair manipulation or a legitimate device for obtaining agreement?

Jung's case study

We learn in the Study that Miss X came to Jung with her problems, seeking him out, having read his works. She feels anxiety and that she is blocked. Upon meeting him, she has a compulsive desire to paint despite not knowing how. He encourages her since he feels it is clearly her unconscious directing her to do so. In her first paintings, she portrays him as a wizard, as he interprets it. He comments:

She did not want to know how liberation might be possible in a general way but how and in what way it could come about for her. And about this I knew as little as she. I know that such solutions can only come about in an individual way that cannot be foreseen.

(Jung 1934/1950, para. 528)

And later, regarding 'these paradoxical and hardly explicable statements of the unconscious,' he comments, 'they are not inventions of any conscious mind, but are spontaneous manifestations of a psyche not controlled by consciousness and obviously possessing all the freedom it wants to express views that take no account of our conscious intentions' (Jung 1934/1950, para. 555).

He points out that spontaneous 'irruptions' are typical of the process. It is his interpretation of the nature of those emotional outbursts by his amplifications that make them meaningful. And being spontaneous, these emotions are also uncontrolled, as he says elsewhere about the unconscious,

As the result of the repressive attitude of the conscious mind, the other side is driven into indirect and purely symptomatic manifestations mostly of an emotional kind, and only in moments of overwhelming affectivity can fragments of the unconscious come to the surface in the form of thoughts or images.

(Jung 1928, para. 323)

Further, he proposes they are a difficulty for the patient in a variety of ways, one being they are not comprehensible to the conscious mind:

the ego momentarily identifies with these utterances, only to revoke them in the same breath. And indeed the things once said when in the grip of an affect sometimes seem very strange and daring. But they are easily forgotten or wholly denied.

(Jung 1928, para. 323)

Spontaneity is indicative of the *purity* of the irruption of emotion in Jung's observance. He assumes that the emotion lacks contrived intention or forethought. These manifestations mark something repressed, and the associated affect makes them visible (or marked). Next, there is the issue of isolating the individual's self-recognition in this display, no matter how the analyst may tailor it all to the patient.

Jung characterises Miss X (a middle-aged unmarried American) as an overly intellectual, self-pitying woman, suffering from childlessness, alienated from her mother's land (Denmark), and overwhelmed by her animus (the masculine element) which is making her ill. Like other women suffering from these problems, she lives among a group of intellectual, unmarried women. As we critique his analysis, we come across problems with it on several levels. It seems he finds a myth that would match so that he can interpret it the way he frames her experiences.

Exploring a black snake that is outside a circle image in her painting (Picture 4), having dismissed the easy solution that it is related to sex (with which she concurs), he reports:

> After this picture, she felt the renewed penetration of the red colour, which she associated with feeling as something disturbing and she now discovered her 'rapport' with me, her analyst (= father), was unnatural and unsatisfactory ... she had to admit she felt very silly and was very silly regardless of what I thought about it.... This admission brought her a feeling of great relief....
>
> (Jung 1934/1950, para. 586)

He continues:

> On the days following, the patient was overcome by feelings of self-pity. It became clear to her how much she regretted never having had any children.... Only when she had completely given way to these feelings could she bring herself to paint another picture. Real liberation comes not from glossing over or repressing painful states of feeling but only from experiencing them to the full.
>
> (Jung 1934/1950, para. 587)

Did this self-pity originate in her feeling herself to be a social failure or from feeling a thwarted personal desire? Given his assumptions about the anima (the feminine principle) and how it plays out in an unmarried woman, he is not fully in a position to know how to read this. And given her immersion in the same cultural matrix, it would be difficult for her to work this out too. Was she keen to subscribe to his theories, and so play to his interpretations? The feelings here are suspect, in other words.

Another angle emerges too: they both dismiss the Freudian symbol of the snake who appears to be unable to penetrate the circle she'd drawn. They both dismiss the 'easy' interpretation of a sexual connotation. Is Jung perhaps countering his objection to Freud finding sex everywhere?

One of the bigger questions about individuation is the issue of knowing what is genuine and what is contrived about an emotion. It is nearly impossible for either analyst or patient to make a judgement on this. Miss X's untrained, spontaneous paintings (which nevertheless somehow developed sophistication as she continued) lead him to determine that her issues were about problems with her mother and her too-highly developed rational self. This longing to reconnect or become unblocked from her attitude about her mother's homeland in Picture 1, for example, is interpreted by Jung as depicting a stated discomfort with and distaste for her mother. The painting shows several spherical rocks and a crudely drawn woman whose feet are firmly embedded in one of the rocks:

The picture shows first of all her imprisoned state, but not yet the act of liberation. So it was there that she was attached to the earth, in the land of her mother. Psychologically this state means being caught in the unconscious her inadequate relation to her mother had left behind something dark and in need of development.

(Jung 1934/1950, para. 526)

She concurs, but is that what it is? Neither Jung nor Miss X figure in any subjective aims or various cultural assumptions that might taint the 'irruptions'. Was she agreeing to his mythologically-led interpretation because she had read much of his work, and knew he would tend in this way? Was she unwittingly setting up a picture to help this analysis?

If interpreted properly and with the knowledge Jung has of mythological symbols and images, the images and emotions they inspire can be made to seem to have a compensatory effect on the one-sidedness of personality. In Jung's theory of the integration of the self, it is axiomatic that one-sidedness is a major flaw. One-sidedness means that parts of what make up the whole of the Self are suppressed and these aspects need probing to unblock the personality. In the Study, he continually regards Miss X's one-sided intellectualising as a flaw, which her paintings disclose

the unconscious tends to regard spirit and matter not merely as equivalent but as actually identical. This is in flagrant contrast to the intellectual one sidedness of consciousness, which would sometimes like to spiritualise matter and at other times to materialise spirit.

(Jung 1934/1950, para. 553)

Her pictures separate these elements unsatisfactorily and so she is troubled just there.

The difficulty here is the supposition about spontaneity and its equation to genuineness. Spontaneity remains an unexamined formula. She came to him originally as if to a wizard (his interpretation of her own analogy, represented in her Picture 1). She has certain assumptions about how to communicate with him. Making certain that she is 'genuine' is just one of those assumptions she plays to, as between patient and analyst. Yet it is one of the crucial signs or marks of a significant step in confronting the unconscious. He does not sense she might be playing his tune – but we may (after all, she had read his works and came to Zurich to study under him) – and she may not realise it either. She was struggling, but 'it is her idea to proceed' with only a few prompts from him, and he comments, 'I could already see what solution the unconscious had in mind, namely individuation, for this is the transformation process that loosens the attachment to the unconscious' (Jung 1934/1950, para. 530). He clearly has suppositions about what he expects.

We see his expectation of what Miss X might be about years before he sets out the Study – ideas already in place in the earlier essay (Jung 1928). He follows a discussion of *persona* with a discussion of the anima which typically, he says, manifests in bursts of emotion that sometimes overtake consciousness (which he associates with rationality). In the Study he comments that Miss X has problems with the animus in her personality; she is fixed on over-intellectualism. Rationality is dispassionate, and so the clear marker of some disruption is manifest in her extreme discomfort with herself. These blurts of feeling that drove her to find him indicate where the blocks are. He does not refer to her thinking process much, but traces her feeling outbursts and amplifies her narrative with references to mythic and occult sources to display that a pure reaction is at stake. In his perspective, in keeping with his cultural world, thinking is 'dispassionate'. His argument develops using a commentary on the anima that is widely contested among Jungians. His attribution of empathy and emotion to the female principle (which is clearly out of sync with post-Jungian and most feminist commentaries) contributes to assumptions he has of Miss X.

The ego, associated with consciousness in his model of the Self, is overcome by emotion– and, as far as the conscious 'side' of the person can tell, there isn't necessarily an obvious purpose to this irruption. The 'other side', the unconscious, has its own autonomous directions and purposes, probably compensatory. And there Jung (1928, para. 323) finds some function: 'the other side is driven into indirect and purely symptomatic manifestations, mostly of an emotional kind, and only in moments of overwhelming affectivity can fragments of the unconscious come to the surface in the form of thoughts or images'.

Once the irruption has occurred you might observe it, but only when it has passed over. You cannot grasp it sooner. He emphasises the spontaneity of these early outbursts as indications of their *purity* which is, I'd propose, another assumption about spontaneity (and the impossibility of reckoning it). Pure, spontaneous emotions lack contrived intention or forethought. There are 'repressed' images and the associated affect assists in making them 'visible' (or marked):

> Our instincts have ridden so infinitely many times, unharmed, over the problems that arise at this stage of life that we maybe sure the transformation processes which make the transition possible have long been prepared in the unconscious and are only waiting to be released.
>
> (Jung 1934/1950, para. 528)

Narratio and affect (part I)

Transformations in action and in personality manifest in ways that are inflected by emotion in stories told to yourself and to others. In the analytic relationship, this story and how it is recounted is the material with which the doctor and patient grapple. Contexts and cultural assumptions play a significant role. The ancients devised techniques to exploit or at least to accommodate those agendas. This accommodation makes *narratio* and other rhetorical terms seem relativist – indeed, rhetoric is considered a relativist endeavour. But it is not. Interactions are situated most specifically for the person in place and time, and in the solutions taken to live in that place and time. This philosophical attitude stretches back centuries in disputes between philosophers and rhetoricians, since a time when the two 'disciplines' separated paths. Individuation engages with a dialectic of ground and time, in the interactions of consciousness and unconsciousness, yet it is not always recognised. By exploring the place of affect in *narratio*, I hope to show that the difficulties were experienced by the ancients in ways that it is instructive to consider.

The Sophists, Gorgias (*c.*485–380 BC) as well as others, were by far the rhetoricians most implicated in using the notion of plausibility or viability as a persuasive goal, rather than cold 'truth' as philosophers aimed to discover. The eighteenth-century rhetorician, Giambattista Vico argued throughout his works that viability was the best humans could do. Latching on to axiomatic interpretations of emotional reaction, as Jung does, would be probed by sophists (albeit in some ways Jung's attitude elsewhere that whatever works in healing is good, is shared with the sophistical doctor, Hippocrates (*c.*460–370 BC)).

Persuasive argument in rhetoric is built most effectively by the plausible intertwining of telling and 'fact' as explored by the first-century Roman pedagogue and rhetorician Quintilian (*c.* AD 35–100), and it is the basis of the art of *narratio*, indeed the art of rhetoric itself. The 'viability' of being a woman comporting herself in a certain way here and now permeates modes of self-presentation and self-exploration. Gorgias explores viabilities in what is his disruptive *epideictic*, the discourse *Encomium for Helen*. Quintilian's lament in Book 6 of *Institutio oratorae* had multiple pragmatic purposes too despite that it moves us and appears genuine due to his skill.

Use of affect in *narratio* was associated particularly with a sophistical approach to persuasion. Was affect always spontaneous and explosive as it was often designed to seem? There was much disagreement among the ancients about this. Was it legitimate to use emotion in arguing a case at all? In fact, Leigh (2004) speculates that there may have been a ban at one time on using passion or pathos in Athenian courts. Rhetors presenting cases were barred from manipulating the jury by using emotion. He suggests that this was an ancillary discussion presented by a contesting school of rhetors, the Stoics, who proposed that the opening remarks, the *peroration*, might be separated into only two parts for best effect. A great disagreement followed.

Chrysippus (*c.*279–206 BC), a Stoic commentator, repudiated the use of affect in persuasion because its subjective component was hard to assess, and it could link you to your adversary in underhand ways. Was that reported sadness planned or genuine? Who was the laughter aimed at? What kind of laugh? Or the anger? And it also had an underhand effect on the audience/jury, distracting them from the main issue at hand. Chrysippus' suggestion is that the *peroration* be separated into two parts: (1) a dispassionate, composed presentation of facts, and (2) at time of determination later in the procedure, bringing up the emotional aspect. In this way a trial could be successfully worked out best with clarity and impartiality.

In contrast, Quintilian and Cicero argued that the *peroration* might include four parts: (1) argument first of all to win the sympathy of the listener, then (2) emphasis on the necessary elements/facts of the case, and then (3) remind the listeners of past/similar event and outcomes, and (4) indeed then, put the listener in an emotional state. Leigh reports on Cicero's account of the case of a Stoic, Rutilius, who was on trial. The rigorous Stoic presented his case in a plain account with 'no groans, no shouting, no weeping,' and was subsequently convicted (Leigh 2004, p. 129). The lesson was clear.

Narratio is a feature of one of the five important canons of rhetoric within the three categories of forensic, deliberative and epideictic rhetoric. It is called *inventio*. The other four canons, as set out in Cicero's *De inventio*, are: *dispositio* (arrangement), *elocutio* (style), *memoria* (memory), *actia* (delivery). As a form of narration, *narratio* inevitably relies on the tropes and unstated, taken-for-granted 'middle terms' embedded in the particular culture. Common sense, common parlance, and cultural norms of behaviour enter here. Indeed, forms of affect are one such category of 'middle terms'.

Unstated assumptions throw up difficulties about personality which are related to the use of *narratio* that I will explore in discussion of Gorgias' *Encomium of Helen* and Quintilian.

Affect as a 'middle term'

Affect and its uses are complex. There are ethical problems as well as cultural differences. As a scientist, Jung had a commitment to dispassion in assessing the results of his psychological enquiries. This scientific attitude initially reflects Aristotle's views: it is a commitment to *logos* but then Aristotle developed an important consideration in his *Rhetoric*: the 'truncated' syllogism, the enthymeme. Aristotle (1926, Book 1 part 1) sets out a persuasive argument for logic as an effective sequence for the rhetor, but suggested that 'probabilities' were the surest routes to obtaining agreement and more natural to the skill and art of rhetoric. A probable 'truth' was the best we could do, given that logical premises were opinion for the most part in any case. Emotion could add truth value to a statement. But it was a dangerous tool because it was unreliable and had to be played carefully.

Affect is a bridging mechanism that we may associate to the 'middle term' – a concept used in setting out the premises of an argument pertinent to the rhetorical equivalent of the syllogism (the logical sequence Aristotle refers to in *Rhetoric* and elsewhere), the *enthymeme*. Vico (1996, p. xx) called the *enthymeme* a 'defective' syllogism because it is derived from the syllogism but misses that third or middle term. The enthymeme constructs equivalence from two terms of comparison. In comparing it to the syllogism, it will become clear how they differ.

The classic example of a syllogism is set out in three terms: 'all men are mortal; Socrates is a man; therefore, Socrates is mortal'. The enthymeme is a 'truncated' syllogism – i.e. a syllogism with an unstated premise: 'Socrates is mortal because he's human'; in other words, that 'middle' term is the unstated premise, which allows the listener or reader to make a connection – what's missing is the proposition that all humans are mortal. In this case, the equivalence of 'human' to 'mortal' is assumed. This missing term/premise is the 'third' or 'middle' term that relies on assumptions of meanings embedded in the beliefs and suppositions of the culture which the rhetor shares with her audience. ('Third' because if it were a syllogism, there would be three explicit and stated terms; the *enthymeme* has two stated and explicit terms, relying on the mediating or 'middle' term which is the 'third' here, missing!)

Affect is linked in dynamic and convincing ways to the enthymeme. Passion – *pathos* as it is called in rhetorical terminology – is effective in setting up the argument, in the *peroration* (its introduction). If it is effectively invoked, the 'third' or 'middle term' brings cultural and everyday grounded-ness to the table; emotion inflects the argument, sets its tone, disrupting a 'logical' formula by inference. In effect, the audience itself supplies a major premise of the proposition making it highly effective by deeply engaging that audience.

However, there was much discussion about the evolution of Aristotle's original idea of the enthymeme. The core point about it is its capacity to evolve alongside the culture. The syllogism is a logical form based on truths; which are in turn based on logical and 'dispassionate' workings-out. By definition, it should not change. But, over time, 'probabilities' began invading 'truths' and as a matter of fact its invasion began right from the inception of the concept of the syllogism. Emotion is a contentious aspect of sequence or of the equations of the enthymeme too. As a short example, Nussbaum (2003, p. 140) points out that sadness is expressed in Balinese culture by laughter – smiling is an emotional display to demonstrate that the reactor is deflecting sadness in this way – and she suggests that it is compensatory, serving to adjust emotional well-being. So when we read a sad story (or hear one), and the teller laughs, or we are directed to laugh, there is a disconnect for us witnessing Balinese reaction. The point is that emotion is culture-specific too.

The enthymeme, or middle term, is an unstated premise and a standard part of *narratio* since a sequence of events relies on our instinctively sharing with the rhetor what might make up a sequence itself. Underlying an order or a reasonable sequence of events are the assumptions of the telling. The rhetor manipulates that sequence if she understands the unstated premises well enough and can use affect to do so. Similarly a patient may engage in emotion telling her story – or in discovering an unconscious block (seeming to be overcome spontaneously by sobbing, for example) – for the purposes of gaining sympathy to herself illicitly, as a display designed to gain attention where it might not be called for, rather than as a marker of 'real' confrontation. As seen, Jung (1934/1950) in his case study insists on the genuineness of spontaneity that his patient displays through her paintings and reflections, which probe her own mental health issues. But it is not so easy.

In his discussion of Quintilian, for whom *narratio* was core to the practice of rhetoric/persuasion, Vico (1996) proposed that the 'middle term' is itself at the heart of the art of rhetoric. Vico followed Aristotle in calling the specific syllogism of rhetorical form, an *enthymeme* (not all commentators were respectful of Aristotle's formula). This assumption about the 'middle term' (stressing here 'middle' as mediation) is directly dependent on contexts or *topos* assumed in a culture. As is apparent, these shifting contexts or cultural *topos* make 'truth' problematic – 'truth' which the logical form, the syllogism, relies on (however, increasingly 'logic' came under tension – over time the idea of the enthymeme began to take precedence over the syllogism in considerations of what 'logic' is; 'logic' came to be seen as formulated by 'opinion' and as having a paradoxical and rhetorical nature; this became increasingly the dominant idea).

To summarise: the 'middle term' of a syllogism, when missing in its 'truncated' derivative form, the *enthymeme*, connects the major premise (first term) to the final premise (the third term). The link derives from contexts expressed often wordlessly in emotion. Emotion could destabilise *syllogisms*, adding irony for example to angry or judgemental statements such as this formula, delivered with a snort by the teller: 'Dogs sniff with their noses. Jack sniffs with his nose. So Jack is a dog.' Enthymemes with their accommodation of 'probability' are more commonplace especially and prevalently in rhetorical statements or sequences of fact. General cultural (or emotional) frameworks provide instinctive underlying parameters within which particulars take on sense, connecting even paradoxically particular 'commonplaces' (which were generally thought to be universal motifs) to the subject – I paraphrase Quintilian (1920) here in *Institutio Oratoriae*: Bk 2.4.30. As Verene (1981) puts it in his discussion of Vico's gloss on Quintilian:

> The art of generating the middle term … makes possible any particular line of reasoning … the middle terms refer to the self-coherence of thought, the ability to connect thoughts conceptually. The *syllogism* is not just a framework for expression of truths in correct form, but a process through which probable truths can be formed.
>
> (Verene 1981, p. 47)

Narratio and affect (part 2)

In its 'truncated' form, the enthymeme deals with coordinates of 'plausible' or 'viable' event; that is, a different category than a 'truth' event. In its sequencing of events, narration – indeed most pointedly its forensic aspect, *narratio*, as played out in a field of assessment like a courtroom – is reliant on audience assumptions. It is people telling their stories with an unrolling future in mind, declarations about how events for them must be seen to play out. In this way, *narratio* is a term from juridical or forensic rhetoric which pre-positions decisions about the future (or proposes to orient a future) by how a story is told;

it is a presentation of how a story might be put to best effect (which is undoubtedly an instinctive aim of individuation too) as a way forward; as a way to live ahead.

Affect plays a different role in the standard rhetorical categories. Past actions that the rhetor uses in deliberative rhetoric to asses and then to incite her audience to new action may provoke violent rage rather than passive indignation. In epideictic, weeping at the heroic activity of the subject of the oration may intervene as a subjective element in helping the rhetor to establish a view of the individual. So it may be used with less controversy.

Forensic rhetoric as displayed in *narratio* is conceived as a means to a preconceived end; and this strategic series aims at a planned sense of how a story and its players develop. You find just what you look for. The rhetor in a courtroom seeks to plant that seed for her purposes. Emotion here is legitimately contrived with a sense of a future goal – seeking to achieve an aim of defending a client.

One example is the one that Vico (1996) raises in his *Art of Rhetoric* (compiled by students based on his lectures). To plead her cause, answering to a charge of theft, a woman brings her children to the court with her to shift her case from a consideration of theft to a visual consideration of the necessity for charity and the demands of poverty. As readers, we approve this manoeuvre (as Vico recounts it) but it would be even better if the children were weeping which would be even more effective! Her poverty and her children's suffering make the argument without words. Weeping is one of the most empathy-inducing affects if used with discretion (Vico 1996, p. 61).

In an authoritative article about Quintilian, O'Banion (1987) argues that for Quintilian *narratio* is core to rhetorical studies in persuasion. His students from an early age were taught to pick out salient facts in people's stories. Fictional tales by Aesop or mythical stories by Homer were used to hone this technique. It is a crucial stage in a kind of argument comprising the *dispositio* (arrangement) which proposes, in the form of a story, a continuity that highlights the sequence of events constituting the 'case'. In the courtroom, *dispositio* is the argument's presentation in full with all elements of persuasion included – not only logical and narratival argument, but also material proofs, witness statements, etc.;

> *Narratio*, as an element in *dispositio*, sets out a dialectic of 'fact' and telling
> … but since 'fact' does not communicate the meaning of the case (*causa*)
> one could say that *narratio* is a dialectic of causes and telling, of motives
> and telling, of situations and the explaining of them.
>
> (O'Banion 1987, p. 343)

The other form of argument, logic, proposes 'a series of coherent "proofs" that emphasize logical coherence' (O'Banion 1987, p. 344). O'Banion explains too that narrative is also embedded in a logical sequence. Finding patterns in stories was a prerequisite to the ability to perceive such patterns in the human dramas in which, and to which, oration was a response. And further, to pick up from earlier discussion here, *narratio* works with bridging by affect to 'the middle term'.

A classic example of the many uses of affect is a dazzling display of rhetorical flourish written by Quintilian in the opening of Book III of *Institutio oratores* (Quintilian 1920). Quintilian describes how he came to write his major work in retirement. Two personally shattering events occurred: the death of his young wife, and the death of his young son whose prowess as a rhetorician was already in evidence. He tells of these events with great sorrow and we are moved. He'd thought he would devote himself to training his son who would become his best friend, according to his principles of pedagogy. The boy had great talent. But there was another agenda. Quintilian says he has taken up writing this book after he stepped down from working for Domitian; he now has time to mourn and write. Truth is, he'd better have had a good reason for that initiative, since it is a resignation that may well have offended the tyrant whose time had come.

As in Gorgias' *Encomium for Helen* (to which I will turn next), we have a dilemma in discerning purposes. Gorgias' work is framed as an exercise in *epideictic*: praise or blame. He uses logical argument addressing the rational process of mind, but underlying it is a predisposition to subliminal emotive persuasion. We are aware of the dialectic of the discussion: sometimes appealing to emotion, otherwise also asking us for judgement, which calls plausibility into question. He makes no appeal to 'truth'. Neither does Quintilian. And we suspect also that this too is a bravura piece written to attract new customers to purchase his services as rhetor. Nowhere is there a warning, for example, to beware of what the gods demand, or to resist the desires that overwhelm you, or to parse out speech so that it does not act as a drug on you, to do something against your will. Similarly, in Quintilian's *peroration*, which leads to a discussion of affect's power to win your point, do we suspect Quintilian's sincerity when we know the personal background? He uses his lamentation as an example of the technique, as a pedagogic exercise; in other words, to counter the claims that emotion is a 'cheap trick'. But how are we to believe him if he's telling the story of his loss for purposes of showing how effective it might be as rhetorical technique? And also he arranges a dangerous tyrant's assessment of his withdrawal from his court (but not quite beyond his reach).

Gorgias has a different use of affect to display in the *Encomium*. It is in Homer's *The Odyssey* that we hear the tale of the beautiful Helen whose adultery and flight with Paris was the cause of the Trojan war. Helen is an emblematic figure, 'collective' in that she has that fixed tarnished status, rigidly held in a time and place – or so it was thought before Gorgias and Euripides (see his play *Helen*, first performed in 412 BC) explored other perspectives.

Helen is 'the beauty that launched a thousand ships', and other women are called 'Helen' with that in mind. Gorgias tells us that Helen is 'a woman concerning whom the testimony of inspired poets has become univocal and unanimous as had the ill omen of her name, which has become tarnished as a reminder of misfortune' (Gorgias, in Sprague 2001, p. 51). Gorgias proposes that Helen should suffer no unjust blame for causing the war, and be exonerated from her infidelity since it was either fate, the gods, logos or Eros (love) which compelled her, and so, she is blameless.

What is considered deviant in a particular time and place might be normative in another time and place. Gorgias argued out Helen's case both ways (the day before he orated his *Encomium* he had already set out the case against her) but it is the defence of her behaviour that brought him crowds and notice. She is either an adulterous woman, or a besieged person, plaything of the gods, suffering her fate in which she is a passive participant. Settling with such multiplicities of perspectives, and deploying meaningful communication accommodating those interiors is what I'd propose individuation is about. But more of that after a brief further exploration of sophistry in telling stories in the sophistic way, with intent.

Narratio and sophistry

Plato may have complained in his *Gorgias* about the rhetor's sophistical practice, which teaches how to argue plausibly both for and against a point of view – and charge money to do so! – but Plato wrote more than one dialogue about that pursuit, and engaged in his own effective powerful speech ploys to make a case against the practice. Telling stories of our lives in the service of achieving goals within the constraints of exigency – the time and place we speak or write from – is the primary frame of human rhetorical practice. Animals may bark or growl, but they don't refer to the narrative of their lives (at least as far as we can tell) to propose their visceral commentary. I'd argue that sophistical rhetoricians particularly concur with Quintilian that *narratio* is a core technique of efficacious communication.

Adept deployment of such a device as *narratio* is not wielded in isolation. When we examine Gorgias' retelling of the tale of Helen, he uses aspects of the framing technique of *inventio* within which *narratio* operates to exonerate her actions, normally thought to have been venal infidelity and perfidy. For Gorgias the sudden decision to follow Paris, her lover refers to an underlying motif of *kairos*, an affective manifestation of a coming together of desire, and action surging up to meet the moment, in space. There is no accounting for *Kairos* – a kind of untethered coming together of action in time and place. The god Amor compelled Helen to follow Paris; or else the power of persuasive talk with equal force, flowing from Paris' mouth – a kind of drug – overcame her to act as she did. Not her fault, then. Gorgias injects pathos into the recounting of her story (who can blame her compliance?) and looks at how she suffered as a result of being uprooted against her will.

She is a daughter from high lineage – a god (Zeus) and Leda – who, with her 'godlike beauty', in many men 'did she work much desire for her love' (Gorgias, frag. 4. in Sprague 2001, p. 5). How could she help being pursued? 'Necessity' compelled her uprooting: rape, or persuaded by speech, or conquered by love. In none of these ways was she complicit. Particularly in the case of speech which is itself 'a powerful lord, which by means of the finest and most invisible body effects the divinest works' (Gorgias, frag. 4. in Sprague 2001, p. 52). As Gorgias puts it:

> Fearful shuddering and tearful pity and grievous longing come upon its hearers, and at actions and physical sufferings of others in good fortunes and in evil fortunes, through the agency of words, the soul is wont to experience a suffering of its own.
>
> (Gorgias, in Sprague 2001, p. 52)

Enchantment and trickery – or magic? Gorgias famous work *On Nature of the Non-Being* sets out further his attitude about the 'plaything' he had made Helen's suffering to represent. She is 'nothing' (a fiction) and so she is 'not being'. Yet, as with other not-beings, she has same status as a 'real' being. To speak of her – emblematic of all beautiful women (since all women are beautiful) relies on a middle term, a bridge about which nothing can be known. By this mechanism, this fiction, 'Helen' is collective, 'universal' as she is non-being, evoked by common discourse and agreement. Perhaps she has more 'being' than individual flesh-and-blood women:

> the nonexistent does not exist; for if the nonexistent exists, it will both exist and not exist at the same time, for insofar as it is understood as nonexistent, it will not exist, but insofar as it *is* nonexistent it will, on the other hand, exist.... The nonexistent, therefore, does not exist.
>
> (Gorgias, in Sprague 2001, p. 43, emphasis in original)

Further, he goes on (I paraphrase here): even if something can be known about it, knowledge about it can't be communicated to others; and even if it can be communicated, it cannot be understood.

True 'objectivity' and emptiness of passion are not possible since the human mind can never be separated from its possessor. Yet passion is a sign of presence, and so moving a listener indicates the presence of a specific kind as communicated by the rhetor or interlocutor. 'We do not reveal existing things to our neighbours but *logos*, which is something other than substances' (Gorgias, frag. 84, in Sprague 2001, p. 52). We reveal only the *logos*, not an existent thing itself. Interacting via *logos* with the non-existent, non-being generates affect if not meaning. Such understanding and use of affect in persuasion is scoffed at by the Stoics. It is a dirty manoeuvre, relying on emotion to scramble judgement.

Quintilian's lament, as mentioned, works also to persuade his audience that his withdrawal was warranted on grounds of pathos. And it served as a pedagogic lesson. It is not a move outside the tenor of the text, however, but it is a seamless part of the discussion of the tenets of rhetoric.

Gorgias' *Encomium* complicates the problematic of the nature of personality in an interesting way. On the surface, attempts at universalising her plight as rape/ abduction victim is best argued out logically, most would agree. And there's another issue: is it not ludicrous to weep for a mythic figure no matter how powerful and astonishing it is? As Hamlet notes, how effective is the power of the actor playing a mythic figure in a play in his uncle's court. And in what sense are we moved? The exploration of Helen's plight, as victim of an overwhelming passion, or the gods' whims in foisting the abduction on her, has an emblematic purpose for Gorgias. He demonstrates the effect of speech on a listener – educating his audience. It is not that we are learning that she is not guilty, but we are focused on the power of speech in his *Encomium*. If that is so, if the sudden imposition of a passion can change the course of history, can a sudden transformative event marked by personal emotion, count as a marker of individuation?

Conclusion

To reiterate, it seems as if Jung's emphasis on the spontaneity of emotion that indicates transformation does not entirely take on an awareness of the contrivances that the use of emotion can involve. The sophistical rhetors especially deploy the energies of *inventio* by building on suggestions of the scope of *narratio* in an argument, and stir up effective emotion, inferring carefully that the assumptions they lean on in their presentation call on subliminal opinion. The spontaneity indicating 'truth' of a mark of transformation may well be calculated for effect but may nonetheless be effective.

References

Aristotle (1926) *Rhetoric* (Translated by J. H. Freese). Cambridge, MA: Harvard University Press.

Jung, C. G. (1928) The relations between the ego and the unconscious. *Collected Works of C. G. Jung* (Vol. 7). London: Routledge.

Jung, C. G. (1934/1950) A Study in the process of individuation. *Collected Works of C. G. Jung* (Vol. 9i). London: Routledge.

Leigh, M. (2004) Quintilian on the emotions (*Institutio Oratoria* 6 Preface and 1–2). *Journal of Roman Studies* 94, 122–140.

Nussbaum, M. (2003) *Upheavals of Thought: The Intelligence of Emotions.* Boston MA: Cambridge University Press.

O'Banion, J. D. (1987) Narration and Argumentation: Quintilian on *Narratio* as the heart of rhetorical thinking. *Rhetorica* 5, 325–351.

Quintilian (1920) *Institutio Oratoria.* Cambridge, MA: Harvard University Press.

Sprague, R. K. (Ed.). (2001) *The Older Sophists.* Indianapolis: Hackett Publishing.

Verene, D. (1981) *Vico's Science of the Imagination.* Ithaca, NY: Cornell University Press.

Vico, G. (1996) *The Art of Rhetoric.* New York: Brill/Rodolpi.

Chapter 9

Co-individuation as an open mandala

Fabrice Olivier Dubosc

In Michel Foucault's (1983) preface to the American edition of Deleuze and Guattari's *Anti-Oedipus* there is a final statement that will sound quite foreign to ears trained in the classical Jungian take on individuation. The quote goes like this:

> Do not demand of politics that it restore the 'rights' of the individual, as philosophy has defined them. The individual is the product of power. What is needed is to 'de-individualize' by means of multiplication and displacement, the layout of diverse combinations. The group must not be the organic bond uniting hierarchized individuals, but a constant generator of de-individualization. Do not become enamoured of power.
>
> (Foucault 1983, p. xiii)

This chapter aims to amplify the above statement and its possible meanings. I shall maintain that the emerging plurality of ethno-narratives and ontologies, the philosophical concept of transindividuation and the anthropological concept of perspectivism, as well as a renewed attention to historical mourning, might help us to unpack the possible meanings of the de-individualising dynamics Foucault had in mind, enriching the idea of 'individuation' with chromatic, plural and relational accents.

De-individualisation stands out as a radical antidote to the 'squaring of the circle' that often informs the hubris of perfectly spherical 'final solutions'. We can find an anthropological manifesto of this perspective in Viveiros de Castro's *Cannibal Metaphysics*:

> Because it is not at all a question, as Derrida opportunely recalled, of preaching the abolition of the borders that unite/separate sign and world, persons and things, 'us' and 'them,' 'humans' and 'nonhumans' … but rather of 'unreducing' [*irréduire*] (Latour) and undefining them, by bending every line of division into an infinitely complex curve. It is not a question of erasing the contours but of folding and making them dense, of diffracting

and making them iridescent.... Chromaticism as the structuralist vocabulary
with which the agenda for its posterity will be written.

(Viveiros de Castro 2014, p. 44)

More humbly, the current intent is to provide here a series of crib sheets including important issues not easily available outside the academy and yet crucial for
contemporary psychosocial research.

Making sense of difference and identity

I hope some of this early philosophical background will be useful in observing
family resemblances with themes developed by Jung and others on individuation.
The first crib sheet owes much to Cisney's (n.d. online) discussion of differential
ontology. The idea of individuation as differentiation, he points out, seems to be
deeply rooted in our philosophical tradition as a sort of statement on the importance and evolution of consciousness. Early philosophy struggled between the concepts of constant transformation (Heraclitus and his river) and permanence
(Parmenides, and his steadfast gaze on the identical), always applying 'reason' to
the understanding of the Cosmos, whether we intend it as abstract analytical
thought or as comprehensive insight. In a variety of ways the early philosophers
confronted difference and identity, as they searched for a rational principle – the
logos – as capable of making something of human experience. We are still struggling with the question they raised: how can we think 'permanence' and 'change'?

In our cultural tradition, 'being' (the object of ontology), thinking, knowledge
and consciousness are strictly related. We tend to discard the extreme abstraction
of Platonic eternal forms and yet we retain a mysterious ability to *perceive* form.
We still struggle with some of Plato's original questioning. We wonder if we
might find a sustainable foundation to knowledge, differentiate it from the mire
of 'opinion' (or so-called 'fake news'), and move beyond its reduction to falsifi-
able correlation. Plato relates Being to the eternal self-identical Form provided
by heavenly archetypes: 'If like things are like by partaking of something, won't
that be the Form itself?' (*Parmenides* 132e on the archetype of Form, see also
Phaedo, *Republic* and *Phaedrus*; e.g. Plato 1961). He also argues in several of
his dialogues (such as *Thaetetus*, *Parmenides*, and *Sophist*) for an Archetype of
Difference. In The Timaeus he speaks of the Soul of the World and relates it to
the process whereby the nature of difference and the nature of identity are mixed
with an original archetype of Being. An archetypal imprinting possibly a better
translation here than 'being' (*Timaeus 35a*). And for individuals things seem
even more complicated in Plato, as the karmic heritages of the soul go further
than family and culture in shaping the challenges of destinies. Yet in spite of the
importance of self-identity (sameness) it seemed obvious to him that difference
could not be thought of in the form of identity but rather as 'self-differentiation',
since the nature of difference is to differ. We have here *in nuce* the principle of
individuation. We could even imagine it as an anticipation of the Deleuzian take

on difference as a relational dimension because, as Cisney shows us, in Plato it is *the archetype of difference that in spite of itself connects all archetypes* in their difference to each other. Although self-identity of forms is obviously crucial, the dialectics of difference is so relevant in Plato that even the Form of the same is not only radically different from the Form of difference but it differs from all other Forms as well!

Aristotle reworked these themes, exploring another perspective focused on the fenomenic world. First of all, he talked of difference as a *specific* difference ('that which is different is different from some particular thing in some particular respect'; *Metaphysics* X.3, quoted in Cisney n.d., online). A difference is what can be perceived through the comparison of things that can be compared. *Otherness* to him was beyond comparison whereas the perception of difference was grounded in the possibility of comparison. This question is still very much present in contemporary anthropological and philosophical reflection on 'absolute otherness' versus knowability based on analogy, self-similarity and homoeomorphic equivalence.

The classical example was: you are *other than* a number, but you cannot say that you are *different from* a number. Aristotle stressed the process of differentiation (*entelechia*) allowing things to develop their self-identity (thus becoming empirically comparable). At the same time he refused to consider difference as an archetype or as something belonging to Being. He said being could be defined in many ways but not from the standpoint of the specific difference between things. He also thought that, from the standpoint of Being, things are what they are, just so. Singular things or even genus (animals, plants) could only be considered from the standpoint of continuity, that is, self-identity. If differences emerge only through external observation, those differences could not belong to Being itself. In other words, he thought difference was in the eye of the beholder. However, it is differentiation that gives Being its 'identity'. The accent once again is on the *process* of self-differentiation rather than on difference: one of the games Being plays is in the passage from potentiality to actuality, bringing forth identity.

The riddle: who interprets who and how can individuation be individual?

In discussing the idea of individuation as self-referential ('I can understand individuation because I am a conscious individuated being'), I shall try to consider different ways to move past the pretence we can 'know' or understand a process, taking for granted that a superior representation of 'conscious' individuation corresponds to a final monadic stage of identity. As we shall see, the ecological crisis is blurring many distinctions and dichotomies that have been taken for granted. The human footprint on the environment and biodiversity has undeniably become a geo-climatic factor, blurring, as a matter of fact, the traditional distinction between a supposedly 'undifferentiated nature' and human culture.

The Sphinx's riddle ('What is the creature that walks on four legs in the morning, two legs at noon and three in the evening?') on the difficulty for the human to understand the a-dualism of its own differences is more cogent than ever. Could the Sphinx's riddle be more 'inclusive' than we have thought beyond the usual characterisation focused on 'the ages of man'? Animal (four legs), human (two legs) and additional artefacts (two legs plus a stick) could be described as part of a continuum. A-dualism is neither monism nor dualism, rather a field of inclusive possibilities: 'What difference does it make that the Sphinx's question is posed from somewhere (slightly) beyond the human?' (Kohn 2013, p. 222).

Postcolonial and critical thinkers are also trying to connect the ecological crisis to the heritage of history without losing track of the deeper psycho-social resources needed to do so. The philosopher and social theorist Achille Mbembe and others remind us that whereas the humanism developed in the Enlightenment was coherent within the context of a colonial project with its reduction of 'the living' into a commodity, there are other narratives and modes of consciousness active in the world. 'In opposing the world of non-humans, humanity opposes itself. It is ultimately in the relationship we have with the whole of 'the living' that we manifest the truth of what we are' (Mbembe 2013, p. 258). For Mbembe, sharing the world with nonhumans was the original 'obligation' assumed by indigenous cultures and ontologies. By seeing such fundamental connection to a broader web of life, the very definition of 'being human' seems to change.

The interdependence of political colonialist attitudes, liberalist agenda and ecological crisis has been highlighted by a number of scholars. As an example I would refer to Alison Jolly's series of anthropological publications on the fragile Madagascar ecosystem (2005–2012):

> [Alison Jolly] knew in detail what the press of rapidly increasing human numbers means to the forests in the situated history of multiple land dispossessions, relocations, violent suppressions, imposition of regimes of private property, insecure markets, a succession of failed national governments, huge solicited and imposed national debt, and broken development promises.
>
> (Haraway 2016, p. 82)

With these complexities in mind I maintain that difference and variety – multiple 'otherness', multispecies worlds, plural ecologies – are central to the core of reality (or 'being'), forcing us to look more carefully at the Cartesian 'border' between Nature and Culture as well as to the evolutionary myth of Western cultural superiority as a founding ground of universalism.

This was strikingly brought home by the healthy shock that anthropology gave to the social sciences in its evolution from an ethnocentric exercise in interpretative hybris to an inventive bricolage aimed at correcting any ethnographer's initial misunderstanding of the meanings shared by her/his informants. Misunderstanding, and also sheer mistranslation, are the basic grounds from which the possibility of communication and dialogical recognition evolve beyond the fixity of ethnocentric solipsistic 'interpretation'.

Moreover, I am intrigued by the idea that the experience of semiosis, of signifying and producing meaning, is not limited to language, much less to our own conceptual ethnocentric world. There are obviously many ways to produce meaning. The problem is the sort of hypnotic anaesthesia making us deaf to the loud but active 'silence' of that very 'Nature' we are constantly hybridising and transforming, closing a blind eye to how much we and the world are being transformed by this very operation. In this respect we have to give an answer to the question the Brazilian anthropologist Viveiros de Castro raised many years ago:

> Anthropology seems to believe that its paramount task is to explain how it comes to know (to represent) its object – an object also defined as knowledge (or representation). Is it possible to know it? Is it decent to know it? Do we really know it, or do we only see ourselves in a mirror?
>
> (Viveiros de Castro 1998/2012, p. 92)

Questioning ethnographic interpretation is the basis for Viveiros de Castro's controversial drive against Western epistemology (our own cultural and disciplinary interpretation of the object) in favour of a *plural ontology*, where everything, including the 'object' of enquiry, is endowed with symbolic agency and contributes to the birthing of different (partially translatable) worlds and not simply to 'worldviews' – contextual 'opinions' – damning us to a sort of a-relational relativism. To think that nature, matter, 'cultures' are endowed with a potential of *relational creativity* is indeed a complete turnabout.

Such an 'ontological turn', as we shall see, has generated controversial debates among scientists, ethologists, anthropologists and philosophers alike. The critical approach to the nature/culture divide has become a transdisciplinary challenge for philosophers of science, cultural theorists, postcolonial thinkers, sociologists and feminists. In spite of rising controversy and some scholars' excessive identification with the 'turn' as paradigmatic, there has been a healthy tension towards overcoming the disciplinarian narcissism of small (or great) differences. In its most radical formulation the question raised by the ontological turn is:

> not just how human phenomena may be illuminated (through structuralism!, no, semiotics!, no, phenomenology!, no, Marx showed the way! etc.), but rather how the phenomena in question may themselves offer illumination. How, in other words, the ways in which people go about their lives may *unsettle* familiar assumptions, not least those that underlie anthropologists' particular repertoires of theory.
>
> (Henare, Holbraad and Wastell 2007, p. 9)

This attitude may, however, also hide a shadow where the 'ontological turn' might be used to give 'ontic' uncritical credit and power to *anything* from techno-algorithmic self-referential bubbles to minority popular subcultures, or microbiological over-amplification. One paradoxical example would be to stress the importance of the bacterial biome in our stomachs, while partially denying other urgent 'matters of concern', such as the drowning of thousands in the seas and deserts of migration. Another aspect of this shadow may lie in a sort of difficulty in dialogical confrontation and negotiation secluding in the end each 'culture' in its own idealised identity-bubble as some forms of idealistic ethnopsychiatry do. This is also a concern Kohn (2014) and others raise in calling for an ethical practice in the Anthropocene.

Rewind: the world as non-being

To further introduce my argument, and to reconsider in the light of these introductory notes the problematic aspect of 'individual' individuation as a *birth of the world through consciousness*, I will consider a brief passage from Carl Gustav Jung's memories of his 1925 journey to Africa – his moment, as he called it, of 'enlightenment'. As he observed the wilds of the African landscape, he saw a number of animals:

> grazing, heads nodding, the herds moved forward like slow rivers. This was the stillness of the eternal beginning, the world as it had always been, *in the state of non-being*; for until then no one had been present to know that it was this world ... here I was now, the first human being to recognize that this was the world....
>
> (Jung 1963, pp. 255–256, emphasis added)

An idea of individuation is implicit in these statements, the idea that only our form of semiosis and consciousness allows the world to *be* what it is. Being and human consciousness are equated. Before Jung *saw* it (he says) the world was in a state of *non-being*. One may wonder if perchance it was this rather luminous and rich 'non-being' itself – something akin to *satori* or *nirvana* – that might have struck Jung. Or the ground of pre-symbolic meaningfulness allowing the enlightenment of emerging form in consciousness.

He did not put it this way: in this formulation, at least, without conscious realisation the world did not exist. And yet we know Jung was rather ambivalent about the value of self-referential consciousness; he often called consciousness itself a 'complex' and was shamanistic enough to imagine a sort of 'holographic' multidimensional new paradigm of consciousness, capable of including 'feeling' (that is, a non-linguistic semiosis shared with much of the animal world).

He was also capable of postulating an emergent widening of consciousness in the ability to perceive meaningful forms (complex or not) emerging from prelinguistic dispositions (archetypes) and constellated unconscious affects. However, he structured his intuition in the frame of the conceptual hierarchical categories that were dominant at his time, cross-referencing Levy-Bruhl's early anthropological notion of *participation mystique* (in his 1910 *How natives think*) with Pierre Janet's psycho-pathological considerations on the *abaissement du niveau mental*, dated 1909.

The term individuation, in any case, indicated for Jung a psychological process fulfilling *individual* destinies through personal ordeals, recovering in a wider form of consciousness something 'primordial', thus making man into that determinate singular being that he is. In sum, the Jungian concept of individuation stressed individual consciousness as a sort of monad reconnecting to a primordial Unity, provided focus is maintained on one's *unique* equation. 'Self-reflection or – what comes to the same thing – the urge to individuation gathers together what is scattered and multifarious and exalts to the original form of the One' (Jung 1954, para 401).

We can contrast this attitude with Simondon's idea that Being *precedes* any individual differentiation and therefore cannot be reduced to a simplified original 'unity'. It is not as if the relational, systemic aspects of individuation were altogether denied but the accent in Jung's account falls mostly on the inner event, although he had the merit of not reducing the reality of being to mere cognitive insight.

Still, in the course of his African journey, he idealised what he perceived as a 'primitive' and 'childlike' symbolisation of consciousness (the 'unconscious homage to the sun' of the Elgonyi, for example). He misunderstood ritual forms such as the *ngoma* rites, which he perceived as a mere dangerous regression into collective frenzy and a lower level of *participation mystique* (Ortiz Hill 1997). Such attitude implied a struggle in facing what he viewed as a radical and regrettable separation between nature and culture. In his critique of Freud, Jung (1928) says that primitive thought is 'perverse' not so much because it is rooted in sexuality but because it has no access to the spiritual singularity of the individual. His aim was to overcome the split.

His idea of the Self was in many ways *holographic.* The American anthropologist Roy Wagner (2001) has defined *holography* as a paradoxical attitude that includes, in a comprehensive identity, the opposite experiences of part and whole in human contingency. However, Jung still struggled in spite of being drawn to a similar holographic understanding of the individual.

One of the cruxes of Jungian theory is his relentless adherence to Kantian philosophy, to the conditioned limits of knowledge; he aspired yet never quite managed to bridge the gap between subject and object. The same struggle applies to the relationship between the I and the Self, which is at the core of his idea of individuation. Sometimes the ego is represented as an emerging complex, coming into its own through recognition of its relative and dependent status. And yet, at the same time, the ego is represented as crucial in its confrontation (Auseinandersetzung) with the Unconscious. All in all, his idea of Being underlying this representation of the psyche remains consistent with the focus on a principle of differentiation as both latent in the matrix and expressed in the result – Aristotelian *entelechia*. The core of it all, the undefinable Self, is both unconscious, undetermined and *the source* of differentiation (cf. Jung 1954, para. 400). And of course it was part of Jung's genius and passionate struggle to imagine a constant living dialectic between the knower and the unknown, although the accent was mostly on the individual ordeal of consciousness faced with overwhelming challenges.

The ontological turn: many worlds in the dance of agency

A while back I mentioned the anthropologist Marilyn Strathern's (1998) seminal book, *The Gender of the Gift*, to a well-read and ethnographically knowledgeable feminist friend. She had not read Strathern yet, but immediately replied: 'Well of course you mean "the gift of gender"'. She misheard as a lapse the reverse formulation, which has condensed how Melanesians conceptualise relationships, giving and personhood.

Strathern explains how gender and things are related in the exchange of gifts, amplifying an idea implicit in the demonstration by the French socio-ethnologist Marcel Mauss that in Maori ritualised exchanges, *things become concepts and active entities* in shaping relationships (Mauss 1925/1966). Mauss cited Maori elder Tamati Ranapiri's communication that *Taonga* (valued articles) were *hau* (the '*spirit* of the gift'). Gifts have power and they are active beyond the Western reduction to 'commodity' or exchange. The interesting thing is that far from interpreting this sentence in the light of dominant ideas, Mauss used it in its reflection on reciprocity and solidarity as the core of social obligation, and applied it to its own conceptualisation of socialism as radical *relational* rather than ideological solidarity.

To explore further how different perspectives may change our own concepts, Strathern showed that for the Melanesians the singular person was not an individual but a 'dividual', embodying in a network of relational exchanges the possibility of plurality. The singular person is a composite. Unity lies elsewhere in the balance and rhythm offered by collective life, not in the individual. Individuation is in the common good. If we were to apply our own ideas of 'the individual' and 'the collective' based on a supposed evolutionary single model of differentiation/individuation, we would fall into a conceptual loop, explaining what we do not understand with our own concepts. In its best version, the ontological turn claims the possibility to access different experiences, different realities (plural), different takes on the human experience of emergence, themselves emerging in an active reciprocal dialogue (and misunderstanding) between bodies (and cultures) rather than through interpretation.

These emergent realities force us to reconsider our own concepts. Although with '*hau*' we are still in the linguistic realm, meaning lies not only in the linguistic representation but in the experience itself. In the gift example, the dominant Western logic of commodity puts emphasis on the nature, quality or usefulness of the objects. It would be impossible to merely use this code to interpret the Melanesian *experience* and the way it offers knowledge about people, relationships and embodied power through gift-making.

In their introduction to their seminal volume on the ontological turn, Amiria Henare, Martin Holbraad and Sari Wastell – strong players in the ontological-turn field – write:

> Against possessive individualism, which turns on the assumption that people are discrete entities that can enter into relations, Strathern has effectively created a new concept of the 'person'.... Her use of the concept 'person' is heuristic in that it under-determines what a 'person' might be, such that it allows (in her case) for attention to be focused on 'relations' rather than entities.
>
> (Henare *et al.* 2007, p. 25)

We shall return to the potential of this 'under-determination' catching up its family resemblance to Simondon's idea of transindividuation as well as to Foucault's stress on de-individualisation.

Resisting interpretation: the rhythm of cognition

As Roy Wagner has extensively sustained, whenever concepts (regarding persons, actions or material things) are suspended, amplified, under-determined or extended, 'they are *ipso facto* transformed into new meanings – an ontological activity' (Henare *et al.* 2007, p. 26; cf. Wagner 1981, p. 39). According to Wagner, worlds, cultures or ontologies – the plurality of generative perspectives – reveal something of the nature of reality, resisting any reduction to unilateral interpretation or translation. This approach also allows a consideration of how a concept can forego transformation when applied to a new context because there is no available and easy translation that the new context can provide. All fieldwork reveals how the intercultural encounter progresses through a complex experience and the gradual clearing of intrinsic misunderstandings and 'false friends' (linguistic, behavioural, or related to non-human dimensions).

The French philosopher Patrice Maniglier (2005) considers the ontological turn as the possibility of rethinking the crucial issue of variability and transformation. He does not dismiss epistemology as intrinsically ethnocentric but upholds that the task of epistemology is *to make of variation a procedure of truth*. Cultural variability can no longer be subjected to a single lens of interpretation but becomes that which resisting interpretation creates a challenging medium of dialogical invention (individuation!). Cultures in this respect are 'ontologies' beyond relativistic worldviews inasmuch as they are perspectives that stand on their own ground and consistency and, through the challenge of such consistency, raise greater symbolic awareness. Interpretation can only be *relational* when it forces engaged partners to question their assumptions, forcing them to redefine 'culture' (or whatever other name to call the dynamics between individual and collective) as an ever-emerging and renewed field of continuity and transformation. How could this happen if cultures (or 'individuated' subjects for that matter) were a sort of final stage of the evolutionary process?

If anthropology becomes a device towards the possibility of 'translation', the anthropological operation itself becomes a constant effort towards 'the decolonization of thought' (Viveiros de Castro 2014, p. 40). The emerging idea is that indigenous people conceptualise in ways we might learn from. Levi Strauss's 'savage thought' is being reconsidered as a rather complex imaginative semiosis. This 'thought' often includes awareness of the limitations of semiosis itself – why should thinking coincide with the Real? And why the real should not include negentropy (the opposite of enthropic disorganisation: life and things becoming more orderly and complex rather than moving towards disorder), i.e. emerging living phenomena including self-organisation and non-linguistic semiosis? In this respect what was termed 'savage thinking' is no longer considered as a mere reflection of structural unconscious signifiers that unwittingly preserve the homeostasis of 'cold societies' but as a form of radical awareness.

Levi Strauss, the great pioneer of anthropological structuralism, initially regarded the relationship with the environment of indigenous groups, resulting in a sort of eco-systemic balance, as the result of an unconscious signifying 'structure' rather than as a *rhythm of cognition* itself. To consider knowledge in the light of such rhythm changes not only our concepts but our very concept of 'concept'. As Bateson had seen, the ecology of ideas is necessary for ecology itself. Psychoanalysis, after all, has partly given its contribution to this shift emphasising the importance of a *negative capability*, accepting the cloud of unknowing any true encounter leads to and resisting the temptation of premature interpretation.

The mythic mode of indigenous thought carries within itself not only the possibility of balance but the possibility of conflict and transformation. The diversity of forms and natures underlies a 'drive to being' common to humans (including animals) that includes:

- Being alive;
- Having to eat and nourish oneself at the expense of other living entities that also have to nourish themselves;
- Having both the drive and the representations necessary to do this;
- A common finitude.

The Upanishads say this, lyrically shunning dualism: 'I am food (object), I am food, I am food! I am the eater of food (subject), I am the eater of food, I am the eater of food!' (Part II, Section 6); and speak of 'the Self which consists of food, the Self which consists of breath, the Self which consists of mind, the Self which consists of understanding' (Part II, Section 5).[1]

According to Viveiros de Castro (1998/2012), in Amerindian 'savage thinking', life is intrinsically pluralistic and tends to an eco-systemic balance inasmuch as it includes the different perspectives and signifying subjectivities in all the living. In Western culture, an example of this pluralistic take reconciling immanence and transcendence (the holographic larger picture that multiple agencies and perspectives allow) can be found in the Book of Revelation: 'and before the Throne there was a sea of glass ... and round about the Throne there were four beasts full of eyes [perspectives] before and behind' (Revelation 4:6). Each perspective is a 'version of the Self'. This makes otherness a sort of relational foundation, possibly in ways that could move forward the intuitions of psychoanalysis and analytical psychology.

Wagner (2010, p. 69ff.) tells us there is a way that the New Guinean Daribi conceptualise the constant struggle with otherness as a dynamic confrontation with an individual anti-twin, a struggle necessary in order to gather enough 'power' (being!) to reinforce and ethically renew the eco-systemic balance of society that is useful to consider in my argument here. The word they use to express the ratio of duality with itself is *sidari-si*. This is akin, he says, to the individual mathematical self-modelling sequence known as the Fibonacci series named for its discoverer, the twelfth-century Italian mathematician Fibonacci. The Fibonacci sequence creates stability through the regular integration of previous numbers in the series it builds ($1+2=3$; $3+2=5$; $5+3=8$ and so forth). In the *sidari-si* this implies turning backwards to gather one's *anti-twin* as a necessary step to move forward. Self-modelling series create stability (buildings built around the 'golden mean' derived from the Fibonacci series are known for withstanding earthquakes). But the anti-twin is not only what Jungians conceptualise as 'the shadow', it is also an altogether different mode and semiosis of confronting reality. A mode rooted, as we shall see, in pre-symbolic deeply relational forms of awareness. A symbolic 'holographic' image can only emerge beyond the mere linguistic symbolisation by including both 'nagual' and 'tonal' in creating and/or connecting to symbols that stand for themselves. The movement backwards is truly something 'other' that also belongs to us, discomfiting the ego's pretence to move forward on his/her own. Potentially we host multiplicities; we must take personal, collective, cultural otherness seriously. This entails the possibility of entering the other's perspective as an anti-twin, without being devoured by it.

As Peter Skafish (2014) states in his introduction to *Cannibal Metaphysics*: 'the dizzying preponderance of perspectives on the self entails that *the other is effectively ontologically prior*, and subjectivation requires assuming, through shamanism and other translational means, the perspective of another' (Skafish 2014, p. 12, emphasis added).

Heritage with no testament: transindividuation

We now consider as a further stage of my argument whether the French philosopher Gilbert Simondon's contribution to the concept of individuation brings us further in understanding the ontology of the variety and transformation at the core of the 'ontological turn'. (For this crib sheet, I am much indebted to Combes 1999.) Simondon (1995) focused on ontogenesis; that is, on how individuated beings come to be, since 'unity and identity apply only to one of the phases of being that follows the operation of individuation' (Simondon 1995, p. 23). He also wondered about which dimensions of being might allow progress transformation, growth, negentropy; i.e. becoming: 'Being as such is whole in each of its phases but with a reserve of becoming' (Simondon 1995, p. 229).

In fact, Simondon regarded the individual as a 'phase' in an unending process of transformation called 'trans-individuation' which has its source in pre-individual abundance and develops into intersubjective awareness. Unity cannot be the source of individual beings since unification points to the continuity of identity; unity is a phase following, not preceding individuation. Simondon tried to answer the following question: if being before individuation cannot be a unity how can we imagine a process moving from such non-unity to the development of individuated beings? The answer he gives is that *being is more than unity* and *more than identity*. Being as a potential of becoming exceeds itself, and in this excess lies the power of transformation.

De-phasing is another crucial concept that Simondon has borrowed from thermodynamics and uses to show how a system can change phases. A system whose nature is becoming can only be a polyphasic system. As Combes (1999, p. 13) states in her introduction to Simondon's work: 'individuals can be considered as beings that come to existence as partial solutions to incompatibility problems between different orders of being'. The given example is how plants connect a cosmic order (the energy of light) with an infra-molecular order (mineral salts, oxygen); and when the plant 'becomes' (individuates), it not only connects these different orders but also contributes to the eco-systemic generation of a symmetric order of the same level (the environment). It is only if we consider a pre-individual being as 'more than one' – that is as a metastable system abounding in potential – that we can consider individuation as a process.

Another key concept in Simondon's (1995) thought is the *transduction* that makes de-phasing possible. Being 'does not possess the identitarian unity of a stable state in which no transformation is possible; being owns a transductive unity' (Simondon 1995, p. 29). There is indeed a sort of wholeness in the overall declination of being's different phases, in its multiple individuations. The idea of *transduction* expresses the dynamics of transformation in a constant systemic interdependence and active relationality. For Simondon, the information underlying a process is not what passes between a transmitter and a receiver (as in information theory) but the way any pre-existing form interacts with other forms in the dynamics of transformation. As an example, he says how a brick moulded from clay, far from being mere 'naked matter', has colloidal properties allowing it to be deformed but maintaining the coherence of its molecular structure – clay holds an 'agency' in this respect. For Simondon, transduction expresses the interdependent, relational processuality inherent in individuation on all levels: physical, biological, psychological, collective.

This perspective challenges the Kantian view of knowledge as dependent only on the structural activity (and intrinsic limitations) of the knower. The stress in Kant is on the limits of knowledge and the conditions of its possibility. In Simondon, the focus is no longer on the limitations of the knowing subject but on the process of individuation as a form of relational knowledge. And such process according to Simondon is *analogical*. 'Individuation of the real external to the subject is perceived by the subject thanks to the analogical individuation of knowledge in the subject' (Simondon 1995, p. 34). This accent on analogy is rather meaningful and on a very different plan if compared with the present 'scientific' emphasis on algorithmic quantifiable efficiency and process control.

In the cognitive process itself, there is a meaningful interaction based on analogy (the power of *associations* and *amplifications* in psychoanalytical terms). Thought itself is in many ways analogical and, according to Simondon, it is one of the phases of being-in-becoming. Transduction 'is a move of the spirit in discovery. This move consists in following being in its generation, in its drive towards the generation of thought *at the same time* as the generation of the object is accomplished' (Simondon 1995, p. 32, emphasis added).

Here, transduction seems to connect the *emerging* ability of consciousness to relate both to *emerging* phenomena while discovering its own emerging apprehension. That this parallel process is accomplished 'at the same time' reminds me of Jung's intuition concerning the emerging of a form of consciousness capable of suddenly recognising emerging constellations. Such generation of thought is not unrelated to pre-symbolic semiotics (indexes and icons according to Peirce) and the way they create complex structures of meaning through analogy (more in the next section). The key concept is that the individual, from the point of view of an ongoing process, is neither self-determined nor a 'final' point of individuation. 'He is the partial and provisional result of individuation inasmuch as maintaining a reserve of preindividual he is still capable of plural individuations' (Combes 1999, p. 67).

This allows us to return to the extract from Foucault opening this chapter: 'The individual is the product of power. What is needed is to "de-individualize" by means of multiplication and displacement, through the layout of diverse combinations.' The kind of 'individual' Foucault has in mind is the result of passive formatting, closed up to further individuation, resisting transformation, focused on whatever little narcissistic imaginary 'power' of his/her own he has structured in cutting itself off from the generative experience of displacement that a dialogical relationship – the deep resonance at the core of co-individuation (the 'group' in Foucault's quote) – allows.

Focusing on interdependence brings to focus *knowledge as relationship*. As Strathern stated, anthropology means studying *relations with relations* (as quoted by Haraway 2016, p. 34). The same goes for other disciplines, and definitely for psychosocial reflection. On the other hand, to imagine individuation as something *substantial, individual and definitive rather than relational and transformative* devalues the cognitive value of relationship, intersubjectivity and co-individuation.

As we shall see, humans are not the only species participating in this transindividual dimension. It is, however, worth noting how in both shamanism and psychoanalytical reconnection with embodied experience, the reverie and other imaginal forms are what connect the human to the transindividual. The stress must be put on the fact that this kind of 'reverie' is not a property of the mind, but something taking place in a 'middle land' between minds and phenomena. This sort of imagining is something quite different from individual subjective fantasy and imaginary comfort; rather, it is objectively dynamised by empathic imaginative confrontation.

Imaginative relationality also points to an inclusive and uncanny form of insight, the sort of 'supernature' that Amerindians and other indigenous people characterise as the wisdom and knowledge of the Forest Spirits (cf. Kopenawa and Albert 2013); such wider active understanding is not dissociated from the interactive web of agencies that includes different forms and states of consciousness. This kind of shamanic reveries founds the 'ecologies of others', connecting the human and the larger implicated environment also emerging from transindividuation.

Shamanic ecologies: more on perspectivism and the semiotic turn

Another way to look at the ontological turn is to consider semiosis as an ongoing process, as Kohn (2013) highlights in his eco-systemic reflections. In exploring the semiotics underlying different levels and hierarchies of relational representations, Kohn draws upon Peirce for whom semiosis is above all relational:

> One of Peirce's most important contributions to semiotics is to look beyond the classical dyadic understanding of signs as something that stands for something else. Instead, he insisted, we should recognize a crucial third variable as an irreducible component of semiosis: signs stand for something in relation to a 'somebody'.
>
> (Colapietro 1989, quoted in Kohn 2013, p. 75)

Kohn underscores how 'superior' human linguistic/symbolic representations are built bottom-up from a semiotic ground we share with the living world. This ground consists of 'indexical' signs (signs directly pointing to something else, such as for example, the message a tree crashing nearby may relay in terms of danger to a monkey) and 'iconic' images (representing a 'just so' with no other referent – something whose quality is not 'difference' but unquestioned evidence – similar to what Wagner calls 'symbols that stand for themselves'). Semiosis seems in fact to begin and end with this sort of 'just so', as in a Japanese haiku or in some of Zen Buddhism's most iconic stories: 'before enlightenment, the mountains and the lake; after enlightenment, the mountains and the lake' (a common metaphor on the process of enlightenment).

Of course, without the symbolic we would not have linguistic, social, cultural, or historical contexts; and yet, says Kohn – and I find resonances here with Simondon – we live in a world that *exceeds* the symbolic (intended here as an evolved linguistic system of signs), and 'this is something our social theory must also find ways to address' (Kohn 2013, p. 38). All life is semiotic and all semiosis is alive, cooperates and fights for life in the carousel of agencies. In important ways, life always signifies something to someone:

> an anthropology beyond the human must find a way to account for the distinctive qualities of human thought without losing sight of its relation to these more pervasive semiotic logics.... Because all experiences and all thoughts, for all selves, are semiotically mediated, introspection, human-to-human intersubjectivity, and even trans-species sympathy and communication are not categorically different. They are all sign processes.
>
> (Kohn 2013, p. 87)

If we understand thinking as nested in this process of signification, life *thinks*; thoughts are alive. This, says Kohn, has implications for understanding who 'we' are. The 'self', even in its most rudimentary ephemeral form, expresses a 'living dynamic by which signs come to represent the world around them to a "someone" – who emerges as such as a result of this process. The world is thus "animate" ' (Kohn 2013, p. 16).

All of these different levels of semiosis have to do with the nested emerging thresholds of form. The similarity of indexes based on experience and habit (the 'just so' of repetition) creates an icon (an unreplaceable image of a meaningful just-so form). The self-organisation of our emerging analogical consciousness connects the systemic relations of the icons that make up our 'just so reality' through webs of habit and repetition. The important conclusion Kohn draws from his Amazonian experience is that 'a symbolic world must be nested in the semiosis of life' (Kohn 2013, p. 55). Recognising this sort of 'grounding' changes our relationship with the world around us, gives us an embodied connection with an 'emergent "us" with all its infinite possibilities' (Kohn 2013, p. 61). The webs of habit and repetition connect emergent iconic representations but thinking is also challenged by the disruption of habit. This constant figure-ground reversal is part of the shamanistic experience throughout the Amazon and Melanesia. Kohn defines these dynamics as 'the open whole'. Emergence is always a 'constellation' but also an open mandala. 'It is only in the realm of the machine that the differentiated part comes first and the assembled whole second. Semiosis and life, by contrast, begin whole' (Kohn 2013, p. 64).

When thought is actively or unconsciously divorced from iconic or indexing levels of semiosis, dissociation results. One consequence of such dissociation is that we take for granted the unnatural adaptive habitat we have built for ourselves, in our reduction of nature to an assemblage of parts, but the anxiety that goes with dissociation ('I think therefore I doubt that I am' to rephrase Descartes) may also help us feel the need to reconnect.

Peirce also gives us another clue for understanding Foucault's idea of dis-individualisation: '[A] person is not absolutely an individual. His thoughts are what he is "saying to himself," that is, is saying to that other self that is just coming into life in the flow of time' (Peirce 1931, quoted in Kohn 2013, p. 87). *Selves just like thoughts are essentially relational, not individual.* It is the imaginal ability to relate to our own emerging and complex self that allows both continuity and transformation. If we consider selective co-evolution as semiotic eco-adaptation, it might help us relate to the counter-intuitive idea that the biological world consists of living thoughts.

In the Amazons, how jaguars *think* – how they see humans – matters a lot! The core narrative of perspectivism, the major anthropological feedback on Amerindian epistemology, is that all sentient beings (animals, humans, spirits) are animate, and although their nature – their bodies – differ they share something akin to personhood:

> Amazonian and other Amerindian peoples (from the Achuar and the Runa all the way up to the Kwakiutl) who live in intense proximity and interrelatedness with other animal and plant species, see these nonhumans not as other species belonging to nature but as PERSONS, human persons in fact, who are distinct from 'human' humans not from lacking consciousness, language, and culture – these they have abundantly – but because their bodies are different, and endow them with a specific subjective perspective.
>
> (Skafish 2014, p. 12)

After Descartes it has become Western common sense to consider the machine (and its potential for 'governance') as the basic blueprint of the cosmos. For animists, the core narrative is that under the animal skin we all share animated intersubjective personhood, the Form of Spirit under an animal guise. Amerindian ontologies are moreover grounded in the idea that any living agency is driven by a sort of eco-systemic hunger. Anything can be food for someone (spirits and animals included). We are all cannibals but we are also at risk of being devoured, turned from a *thou* into an *it.*

The other's perspective can eat you up. Yet we can move in awe – in fear and trembling – in an enchanted world of negotiated possibilities. The human relation to both destructive drives and fears is not repressed but actively grounded in this web of agencies. Of course the immanent complexity of life sets the conscious task of avoiding (or postponing) being devoured. As already underscored, the question is how to gain access to the other's perspective and come out of it alive. Perspectivism is not relativism but the relational ecology of different perspectives (and worlds) sharing a common ground: being. The interreligious philosopher Raimon Panikkar characterises this as the passage from the relativity of reality to the reality of relationality. In short, the Amerindians characterise being as the primordially *human* (relational) ground of all *embodied* differentiation (multinaturalism rather than multiculturalism).

What seems relevant here is how much an intersubjective process of co-individuation involves first of all recognising the 'other's' agency. The Gospel parable of the Good Samaritan is a good example of this reversal. When asked, 'who is my neighbour?' Jesus' answer pointed not to the poor beaten victim, but to a hated Samaritan (considered 'inferior' by the religiously correct), showing how this 'other' was not to be the passive object of our attention but was endowed with great or even greater agency. To consider the victim as the category worthy of being 'our neighbour' – inasmuch as it is a victim in a state of minority, hence deserving our help – would cancel the victim's own subjectivity, the recognition of the other as able to co-create rather than being the recipient of our superior humanitarian stance. History is woven with instances where even in the most dire situations the subaltern attempt cultural resistance, transformation, becoming through performative thinking and agency. In this age, the recognition of transindividual agency seems to be acquiring an ever deeper ecosystemic urgency.

A turn in the maze: Anthropos in the Anthropocene

It is not difficult to relate past narratives on individuation with heroic narratives where Anthropos and Self are connected, in the mysterious *entelechia* generating 'the human'. It is well known that Jung took the Anthropos as the privileged paradoxical archetypal image of the Self – at once the perfect 'spherical' (global/ universal) monadic 'true man', and the unconscious ground of its development. It was certainly part of Jung's genius to reconnect the alchemical production of the Anthropos with the philosophical 'Stone', the 'Tree', or with the gnostic 'Snake' – non-humans all – an accent on the personal/universal incarnation of an oxymoron: a divine-preconscious (or possibly supra-conscious) totality being realised in the monadic individual.

It is the view of the Anthropos as a product of cultural evolutionary difference (the 'enlightened' Western difference as universalised human essence) that is today in question. The term Anthropocene indicates the crucial factor of the human impact in the present geo-climatic age, the impact on climate and global warming. In contemplating Gaia's discontent and intrusion, Latour (2017) and Stengers (2015) tell us we are not dealing with a simple dichotomy, man/nature, but with a nature that is constantly modified and even hybridised by human actions. Gaia includes its own shadowy negative version. The kind of Gaia, as it were, that returns *karmic* actions to Man is not some idealised Mother Nature. 'She' is already humanised, transformed, hybridised. A classic example is how antibiotics have contributed to the development of resistant super-bacteria against which there is no cure. Gaia *interferes* with the description modernity would make of its progressive destiny. It is no longer possible to believe in a dialectical evolutionary history and many underlying divisions are being challenged by the geoclimatic crisis: man/world, culture/nature, political economy/ geology.

In his seminal discussion of historical consciousness as confronted by the Anthropocene crisis, Dipesh Chakrabarty sustains the idea that our collective self-understanding as a specie may be crucial for our survival, but adds:

> Who is the we? We humans never experience ourselves as a species. We can only intellectually comprehend or infer the existence of the human species but never experience it as such. There could be no phenomenology of us as a species. Even if we were to emotionally identify with a word like *mankind*, we would not know what being a species is, ... one never experiences being a concept.
>
> (Chakrabarty 2009, p. 220, emphasis in original)

Many have eschewed the use of the term Anthropocene with its implication of a collectively responsible humanity. Alternative names have been suggested such as Eurocene, Anglocene, Capitalocene. Haraway (2016) prefers looking at the transition towards a new Age of the Earth, and speaks of Cthulucene: 'Living-with and dying-with each other potently in the Chthulucene can be a fierce reply to the dictates of both Anthropos and Capital' (Haraway 2016, p. 2).

One could ask with Chakrabarty 'Who is this Anthropos?' Is there really a collective humanity that has inscribed its global effect on the Earth or should we rather consider that there may – or may not – be 'an Anthropos in the making' still stuttering as we attempt to face the *global* dimension of the problem? Some have even suggested that the term Anthropocene has a colonial aura because to maintain that the Anthropos, the collective *summa* of humankind, is responsible, really amounts to saying that the responsible segment represents the *essence* of humanity. This is precisely the way Europeans represented themselves and their cultures throughout the colonial period. Chakrabarty and others suggest that a responsible Anthropos does not yet exist and can only emerge from a comparative anthropology and from the cosmopolitical negotiations it implies (cf. Stengers 2010, 2011). And yet it seems clear that the intrinsic trans-human devouring drive has gone out of bounds in a large area of human collectives both socially and psychologically.

If we consider anthropology as a comparative discipline rather than 'the merely critical non-constructive position anthropology is most often comfortable with' (Skafish 2014, p. 10) we can reframe it as an *effort at translation through initial misunderstanding* operating as a sort of prism allowing us to acknowledge in the diffraction wavelengths of different colours. The same goes for the Anthropos: there are thousands of ways in which the 'human' is conceived, facets we might discover by being initially *lost in translation*. As Latour (1993) said, we cannot conceive a history of the Anthropocene without an anthropology putting the

Moderns' take on techno-progress in its place. In other words, the perspective of modernity becomes one among many other provincial perspectives that confront it. Any 'us' in question must be thought of as 'others among others' and transdisciplinary narratives must be wide enough to accommodate this variability.

In this respect it is worth remembering what the eco-feminist sci-fi and fantasy writer Ursula Le Guin (1989) said in her call towards a new version of the Grail Quest: no longer only the search for *anima* through an idealised hero's journey, but the *carrier bag* of co-individuation. The first (cultural/human) tool, says Le Guin, was probably not the romanticised bone-weapon of Kubrick's movie *2001: A Space Odyssey*, depicting the ascent of man through violent drives all the way to the spaceship, but a recipient, a container capable of holding gathered products. And so, says Le Guin, it wasn't the spear or the hunter's meat that made the difference; it was the holder, the gatherer's Grail. And yet the exciting stories were the hero's stories, the hunter's stories, the spear stories. Long before the concept of the ontological-turn was coined, Le Guin saw in storytelling the possibility of telling a different kind of story. She claimed a novel might resemble a sack, a bag, a medicine bundle

> full of beginnings without ends, of initiations, of losses, of transformations and translations, and far more tricks than conflicts, far fewer triumphs than snares and delusions; full of spaceships that get stuck, missions that fail, and people who don't understand.
>
> (Le Guin 1989, p. 153)

I do not need to further stress the relevance of Le Guin's 'carrier bag theory of fiction', rooting for narratives and indeed transdisciplinary attention to matters of concern wide enough to accommodate all kinds of differences and well rooted in our common human heritage.

I think that Jung himself had an inkling of this when, in a 1959 interview with Georges Duplain (first published in the *Gazette de Lausanne*), he considered the passage to the Age of Aquarius as symbolised by the Aquarius's pitch and a relevant switch from content to container (Jung 1977). De-individualisation might be a tool to multiply perspectives, if we consider individualisation as always somewhat *identification with content*. De-individualisation, of course, would stand as the opposite of de-humanisation. However, another strand of Jung's forecast on the transition from Pisces to Aquarius – foreshadowed in his monograph *Aion* (Jung 1951) – imagined the passage from one age to another as a radical acknowledgement of the reality of evil:

> the approach of the next Platonic month, namely Aquarius, will constellate the problem of the union of opposites. It will then no longer be possible to write off evil as the mere privation of good; its real existence will have to be recognised.
>
> (Jung 1951, para 141)

The flash of history in the moment of danger and the threshold of mourning

My intent has been to share a journey, to provide a way *into* rather than *out of* the maze of questions that I felt opened when I began reading about the onto-logical turn, perspectivism and transindividuation. I have tried not to lose the thread that I suggested my argument would follow: the paradoxical call to de-individualise. In the open mandala of transindividuation, the emerging 'I' of 'individuated' consciousness should not overrule the 'dividual self' nor the inter-subjective web of agencies that constantly recreates a world.

In Simondon, as well as in Kohn, individuation has crucially become the indi-viduation of *life and co-evolution*, the overall intertwined possibility of survival superseding the 'separate' historical individuation of humankind although the species may, after all, be the proper name for 'an emergent, new universal history of humans that flashes up in the moment of the danger that is climate change' (Chakrabarty 2009, p. 221).

There has been, throughout my bricolage, another underlying crucial thread I mentioned at the beginning but that has mostly remained latent and that I need to make explicit in order to give sense to my conclusions: the thread of historical and ecological mourning. This aspect has in many ways been taken up by postcolonial and critical thinkers who in the wake of Chakrabarty's article have reacted saying: to what extent can we afford to forget history when dealing with the challenges facing the collective future of humanity and countless other species? Some have wondered if the supposed 'equalising drive' in a climatic global catastrophe could become another force of histor-ical erosion, erasing the very articulations we need to contemplate in order to face what needs repairing (Baucom 2014). The risk is erasing, as it were, dis-equality – the unequal play of forces in history that are not only at the core of the issue but will continue even in the semi-apocalyptic thrall of future eco-disasters. Should we just ignore the roots of the current de-humanisation? Isn't our human history what reveals our current predicament? Hasn't History got its own Fibonacci series? And isn't the ability to mourn the ability to recog-nise where reparation is due? Co-individuation and the ability to mourn and face history seem to me deeply related.

This concern with history appears crucial at a time when the forces of de-humanisation indeed evoke some of the direst Aquarian aspects of that 'emerg-ing evil' that Jung had predicted, as the opposites of humanisation and de-humanisation face each other as heralds of the Age of Aquarius.

To put it differently (and with the idea of individuation as relational trans-formation indeed in mind): isn't there a 'constellation' connecting present events to the past? Is climate change, for example, related to colonialism's turning the living into commodities at an unprecedented scale? We could also follow a similar thread in considering the Holocene as the long period when places of refuge still existed for both cultural and biological diversity. This historical consideration would allow us to see the Anthropocene as the critical point where most *refugia*, and the very possibility of ecosystemic regeneration after desertification, will become impossible (Tsing 2015).

So, in the mandala we have drawn around the issue of co-individuation, how do we orient our feeling in confronting the past and its heritage? Is there 'a secret agreement between past generations and the present one' (Benjamin 1999, pp. 245–246)?

Introducing a journal's special issue on climate change and the production of knowledge, Baucom and Omelsky write:

> We have arrived at an impasse of non feeling and nonreflexivity, rendering us 'structurally alien' to 'our own apocalypse,' … But despite this apparent foreclosure of affect, the question of feeling persists throughout this collection. What animates many of these essays are the ways in which climate change discourse has not simply reshaped the order of knowledge, but how it has done so in the service of this elusive figure of 'feeling'.
>
> (Baucom and Omelsky 2017, p. 16)

Even Jung's attention to historical periods as long term 'constellations' of consciousness (collective Ages implying the possible evolution/involution of humanity's individuative adventure) speaks of a form of dialectics quite different from the Hegelian or Marxian philosophical vulgate. For Walter Benjamin, true dialectics can take place only when the mind is able to bring time to a 'standstill' – when time, as it were, stops in order to enter into a *constellation* with the past, to make room in the now to the awakening content of re-memoration, sometimes even to the shocking re-memoration of unfulfilled, avoided historical heritages and challenges. This is the concept of historical mourning I am trying to relate to the individuation.

In cross-referencing Jung and Benjamin I can see an emerging urgency to recognise emerging unconscious content embedded in history. Benjamin does not dismiss the evolutionary potential of the repressed negative in history, nor the conflict between masters and slaves of all generations – his, however, is a different kind of dialectics. The key passage elucidating his paradoxical idea of *dialectics at a standstill* is the following:

> It's not that what is past casts its light on what is present, or what is present its light on the past; rather, image is that wherein what has been comes together in a flash with the now to form a *constellation*. In other words, image is dialectics at a standstill. For while the relation of the present to the past is a purely temporal, continuous one, the relation of what-has-been to the now is dialectical: it is not progression but image, suddenly *emergent*. – Only *dialectical images* are *genuine images* (that is, not archaic); and the place where one encounters them is language.
>
> (Benjamin 2002, p. 462; emphasis added)

In his take on history, each 'age' would transmit via the collective unconscious the dynamics of its repressed, undigested, unsettling and traumatic content to the next. The historian must therefore become in a way an interpreter of dreams in order to be there at that mysterious rendezvous with past generations. The offence of uncelebrated life symbolised by 1000 unburied lives sank under the Mediterranean in resonating with the history of slave trade, or the connection between the use of the living in colonialism and our unbalanced exploitation of natural resources, might be examples of what Benjamin called a 'true image', i.e. an image capable of shaking us from sleep, awakening to the perception of a mysterious rendezvous among generations that resonates with unredeemed crucial past issues speaking, as it were, to our present. Synchronicity may have something to do with this. Dreams and re-memoration also.

I will therefore conclude with the issues of mourning. There is an emerging transcultural growing awareness for the need of a 'dialogue with the dead'. This is closely connected with a common challenge in caring for our co-vulnerability. As Butler (2012) aptly states, the crucial question is *which lives are already considered non-lives, or only partially alive, or already dead, or lost, even before any outright destruction or loss.* As a fact, whenever vulnerability is handled within a mere economic procedural cost/benefit logic we are not far from Nazi eugenic policies. Vulnerability, on the contrary, should be considered – outside of any cult devoted to traumatic memory – as our common social foundation. Valuing life as embodied form implies a different dialogue with 'deep time'. The need for mourning and a 'dialogue with the dead' emerges thus in all its poignancy. Such inclusive form of mourning also acknowledges the emergent vulnerability of the Earth (Robertson 2015). I suggest that the call to feeling and mourning can provide the needed mediation between the ontological turn and the urgency to rekindle critical attention to historical constellations. To me this is what co-individuation is all about. I find no better way to close than with Haraway's take on mourning:

> Outside the dubious privileges of human exceptionalism, thinking people must learn to grieve-with. Mourning is about dwelling with a loss and so coming to appreciate what it means, how the world has changed, and how we must *ourselves* change and renew our relationships if we are to move forward from here. In this context, genuine mourning should open us into an awareness of our dependence on and relationships with those countless others being driven over the edge of extinction.... Staying with the trouble does not require such a relationship to times called the future. In fact, staying with the trouble requires learning to be truly present, not as a vanishing pivot between awful or edenic pasts and apocalyptic or salvific futures, but as mortal critters entwined in myriad unfinished configurations of places, times, matters, meanings.
>
> (Haraway 2016, p. 38, emphasis in the original)

To paraphrase Haraway again, until sympoiesis (a word she and others use to express the unpredictable dynamics of co-evolution) with the dead and with our historical past won't be acknowledged, sympoiesis with the living will be radically incomplete. This form of historical empathy is nothing other than the access to mourning in its connection with the ongoing-ness of life. This may be the best answer to the temptation of 'becoming enamoured with power'.

Note

1 *The Upanishads* (trans. M. Müller, 1879). Available: www.sacred-texts.com (accessed 10 July 2018).

References

Baucom, I. (2014) History 4: Postcolonial method and anthropocene time. *Cambridge Journal of Postcolonial Literary Inquiry* 1, 123–142.

Baucom, I. and Omelski, M. (2017) Knowledge in the age of climate change. *South Atlantic Quarterly* 116, 1–18.

Benjamin, W. (1999) *Illuminations.* London: Pimlico.

Benjamin, W. (2002) *The Arcades Project.* Harvard: Harvard University Press.

Butler, J. (2012) Can one lead a good life in a bad life? Available: https://thats1.files.wordpress.com/2012/10/butler_adorno_prize.pdf (accessed 31 July 2018).

Chakrabarty, D. (2009) The climate of history: four theses. *Critical Enquiry* 35, 197–222.

Cisney, V. W. (n.d.) Differential ontology. *Internet Dictionary of Philosophy.* Available: www.iep.utm.edu/diff-ont/ (accessed 31 July 2018).

Combes, M. (1999) *Simondon. Individu et collectivité. Pour une philosophie du transindividual.* Paris: Presses Universitaires de France.

Foucault, M. (1983) Preface. In: G. Deleuze and F. Guattari, *Anti-Oedipus: Capitalism and Schizophrenia.* Minneapolis, University of Minnesota Press.

Haraway, D. (2016) *Staying with the Trouble: Making Kin in the Cthulucene.* Durham: Duke University Press.

Henare, A., Holbraad, M. and Wastell, S. (2007) Introduction. In: A. Henare *et al.* (eds), *Thinking Through Things: Theorising Artefacts Ethnographically.* London, Routledge.

Jung, C. G.: Unless otherwise stated, the following are from *The Collected Works of C. G. Jung* (CW). London: Routledge & Kegan Paul/Princeton, NJ: Princeton University Press:

Jung, C. G. (1928) On psychic energy. (CW 8).

Jung C. G. (1951) *Aion.* (CW 9ii).

Jung, C. G. (1954) Transformation Symbolism in the Mass. (CW 11).

Jung, C. G. (1963) *Memories, Dreams, Reflections.* New York: Pantheon Books.

Jung, C. G. (1977) *C. G. Jung Speaking: Interviews and Encounters.* Princeton: Princeton University Press.

Kohn, E. (2013) *How Forests Think: Toward an Anthropology beyond the Human.* Berkeley: University of California Press.

Kohn, E. (2014) Toward an ethical practice in the Anthropocene. *HAU: Journal of Ethnographic Theory* 4, 459–464.

Kopenawa, D. and Albert, B. (2013) *The Falling Sky Words of a Yanomami Shaman.* Harvard: Harvard University Press.

Latour, B. (1993) *We Have Never Been Modern*. Cambridge: Harvard University Press.
Latour, B. (2017) *Facing Gaia. Eight Lectures on the New Climatic Regime*. Cambridge: Polity Press.
Le Guin, U.K. (1989) The carrier bag theory of fiction. In: *Dancing at the Edge of the World: Thoughts on Words, Women, Places*. New York: Grove Press.
Maniglier, P. (2005) La parenté des autres. *Critique* 701, 758–774 (in French).
Mauss, M. (1925/1966) *The Gift: Forms and Functions of Exchange in Archaic Societies*. London: Cohen and West.
Mbembe, A. (2013) *Critique de la raison nègre*. Paris: La Decouverte (in French).
Ortiz Hill, M. (1997) C. G. Jung in the heart of darkness. *Spring* 61, 125–133.
Plato (1961) *The Complete Dialogues of Plato*. Princeton, NJ: Princeton University Press.
Robertson, C. (2015) Well-being of misfortune: accepting ecological disaster. Available at: www.climatepsychologyalliance.org/explorations/papers/68-well-being-of-misfortune-accepting-ecological-disaster (accessed 31 July 2018).
Simondon, G. (1995) *L'Individu et sa genèse physico-biologique*, 2nd edn. Paris: PUF, Coll. Épiméthée (in French).
Skafish, P. (2014) Preface. In: E. Viveiros de Castro (Ed.), *Cannibal Metaphisics*. Minneapolis: Univocal Publishing.
Stengers, I. (2010) *Cosmopolitics I*. Minneapolis: University of Minnesota Press.
Stengers, I. (2011) *Cosmopolitics II*. Minneapolis: University of Minnesota Press.
Stengers, I. (2015) *In Catastrophic Times, Resisting the Coming Barbarism*. London: Open Humanities Press.
Strathern, M. (1998) *The Gender of the Gift: Problems with Women and Problems with Society in Melanesia*. Berkeley: University of California Press.
Tsing, A. (2015) *The Mushroom at the End of the World: On the Possibility of Life in Capitalist Ruins*. Princeton, NJ: Princeton University Press.
Viveiros de Castro, E. (1998/2012) *Cosmological Perspectivism in Amazonia and Elsewhere*. Four lectures delivered at the Department of Social Anthropology, University of Cambridge. February–March 1998. HAU Masterclass Series, Vol. 1. Available at: http://haubooks.org/cosmological-perspectivism-in-amazonia/ (accessed 31 July 2018).
Viveiros de Castro, E. (2014) *Cannibal Metaphysics*. Minneapolis: Univocal Publishing.
Wagner, R. (1981) *The Invention of Culture*, 2nd edn. Chicago: University of Chicago Press.
Wagner, R. (2001) *An Anthropology of the Subject*. Berkeley: University of California Press.
Wagner, R. (2010) *Coyote Anthropology*. Lincoln: University of Nebraska Press.

Chapter 10

Challenges to dialogicality and individuation in techno-digital culture

Vincent W. Hevern

At the end of the central hallway on its second floor the recently refurbished Rijksmuseum in Amsterdam welcomes visitors to view Rembrandt's 1642 masterpiece, *The Company of Captain Frans Banning Cocq and Lieutenant Willem Jan Ruytenburch*, commonly known as *The Night Watch* (Kiers and Tissink 2000). The museum describes this massive canvas (363 × 437 cm or 11.9 by 14.3 feet) as 'a painting that has gone down in history as marking the turning point in his career and as the superlative example of his creative genius' (Rijksmuseum 2018). My first sight of *The Night Watch* came in 2000 on my first trip to Amsterdam. It was in the mid-morning and I sat down on a bench to look at the painting. Next to me I found a young college student who was sleepy and having trouble staying awake. We got talking and he told me that he had just landed at Schiphol Airport that morning as part of an American university choral group. While they were going to give a series of concerts in Europe, they also had some school research assignments to complete. He took out of his jacket a printed sheet of paper and showed me what he was supposed to do. It involved analysing several important works of art in the Rijksmuseum, including *The Night Watch*, to understand what the artist was trying to capture. He was having trouble concentrating on the painting because he was so tired. I found myself suggesting some of my own impressions of what Rembrandt was doing on that vast canvas. He quickly took out a pencil and began to write down my observations. He seemed grateful that my off-the-cuff remarks served as a prompt for what he needed to accomplish.

Jump head more than a decade to December of 2014 and that same setting. Across the internet, social media widely shared the image of six young adolescents, all sitting with their backs to the clearly visible Rembrandt painting, hunched over, and staring intensely at their mobile devices (Molloy 2016). Photographer Gijsbert van der Wal had observed these students, posted the picture to a social media site, and comments online exploded from a worldwide audience. On the face of it, here was a group of teenagers seemingly distracted by their smartphones and ignoring the masterpiece behind their backs. For many commentators this served as a fitting example of the negative impact of digital technology. With the opportunity to savour directly one of the great works of European art, these young people appeared far more interested in the content of the small screens in their hands. Yet, digging deeper, it seems that these students might actually have been either looking at the museum's own app to explain the artwork or were checking up on what their assignment required them to do in *The Night Watch* gallery (Molloy 2016). May I suggest, though, whether we accept the negative or positive explanation for that image, among the most important messages it conveys has to do simply with the mediation of attention: that digital technology such as the smartphone has embedded itself thoroughly into our conscious lives no matter where we find ourselves and we turn our attention to digital media instinctively and usually without much hesitation (Wu 2016).

Indeed, in a newly published novel about Native American Indians in California, *There There* by Tommy Orange, the author describes one character, Orvil Red Feather, as being brought up with so little sense of his heritage that he had to absorb it all virtually online, from 'watching hours and hours of powwow footage, documentaries on YouTube, by reading all that there was to read on sites like Wikipedia, PowWows.com, and Indian Country Today' (Orange 2018, p. 121). I find most remarkable the notion that this description of that character's behaviour would have made little or no sense 15 years ago but we understand it today immediately. Yet, the pervasive and transformative role of media technology in the last several decades should not ultimately be surprising. As Van Den Eede (2011) argues:

> Our social lives are bathed in technological mediation. This we notice every day, from our waking hours scrolling through our Facebook News Feed to our last e-mail check just before we take off to bed, or in bed. See teens flashing their thumbs at light speed over mobile phone buttons, always in touch. Observe how more and more of our daily communication – administration, shopping, planning – is inconspicuously transferred to the realm of the Internet. Notice the umpteen devices, boxes, wires, antennas, satellites, companies, contracts – standing between us and a friend. Yet what *do* we notice still?
>
> (Van Den Eede 2011, p. 139)

Van Den Eede's question highlights the degree to which technology, once adopted within a culture, becomes transparent to its users. It disappears from immediate consciousness. And, in the process of using such technologies, humans often become unaware of the ways in which their lives are being shaped and affected by the tools they are using.

In both popular media and scholarly research over the last decade, we find ourselves confronted repeatedly by the question: is mediated attention problematic? And, usually even the gentlest of answers suggests there is some cause for alarm. In two national surveys of randomly-selected respondents, the Pew Internet Research Project found a rise in concern by US adults who judge that their own online experience is mostly beneficial, but are beginning to doubt if the internet itself may be negatively affecting society (Smith and Olmstead 2018). While 88 per cent of Americans believe that the internet has been mostly a 'good thing' for themselves, almost 30 per cent respond that the internet has been either 'a bad thing' or has had a mixed 'good and bad' impact upon society. Similarly, almost a quarter of US teens believe online social media has had mostly a negative effect on their lives because of experiences such as bullying, lack of in-person relational contact, and other difficulties (Anderson and Jiang 2018). In 2018, another Pew survey of a sample of 10,000 technology experts, scholars, and health specialists received 1150 responses to questions asking about the impact of digital media over the decade ahead (Anderson and Rainie 2018). The report informs that

> some 47% of these respondents predict that individuals' wellbeing will be more helped than harmed by digital life in the next decade, while 32% say people's wellbeing will be more harmed than helped. The remaining 21% predict there will not be much change in people's wellbeing compared to now.
>
> (Anderson and Rainie 2018, p. 2)

Such judgements are not simply confined to North America. Teenagers and young adults in the UK also point to social media as a distinctively mixed blessing (Economist Data Team 2018, using data from RSPH 2017). These young respondents cite negative aspects of major social media outlets such as Instagram, Snapchat, Facebook and Twitter as including increased problems with adequate sleep, a pervasive fear of missing out in social interactions, bullying, body image issues, anxiety, depression, and loneliness. Social media, they believe, also generate some positive benefits, including increased self-expression, self-identity, emotional support and community building, among others.

Some researchers question whether digital media are psychologically pathological and answer increasingly in the affirmative. Psychologist Adam Alter (2017) published a controversial volume entitled *Irresistible* (Brabazon 2017; Kirkus Reviews 2017; Turner 2017) and posits a singularly negative evaluation of these media. He proposes that today's online world has been shaped fundamentally by technologies designed to foster behavioural addictions such as impulse buying, the consumption of pornography, and online gaming and gambling. Associated with these addictions are marked and increasing levels both of social isolation and depression as well as growing levels of narcissism and lack of empathy among younger people. As noted further in this chapter, Alter's is not the only voice with such strong concerns (e.g. Lin *et al.* 2016; Twenge *et al.* 2017).

One reasonable response to such reports might be to label them all a form of moral panic: the feeling of fear spread among a large number of people that some evil threatens the wellbeing of society (Cohen 1972). Commentators have observed that every major media innovation in human history has been associated with moral denunciation: in *The Phaedrus*, Plato expressed concern about the coming of writing; with the invention of moveable type and the printing press, the Catholic Church felt itself threatened by the publication of vernacular translations of the Bible; and from the beginning, almost every techno-digital advance has evoked a dystopian judgement (Goode and Ben-Yehuda 1994; Markey and Ferguson 2017). As Turner (2017) commented in her review of Alter's (2017) alarming assessment of digital media's influence,

> I am reminded of our parents' fears that endless TV would give us square eyes and turn us into drooling morons. These worries seem quaint now: humans adapt. We are yet to discover how that baby in New York with her tech-distracted parents, who will shortly be fed her own tech distractions, grows up; a native of two clashing worlds.
>
> (Turner 2017, p. 11)

Echoing Turner's (2017) caution about future adaptation and despite the ominous concerns reflected by some commentators, this chapter acknowledges that a definitive answer to the overall question of media's psychological and personal impact as a general and enduring phenomenon is not yet available. Indeed, digital technology in the past quarter-century has unfolded in such a dynamic and changing manner that researchers have had difficulty in keeping pace with or describing the nature of the digital-social universe itself, as well as estimating its effects upon the inhabitants of that universe. Nonetheless, several interconnected pathways promise to open the possibility of better assessing the relationship between the emerging techno-digital landscape and integral human wellbeing in order to come to an informed, if interim judgement. More specifically, I propose (a) to use a media ecological framework (Meyrowitz 1998) to understand the emergence and nature of contemporary digital media; (b) to advance an understanding of human wellbeing and integration grounded in a contemporary narratively-oriented theory of personality, Hermans' *dialogical self and positioning theory* (DSPT; Hermans and Gieser 2012; Hermans, Kempen, and Van Loon 1992); and (c) to deploy these notions to estimate in preliminary fashion some notable effects of techno-digital technology on its users.

Contemporary digital media from a media ecology perspective

What might be a fruitful stance from which to understand the techno-digital world in which we now live? In an effort to achieve greater literacy regarding communication phenomena, Joshua Meyrowitz (1998) argues that contemporary media might be approached from three different frameworks. The oldest and usual method examines the *content* delivered to the users of media itself and, in turn, looks for a kind of dose-dependent effect upon those users due to that content, an applied experimental technique. A second approach considers each form of media (cinema, television, video games) to be a kind of *language* with its own grammar and presentation style (Manovich 2001). In the analysis of digital media's impact upon the development of the individual person, this has proven not to be a particularly helpful frame. Rather, as I have previously proposed (Hevern 2012a), the entire array of media at any particular point in human history forms an ecology or comprehensive environment within which humans function on a day-to-day basis, the third approach Meyrowitz (1998) highlights. This *media ecology* framework (Strate 2017) contends that the differing parts of the physical, technological and human life-worlds each function as complex interactive systems. These systems involve dynamic processes of change, growth, decay, and so on as they seek to achieve diverse goals. Further, applying Marshall McLuhan's (1964/1994) central insight, digital and communications media form extensions of at least three fundamental human systems: our sensory-perceptual apparatus, our cognition, and our motor-expressive abilities.

What then has been the ecology of the techno-digital world over the past two decades? The overview here argues that it has changed, particularly in the last 10 to 15 years, in profound ways (Ankerson 2018). Some readers may be old enough to remember the advent of the personal computer in the 1980s and early 1990s, when Apple and IBM first fought to bring the digital revolution to the desktop in the form of the Apple II Plus, the PC, and the early Macs. But those early innovations opened up to a far broader set of services and functions among digital technologies over roughly the last generation (Levinson 2014; Siapera 2018).

The last decade of the twentieth century marked the advent of the *fundamental physical and notional structures* of today's techno-digital culture. These rest upon the invention of the World Wide Web (WWW) by Tim Berners-Lee between 1989 and 1991 and advances in central processing unit microchips (Gillies and Cailliau 2000). The WWW taught us the idea of hyperlinked connectivity whose usefulness was profoundly enhanced by services such as Google (1998) and Wikipedia (2001; these and subsequent dates represent the first appearance or launch of the named devices and services). This was the period in which the first cell phone technologies emerged (1992) and when mobile devices such as the Palm Pilot (1996) and Blackberry (1999) personal assistants as well as the iPod (2001) portable media player proliferated. From the mid-1990s to the mid-2000s, Silicon Valley and other venture capitalists advanced what we might generally describe as a *digital entrepreneurial vision*. Amazon (1994) in the US and the Alibaba Group (1999) in China are examples of how successful that vision could be. These efforts were motivated by the goal of generating profit by offering a diverse array of digital services and commercial goods. Many initial online businesses appeared and quickly disappeared in the (in)famous 1997–2001 'dot com bubble' of inflated and unrealistic expectations (Cassidy 2002). However, those companies that did survive the bubble transformed the techno-digital world from the mid-2000s until today by joining together in a unique constellation of four interacting components. This has been the generation of *smartphones and tablet computing*: each such device has brought with it portability, multi-functionality, and the possibility of constant connectivity with media content. All of the major social media sites and services we use today – Facebook (2004), YouTube (2005), Twitter (2006), Instagram (2010), Snapchat (2011) – are less than 15 years old. The earlier worlds of personal webpages and blogging, which were so prominent in the 1990s and early 2000s, no longer really exist as crucial online platforms (Ankerson 2018). *Cloud computing services* – still emerging today – permit the inexpensive storage of both personal and business data in massive quantities. And, throughout this entire period, online services and sites have been *consolidated and monetized* by a relatively small number of the new major media corporations. As we approach the end of the second decade of the twenty-first century, these elements comprise the techno-digital environment within which so many persons across both the industrialized and developing world live life daily.

Human wellbeing and Hermans' dialogical self

The foundations of techno-digital media emerged at roughly the same time (the late 1980s and early 1990s) that the Dutch psychologist Hubert Hermans and his collaborators first outlined the concepts underlying the theory of the dialogical self and what has now emerged as dialogical self and positioning theory. The roots of DSPT lie in both American pragmatist thinking about the self – particularly William James' (1890/1981) notion of the self as social – and the European intellectual tradition of thinkers such as Mikhail Bakhtin and Martin Buber, who stressed the centrality of voice and dialogue in human existence (Hermans and Gieser 2012). DSPT can be distinguished from personality theories that reflect a strongly individualist conception of the self. Such theories argue that the *I* functions 'as a relatively bounded and autonomous entity, complete in and of itself, existing separately from others and the surrounding social context … largely uninfluenced by the presence of others … [and] relatively unchanging and constant across situations' (Heine 2001, p. 886). In contrast, Hermans and Gieser (2012) propose that

> the dialogical self can be conceived of as a *dynamic multiplicity of I-positions*. In this view, the *I* emerges from its intrinsic contact with the (social) environment and is bound to particular positions in time and space. As such, the embodied *I* is able to move from one position to the other in accordance with changes in situation and time. In this process of positioning, repositioning and counter-positioning, the *I* fluctuates among different and even opposing positions (both with the self and between self and perceived or imagined others), and these positions are involved in relationships of relative dominance and social power.
>
> (Hermans and Gieser 2012, p. 2, emphasis in original)

This self may express a range of positions at differing times and contexts which support or contradict, challenge or overwhelm, undermine or cooperate with other positions.

Since the turn of the twenty-first century, the early formulation of DSPT has continued to develop and forms what Hermans (2018, p. 9) judges to be as 'an open and flexible bridge' by which differing conceptual systems in the social and psychological sciences might be connected. Specific applications of DSPT have ranged across research and applied domains as diverse as clinical and counselling psychology (Hermans and Dimaggio 2004), cultural psychology (Ahammed and Cherian 2015; Hermans 2001), education (Meijers 2013), and developmental psychology (Hermans 2012). In its role as a bridging theory, DSPT can elucidate strategies, some healthy and others less so, by which individuals function within today's techno-digital environment.

Among various types of positions within DSPT, two forms – *meta-positions* and *promoter positions* – have been central in understanding how the individual self maintains a sense of unity while, at the same time, developing and changing. As Hermans (2018, p. 400) explains, *meta-positions* allow 'a helicopter view of other positions and their patterning and [they] offer a long-term and cross-situational perspective'. *Promoter positions* function dynamically by 'organizing and giving direction to the development of other positions in the repertoire and are able to generate new ones' (Hermans 2018, p. 400). Within the dialogical self, however, there are positions that may either exist non-consciously, that is, below the level of consciousness or have been disowned in the case of *shadow positions* that are rejected as unacceptable. Extending positioning theory in his most recent volume, Hermans (2018) identifies a new and influential notion of the *over-position* which he describes as 'exaggerating a position to a degree that the balance in the self is lost due to the lack of effective counter positions' (Hermans 2018, p. 400). When this happens, an individual is threatened by what he terms an '*I-prison*'. The dominance of an over-position has effectively shut or drowned out communication and dialogue among the multiplicity of positions in the self.

How might we relate these different types of positions in the dialogical self to the question of wellbeing in the environment of digital media? DSPT does not explicitly use the Jungian term 'individuation' to denote a final or desired goal for the development of the person across the lifespan (for points of similarity and difference between DSPT and Jungian perspectives see the series of essays in Jones and Morioka 2011). Nonetheless, Hermans (2018), in contrast to the risks associated with a narrowing of I-positions or 'the homogenization of the self' (Hermans 2018, p. 255), does outline a broad understanding of what underlies happiness and subjective wellbeing as fundamental goals for personality development. The constituent elements, leading to 'heterogenization' of the self, involve four factors: positive emotion, negative emotion, domain satisfaction, and life satisfaction (Hermans 2018, p. 261). These factors arise from 'a multiplicity of I-positions' (Hermans 2018, p. 257) across 'a multiplicity of domains'

(Hermans 2018, p. 259) and require what Hermans (2018, p. 264) terms 'emodiversity' or an 'affective enrichment of the self'. As such, DSPT advances the idea that our wellbeing requires attention not only to positive but also to negative emotions so that individuals can tolerate distress (Kashdan and Biswas-Diener 2014) in many different settings:

> distress tolerance is found in those who do not shy away from anger, guilt, or boredom just because they feel bad. Instead they are able to withstand the discomfort of those experiences and – when appropriate – even draw from this darker palette of emotions.
>
> (Hermans 2018, p. 266)

Further, the loss of diversity in the I-position repertoire may lead both to the scapegoating of others or the construction of an 'enemy image' against others of a 'different race, religion, culture, age, or appearance' (Hermans 2018, p. 271). In either case individuals reject what form shadow positions in themselves and fail to develop more integrative meta-positions that include these elements. In so doing they fall victim to a kind of 'psychological blindness' (Hermans 2018, p. 275) at odds with reality and a blockage in their ability to respond appropriately to others in their social worlds. Thus, in order to achieve adequate levels of wellbeing or individuation in a non-Jungian sense, DSPT contends that individuals need to overcome, minimize or reject narrowness or significant imbalances among the diverse positions of the self; embrace what is hidden, disavowed, or otherwise splintered from consciousness; and, seek an integrative movement or synthesis among the self's potential multiplicities.

Techno-digital technology's effects on its users

How do these themes relate more specifically to our current techno-digital media culture and how it affects users of these technologies? Hermans (2018) points to part of the answer, but I suggest he stops somewhat short in identifying how media today have begun to undermine processes of individuation or, as he terms it, 'heterogenizing the self'. He rightly identifies the global dominance of the market economy which has demonstrated a remarkable ability to infiltrate into multiple niches of contemporary society. To demonstrate processes of marketization, Hermans incorporates the work of Schimank and Volkmann (2012) who portray modern society as functionally differentiated into 12 subsystems or what they term 'subuniverse[s] of meaning'. These subsystems involve politics, economy, religion, science, art, education, health care, journalism, law, the military, sports, and intimate relations. Countering Hermans, I suggest that the differentiation of these subsystems over the last decade as significantly bounded realities has been undermined and they have been transformed into a far more interlocking and interdependent techno-digital system with media at its centre.

Over-positioning and the digital media self

Hermans (2018) notes a series of distinctive selves that have been described in the last several decades as characteristic of contemporary society. These include Kelly's (2006) emerging 'entrepreneurial self', Hamilton's (2010) 'consumer self', Phil Cushman's (1990) 'empty self' and Kasser and Ryan's (1993) identification of the shadow sides of the American dream. All of these selves illustrate 'expressions of a society that is subjected to a process of over-positioning economical thinking' (Hermans 2018, p. 204) while each of these 'selves' might further be considered 'a position that the self can take among different other positions' (Hermans 2018, p. 231). Hermans' analysis points to over-positioning as a process primarily involving economical thinking. I argue, however, that the over-positioning we experience now goes beyond the economic to a broader array of concerns. More specifically, a new form of over-positioning arises from and is mirrored in the self by the interpenetrative processes of our techno-digital media landscape as an increasingly unified human ecological system. This system involves at least three fundamental facets that combine economic and other factors in its functioning. First, techno-digital media culture deploys comprehensive psychological and marketing strategies in order to capture ever-increasing levels of our individual attention and personal data (Wu 2016). Second, this ecological system obtains more and more of that attention as seen in residual attitudes such as 'fear of missing out' from the stream of social media (the so-called 'FOMO' experience) or the priority of media over 'in real life' (IRL) contact on an everyday basis (Elhai *et al.* 2016). And, third, this system is motivated by both the financial and entrepreneurial goals of advanced capitalism (rather than more individual or personal goals of earlier times; Siapera 2018).

The profound degree to which our world has been altered is underscored by Coudry and Hepp's (2017) sociological argument that reality today is being constructed by what they term 'deep mediatization and the media manifold' (Coudry and Hepp 2017, p. 53). These concepts mirror 'our embedding in today's extremely complex media environment. The set for media and information possibilities on which a typical social actor, at least in rich countries, can now draw is almost infinite, and organized on very many dimensions' (Coudry and Hepp 2017, p. 56). Further, inhabitants of this techno-digital world are positioned 'within a much larger institutionalized environment of interdependent media', which creates 'a situated complexity of that actor's everyday choices of media' (Coudry and Hepp 2017, p. 56). From another perspective, the developmental psychologist Zheng Yan (2018) contends that the introduction of smartphones into the lifeworld of children and adolescents 'can be conceptualized as an *unparalleled complex developmental phenomeno*n that features multi-faceted, … multilayered, … and multiprocessed processes' (Yan 2018, p. 7, emphasis added). Developing personhood in the twenty-first century takes place in an environment never previously encountered in human experience.

The emergence of a techno-digital media over-position in the past decade can be illustrated by contrasting earlier attempts by myself and others to apply dialogical self theory to cyber-culture. In the late 1990s and early 2000s, we referred to positions such as 'I as blogger' or 'I as personal webpage creator' or 'I as emailer or texter' or even 'I as Facebook user' (e.g. Hevern 2004; Dillon 2010). Such more narrowly-focused I-positions have given way today to an almost endless series of techno-digital activities undertaken by the same individual; hence, it is now possible to describe an array of I-positions linked to techno-digital media which include the I as a digital media addict, agent, commentator, consumer, correspondent, critic, customer, cyber-bully, end-user, enjoyer, fan, friend, influencer, lurker, maker, merchant, pleasure seeker, producer, fake-news reporter, researcher, socializer, trader, troll, user, vendor, cyber-bully victim, viewer and witness. This conglomerate of online behaviours and roles (many others could also be added) points to how techno-digital culture has become ubiquitous, functions for multiple purposes, and finds expression in moderate to quite extreme degrees of involvement.

Captured attention

Data bear out how much media, and increasingly digital media, have captured our attention. In the first quarter of 2018, the average American adult spent 11.06 hours or 46 per cent of a 24-hour day attending to all forms of media – at home or the office, during travel or at leisure (Nielsen Company 2018). Young adults between 18 and 34 years old averaged 4.51 hours daily using digital media (18.8 per cent of a whole day) while among those 35 to 49 years old digital use rose to 4.98 hours daily (20.8 per cent of a whole day; Nielsen Company 2018). Further, between 2012 and 2018, the use of portable, hand-held mobile devices has more than doubled to 3.4 hours or 14 per cent of each day (calculated from data at Statista 2018). In this past decade, technology has had

> a singular goal of completely conquering our eyes. It has given us phones with ever-bigger screens and phones with unbelievable cameras, not to mention virtual reality goggles and several attempts at camera-glasses. Tech has now captured pretty much all visual capacity.
>
> (Manjoo 2018)

In my own undergraduate classes on psychology and digital media since 2014, each year students report increasing time spent using applications on mobile phones, checking social networks such as Facebook or Snapchat, and reading social media postings. Mirroring the experience of their peers nationally, they acknowledge using their mobile phones or texting more than once an hour, day in and day out, every day of the week.

Narrowing of social exchange

The expansion of digital media in the past generation has afforded its users the possibility of accessing an almost unlimited range of information, viewpoints, and communities, whether political, social, religious, scientific, or otherwise. Nonetheless, this diversity of online communities, news sources, and platforms for potential dialogue has paradoxically been met by some tendencies which narrow the range of social exchange. On the one hand, the American legal scholar, Cass Sunstein (2017), points out that profound political polarization and the decision to limit exposure to viewpoints congenial to one's own (sometimes termed *homophily*) are not predominant characteristics of online environments. In fact, based on a US national probability sample generated in 2012, Lee *et al.* (2014, p. 714) suggest that 'It is likely that social media indeed facilitates an individual's exposure to diverse perspectives when she is on Facebook, Twitter, or other social media sites'. On the other hand, when those same data are examined to judge the impact of strongly-held negative reactions to members of opposing political parties (Democrat vs. Republican) – what the authors term 'affective polarization' – the results are different:

> most cross-cutting interactions on SNSs [social networking sites] occur between non polarized partisans, that is, those who evaluate the two parties on similar terms or who may dislike the party they identify with even more than they dislike the opposing party ... cross-cutting discussions occurring on SNSs lack involvement from each party's most polarized partisans.
>
> (Heatherly *et al.* 2016, p. 14)

Further examples for a narrowing of social exchange can be seen in a variety of contexts, but perhaps most profoundly in the form of cyberhate websites (Quant and Festl 2017; Schafer 2002). Such sites 'spread (mis)information, extremist viewpoints, and ideological messages' (Quant and Festl 2017, p. 3) and may advocate for positions such as White nationalism, neo-Nazism, male supremacy, anti-Muslim, anti-immigrant, or anti-LGBT policies, and others. Hevern (2012b) has suggested that these sites reflect a form of extreme monologicality grounded in three tactics that DSPT suggests the self might use to cope with political, economic or cultural uncertainty in the contemporary world: giving the lead to one powerful position, boundary sharpening, and position multiplication (Hermans and Hermans-Konopka 2010). These tactics allow individuals to leverage affordances for *anonymity, isolation* and *exclusivity* in online communication. In sum, whether expressed by extreme partisan polarization or the tactics displayed on cyberhate sites and their like, a notable proportion of users function within the techno-digital world in ways that narrow or otherwise filter out what they are willing to engage with, confront, or acknowledge in themselves and others.

Imbalanced media use in adults and youngsters

As social media first emerged in the early 2000s, multiple researchers identified what is termed 'the Facebook Effect' – that is, the higher the use of Facebook, the greater the level of reported subjective distress, especially depression. In 2013, Rosen and his colleagues summarized the literature by claiming 'there is now extensive evidence documenting a relationship between depression and excessive texting, viewing video clips, video gaming, chatting, e-mailing, listening to music and other media uses' (Rosen *et al.* 2013, p. 1243). However, over the past five or so years, other researchers have challenged the notion of a uniform 'Facebook Effect' by identifying a co-variant relationship that earlier researcher overlooked. For example, the work of Ariel Shensa and her colleagues (2017) at the University of Pittsburgh Medical Center has focused upon a large group of young American adults between 19 and 32 years old. They found 44 per cent in their sample engaging in excessive social media use with 14 per cent showing clearly problematic forms of use. Contrary to the 'Facebook Effect', it was *not* the overall time online that defined the link between media use and depression, but rather a set of six problematic behaviours of social media use that were associated with depression. Identified in earlier research by Andreassen *et al.* (2012), all six of these behaviours appear to involve addictive qualities: salience or the urge to use, modification of the user's mood, increasing tolerance, withdrawal feelings when not using, clearly negative impact of use on major life demands, and a tendency to relapse to use despite the desire not to. These data illustrate precisely what Hermans identifies as an over-position that arises in the constant use of techno-digital media among a sizable random sample of young American adults. Note that the over-position identified here is not universal but is reflected in a minority proportion of these younger people. Indeed, a further nuance to what comprises a digital media over-position comes with a more recent report by Shensa *et al.* (2018). Here, the researchers note that the relationship between social media use and depression is moderated by a third variable: more specifically, the number of social media contacts with whom a user has actual closeness in real life. The lack of face-to-face contact increases significantly the risk of depressive symptoms in social media users. The narrowing of one's social life to a predominantly online environment negatively affects overall psychological functioning.

What about the wellbeing of even younger people who are also avid social and digital media users? In that unique techno-digital developmental context identified by Yan (2018), what are pre- and early adolescents experiencing? Jean Twenge and her colleagues (2018) reported a study of 8th and 10th grade American students (that is, roughly 13 to 16 year olds) and their sense of wellbeing across the decade beginning in 2006. I caution as I would with my own students that correlational data do not prove causation. But, when comparing students across this period in terms of their adoption of smartphones and amount of time spent online (as well as using general US unemployment as a kind of economic contrast variable since lowered levels of unemployment have been associated with increasing feelings of wellbeing), something rather striking appears to emerge after 2012: as both smartphones and time spent online rises, the level of low psychological wellbeing self-reported by these students shows a rapid ascent as well. And, 'across the 14 domains of life satisfaction [tracked in this research], the largest declines between 2012 and 2016 appeared in satisfaction with life as a whole, friends, amount of fun, self, and personal safety' (Twenge *et al*. 2018, p. 3). Again, the narrowing of the range of behaviours in favour of a particular way of engaging in daily life through media seems to impede multiple facets of social and personal growth.

'Technoference' and distracted parenting

A final consideration of the impact of over-positioning arises when considering the role of digital media within the dynamics of the family home. Developmental psychology puts parent–child face-to-face (FTF) communication as a central element in the psychological, social and educational maturation of offspring. Yet there is mounting evidence that some parents are so engaged in their own media use that they have decreased the degree to which they attend to their own children. From a broader perspective among younger people and adults, researchers have documented how the very presence of a smartphone or other digital device within a conversational setting tends to degrade the quality of dyadic communication, including overall levels of empathic concern (Misra *et al*. 2014; Przybylski and Weinstein 2012). What of the context of child–parent communication? Turkle's (2012) interviews with 300 children and 150 parents in the US underscore the distress experienced by children when their parents fail to engage in FTF conversations with them. In her subsequent research she identified extensive discontent arising from a kind of vicious circle involving digital, specifically smartphone, technology:

> Parents give their children phones. Children can't get their parents' attention away from their phones, so children take refuge in their own devices. Then, parents use their children's absorption with phones as permission to have their own phones out as much as they wish.
>
> (Turkle 2015, quoted in Franzen 2015, para. 5)

The impact of this media-distracted parenting is a relatively new research field, but Kildare and Middlemiss (2017) summarize major findings in the recent literature: parental use of media often demonstrates that

> the continual connections provided by phones combined with the social pressure to respond quickly to calls/messages disrupt[s] parent–child interactions. Parents who use their phones during parent–child interactions are less sensitive and responsive both verbally and nonverbally to their children's bids for attention.
>
> (Kildare and Middlemiss 2017, p. 579)

Further, children ignored by media-distracted parents are more likely to engage in risky behaviours to gain attention while overall levels of intra-familial conflict tend to be higher. Consider the content of a Facebook posting by a teacher of 2nd graders (that is, seven- and eight-year-old children) which was widely shared online (WKBW Staff 2018). When that teacher asked her 24 students to write about the invention that they wish had never been created, four students wrote on the same theme: smartphones. One child expressed these feelings:

> If I had to tell you which invention I don't like, I would say that I don't like the phone. I don't like the phone because my parents are on their phones every day. A phone is sometimes a really bad habet [*sic*]. I hate my mom's phone and I wish she never had one. That is an invention that I don't like.

The crucial dialogicality of childrearing and development can be bypassed when parents themselves become so engaged in using such media that they neglect interacting with their kids, a process recently labelled as 'technoference' by child developmental researchers (McDaniel and Radesky 2018).

Concluding remarks

Fourteen years ago at a conference on DSPT in Warsaw, psychologist Mick Cooper questioned me in a pointed fashion about whether my comments about the dialogical self and online environments were simply too positive and optimistic. He was sceptical of the overall promise for human flourishing that lay in the impact of online media. While I would defend what I had to say then, I would answer Mick's question today in a different fashion. In detailing in this chapter how techno-digital culture challenges dialogicality and individuation, I would now situate any assessment of such challenges as conditioned by the unfolding of a particular narrative. Techno-digital media has infiltrated our lives in ways we did not and could not have anticipated clearly at the turn of the twenty-first century. Its very omnipresence is not merely an instance of a circumscribed factor affecting our psychological lives, but reflects a far broader ecological world within which we have come to function at varying levels of engagement. Earlier research models estimated the impact of digital technology by categorizing the internet or its components as individual variables and quantified their effects on specified aspects of psychological activity and personal behaviour. Yet, as Coudry and Hepp (2017, p. 35) conclude, 'mediatization also refers to qualitative dimensions, that is, to the social and cultural differences that mediated communications make at higher levels of organizational behaviour complexity' and, thus, 'the internet' has become 'a deeply commercialized, increasingly banal *space for the conduct of social life itself'* (Coudry and Hepp 2017, p. 50, emphasis in the original).

Recent research findings, some of which have been offered here, resist summary judgements of techno-digital media as either overwhelmingly or unilaterally negative or positive. Rather it appears that significant numbers of us find the emerging digital ecology so compelling that our daily lives and social activities become unbalanced in ways that were never true previously. While not valid for the majority of individuals, the position of 'I as techno-digital media user' may be transformed into an over-position for some significant minority of today's media consumers. Such a transformation tends to drain away the psychological energies necessary to engage in the kind of broad dialogical conversations necessary to advance reasonably healthy individuation or wellbeing. The challenge of the years ahead involves helping others or even ourselves who have adopted such an over-position to find a way back to a more balanced dialogicality within ourselves and across society.

References

Ahammed, S. and Cherian, I. (Eds.) (2015) Eastern perspectives on the dialogical self [Special issue]. *International Journal for Dialogical Science* 9(1). Online. Available: http://ijds.lemoyne.edu/journal/9_1/index.html.

Alter, A.L. (2017) *Irresistible: The Rise of Addictive Technology and the Business of Keeping us Hooked*. New York: Penguin Press.

Anderson, J. and Rainie, L. (2018) *The Future of Wellbeing in a Tech-saturated World*. Pew Research Center. Available at www.pewinternet.org/2018/07/03/stories-from-experts-about-the-impact-of-digital-life (accessed 31 July 2018).

Anderson, M. and Jiang, J. (2018) *Teens, Social Media & Technology 2018*. Pew Research Center. Available: www.pewinternet.org/2018/05/31/teens-social-media-technology-2018/ (accessed 6 July 2018).

Andreassen, C. S., Torsheim, T., Brunborg, G. S. and Pallesen, S. (2012) Development of a Facebook addiction scale. *Psychological Reports* 110, 501–517.

Ankerson, M. S. (2018) *Dot-com Design: The Rise of a Usable, Social, Commercial Web*. New York: NYU Press.

Brabazon, T. (2017) Review of 'irresistible: why we can't stop checking, scrolling, clicking, and watching'. *Times Higher Education*. Available: www.timeshighereducation.com/books/review-irresistible-adam-alter-bodley-head (accessed 6 July 2018).

Cassidy, J. (2002) *Dot.con: The Greatest Story Ever Sold*. New York: HarperCollins.

Cohen, M. (1972) *Folk Devils and Moral Panics: The Creation of the Mods and Rockers*. London, UK: Granada Publishing.

Coudry, N. and Hepp, A. (2017) *The Mediated Construction of Reality: Society, Culture, Mediatization*. Malden, MA: Polity Press.

Cushman, P. (1990) Why the self is empty: toward a historically situated psychology. *American Psychologist* 45, 599–611.

Dillon, L. (2010) Listening for voices of self: digital journaling among gifted young adolescents. *Qualitative Research Journal* 10, 13–27.

Economist Data Team (2018) How heavy use of social media is linked to mental illness. *The Economist*. Available: www.economist.com/graphic-detail/2018/05/18/how-heavy-use-of-social-media-is-linked-to-mental-illness (accessed 6 July 2018).

Elhai, J. D., Levine, J. C., Dvorak, R. D. and Hall, B. J. (2016) Fear of missing out, need for touch, anxiety and depression are related to problematic smartphone use. *Computers in Human Behavior* 63, 509–516.

Franzen, J. (2015) Review of 'Reclaiming conversation: The power of talk in a digital age' by Sherry Turkle. *New York Times*. Available: www.nytimes.com/2015/10/04/books/review/jonathan-franzen-reviews-sherry-turkle-reclaiming-conversation.html (accessed 6 July 2018).

Gillies, J. and Cailliau, R. (2000) *How the Web was Born: The Story of the World Wide Web*. New York: Oxford University Press.

Goode, E. and Ben-Yehuda, N. (1994) Moral panics: culture, politics, and social construction. *Annual Review of Sociology* 20, 149–171.

Hamilton, C. (2010) *Requiem for a Species: Why We Resist the Truth about Climate Change*. London, UK: Routledge.

Heatherly, K. A., Lu, Y. and Lee, J. K. (2016) Filtering out the other side? Cross-cutting and like-minded discussions on social networking sites. *New Media & Society* 19, 1271–1289.

Heine, S. J. (2001) Self as cultural product: an examination of East Asian and North American selves. *Journal of Personality* 69, 881–906.

Hermans, H. J. M. (Ed.) (2001) Culture and the dialogical self: theory, method and practice [Special issue]. *Culture & Psychology* 7(3).

Hermans, H. J. M. (2012) Dialogical self theory and the increasing multiplicity of I-positions in a globalizing society: an introduction. *New Directions for Child and Adolescent Development* 137, 1–21.

Hermans, H. J. M. (Ed.) (2015) Dialogical self in a complex world: the need for bridging theories. *Europe's Journal of Psychology* 11, 1–4.

Hermans, H. J. M. (Ed.) (2018) *Society in the Self: A Theory of Identity in Democracy*. New York: Oxford University Press.

Hermans, H. J. M. and Dimaggio, G. (Eds) (2004) *The Dialogical Self in Psychotherapy*. New York: Brunner-Routledge.

Hermans, H. J. M. and Gieser, T. (Eds) (2012) *Handbook of Dialogical Self Theory*. Cambridge, UK: Cambridge University Press.

Hermans, H. J. M. and Hermans-Konopka, A. (2010) *Dialogical Self Theory: Positioning and Counter-positioning in a Globalizing Society*. New York: Cambridge University Press.

Hermans, H. J. M., Kempen, H. J. G. and Van Loon, R. J. P. (1992) The dialogical self: beyond individualism and rationalism. *American Psychologist* 47, 23–33.

Hevern, V. W. (2004) Threaded identity in cyberspace: weblogs and positioning in the dialogical self. *Identity* 4, 321–335.

Hevern, V. W. (2012a) Dialogicality from the media ecology perspective. Paper presented at *the Seventh International Conference on the Dialogical Self*, Athens, Georgia, October 2012.

Hevern, V. W. (2012b) Dialogicality and the internet. In: H. J. M. Hermans and T. Gieser (Eds), *Handbook of Dialogical Self Theory*. New York: Cambridge University Press.

James, W. (1890/1981) *The Principles of Psychology*, Vol. 1 (F. Burkhardt, Ed.). Cambridge, MA: Harvard University Press.

Jones, R. A. and Morioka, M. (Eds) (2011) *Jungian and Dialogical Self Perspectives*. New York: Palgrave Macmillan.

Kashdan, R. B. and Biswas-Diener, R. (2014) *The Upside of your Dark Side*. Toronto, ON: Hudson Street Press.

Kasser, T. and Ryan, R. M. (1993) A dark side of the American dream: correlates of financial success as a central life aspiration. *Journal of Personality and Social Psychology* 62, 410–422.

Kelly, P. (2006) The entrepreneurial self and 'youth at risk': exploring the horizons of identity in the twenty-first century. *Journal of Youth Studies* 9, 17–32.

Kiers, J. and Tissink, F. (2000) *The Glory of the Golden Age: Dutch Art of the 17th Century*. Amsterdam, the Netherlands: Waanders Publishers/Rijksmuseum.

Kildare, C. A. and Middlemiss, W. (2017) Impact of parents mobile device use on parent-child interaction: a literature review. *Computers in Human Behavior* 75, 579–593.

Kirkus Reviews (2017) Review of 'Irresistible: the rise of addictive technology and the business of keeping us hooked by A. Alter'. Available: www.kirkusreviews.com/book-reviews/adam-alter/irresistible-rise/ (accessed 6 July 2018).

Lee, J. K., Choi, J., Kim, C. and Kim, Y. (2014) Social media, network heterogeneity, and opinion polarization. *Journal of Communication* 64, 702–722.

Levinson, P. (2013) *New New Media* (2nd edn). Boston, MA: Pearson.

Lin, L.Y., Sidani, J. E., Shensa, A., Radovic, A., Miller, E. *et al.* (2016) Association between social media use and depression among U.S. young adults. *Depression and Anxiety* 33, 323–331.

Manjoo, F. (2018) We have reached peak screen. Now revolution is in the air. *New York Times*. Available: www.nytimes.com/2018/06/27/technology/peak-screen-revolution.html (accessed 6 July 2018).

Manovich, L. (2001) *The Language of New Media*. Cambridge, MA: MIT Press.

Markey, P. M. and Ferguson, C. J. (2017) *Moral Combat: Why the War on Violent Video Games is Wrong*. Dallas, TX: BenBella Books.

McDaniel, B. T. and Radesky, J. S. (2018) Technoference: parent distraction with technology and associations with child behavior problems. *Child Development* 89, 100–109.

McLuhan, M. (1964/1994) *Understanding Media: The Extensions of Man*. Cambridge, MA: MIT Press.

Meijers, F. (Ed.) (2013) Education and the dialogical self [Special issue]. *International Journal for Dialogical Science* 7(1), online. Available: http://ijds.lemoyne.edu/journal/7_1/index.html.

Meyrowitz, J. (1998) Multiple media literacies. *Journal of Communication* 48, 96–108.

Misra, S., Cheng, L., Genevie, J. and Yuan, M. (2014) The iPhone effect: the quality of in-person social interactions in the presence of mobile devices. *Environment and Behavior* 48, 275–298.

Molloy, M. (2016) The real story behind a viral Rembrandt 'kids on phones' photo. *Telegraph*. Available: www.telegraph.co.uk/news/newstopics/howaboutthat/12103150/Rembrandt-The-Night-Watch-The-real-story-behind-the-kids-on-phones-photo.html (accessed 6 July 2018).

Nielsen Company (2018) *The Nielsen Total Audience Report. Q1 2018*. Available: www.nielsen.com/content/dam/corporate/us/en/reports-downloads/2018-reports/q1-2018-total-audience-report.pdf (accessed 1 August 2018).

Orange, J. (2018) *There There*. New York: Alfred A. Knopf.

Przybylski, A. K. and Weinstein, N. (2012) Can you connect with me now? How the presence of mobile communication technology influences face-to-face conversation quality. *Journal of Social and Personal Relationships* 30, 237–246.

Quant, T. and Festl, R. (2017) Cyberhate. In: P. Rössler (Ed.), *The International Encyclopedia of Media Effects* [Online reference] New York: Wiley.

Rijksmuseum (2018) Night Watch Gallery. Available: www.rijksmuseum.nl/en/general-information/building-and-presentation/night-watch-gallery (accessed 6 July 2018).

Rosen, L. D., Whaling, K., Rab, S., Carrier, I. M. and Cheever, N. A. (2013) Is Facebook creating 'iDisorders'? The link between clinical symptoms of psychiatric disorders and technology use, attitudes and anxiety. *Computers in Human Behavior* 29, 1243–1254.

Royal Society for Public Health (RSPH) (2017) Status of mind: social media and young people's mental health and wellbeing. Available: www.rsph.org.uk/our-work/campaigns/status-of-mind.html (accessed 6 July 2018).

Schafer, J. A. (2002) Spinning the web of hate: web-based hate propagation by extremist organisations. *Journal of Criminal Justice and Popular Culture* 9, 69–88.

Schimank, U. and Volkmann, U. (2012) *The Marketization of Society: Economizing the Non-economic.* Bremen, Germany: University of Bremen.

Shensa, A., Escobar-Viera, C. G., Sidani, J. E., Bowman, N. D., Marshal, M. P. and Primack, B. A. (2017) Problematic social media use and depressive symptoms among U.S. young adults: a nationally-representative study. *Social Science & Medicine* 182, 150–157.

Shensa, A., Sidani, J. E., Escobar-Viera, Chu, K.-H., Bowman, N. D., Knight, J. M. and Primack, B. A. (2018) Real-life closeness of social media contacts and depressive symptoms among university students. *Journal of American College Health* 30 March 2018, 1–8.

Siapera, E. (2018) *Understanding New Media* (2nd edn). Thousand Oaks, CA: Sage.

Smith, A. and Olmstead, K. (2018) *Declining Majority of Online Adults Say the Internet has been Good for Society.* Pew Research Center. Available: www.pewinternet.org/2018/04/30/declining-majority-of-online-adults-say-the-internet-has-been-good-for-society/ (accessed 6 July 2018).

Statista (2018) Average daily media use in the United States from 2012 to 2018, by device (in minutes). Available: www.statista.com/statistics/270781/average-daily-media-use-in-the-us/ (accessed 6 July 2018).

Strate, L. (2017) *Media Ecology: An Approach to Understanding the Human Condition.* New York: Peter Lang.

Sunstein, C. (2017) *#republic: Divided Democracy in the Age of Social Media.* Princeton, NJ: Princeton University Press.

Turkle, S. (2012) *Alone Together.* New York: Basic Books.

Turkle, S. (2015) *Reclaiming Conversation: The Power of Talk in a Digital Age.* New York: Penguin.

Turner, J. (2017) Social media: how to fight back: Review of 'Irresistible: Why we can't stop checking, scrolling, clicking, and watching.' *The Times,* 25 February 2017 (p. 11).

Twenge, J. M., Joiner, T. E., Rogers, M. L. and Martin, G. N. (2017) Increases in depressive symptoms, suicide-related outcomes, and suicide rates among U.S. adolescents after 2010 and links to increased new media screen time. *Clinical Psychological Science* 6, 3–17.

Twenge, J. M., Martin, G. N. and Campbell, W. K. (2018) Decreases in psychological wellbeing among American adolescents after 2012 and links to screen time during the rise of smartphone technology. *Emotion,* Online first; doi: 10.1037/emo0000403.

Van Den Eede, Y. (2011) In between us: on the transparency and opacity of technological mediation. *Foundations of Science* 16, 139–159.

WKBW Staff (2018) I wish my mom's cell phone was never invented: child's essay goes viral. 24 May 2018. Available: www.wkbw.com/news/i-wish-my-moms-cell-phone-was-never-invented-childs-essay-goes-viral (accessed 6 July 2018).

Wu, T. (2016) *The Attention Merchants.* New York: Knopf.

Yan, Z. (2018) Child and adolescent use of mobile phones: an unparalleled complex developmental phenomenon. *Child Development* 89, 5–16.

Chapter 11

Narratives of transformation

The Structural Dream Analysis method

Christian Roesler

Identity can be seen as the construct that provides the person with a sense of continuity of being over time. It also creates a sense of coherence, so that the divergent experiences of the person over their life course form an interconnected whole. Finally, identity gives meaning to one's experiences and to life as a whole. The theory of narrative identity (Gergen and Gergen 1987; Josselson and Lieblich 1995) adds to this perspective by pointing to the importance of autobiographical narratives in the construction of one's identity. By telling and retelling one's life stories, the person creates personal identity. This narrative approach has had a major impact on the humanities and the social sciences in the last few decades (Chamberlayne 2000) and has also found its way into analytical psychology (Covington 1995). It can be demonstrated that personal life stories are also influenced by archetypal story patterns, which provide templates for creating meaning in one's life (Roesler 2006).

This points to the unique viewpoint taken in Jungian psychology, which stresses that the conscious ego is not the only author of the person's life story and identity. The term individuation, coined by Jung (1928), is defined as a process of transformation of the personality over the life course, aiming at the potential wholeness of the person, and thus providing meaning in life. This process is seen as a continuous dialogue between the conscious ego and the unconscious. In this process the unconscious is seen as a supportive force for personality development. This is manifested, for example, in dreams in which the unconscious provides additional information to consciousness by way of symbols and patterns (Jung 1948).

This viewpoint of analytical psychology, somehow, contrasts with the approach usually taken in narratology, in which the person telling and retelling his/her life stories is regarded as the author, maybe not of their lives, but of the meaning of the events in the life course reflected in one's identity. In the perspective of analytical psychology, a 'second author' can be found in the unconscious of the person, who adds to the formation of identity by communicating with consciousness by the way of symbols. In the practice of Jungian analysis, therefore, the transformation of the personality is not only supported by the dialogue between analyst and client, but the analyst will also focus on the intrapsychic communication between consciousness and the unconscious. The individuation process in this sense manifests in this intrapsychic communication between the conscious ego and the symbols – and sometimes symptoms – coming from the unconscious, which are often experienced by the person not as supportive, but sometimes even disturbing. Jung has pointed out that individuation can be seen as an autonomous force manifesting over the life course, and many people even in today's society never become conscious of this intrapsychic exchange. Jungian analysis, which attempts to bring this intrapsychic communication to consciousness and support a process of full integration of the different perspectives of conscious ego as well as the unconscious, can be seen as a very special case of individuation in the sense of active inner work. Nevertheless, many people, even if they never make use of psychoanalysis, experience some sort of this intrapsychic exchange by way of their nightly dreams.

In the psychoanalytic tradition, the work with dreams has always had an important role in the treatment of psychological disorders and is still considered as the royal road to the unconscious (Fosshage 1987). Even though quite different approaches to the interpretation of dreams have developed in the different psychoanalytic schools, there is general agreement that dreams give access to an understanding of the unconscious roots of psychological problems as well as to therapeutic pathways. The dream can be seen as a subtext which points to the core conflicts underlying neurosis and it also contains constructive impulses for overcoming the problems. Nevertheless, there is a strong lack of systematic investigations into the meaning of dreams and their connection to process in psychotherapy and to individuation as a whole.

Structural Dream Analysis (SDA) is a narratological method for analysing the meaning of dream series in analytical psychotherapies. For the application of SDA, dreams are understood as narratives. In the psychoanalytic encounter, the patient usually presents a dream in the way of telling a story about what happened during sleep, so dreams in psychotherapy can be seen as narratives (Boothe 1994). The dream as an inner world phenomenon – which is never accessible for research – has to be differentiated from the narrated form: a text. From a linguistic point of view, the genre of this text is a narrative. In narratology, a narrative is defined as a development from a starting point, which often features a problem that needs repair or solution; the narrative goes through ups and downs, generally arriving at the solution of the problem or the valued endpoint of the story (Gülich and Quasthoff 1985).

Psychoanalytic dream theory

In the last few decades there has been a reconceptualization of psychoanalytic dream theories influenced by insights from empirical dream research. This has led to a convergence of contemporary Freudian theories of the dream towards Jung's understanding of the dream (e.g. Fosshage 1987; Levin 1990). Referring to Barrett and McNamara (2007), the results of empirical dream research can be summarized in the following theory of dreaming: in the dream the brain is in a mode where it does not have to process new input but can use larger capacities for working on problems and finding creative solutions. The dream focuses especially on experiences in waking life that have emotional meaning for the dreamer. The dreaming mind can find solutions for problems more easily compared with waking consciousness because it is able to connect different areas and functions of the brain. This supports the viewpoint taken by Jung (1934, 1948), which sees the psyche as a self-regulating system and the dream as a spontaneously produced picture of the current situation of the psyche in the form of symbols. Jung differentiates between a 'subjective' level and an 'objective' level. In the first perspective, the figures and objects of the dream are interpreted as being representatives for parts or qualities of the dreamer's personality (especially conflictual parts, i.e. complexes), whereas in the objective perspective they are seen as representing persons or entities existing in reality. In dreams, the unconscious psyche attempts to support ego consciousness and foster a process of personality integration by pointing to parts of the psyche not yet integrated into the whole of personality, or to indicate unresolved conflicts. Through dreams, the unconscious, because it contains a more holistic knowledge about the development and integration of personality, brings new information to consciousness, which can then be integrated if a conscious understanding of the information is possible. This is the aim of dream interpretation in psychotherapy. So Jungian dream interpretation focuses on the relationship of the dream ego (i.e. the figure in the dream which the dreamer experiences as 'myself', psychoanalytically representing ego consciousness) to the other figures in the dream. This gives an indication through the imagery of the capability of the ego to cope with emotions, impulses and complexes (being represented in this symbolic form in the dream), and the strength of ego consciousness. As the information in dreams appears in the form of symbols and images it needs translation to be understood by the conscious ego. For this aim Jung developed the method of 'amplification': the symbolic form is enriched with information coming from cultural parallels, the meaning the symbol has in different cultures, mythologies, religious traditions, and spiritual belief systems. Through amplification a network of meaning is constructed around the symbol; the aim is not so much to give a precise interpretation of the symbol but more to stimulate processes in the dreamer to become more conscious of potential solutions offered by the dream.

Empirical dream research

Many insights from empirical dream research support this view of the dream (for more details, see Roesler 2018). Hall and Van de Castle (1966) argued that it is possible to draw a personality profile based only on dreams of the person. In a study on dreams of persons with multiple personality disorder, Barrett (1996) was able to demonstrate that the split-off parts of the personality appeared personified in the dreams. There is a high continuity among the themes in the dreams of a person over a long period of time (Levin 1990). Cartwright (1977) found that the themes in the dreams change when a person goes through psychotherapy. Greenberg and Pearlman (1978) compared the content of dreams of patients currently in psychoanalysis with the protocols of therapy sessions from the time of the dream and found a strong connection between the themes in the dreams and in psychotherapy. The dream can be read as a report about the current conflictual themes in the waking life of the dreamer. Schredl (2007) found a correlation between the motifs of flying and of falling in dreams and neuroticism scales. Palombo (1982) could show that analysands reprocess contents from the last analytical session in the following dreams. Popp, Luborsky, and Crits-Christoph (1990) investigated dreams and narratives from therapy sessions with the methodology of the Core Conflictual Relationship Theme. They found that both narratives and dreams were structured by the same unconscious relationship patterns.

So there is some evidence for the above-mentioned psychoanalytic theories of dreaming and their role in psychotherapy. Nevertheless, there is a strong need for more systematic studies on the relationship between the content of dreams of a person, namely the development of recurrent themes and figures in a series of dreams, and the course of psychotherapy, namely the development of core conflictual themes of the patient and the overall development of the personality. In Germany, there is a tradition in psychoanalysis for developing elaborated coding systems for dream content and their use in studies investigating processes in psychotherapy (e.g. Moser and von Zeppelin 1996). To understand meaning conveyed by the dream, it has to be interpreted. In the psychodynamic schools of psychotherapy this interpretation of dreams takes place in an interaction between therapist and client. For a systematic research on the meaning of dreams it would be necessary to have a method of interpretation which produces more objective and reliable results. The method of SDA is an attempt in this direction.

Structural Dream Analysis (SDA)

In psychotherapeutic processes, dreams point to the core problems or conflicts, but they also contain elements to solve these problems. SDA sees the dream as a narrative. In narratology, a narrative is defined as a development from a starting point, which often is a problem that needs repair or solution. The narrative goes through ups and downs leading to the solution of the problem or a valued endpoint to the story (Gülich and Quasthoff 1985). Similarly, the dream is a short story about how the protagonist, in most cases the dream ego, processes a problem. During the course of a psychotherapy the analyst assumes that the series of dreams follows an inner structure of meaning. SDA aims at identifying this inner structure of meaning from the series of dreams alone without referring to additional information about the dreamer, the psychodynamics or the course of psychotherapy. This also means that SDA is not at all concerned with the process of interpretation of the dreams in the context of psychotherapy and how this is conducted in the exchange of analyst and client. In contrast, SDA focuses on the structural patterns inherent in the dreams and how these patterns transform over the series of dreams, as well as how this parallels transformative processes over the course of therapy.

The meaning conveyed by the dream is analysed in a systematic series of interpretive steps, which makes use of analytic tools developed in narratology (Lieblich *et al*. 1998); in particular, two earlier methods of narrative analysis were incorporated into the SDA study:

1   The Russian researcher Vladimir Propp (1928/1958) developed a method called Structural analysis or Functional analysis, and applied it to fairy tales. Each fairy tale is divided into its functional parts (e.g. 'The King is ill and needs healing'; 'The hero fights the Dragon') and each functional part receives an abstract symbol, e.g. a letter or number. As a result each fairy tale can be written as an abstract formula of symbols and then different fairy tales can be compared regarding their structure.

2   Brigitte Boothe (1994) of the University of Zürich developed the narrative method, JAKOB, for the analysis of patient narratives from analytical psychotherapies and their development over the course of psychotherapy. An important element in this method is to analyse the role that the narrator takes in the narrative in terms of activity versus passivity and his/her relation to other protagonists in the narrative.

SDA also makes use of amplification, which was systematized in the form of a manual. The interpreters, who are blinded regarding all other information about the case, receive a series of 10 to 20 dreams covering the whole course of a psychotherapy, ideally marking core points and topics. The dreams are provided by practising analysts who also write a case report about the psychopathology and psychodynamics of the patient involved as well as about the development of core conflicts and themes in the course of the therapy.

In the ongoing study, it was hypothesized that the connection between dream content and the psychological problems of the dreamer would be revealed in the relationship of the dream ego to the other figures in the dream, and in the extent of the dream ego's agency, i.e. its capability to act, to execute willpower and to cope with problems in the dream. This would serve as a support for Jung's theory of dreaming and its role in the individuation process.

Overview of the research methodology

(For more details, see Roesler 2018.)

1   *Segmentation of the narrative.*
2   *Episodic models.* As described above, a narrative consists of a starting point, a development and a conclusion; this basic structure can be differentiated

into different dynamic models. In SDA, 10 different episodic models (Boothe 1994) are used to describe the dynamic of the development in the dream narrative:

2.1   Continuity: a static image, no destabilizing momentum.

2.2   Climax: a process of growth and optimization.

2.3   Anticlimax: a process of decline.

2.4   *Restitutio ad integrum* (after deintegration): after deintegration a return to normal conditions.

2.5   *Restitutio ad integrum* (after climax): after climax a return to normal conditions.

2.6   Approbation: validation after denigration, by successfully passing an examination or test.

2.7   Frustration: after a short gradation there is strong degradation.

2.8   Chance: positive development; the protagonist adapts to conditions and stabilizes.

2.9   Anti-Chance: negative development; the protagonist adapts to negative conditions and stabilizes.

2.10 Unexplainable changes: the normal course of the narrative is disrupted, something unexpected happens.

3   *Fate of the protagonist.* The dream narratives are analysed regarding the position the dream ego takes in relation to other figures and objects in the dream:

3.1   Only ego initiative: in all phases of the narrative the ego has the initiative; the ego is always in the subject position.

3.2   Only other's initiative: only other agents have the initiative throughout the narrative; the ego is never in the subject position.

3.3   Loss of initiative: initially the ego has the initiative, also parallel to other figures, but at the end is in a passive position.

3.4   Regain the initiative: the ego is at the beginning and at the end in the initiating position; during the course of the narrative the ego loses the initiative to other actors.

3.5   Embedded in others' initiative: the ego is from time to time in the course of the development in the initiative position, but not at the beginning and not at the end.

4   *Functional analysis* (following Propp). In this step, each dream is segmented into its functional parts and each part receives an abstract symbol. Here, the interpreter has to decide how far the abstraction of the narrative segment should go. The aim here is to reduce the dream narrative down to its structural elements so that they become comparable. Originally in the application of SDA the definition of structural elements had to be developed for each new series of dreams. After a superordinate analysis of 15 completed cases was conducted, it was possible to identify six general types of

dreams and their role in the psychotherapy process (Roesler, under review). In the exemplary dream series presented below, one of these types (the dream ego is threatened) and its development over the dream series is demonstrated.

5   Integrating the above steps into a structural framework describing the whole dream series.

6   *Amplification of core symbols.* Symbols that appear in several dreams or have a central position to the dream series are analysed using symbol dictionaries and translated into a hypothesis of their psychological meaning.

7   Amplifications are included into the framework of the dream series.

8   Overall interpretation of the meaning of the whole dream series in psychological language.

Case example

To illustrate the application of the method and how it can identify a typical pattern in the dreams as well as its development over the course of therapy, the following case example is presented.

The client is a young man (30 years of age). Before starting psychotherapy the client was imprisoned having committed physical violence in more than 100 cases. Being not openly violent anymore after imprisonment, he suffered from feelings of strong tension, unrest and emptiness that were almost unbearable, against the background of severe depression. The only means to deal with these depressive states was a strong compulsion to consume pornographic media, especially those containing physical violence towards women.

The client came from a broken home. The father suffered from severe alcoholism and tended to be violent against his wife and children. On several occasions the client experienced fear of death and was almost killed by his father. The father also seems to have been suffering from a sexual obsession: he collected pornographic videos in large numbers and stored them in his bedroom. This aspect of the father's life was always fascinating for the client. The mother grew up in the former Yugoslavia and was never able to speak German properly; it might be that the mother was slightly mentally disabled. The client stated that 'she was too dumb to understand what I needed'. In adolescence, the client was taken out of his family by the welfare authorities because of the difficult situation and was put in care. Later, he joined a group of hooligans and committed a large number of violent crimes. In prison the client experienced a religious conversion and became member of a fundamentalist Christian sect. He came into psychotherapy with the explicit intention of overcoming his aggressive impulses. His intimate relationships often followed a sado-masochistic pattern.

Psychodynamics. The client seems to have experienced severe abandonment, helplessness and anxiety in childhood. The frustration of his basic needs has led the client to compensatory aggression. From the psychodynamic viewpoint the client suffers from severe depression based on a narcissistic disorder connected with a strong sexual drivenness towards violent contact with women. There is a deep contempt in the client towards women, originating on the one hand from the frustration experienced with the mother, but also influenced by the father's sexual obsession. The denigration of women also seems to have the function of defence against depression. The religious conversion has equipped the client with a strong superego which helps him to control himself in social life, nevertheless this does not solve the inner conflicts. There is a very strong and violent destructive complex in the psyche which formerly was dealt with by directing it outwards to other people, now it goes up against the ego.

Course of therapy. In the first years of therapy the focus was on helping the client to formulate his needs and feelings and to communicate them in social relationships, which helped to decrease the pressure of frustration aggression. In the transference the therapist came into the position of the threatening father. The experience of security in the therapeutic relationship, which also included a certain control over the analyst, helped to integrate these experiences and strengthen ego functions. In the course of therapy the relationships with women changed and the client became capable of building a marriage and family. When his first son was born the client experienced such panic that he felt aggressive impulses towards the infant. By working through these impulses and their connection to early experiences in life, the inner pressure of frustration and aggression slowly receded. At the end of therapy the client was living in a very solid social, family and job situation. From time to time the client still needs to use violent pornographic videos to control his inner states of emptiness and frustration. In social life the client is now fully adapted. The low-frequency therapy took six years with two minor interruptions, and 206 hours.

Over the course of therapy, the client presented a large number of dreams, from which the following series was selected, covering the whole period of time. The dreams originally were written down by the dreamer in German and handed over to the therapist; the translation follows the original style of the client.

> *Dream* 1. I walked down the street in the darkness, on both sides small houses behind fences. Lots of barking dogs jumped against the fences. I was frightened but then I became brave. I barked like a dog myself aggressively and the dogs immediately fell silent.

> *Dream* 2. I am on my way with my bicycle up a hill. It is demanding. Around me are large trees, it's like in the mountains. Arriving on top there is a little white poodle, it barks, it is on a leash. I'm driving home downhill in sharp curves. Doberman dogs are behind me, I cannot get rid of them because of the curves. They run at my side and bark at me. Then it is light and sunny, arriving on the pass it's beautiful. There is a restaurant, like in Italy, beautiful houses. On top of the pass the black dogs are coming.

Dream 3. There is a still water, a river? There is a little bridge, somebody on the other side. He falls into the water, he somehow slipped as if under a log. I pull him out, but first I hesitate. He is like dead. But that guy has a sharp knife and he cuts the other helper's throat. I flee.

Dream 4. In black and white: at a nearby train station. A girl and another person, who seems to be masochistic, and a very energetic black dog. The dog pulls the other person into the little pond, then pulls the person out of the water and up the hill. The person gives himself a blow job, then to the dog. Then I am at the foot of a tall building. I say: the dog must be put on a leash. The masochistic person says: you have to stroke the dog. I say: no, it must be put on a leash and then removed. The masochistic person is angry and goes into the tall building. The other person says: you have to follow him, he is sad. The dog smells, I put him on a leash but it is disgusting.

Dream 5. An elderly, badly smelling dog is with me and my girlfriend in Paris. It just found us. We get on the bus, the badly smelling dog could not go with us, we left it outside. We are already outside of the city limits, but will return to the city on the highway. The dog would not have been able to come along behind us.

Dream 6. I was the manager of a café in the house. I was promoted like Joseph in the house of Potifar. Everybody says goodbye to a father with his little son, he's in the backyard. There is an elderly man with a Pitbull. He says: I can show you how evil the dog is. But I just had to go. I walked into a vineyard. The dog runs from its leash and goes behind me, but I jump over fences and walls. The path goes uphill through the yard and back down on the other side.

Dream 7. In a country restaurant. Two Romanians come in and start begging. I remember: the last time the two of them were masked and committed a robbery. I drive away with the motorcycle. I want to report to the police, because now I know their faces.

Dream 8. A little baby is in danger. I cover it with newspaper and carry it with me through a sewerage system. Then I forget about it and leave it somewhere. But then I realize that the baby is missing and go back and find it again. I carry it with me and feed it. I think: the baby is so small, it should get mother's milk, but I can just feed him solid food.

Dream 9. I'm sitting on the couch in the garden. A man with two bottles of beer is by my side and offers one to me, maybe my father? I get the feeling of being unfair to the other person. We are having a beer together.

Dream 10. My father dies at the age of 49 years. I'm not moved at all. It was strange that he died so young. We don't have such a long life as my grandma with her 102 years of age.

Dream 11. I saw a giant toe and found it is my toe. The skin on the nail was grown very wide. I thought: this has to be removed. It could be moved back easily. There was another level of skin below, this one could be taken off easily, too. I was surprised that it did not hurt. Below the skin were very small black worms, everything was rotten, but you could remove it without difficulty. Below that everything was new.

Results of Structural Dream Analysis

Episodic models and fate of the protagonist

On both levels of analysis there is a certain development from patterns of decline in the first half of therapy to patterns of approbation or chance which could be called more optimistic. Regarding ego initiative there is a development from patterns of loss of initiative or the ego being subjected to others' initiative to patterns dominated by ego initiative. Psychologically speaking there is a certain development from a situation in which the ego is more of a victim of conditions or others' initiative to a situation where ego consciousness is more capable of taking over initiative and controlling the situation.

Functional analysis

These results are further supported by the results of functional analysis. Repetitive structures that were marked are now extracted:

Dream 1: threat, constructive strategy
Dream 2: threat, pursue, flight, threat
Dream 3: help/support, threat, flight
Dream 4: disgust
Dream 5: pursue, disgust, pursue
Dream 6: threat, pursue, flight, end pursue
Dream 7: pledge for help/support, threat, constructive strategy
Dream 8: pledge for help/support, help/support, inadequate measures
Dream 11: wish for modification, modification, renewal/regeneration

Amplification of major symbols

To combine the above structural elements of the dreams with content in the next step, the meaning of the central symbols of the dreams will be analysed by using Jung's original method of amplification. To arrive at a scientific approach to the interpretation of symbols via amplification in the application of SDA, this step is clearly defined. Amplification of symbols is restricted to the use of a set of symbol dictionaries (e.g. Cooper 1978) which give information about the cultural background of symbols in the sense of their use and understanding in religious traditions, mythology, cultural beliefs etc. This is to certify that interpretation of the symbols is done in as objective a way as possible.

This step of interpretation is applied only to a very restricted number of symbols, ideally those that appear repeatedly in the dreams or seem to be especially important to the series of dreams. In the case presented here, the dominating symbol is the dog:

In a number of cultures the dog is related to death. In old Egypt and Greece the dog guards the underworld and is a mediator between the worlds of the living and the dead (Anubis, Cerberus). Those gods either living in the dark or being ambiguous figures often appear in the form of dogs. The dog clearly has ambiguous meaning: on the one side it is connected with wisdom, grace and religion, especially the white dog; on the other hand the dog is connected with primitive affects, impurity, vice and envy, especially dark dogs. Also the dog is related to sexuality, because dogs in the streets are promiscuous. In some cultures the dog appears as ancestor and creator of man and of civilization because of the wisdom and the sexual power that is related to it.

The above findings just give information about the field or context of meaning of the symbols. In the next step this has to be integrated in the structure of the dream series. This is clearly the more psychological step in the interpretation, which makes use of psychological and psychodynamic concepts. Still this step of interpretation attempts to stay as objective as possible, therefore the aim here is not to formulate definite interpretations of the dreams but to translate the above structures into a psychological language. As mentioned earlier, dreams do not represent a linear structure of development but usually take up symbols and patterns repeatedly which undergo a process of transformation. In this step of interpretation it should be attempted to reconstruct this repetitive use of symbols and patterns in the dreams and the transformative process, if there is any. The focus here is on more general topics appearing repetitively in the dreams.

For the dream series presented here this is exemplified in the repetitive appearance of the pattern 'threat by dogs'.

In the first half of the process the ego is confronted with threatening aspects, symbolized by dogs. From the amplification of the symbol, these aspects can be characterized as having an aggressive and destructive, even murderous character; also they seem to be connected with sexuality. Finally, they carry a certain ambiguity, changing between aggressiveness and helpless neediness. In the beginning the ego is threatened by these aspects and experiences strong fear, it is not capable of coping with these aspects but flees from them. In the beginning even flight is not always successful but the ego gets caught and overwhelmed by these destructive aspects.

The negative complex leading to aggression and sexual compulsiveness of the client can easily be identified in the symbol of the threatening dogs, also because the dog symbolically is connected with sexuality; on the other hand the image of the pursuing dogs is a very direct expression of the experience of the violent father. This is a striking example for the fact that in dreams the major pathological complex is symbolized, not only by way of the symbol but also by way of the pattern, i.e. the position the dream ego takes in relation to this complex. Here, the dream ego is totally overwhelmed by the threat and the only strategy it has is flight, and even this is not always successful. From a psychoanalytic perspective, this is an image for a weak ego structure which, at least initially, has no strategy to cope with the complex, which leads to aggressive impulsiveness and compulsive sexuality.

In the further course of the dream series the shadow aspects begin to lose their threatening character. The ego now experiences disgust regarding these parts of the psyche and rejects them. This marks a change in the pattern, as the ego is no longer threatened by the complex, but tries to distance itself from it and rejects it. This can be seen as a result of therapy, which has strengthened the ego, which is now capable of facing the complex, which is still not integrated.

Now a new thematic field is introduced. It is centred on situations where the ego is asked to act in a helpful and supportive way and to be active. Some pledges for help appear to be dangerous, because these parts of the psyche that ask for help are also destructive powers. The ego therefore is in danger of supporting destructive energies and being itself destroyed in the process. It can be assumed that in this change the original ambiguity of the shadow aspects is contained and they move towards the helpless and needy side. So the psychological development now asked for is for the ego to take a more integrative stance towards these parts of the personality, and not reject them.

In the image of the infant needing help these parts have finally lost their destructive aspects and the ego meets a pure, positive part of the psyche which points to a new beginning. These parts of the psyche need support but the ego has some difficulty in overcoming disgust and rejection and finding a supportive and accepting attitude towards these parts. Then the ego realizes more and more how these parts have to be cared for, even though some of the necessary means and strategies are still missing. Towards the end of the dream series the ego actively takes part in a process where some parts of the psyche experience a process of death and renewal. These aspects of the psyche can be associated with willpower and intention.

In the course of therapy, the dreamer becomes increasingly conscious of the neediness and helplessness behind the destructive complex, which culminates in the image of the helpless infant. To the extent that the client can accept these needs and take care of them the ego gains control over the complex and the destructive aspects become integrated. In the end, with the symbol of renewal, a new state of ego strength and wilful control over the personality is established.

It is important to note that not only does the character of the symbolization of the complex change over the course of the dream series. The pattern also changes; that is, the position the dream ego takes in relation to the unintegrated parts of the personality. The pattern 'the dream ego is threatened', which was found in a number of dream series in the overall study, is generally connected with a very weak ego structure of the client, and strong pathological complexes, which are split off from the conscious personality. In those cases in which therapy was successful, a similar pattern of transformation could be observed: initially, the dream ego has no other strategy than to flee, which slowly transforms into the ego facing the threat, sometimes even actively fighting against the threatening figures, which can be seen as an image for the ego gaining strength. Over the course of the dream series, the character of the threatening figures changes, usually losing their threatening character, and finally being integrated into the personality. A very interesting point is that in a number of cases, as in the one presented here, the image of a (newborn) child appears, usually in the middle part of the series, marking a turning point. This points to Jung's observation that the archetype of the (divine) child is an image for turning points in the individuation process, which initiates a major transformation of the personality and opens the gate to the future.

Conclusion

It can be summarized as a result of the SDA research project, that there are clear parallels between the psychological situation of the client, especially the extent of ego strength and the existence of pathological complexes, and the imaginary of the dreams. It is not only the symbolism in the dreams, but also the structural pattern which pictures the inner world of the dreamer.

A typical pattern could be identified in the cases that were analysed in the project: initially the dream ego is threatened by a dream figure representing a complex – the ego applies inadequate measures (flight, paralysis) and the threat persists. This pattern changes over the course of therapy to a pattern where the dream ego can manage the threatening figure with a constructive strategy and the threat vanishes or is incorporated. Threatening animal figures become human (as in the exemplary case above).

In all cases, strong parallels between the symbolism of the dreams and the themes in therapy were found. Thus, the usual approach in Jungian psychology to dreams, to interpret the symbolism of the dream images, could be expanded by adding the structuralist viewpoint presented here. Important information is conveyed by the dream, in the sense of a dialogue between the unconscious and ego consciousness fostering the individuation process, by the pattern in which the dream ego relates to other figures in the dream.

It has become quite clear in the above example that in the image of the threatening dogs a major complex of the person is personified. In the early phase of the dream series (and the therapy) this pathological complex is strongly split off from ego consciousness. The fact that the dreams present this split in the personality to the client's consciousness in a very drastic picture, connected with strong emotions, can be seen as a striking example of Jung's idea of the individuation process, because here the unconscious tries to confront the ego with an unsolved problem in the personality. It is as if the unconscious would attempt to communicate to ego consciousness that there is an unsolved problem which the person has to deal with. Later in the process, by way of the symbol of the newborn child which the dreamer has to care for, again there is a striking example of the transformative force coming from the unconscious. It can be assumed that the client would not have been able to thematize both the split in the personality as well as the image of a new future.

As was pointed out above, this contrasts with the usual understanding in the narrative approach, in which the person telling his/her story is regarded as the author of their narrative identity. Already Freud pointed out that the ego is by far not the boss in the house of personality. It could be said that, from the viewpoint of individuation, two independent storylines come together, and the problem that has to be solved in therapy is to integrate the two streams into a new synthesis. The storyline coming from the unconscious, e.g. by way of dreams, confronts the ego with a different perspective on its own being, often puzzling, sometimes disturbing or even frightening. It could be said that if we put Jung into the frame of narratology, his message is: listen to the stories from below, allow them to question the ego's viewpoint, and try to integrate them into your life's storyline.

References

Barrett, D. (1996) Dreams in multiple personality. In: D. Barrett (Ed.), *Trauma and Dreams*. Cambridge, MA: Harvard University Press.

Barrett, D. (2001) *The Committee of Sleep. How Artists, Scientists, and Athletes use Dreams for Creative Problem-Solving*. New York: Crown.

Barrett, D. and McNamara, P. (eds) (2007) *The New Science of Dreaming*. Westport: Praeger.

Boothe, B. (1994) *Der Patient als Erzähler in der Psychotherapie*. Göttingen: Vandenhoek & Ruprecht.

Cartwright, R. D. (1977) *Night Life*. Englewood Cliffs: Prentice-Hall.

Chamberlayne, P. (Ed.) (2000) *The Turn to Biographical Methods in Social Science*. London: Sage.

Cooper, J. C. (1978) *Dictionary of Traditional Symbols*. London: Thames and Hudson.

Covington, C. (1995) No story, no analysis? The role of narrative in interpretation. *Journal of Analytical Psychology* 40, 405–417.

Fosshage, J. L. (1987) New vistas on dream interpretation. In: M. Glucksman (Ed.), *Dreams in New Perspective. The Royal Road Revisited*. New York: Uman Sciences Press.

Gergen, K. J. and Gergen, M. M. (1987) The self in temporal perspective. In: R. P. Abeles (Ed.), *Life-span Perspectives and Social Psychology*. London, Hillsdale: Erlbaum.

Greenberg, R. and Pearlman, C. (1978) If Freud only knew. A reconsideration of psycho-analytic dream theory. *International Review of Psycho-Analysis* 5, 71–75.

Gülich, E. and Quasthoff, U. (1985) Narrative analysis. In: T. A. van Dijk (Ed.), *Handbook of Discourse Analysis, Vol. II: Dimensions of Discourse*. London: Academic Press.

Hall, C. S. and Van De Castle, R. L. (1966) *The Content Analysis of Dreams*. New York: Appleton-Century-Crofts.

Josselson, R. and Lieblich, A. (Eds) (1995) *Interpreting Experience: The Narrative Study of Lives*. London: Sage.

Jung, C. G.: The following are from *C. G. Jung, Gesammelte Werke* (GW) Olten: Walter. *The Collected Works of C. G. Jung.* (CW). London: Routledge & Kegan Paul/Princeton, NJ: Princeton University Press.

Jung, C. G. (1928) *Die Beziehungen zwischen dem Ich und dem Unbewußten.* (GW 7). The relations between the ego and the unconscious. (CW 7).

Jung, C. G. (1934) *Die praktische Verwendbarkeit der Traumanalyse.* (GW 16). The practical use of dream-analysis. (CW 16).

Jung, C. G. (1948) *Allgemeine Gesichtspunkte zur Psychologie des Traumes.* (GW 8). General aspects of dreams psychology. (CW 8).

Levin, R. (1990) Psychoanalytic theories on the function of dreaming. A review of the empirical dream research. In: J. M. Masling (Ed.), *Empirical Studies of Psychoanalytic Theories.* Hillsdale, NJ: Erlbaum.

Lieblich, A., Tuval-Mashiach, R. and Zilber, T. (1998) *Narrative Research.* London: Sage.

Moser, U. and von Zeppelin, I. (1996) *Der geträumte Traum. Wie Träume entstehen und sich verändern.* Stuttgart: Kohlhammer.

Palombo, S. R. (1982) How the dream works. The role of dreaming in the psychotherapeutic process. In: S. Slipp (Ed.), *Curative Factors in Dynamic Psychotherapy.* New York: McGraw Hill.

Popp, C., Luborsky, L. and Crits-Christoph, P. (1990) The parallel of the CCRT from therapy narratives with the CCRT from dreams. In: L. Luborsky and P. Crits-Christoph, (Eds), *Understanding Transference. The CCRT Method.* New York: Basic Books.

Propp, V. I. (1928/1958) *Morphology of the Folktale.* Bloomington, IN: Indiana University Press.

Roesler, C. (2006) A narratological methodology for identifying archetypal story patterns in autobiographical narratives. *Journal of Analytical Psychology* 51, 574–596.

Roesler, C. (Ed.) (2018) *Research in Analytical Psychology: Empirical Research.* London: Routledge.

Roesler, C. (Under review) Dream content corresponds with dreamer's psychological problems and personality structure and with improvement in psychotherapy. A typology of dream patterns in dream series of patients in analytical psychotherapy.

Schredl, M. (2007) *Träume. Die Wissenschaft enträtselt unser nächtliches Kopfkino.* Berlin: Ullstein.

Chapter 12

Narrating the archetypal images

The road less travelled

Inna Semetsky

Two roads diverged in a wood, and I –
I took the one less traveled by,
And that has made all the difference.
(Robert Frost)

Introduction: the role of images

A symbolic approach to the unconscious is the crux of Jung's depth psychology. Symbols represent more than their literal and immediate meanings. They are effective because they act as '*transformers*, their function being to convert libido from a "lower" into a "higher" form' (Jung 1952a, para. 344, emphasis in original). In contrast to solely theoretical knowledge, it is the libidinal economy of the unconscious that effectuates the participation of the human psyche in the symbolic process of individuation. The unconscious is not reduced to its largely repressed acquisitions during individual lifetimes but has a collective dimension in terms of *objective* psyche – the collective unconscious populated by archetypes as formal skeletal structures common to humankind. Archetypes, being 'structural elements of the psyche ... possess a certain autonomy and specific energy which enables them to attract, out of the conscious mind, those contents which are better suited to themselves' (Jung 1952a, para. 344), and are charged with psychic or spiritual energy exceeding Freud's sexual libido. In contrast, 'psychic energy is a very fastidious thing which insists on fulfilment of its own conditions' (Jung 1943, para. 76). The collective unconscious is transpersonal thus surpassing the scope of traditional Freudian psychoanalytic conception and comprising 'the psychic life of our ancestors right back to the earliest beginnings. It is the matrix of all conscious psychic occurrences' (Jung 1929, para. 230). The vague and unconscious forms are to be filled with informational content embedded within real, flesh-and-blood, human experiences in the phenomenal world while being determined by the activity of the dynamical patterns manifesting as universal motifs in human actions. The contents of the unconscious are paradoxical and ambiguous; they require interpretation in order to be discovered. Jung was explicit that

The *via regia* to the unconscious ... is not the dream, as [Freud] thought, but the complex, which is the architect of dreams and of symptoms. Nor is this *via* so very 'royal,' either, since the way pointed out by the complex is more like a rough and uncommonly devious footpath.

(Jung 1948, para. 210)

Complexes as the expressions of deep psychic life partake of 'Descartes' devils and seem to delight in playing impish tricks' (Jung 1948, para. 202) leading to the fragmentation of personality. They form splinter psyches, the fractured pieces of which are to be integrated into consciousness within the psyche made whole. It is the archetype of wholeness – or Self – that implicitly guides us towards 'the ultimate integration of conscious and unconscious, or ... the assimilation of the ego to a wider personality' (Jung 1945/1948, para 557) in the process of individuation. Jung emphasized that 'complexes can *have us*' (Jung 1948, para. 200, emphasis in original), and a feeling-tone complex is:

the *image* of a certain psychic situation.... This image has a powerful inner coherence, it has its own wholeness and ... a relatively high degree of autonomy, so that it is subject to the control of the conscious mind to only a limited extent, and therefore behaves like an animated foreign body in the sphere of consciousness.

(Jung 1948, para. 200, emphasis in original)

The unconscious is capable of spontaneously producing images 'irrespective of wishes and fears of the conscious mind' (Jung 1952b, para. 745). Jung referred to the so-called Faustian question when 'the ego must ... ask "How am I affected by this sign?"' (Jung 1958, para. 188), that is, by one or another invisible archetype or the constellation of the activated archetypes within the individuating process. The alternative – devious – path to individuation is marked by archetypal images and, even if archetypes per se do escape their immediate representation in consciousness, the interpretive symbolic process of discovering their hidden meanings

is an experience *in images* and *of images*.... Its beginning is ... characterized by one's getting stuck in a blind alley or in some impossible situation and its goal is ... illumination of higher consciousness, by means of which the initial situation is overcome.

(Jung 1934/1954, para. 82, emphasis in original)

Taking the less travelled road

This chapter focuses on the rarely taken path to individuation: creating the narrative by reading and interpreting the Tarot images (Semetsky 2011, 2013). Jung asserted that despite their 'obscure origin ... the set of pictures on Tarot cards were distantly descended from the archetypes of transformation' (Jung 1934/1954, para. 81) that represent 'typical situations, places, ways and means' (Jung 1934/1954, para. 80) in addition to manifesting as active personalities in dreams. Sally Nichols, who was Jung's student in Zurich, has explicitly connected archetypes with the Tarot images; and Jung's biographer Laurens van der Post pointed out Nichols' 'profound investigation of Tarot, and her illuminated exegesis of its pattern as an authentic attempt at enlargement of possibilities of human perceptions' (in Nichols 1980, p. xv). Jungian psychologist Irene Gad (1994) considered Tarot archetypal images to be 'trigger symbols, appearing and disappearing throughout history in times of transition and need' (Gad 1994, p. xxxiv). Edinger (1992) mentioned Tarot cards in the context of his analysis of Jung's *Answer to Job*; and Whitmont (1985) pointed out that solely verbal methods may not be sufficient as the development of psychic awareness. Contemporary post-Jungian Andrew Samuels (1985) refers to 'systems such as that of the *I Ching*, Tarot and astrology' as possible, even if uncertain, resources in analysis, and quotes Jung as saying,

> I found the *I Ching* very interesting.... I have not used it for more than two years now, feeling that one must learn ... or try to discover (as when one is learning to swim) whether the water will carry one.
>
> (Samuels 1985, p. 123)

Among multiple esoteric practices that in the anti-dualistic, anti-Cartesian, manner unite matter and mind, consciousness and the unconscious, alchemy was perhaps the one most researched by Jung: across his corpus, Jung referred to the axiom of Maria Prophetissa, a third-century alchemist, as a metaphor for the process of individuation. Jung was adamant that alchemy purports to fill in the gaps in the religious dogma that demonstrate a tendency towards the masculine with the opposite, compensatory tendency of invoking 'the chthonic femininity of the unconscious' (Jung 1944a, para. 26). Jung considered Eros to be the feminine principle of relatedness, of binding, in contrast to detached reason or Logos. In Jung's dreams, he remarked, the figure of Philemon, his male spiritual guide, was accompanied by a female figure as a personification of soul. Jung shared a Gnostic vision of Wisdom-Sophia as the Bride of Christ who can bring Sophia back into Pleroma (fullness of being) while educating humankind in deep inner knowledge. Psychic residues are formed by recurrent experiences and are laid down in the archetypal structures, but as systems of readiness for action, those structures themselves in a self-referential, indirect, manner can 'exert an influence on experience, tending to organize it' (Samuels, Shorter and Plaut 1986, p. 24) in a novel manner thus effecting transformations and creating new possibilities in the phenomenal world.

Jung maintained that self-knowledge remains an indispensable basis of adult development and emphasized the indirect approach to its attainment by means of symbolic mediation: 'Of the unconscious we can learn nothing directly, but indirectly we can perceive the effects that come into consciousness' (Jung 1928a, para. 112). Similar to dreams, Tarot images lay down a 'route to the unconscious. This alternative route uses some of the materials, shapes, signs, and symbols used by artists and our dreams.... The major arcana ... are visual aids to the unconscious. They are vivid shorthand portraits' (Hederman 2003, p. 27). The libidinal expressions of the unconscious precede and exceed the verbal language of conscious mind: 'it is not the personal human being who is making the statement, but the archetype speaking through him' (Jung 1963, p. 352) via the language of images. Narratives of all kinds represent specifically women's ways of knowing (Belenky *et al.* 1986) that can bridge the gap between the cognitive, moral and emotional dimensions in the course of personality development. Narrating the unconscious and bringing it to consciousness is possible by virtue of transcendent function that conforms to the principle of *coincidentia oppositorum* via the movement 'out of the suspension between opposites ... that leads to a new level of being, a new situation. The transcendent function manifests itself as a quality of conjoined opposites' (Jung 1958, para. 189). Sure enough, archetypes are 'located' at the *psychoid* level that reflects the presence of the animating, spiritual and numinous, power in the material reality creating one unified world, *Unus Mundus.*

Jung pointed to amplification as a cornerstone of his analytical method so that we may 'supply these fantastic images that rise up so strange and threatening before the mind's eye with some kind of context so as to make them more intelligible' (Jung 1944a, para. 38). It is the task of an authentic Tarot reader as a 'bilingual' interpreter to amplify the unconscious contents of the psyche by narrating the imagery pregnant with symbolic significance. The pictures, when laid down in a particular spread, comprise an unorthodox text that as such has its own syntax and semantics even if not in a written alphabetic form. The relationship between word and image has long been controversial. Yet, 'Before there was writing there were pictures' (Shlain 1998, p. 45), and one image indeed may be worth many thousands words. The perceived dualisms that contrast Dionysus with Apollo, mystical thought with scholastic thought, magic with science, or right brain with left brain, surrender themselves to a symbolic approach that demonstrates holistic thinking historically associated with the feminine mode of expression and affirms the paradoxical presence of *synthesis* in Jungian *analysis*. Reading the images is possible via the shift to the right hemisphere which is permeated by intuitive states that 'are *authentic*.... An internal voice verifies the experience ... The right hemisphere is ... the portal leading to the world of the invisible' (Shlain 1998, p. 19, emphasis in original).

Making the invisible visible – becoming aware of the unconscious – is the prerogative of Tarot readings that demonstrate the synchronicity principle in action. Synchronistic occurrences indicate that 'psyche and matter are two different aspects' (Jung 1947/1954, para. 418) of the unified world that abandons our habitual 'either-or' perception of dualistic categories. The integration of the unconscious 'presents a way of moving from "either-or" to "and" by going beyond the limitations of logical discourse or common-sense.... The experience of "and-ness" is central to psychological change' (Samuels 1985, p. 59). The concept of synchronicity was developed by Jung in collaboration with physicist and Nobel laureate Wolfgang Pauli who envisaged the development of theories of the unconscious as overgrowing their solely therapeutic applications by being eventually assimilated into the mainstream natural science. He considered the unconscious analogous to the notion of 'field' in physics (Pauli 1994) and envisaged the gradual discovery of a *neutral* language (in Meier 2001) that functions symbolically to describe an invisible reality which is inferable indirectly through its visible effects. Such symbolic language would reflect a unified psychophysical reality of the archetypes in the form of images, ideograms, or 'arcana'. Arcanum (singular) partakes of the Latin *arca* as a chest; *arcere* as a verb means to shut or to close; symbolically, Arcanum is a tightly shut treasure chest holding a secret: the hidden meaning of experience. In reference to Greek etymology, Arcanum relates to *arce* that means origin or inception. The archetypal images are primordial – *original* – and, as rising from the depth of the psyche, they may have inspired the artists who designed the Tarot pictures.

Arcanum refers to an often missing or obscured element in our experience, which is necessary to know, to discover in practical life so as to individuate and become able to creatively solve real-life problems situated in the midst of experiential situations, hazardous events, and our complex relationships with others especially when we face decisions and choices or encounter moral dilemmas. The reality of such implicit 'self-subsistent "unconscious" knowledge' (Jung 1952c, para. 931) of what we are meant to be and where we stand along the path to individuation demonstrates itself empirically in the archetypal constellations of Tarot images even as the interpretation of images surpasses fixed factual knowledge which is known by a solely 'cognitive act [that] has "grasped" it' (Jung 1942/1954, para. 417). As enriched with imagination and intuition, interpretation creates

> something that is ... in the process of formation. If we reduce this by analysis to something that is generally known, we destroy the true value of the symbol; but to attribute hermeneutic significance to it is consistent with its value and meaning.
>
> (Jung 1916, para. 492)

Roberts (1987), in his verbatim account of Tarot readings, including a reading for, and a dialogue with, Joseph Campbell, suggests that

> the ultimate importance of Tarot is that it is a symbolic system of *cosmic*, *moral*, and *natural* laws, each of which has the same underlying principle, *operating in all areas relevant to human endeavour*, and which ties together all three systems.
>
> (Roberts 1987, p. 7, emphasis in original)

The language of the unconscious

A typical Tarot deck comprises 78 pictures, 22 so-called Major Arcana (see Figure 12.1) and 56 Minor (see Figure 12.2 later). What is called a Tarot layout or spread is a particular pattern of the cards. Each position in the sequence of pictures constituting a given layout has some specific connotations as well as temporal nuances and thus creates a specific context within which the narrative is created. As such, Tarot 'speaks' in a mythic format of the symbolic – universal or *neutral* – language full of deep, even if initially opaque, meanings. This language crosses over the barriers between different native languages, conflicting beliefs and incommensurable values immortalized in the symbol of 'the heaven-high tower of Babel that brought confusion to mankind' (Jung 1952a, para. 171). In the framework of projective hypothesis, Tarot readings may be compared with the sandplay technique (cf. Ryce-Menuhin 1992) used today not just for children but adults as well. Psychologically, a projective technique that externalizes one's inner reality in some material medium is a means for organizing a person's unique experience. Emotions, hopes, fears, interpersonal relationships, intra-psychic conflicts, immediate environment are projected in the layout as the symbolic expression of the unspoken and unconscious. Thus, Tarot can be looked at as a supplementary source of valuable therapeutic material.

By means of projecting the life-world of beliefs, hopes, or unconscious desires, Tarot collects 'data' that emerge and can be read and interpreted even though 'every interpretation necessarily remains "as-if"' (Jung 1940, para. 265). Indeterminacy abounds, 'certain fundamental meanings ... can only be grasped approximately' (Jung 1947/1954, para. 417), because archetypes express themselves via the 'images of contents which ... transcend consciousness.... [But their] contents are real ... they are agents with which it is not only possible but absolutely necessary for us to come to terms' (Jung 1952a, para. 114). In this respect the layout of images appears to not only parallel but even surpass the Rorschach test in terms of demonstrating both interpersonal and intra-psychic transactions. In the course of the archetypal journey through the array of Tarot pictures, certain situations and the feelings associated with them are being externalized and provide an opportunity to literally *see* them when they are spread in one or other pictorial layout. For Jung, meanings and image are identical in a sense that as images unfold, their meanings become clear. Still, the descriptions of the Arcana presented below are only *general.* The same images pertaining to different individuals, situations and contexts acquire specific meanings, thus combining universality with particularity.

The first picture of the Major Arcana is the Fool – a symbol of the very beginning of individuation: the number associated with this card is zero. It is the archetypal *puer aeternus*, a symbol of novelty and unlimited possibilities populating the abyss of experiences just a step away. In the Tarot picture, the Fool stands on top of the mountain, at the edge of the abyss. Its self-reflective

Figure 12.1 Major Arcana.

consciousness has not yet been developed and, according to Jung, the ego may be standing on a shaky ground. Yet, asked Jung, how 'can one … attain wisdom without foolishness?' (Jung 1944b, para. 953). In the journey from zero to the last Arcanum XXI, the Fool's very identity will be contested and will reappear in the guise of the names for other Arcana in the deck. Finding itself amidst novel, yet unknown experiences, the Fool can become the Magician, Arcanum I, a symbol of successful accomplishment of goals. The four magical tools in the picture are represented by cup, wand, pentacle and sword corresponding to four elements of nature available to the Magician-the alchemist: fire, earth, water and air, all brought together in the *Unus Mundus* when combined with the fifth, quintessential and spiritual, element so as to, in the Gnostic tradition, free a human spirit from the constraints and limitations of the material world. Alternatively the four tools correspond to four Jungian functions.

We should remember that for Jung all archetypes have light and dark aspects, and the dark side of the Magician is the Trickster archetype. Importantly, it is only in the actual practical context of the hermeneutic process embedded in Tarot readings that we can distinguish between the archetypes' light and dark aspects in each concrete case. While the Magician's actions are wise and ethical, its nemesis the Trickster may easily coerce people into playing its games and performing its tricks. The Magician is the symbol of unification first prophesized in the Hermetic text *Tabula Smaragdina* (Emerald Tablet): *That which is above is like to that which is below and that which is below is like to that which is above, to accomplish the miracles of one thing.* The Magician's right hand holding the wand points upwards, to the skies, and the left hand is pointing to the earth as a symbol for *putting into practice* the Hermetic maxim, the temporal correlate of which partakes of Nietzsche's principle of eternal recurrence: *That which was is as that which will be, and that which will be is as that which was.* Each archetype demonstrates the feature of anticipation and determines 'the nature of the configurational process and the course it will follow, with seeming foreknowledge, or as though … in possession of the goal' (Jung 1947/1954, para. 411). An important function operative in the psychological process was, for Jung, compensation as a tendency of the unconscious to maintain balance and stay in a homeostasis with the conscious mind for the purpose of self-regulation. But the archetypal dynamic also functions prospectively and prophetically in terms of 'anticipating a psychological direction or development extrasensorily, affording one information about an occurrence outside of the awareness of one's five senses; and … predicting a future occurrence' (Hopcke 1992, p. 26). The interpretation of Tarot images demonstrates a symptomatic that not only serves a diagnostic purpose but also performs a prospective, prognostic function. Tarot readings possess a sort of foreknowledge that differs in principle from vulgar fortune-telling – yet affords a great divinatory potential! Non-incidentally, Jung used the marker 'Janus-faced' for the unconscious which, on one side, points backwards toward the prehistoric instinctual world while its other side is oriented to the potential future that as such the unconscious always already anticipates.

The Arcanum II is called The High Priestess. She is the Egyptian Isis, the goddess of the rainbow as a symbolic bridge between heaven and earth. To fully individuate, we need to lift the veil of Isis, to learn the universal language of images, thus ourselves partaking of magicians or priestesses. The High Priestess is a symbol of female intuition and spiritual life that embodies the feminine principle complementary to the essentially masculine instrumental rationality prevalent in the modern world. As Sophia (in Greek philosophy) or *Shekhinah* (in Jewish mythology), she represents Wisdom contained in the scroll on her lap. Her task is to unfold the scroll so as to reveal to the Fool the hidden secrets of Gnostic knowledge long lost in the scientific (and overly masculine) rationality. The High Priestess holds the keys to the lost speech that describes the true nature of things in a symbolic, Edenic, neutral language 'known' by Adam before the Fall. She signifies the invisible and secret knowledge as opposed to the sensible and empirical; yet she can potentially express herself, thus making the invisible present. This is the distinguishing feature of Tarot, as we said earlier: the ability to transcend the invisible and make it visible.

The archetype of the Great Mother is represented by Arcanum III and is called the Empress. Pauli, in his letters to Jung (Meier 2001), addresses the Mother archetype as corresponding to the instinctive and unconscious idea of the human relationship. In the actual layout, the Empress often indicates pregnancy. Yet, the dark, chthonic or wicked aspect of the Mother archetype may manifest in real life as being excessively overprotective or, vice versa, too demanding for the Fool who may as a result demonstrate regression, arrested development, and the lack of confidence. The next Arcanum IV represents the omniscient and powerful Father archetype. The Fool stops being a victim of its own weak ego by learning the lesson of self-assertion – but sometimes even to the point of aggression as power and control issues tend to become dominant. Confusion between sex roles may take place as the Emperor and the Empress demonstrate the Jungian archetypes of anima and animus in action.

At the next level, the archetypal figures turn into social roles: the innocent Fool, while traveling, has lost its spirit, put on a mask and became guided by the archetype of Persona, a symbol of conformity and adjusting to societal standards and norms. The personality behind Persona may be of an obsessive-compulsive type, intolerant or passive-aggressive. A socially adapted mask may become overused to the extent of becoming a second face, to the total detriment of personality, to the neglect of inner life. Jung called this process Persona identification and considered it to be a frequent cause of psychological disorders. Persona can be identified with the Arcanum V called the Hierophant as the masculine counterpart to the High Priestess. The Hierophant (also called the Pope in some decks) represents law and order, establishment, and fundamentalism. In the readings, it sometimes indicates set in stone marriage. The imagery of the next Arcanum VI, the Lovers, represents a time for choice. Standing at the crossroads, the Fool may face a moral dilemma. In the story of Eden, the knowledge of good and evil – that is, our capacity for ethical decision-making – is symbolically related to the Tree of Knowledge with the verb 'to know' having deep erotic overtones. For Jung,

> Eros is a questionable fellow [who] belongs on one side to man's primordial animal nature [and] [o]n the other side … is related to the highest forms of the spirit. But he only thrives when spirit and instinct are in right harmony
>
> (Jung 1943, para. 32)

Such harmonious duality is symbolized by the Lovers. The Lovers indicate that the Fool is likely to make a right choice, a good decision – and especially when carried forward by the Chariot, Arcanum VII, as a symbol of controlling one's emotions and correcting the course of action by means of keeping the two horses, symbolizing the forces of creative and destructive psychic energy, in balance.

With the newly found strength and fortitude as per Arcanum VIII, Strength, the Fool becomes able to tame a lion, a fiery animal as a symbol of being 'swallowed by the unconscious' (Jung 1944a, para. 277), often with the help of counselling, as happens when this picture appears in a particular Tarot layout. Then it is ready to meet the Hermit, Arcanum IX. That is when, at the beginning of the mid-life cycle of the individuation process, self-examination and reflection produce an examined versus unexamined (read: lacking meaning) life. It is the Hermit who embodies the ancient 'Know Thyself' principle, symbolic of the search for the individuated Self. The Hermit's lantern in the picture illuminates and brings into consciousness the seeds of Gnostic knowledge. This image partakes of the Jungian archetype of the Wise Old Man and its meaning is often solitude, isolation from others in lieu of intense connection with nature for the purpose of silent meditation and self-reflection. It is a deep spiritual meaning that from now on guides the Fool, and the Wheel of Fortune (Arcanum X) starts to turn, indicating a turning point on the road to individuation. The movement of the wheel is not brought about by force. The wheel is turning effortlessly so that the old is discarded giving room to the new. But the Fool's own actions may help or hinder the turning of the wheel which may as a result reverse its course. It is time for the retribution of karma or, alternatively, for distributive justice represented by Arcanum XI, Justice. The image of the blindfolded female figure holding the scales carries the message that she is putting into practice the Jungian function of feeling reflecting precise value judgement in the context of a particular situation. Yet, it is not that Justice rules blindly in accord with the universal moral law. For Jung, 'morality was not brought down on tables of stones from Sinai and imposed on people, but is a function of the human soul, as old as humanity itself' (Jung 1943, para. 30). The diversity of experiential situations that abound in life disrupts preconceived judgements based on a strict moral code. In his introduction to Neumann (1969), Jung stressed that the presupposed universal rules of human conduct are 'at most provisional solutions, but never lead to those critical decisions which are the turning points in a man's life' (Jung 1949, para. 1412); that 'The formulation of ethical rules is not only difficult but actually impossible because one can hardly think of a single rule that would not be reversed under certain conditions' (Jung 1949, para. 1413) and that

> through the new ethic, the ego-consciousness is ousted from its central position in a psyche organized on the lines of a monarchy or totalitarian state, its place being taken by wholeness or the Self, which is now recognized as central.
>
> (Jung 1949, para. 1419; see also Neumann 1969, pp. 13–18)

Human ethical choices sometimes demand a sacrifice, symbolized in the image of the Hanged Man, Arcanum XII, with the figure in the picture suspended between the sky and the ground without a solid foundation under its feet. This is a testing period accompanied by the loss of direction. The Hanged Man presents a challenge of a helpless moment; yet, sacrificing the old set of beliefs and reversing the point of view brings forth a new level of awareness. Jung would have agreed: 'A great reversal of standpoint, calling for much sacrifice, is needed before we can see the world as "given" by the very nature of the psyche' (Jung 1935/1953, para. 841). The ultimate sacrifice is death itself, and Jung pointed out that many initiation rites often include a figurative death as a symbol for the reversal of values so as 'to restore to the soul the divinity it lost at birth' (Jung 1935/1953, para. 842). Sure enough, the Arcanum XIII that follows the Hanged Man is called Death, a symbol of transformation, transition, change and renewal. Old and restrictive viewpoints, a stagnant environment, whatever was status quo for the Fool, are now in the process of evolution. The Fool is about to leave the old ego behind, and the dynamic of this process may be quite painful. It is in the symbolic death that the ego encounters a confrontation with the potential Self. Edinger noted that 'the vicissitudes of psychological development can be understood in terms of the changing relation between ego and Self at various stages of psychic growth' (Edinger 1992, p. 4), and the Fool's archetypal journey represents the progressive evolution of consciousness. But do not rush, advises Temperance, Arcanum XIV, a symbol of moderation and patience. The maxim 'Nothing in excess' as the virtue of Temperance was as much celebrated in the Hellenic world as the 'Know Thyself' principle; both were inscribed on the Temple of Apollo at Delphi. The challenging task of the ego transcending toward the Self can often usurp one's power. The Fool may feel enslaved by a symbolic image of the Devil, Arcanum XV, as the archetype of the Shadow. The conscious brightness of ego-centredness always casts its own shadow that consists of impulses, complexes, shameful desires, denials, self-indulgence, or being a slave to one's primitive instincts. The chains in this image are symbolic of sexual compulsion, poor impulse control or low frustration tolerance. It may be a fear, a superficial complex of superiority when in fact one feels inferior. In the context of interpersonal relationships, the Devil may point to co-dependency issues. Intra-psychically it may be a deeply ingrained fear of breaking loose, like battered spouses afraid to leave and, overwhelmed by submissiveness or sexual/economic dependency, continuing to stay in an abusive relationship. As the archetypal figure, the Shadow calls for a deep exploration so that its presence in the psyche and its poisonous quality is recognized and integrated into consciousness. Otherwise it may fall deeper and deeper into the unconscious where it will continue to work even if denied to oneself. Archetypes are surely 'the ruling powers' (Jung 1943, para. 151).

The awareness of the collective Shadow is equally necessary. At the level of culture and society, the Shadow encompasses those outside the norms of the established moral or legal order and social system such as 'criminals, psychotics, misfits, scapegoats' (Samuels 1985, p. 66). It is not only that these figures belong to the category of outsiders – significantly, it is dominant culture itself that fails to assimilate its own Shadow and as a result often implements the scapegoat policy. While ego-consciousness focuses on indubitable and unequivocal moral principles, these very principles crumble under the '*compensatory significance of the shadow* in the light of ethical responsibility' (Jung 1949, para. 1410, emphasis in original; in Neumann 1969, p. 12), the neglect of which tends to precipitate multiple evil consequences in the world. The unconscious Shadow rules one-sidedly unless integrated into the whole of personality. In the absence of integration it can create a sealed aggressive world until starting spontaneously to act out, often in the form of destructive climax or psychotic breakdown. Referring to real-life events of the archetypal scope, Jung invoked the mythology of the Nordic God Odin, or Wotan, and commented that it was changed into the devil by Christendom. The symbolic Wotan tends to go underground and remain invisible but still dormant in the collective unconscious. The collective Shadow partakes of the 'impersonal, imperceptible but terrific power.... This ghastly power is mostly explained by fear of the neighbouring nation' (Jung 1947, p. 78, apropos the horrors of World War Two), the projection of their own Shadow that results in closing borders and building walls. The Devil is one of the most powerful symbols in the Tarot deck and a detailed exploration of its connotations, if this card comes up in a reading, will in turn empower the person! But because it is not easy to break out of the Devil's chains, the new awareness may come in the form of a shock as manifested by the Tower, Arcanum XVI, which breaks everything that is counterproductive to the Fool's journey ahead. This image 'heralds an individuation crisis, a major step in psychological development which requires that old conditions be destroyed to make room for the new' (Edinger 1992, pp. 80–81).

In the Tarot feminist interpretation (Gearhart and Rennie 1981), the Tower signifies radical intervention, revolution, overthrowing of false consciousness, violent social conflict and change, destruction of the old order on a grand scale, and release from imprisonment in the phallic structure during the very process of its demolition. The complex process of individuation can take us to the limit of endurance as exemplified in the preceding Arcanum (Death). Time may appear to stand still (Temperance) especially when we stay in bondage to the archetypal Shadow in the image of the Devil. So sometimes we have to be hit by symbolic lightning to break the towering prison of the outlived habits. It might be a moment of the sudden truth shaking one's security – yet providing illumination, a light of awakening, represented by the Star, Arcanum XVII. The naked woman pouring waters in the midst of organic nature represents purification by the stream that washes away the remnants of dark matter, the explosion of which was manifested in the imagery of the preceding Tower. The Star of hope, healing, inspiration and spiritual baptism is now accompanying the Fool. For Jung, just 'as evening gives birth to morning, so from the darkness arises a new light, the *stella matutina*' (Jung 1943/1948, para. 299). But that is where one must pay attention to the warning sign of the Moon, Arcanum XVIII. After the hopefulness symbolized by the Star, the Fool is distracted by the cold light of the Moon, sometimes succumbing to illusions or even delusions. Obscurity is here like a fog between the ego and the Self. This image correlates with Jung's notion that the individuation process may become dangerous in case the unconscious totally takes over the psyche. There is an importance nuance here, though: the problem is not so much that the unconscious may possess one's psyche, but that such possession occurs when one's current level of consciousness is too low to accommodate the upheavals of real life with its conflicting experiences and turbulent relations. Still, after the moonlit night, the Fool can be reborn in the image of the Sun (Arcanum IXX). The *puer* has grown up and now embodies the archetypal divine child as a symbol for Rebirth, a child always already been born into the wholeness of the Self.

The next Arcanum XX is Judgement, a symbol of resurrection when the sound of the trumpet in the picture leads to the soul's spiritual awakening and also to the body's symbolic reincarnation into new experiences and becoming free to act in a new way in real life. The symbolism of the Judgement indicates self-renewal, vivification of life and integration into the world when, as Marie-Louise von Franz put it, waking up from Hades and standing up from the grave (as, non-incidentally, is portrayed in this picture). The Gospel song says that Gabriel's trumpet calls us toward the New Jerusalem as a symbol of spiritual restoration, a futuristic goal of humanity – and, respectively, the end of the Fool's quest portrayed in the last Arcanum, XXI, called the World. The feeling of taking upon ourselves ethical responsibility *in* the world and *for* the world is embodied in this image, also called the Universe in some decks. The circular mandala in this image conveys the meaning of having completed the search for the individuated Self – but with a qualification. It represents a continuum, that is, the idea that individuation is a never-ending process in the changing circumstances of experience. The ever-expanding and varying multitude of experiential situations and events always presents new challenges: the story of the Fool's journey describes, in a symbolic form, the real-life journeys of us, human beings who must learn many existential lessons. At the deeper level, the image of the Fool indicates a divine spark, a trace of spirit in matter that becomes fully integrated in the imagery of the World. It is the integration of the unconscious by means of narrating the meanings of images that ultimately creates

[The] widened consciousness [which] is no longer that … egotistical bundle of personal wishes, fears, hopes, ambitions which always have to be compensated or corrected by the unconscious counter-tendencies; instead it is a function of relationship to the world of objects, bringing the individual into … indissoluble communion with the world at large.

(Jung 1928b, para. 275)

For Jung, the Self is not simply the centre of the personality but the whole circumference partaking of the mandala in the picture of the World as a symbol of conscious and unconscious aspects integrated together, thereby creating psychic wholeness. The dancing female figure surrounded by a garland relates to the Dionysian mysteries, to joy and fulfilment, to the fullness of Pleroma, to soul or anima discovered in the rational, Apollonian, world. The totality of the psyche exceeds our mortal bodies and encompasses immortal souls blending into the ultimate archetype of the Self in unity with the world soul, *Anima Mundi*. The World conveys the metaphysics of the universe as a rhythmic process, a series of creative acts. Still, as subjected 'to the interference … of the autonomy and numinosity of archetypal processes' (Jung 1963, p. 53) we may never reach the World in our search for Gnosis during our lifetime. The field of collective unconscious can never be fully exhausted because of the archetypes' 'almost limitless wealth of reference' (Jung 1934/1954, para. 80). The wholeness and oneness with the World may be an ideal limit, and the archetypal Fool will continue its pilgrimage starting again from *zero* and encountering the symbolism of Tarot Arcana again and again: it is 'only possible to live the fullest life when we are in harmony with these symbols; wisdom is a return to them' (Jung 1930–1931, para. 794). Each new product of integration is bound to be 'challenged from within. So if there is a merger, it is to be seen as the starting point for a further dynamic' (Samuels 1985, p. 48) represented by the various constellations of Tarot images in specific layouts as a function of new experiences, diverse situations, relationships with significant others, and novel empirical contexts.

The journey through Major Arcana is complemented by the multiplicity of practical real-life concerns embodied in Minor Arcana (Figure 12.2). The symbolism of the four suits in the deck relates to four Jungian functions: intuition is strongly present in cups, sensation is linked to pentacles, thinking is correlated with a sharp sword, and feeling is likely to manifest by wands. Minor cards reflect typical human emotions such as love, trust, fulfilment – but also frustration, anger, depression, 'pain in the neck', fantasizing, insecurity, anxiety, confusion, exhaustion, being overwhelmed, etc – and narrating the images brings those issues and affects into sharp focus.

For example, the image of the Five of Cups with its sad figure in a black cloak presents us with the feeling of loss, sorrow or mourning. The three cups in front of the central figure are obviously empty, carrying the message of futility and wasted efforts. Yet, should the figure turn around, they would see two full cups standing

Figure 12.2 The Minor Arcana.

erect and representing new knowledge, new fulfilment, a different point of view or perspective. The Three of Swords is one of the most dramatic pictures, literally portraying a crying and broken heart as a result of being pierced by three swords. It depicts separation, severance, divorce, and similar experiences. It may also indicate a surgical intervention, quite often open-heart surgery. In either case, the experience is painful. The imagery of the Ten of Wands brings human endurance to the brink: the figure is struggling under the heavy load on its shoulders. The Minor Arcana tell us multiple stories about feeling happy or being sad, making plans or breaking promises, becoming engaged or getting out of an abusive relationship, starting a new venture or experiencing separation anxiety. The list is endless, and the real-life situations always create new contexts and encounters that call for new evaluations, new meanings, and deep self-knowledge.

The case study, in brief

Jung's depth psychology in its practical sense incorporates 'the paradigm of an *active, interventionist therapist*' (Samuels 1985, p. 197, emphasis in original) who facilitates a session by means of interpreting images that appear as unconscious material in the analysand's dreams, or in the course of active imagination – or in artefacts such as drawings or pictures, including the Tarot images. Below is the Tarot layout for 'Anita' (Figure 12.3) who wanted to have a reading for an unspecified family problem. While Anita inquired whether the reading would reflect on her husband, she provided no other information prior to the reading. Her narrative is one of 15 documented case-studies earlier analysed in detail (Semetsky 2011) and is reproduced here with the permission from the publishers and in its heavily abbreviated form. The descriptions of the cards' positions in Figure 12.3 are also largely omitted. Not all archetypal constellations are narrated either, for brevity.

The central position – the very problematic issue for Anita – was indeed taken by the Emperor representing the male energy of the Father-figure, the omnipotent animus. Yet, in case of being 'anima/animus ridden' (Hopcke 1992, p.91), the individuals may display the elements of psychopathology. Driven by the overacting animus, it was extremely important for Anita's husband to maintain his status as the head of the family, but – being 'crossed' by the Ace of Swords – there was a constant struggle to overcome multiple obstacles. Anita's husband unconsciously needed to compensate and prove himself worthy by projecting the strength of character in the image of the King of Swords. Did he feel that he was unjustly treated, as suggested by the Seven of Swords? Anita confirmed that a job he expected to get was taken by someone else. Thus, her husband's feeling of defeat, in view of his desire to be the breadwinner who can support his family and keep it safe and secure (the Ten of Pentacles), was a truly emotional issue affecting his psyche. While her husband was trying to carry the load of his responsibilities all by himself, Anita – in sharp contrast with the rest of the cards – manifested total gloom and hopelessness as depicted by the Ten of Swords in the overall position. She appeared to be overwhelmed with the feeling of their

Figure 12.3 Anita's layout.

family being ruined as if cursed with bad luck. Unable to contain her emotions, she displayed rather destructive behaviour (the Five of Swords). She seemed to fight with her spouse, blaming him for all misfortunes instead of supporting him. Anita confirmed that they argued: she did blame him and, sure enough, accused him of having been cursed. The negative energy projected by Anita was making her spouse's burden even heavier, reaching the point of becoming unbearable (the Ten of Wands) as if one more straw would break his back! Did he threaten to leave but stayed at home because of the children? The Knight of Swords tends to manifest the hastily thought and impulsive behaviour; yet, it was contained by the Page of Cups that embodied the image of the children.

Under the circumstances, Anita needed to accept the present limitations and to hold on tightly (the Four of Pentacles) to what was most important: her family. She needed to be the one to organize her willpower in order to get out of the current conflict. The image of the Chariot promised that she should be able to control her negative emotions while the Magician, functioning as a guardian angel, will be protecting their family and symbolically providing the tools to reassure and empower Anita. Controlling her emotions should enable Anita to get out of the self-imposed feeling of being in a vicious circle (the dark side of the archetypal World) of bad luck. At this point Anita, free-associating with the reading, interjected saying that her husband's misfortune started with the recent death of his father. Indeed, the Emperor that embodies the Father archetype may also manifest as an actual father in real life. Anita said how important it was for her to hear her own voice and that she was now getting an insight with regard to what really created the problem. The Ten of Cups represented the image of a happy family life based on mutual support, and the Four of Cups provided important advice: in the case of a new job opportunity, instead of putting pressure on her husband and thus increasing his tension and anxiety, Anita should let go, thus preventing it becoming the problematic issue even if a job is not offered to him at this time. But, Anita asked, how could she get out of the blackness of her current state of mind? She picked up a card from the deck that, upon turning it face-up, happened to be the Page of Pentacles. It carried the message from the collective unconscious that her studies (she was a graduate student) and the whole learning environment would provide a support system. With the past, present and potential future combined together in the same layout, Anita was able to not only observe the unconscious factors in her psyche but, significantly, self-reflectively also *participate* in the archetypal process of becoming aware of the unconscious and acquiring much needed self-knowledge that afforded her an insight into the meaning of both her own and her significant other's experience. Her narrative reinforced the value of images that created 'the true iconoclast ... which explodes [with] allegorical meanings, releasing startling new insights' (Hillman 1989, p. 25) and encouraging Anita to take actions that were earlier unthinkable.

A concluding remark

The hermeneutic of Tarot allows us to 'hear' a subtle voice of the unconscious as the 'most natural thing imaginable.... You can describe it as mere "associating" ... or as a "meditation" [and] a real colloquy becomes possible when the ego acknowledges the existence of a partner to the discussion' (Jung 1940/1950, paras. 236–237). Still, the process of narrating the pictorial text is not without its nuances. Surely, archetypes are units of meaning that are subject to being 'apprehended intuitively' (Jung 1940, para. 302), and it is nearly impossible to dig out a single archetype from the living tissue of the psyche. Thus, a 'situational variable' represented by a reader is of paramount importance and demands the presence of ethical responsibility coupled with integrity, sensitivity and intuition. Jung described intuition as a particular psychological non-rational function that transmits perceptions in an unconscious way, and the conscious mind is 'extended forward by intuitions which are conditioned partly by archetypes' (Jung 1944a, para. 175). As June Singer (1985) commented, Jungian analysts must be seasoned and scorched in addition to being wise and compassionate. Analogously, only a genuine reader, who *lived through* the meanings of the archetypal images in her own experience, the traumatic events notwithstanding, will be able to guide people seeking a Tarot reading: one cannot take others further than where one has already travelled. The reader must be individuated; her unconscious must be integrated: this is a necessary precondition for conducting readings and narrating pictorial stories. Perhaps that's why Tarot as a cultural practice has historically had such a dismal reputation: rarely readers satisfy this condition. Nor are they trained mental health professionals, Jungian analysts notwithstanding. Rather than empowering people, they may in fact propagate their clients' fears and anxieties or, worse, mislead them by rigid and forceful 'instructions' thereby closing multiple opportunities that people would have taken if not for their 'fortune' being already 'told'. Indeed, 'psyche matters' (Romanyshyn 2007, p. 38): the unconscious is embodied in the material medium of the Tarot pictures and, respectively, real life decision-making is embodied in the archetypal symbolism, thus demonstrating the significance of Jungian phenomenology of the Self.

Note

All illustrations are from the Rider-Waite Tarot Deck. Reproduced by permission of US Games Systems Inc., Stamford, CT, USA. © 1971 US Games Systems, Inc. Further reproduction prohibited.

References

Belenky, M. F., Clinchy, B. M., Goldberger, N. R. and Tarule, J. M. (1986) *Women's Ways of Knowing*. New York: Basic Books.
Edinger, E. (1992) *Ego & Archetype: Individuation and the Religious Function of the Psyche*. Boston & London: Shambhala.
Gad, I. (1994) *Tarot and Individuation: Correspondences with Cabala and Alchemy*. York Beach, ME: Nicholas-Hays.
Gearhart, S. and Rennie, S. (1981) *A Feminist Tarot*. Boston: Alyson Publications.
Hederman, M. P. (2003) *Tarot: Talisman or Taboo? Reading the World as Symbol*. Dublin: Currach Press.
Hillman, J. (1989) *A Blue Fire: Selected Writings by James Hillman*. Edited by T. Moore. New York: Harper Collins.

Hopcke, R. H. (1992) *A Guided Tour of the Collected Works of C. G. Jung*. Boston & London: Shambhala.

Jung, C. G.: Unless otherwise stated, the following are from *The Collected Works of C. G. Jung* (CW) London: Routledge & Kegan Paul/Princeton, NJ: Princeton University Press:

Jung, C. G. (1916) The structure of the unconscious. (CW 7).

Jung, C. G. (1928a) Child development and education. (CW 17).

Jung, C. G. (1928b) The relations between the ego and the unconscious. (CW 7).

Jung, C. G. (1929) The significance of constitution and hereditary in psychology. (CW 8).

Jung, C. G. (1930–1931) The stages of life. (CW 8).

Jung, C. G. (1934/1954) Archetypes of the collective unconscious. (CW 9i).

Jung, C. G. (1935/1953) On the 'Tibetan Book of the Dead'. (CW 11).

Jung, C. G. (1940) The psychology of the child archetype. (CW 9i).

Jung, C. G. (1940/1950) Concerning rebirth. (CW 9i).

Jung, C. G. (1942/1954) Transformation symbolism in the Mass. (CW 11).

Jung, C. G. (1943) On the psychology of the unconscious. (CW 7).

Jung, C. G. (1943/1948) The spirit Mercurius. (CW 13).

Jung, C. G. (1944a) *Psychology and Alchemy*. (CW 12).

Jung, C. G. (1944b) The holy men of India. (CW 11).

Jung, C. G. (1945/1948) On the nature of dreams. (CW 8).

Jung, C. G. (1947) *Essays on Contemporary Events*. London: Kegan Paul.

Jung, C. G. (1947/1954) On the nature of the psyche. (CW 8).

Jung, C. G. (1948) A review of the complex theory. (CW 8).

Jung, C. G. (1949) Forward to Neumann: 'Depth psychology and a new ethic'. (CW 18).

Jung, C. G. (1958) The transcendent function. (CW 8).

Jung, C. G. (1952a) *Symbols of Transformation*. (CW 5).

Jung, C. G. (1952b) Answer to Job. (CW 11).

Jung, C. G. (1952c) Synchronicity: An acausal connecting principle. (CW 8).

Jung, C. G. (1963) *Memories, Dreams, Reflections*. New York: Pantheon Books.

Meier, C. A. (Ed.) (2001) *Atom and Archetype: The Pauli/Jung Letters, 1932–1958.* Princeton, NJ: Princeton University Press.

Neumann, E. (1969) *Depth Psychology and a New Ethic*. London: Hodder & Stoughton.

Nichols, S. (1980) *Jung and Tarot: An Archetypal Journey.* York Beach, ME: Samuel Weiser.

Pauli, W. (1994) *Writings on Physics and Philosophy*. Berlin: Springer-Verlag.

Roberts, R. (1987) *The Original Tarot and You*. San Anselmo, CA: Vernon Equinox Press.

Romanyshyn, R. (2007) *The Wounded Researcher: Research With Soul In Mind*. Spring Journal Books.

Ryce-Menuhin, J. (1992) *Jungian Sandplay: The Wonderful Therapy*. London: Routledge.

Samuels, A. (1985) *Jung and the Post-Jungians*. London & New York: Routledge.

Samuels, A., Shorter, B. and Plaut, F. (1986) *A Critical Dictionary of Jungian Analysis*. London & New York: Routledge.

Semetsky, I. (2011) *Re-Symbolization of the Self: Human Development and Tarot Hermeneutic*. Rotterdam: Sense Publishers.

Semetsky, I. (2013) *The Edusemiotics of Images: Essays on the Art-Science of Tarot.* Rotterdam: Sense Publishers.

Shlain, L. (1998) *The Alphabet versus the Goddess: The Conflict Between Word and Image.* New York: Viking.

Singer, J. (1985) The Education of the Analyst. In M. Stein (Ed.), *Jungian Analysis.* Boston & London: Shambhala.

Whitmont, E. (1985) Recent influences on the practice of Jungian analysis. In M. Stein (Ed.), *Jungian Analysis.* Boston & London: Shambhala.

Index

active imagination *see* imagination
Adler, Alfred 24, 95
affect 4, 21, 149–150, 153, 161, 168, 183, 233; primitive 215; turn to 7, 26; *see also* emotions; *narratio*
affective 10, 22, 160, 194; 'polarization' 197; *see also* emotional
agency 16, 47, 73, 74, 167, 170, 174, 178, 179, 209
alchemy 22, 61, 101, 125, 134, 222
Allport, Gordon 23–24
amplification 69, 72, 94, 106, 150, 175, 207, 209, 211, 214–215, 223
analytical psychology 1, 4, 6, 10, 53, 92–93, 95, 108–109, 116, 134–135, 173, 205, 206; *see also* Jungian psychology
anima 59, 88, 92, 133, 144, 151, 153, 181, 228, 233, 235
animus 17, 133, 150, 153, 228, 235
Anthropocene 7, 168, 179–180, 183
anthropology 5, 166, 167, 172, 175, 177, 180
Anthropos 179–180
anxiety 39, 52, 61, 63, 149, 189, 211, 233, 235, 237
Aquarius, age of 118, 181, 182
archetype 10, 21, 23, 168, 220, 221–225, 227, 231, 233, 237–238; child (divine) 217; Father 228, 237; Mother 228; in Plato 164–165; *puer* 133, 144–145, 225, 232; Shadow 230–231; Trickster 15, 133, 227; Wise Old Man 229; *see also* anima; animus
Aristotle 18, 78, 87, 115, 127–128, 155, 156–157, 165
Augustine, Saint 3, 42, 43, 71–72, 75, 76–77, 81, 82–83, 85–86, 88; *Confessions* 3, 42, 43, 71, 75–76, 77, 83

autobiography: as argumentation 74–75; as narrative 2, 71–74, 82–83; *see also* self-narration; self-narrative
Autobiography see Vico, Giambattista

Bachelard, Gaston 27
Bakhtin, Mikhail 5, 12–13, 15, 27, 88, 192
Bartlett, Frederic Charles 16, 17
Benjamin, Walter 71–72, 76, 183–184
bereavement *see* grief
Bruner, Gerome Seymour 5, 18–20, 27, 35
Buddhism 58, 176

Campbell, Joseph 119, 224
Cartesian 13, 15, 27, 77–78, 166, 222; mind-body problem 14–15; *see also* Descartes
Christianity 85, 104, 117, 134; Judeo-Christian 114, 123; *see also* myth, Christian
co-individuation 175–176, 179, 181, 182–183, 184
collective unconscious *see* unconscious, the
compensation 108, 227
complex (autonomous) 20, 45, 81, 84, 104, 107, 168, 207, 212, 216–217, 221, 230; *see also* constellation; ego-complex
constellation 20, 47, 175, 177, 178, 183–184, 221, 224; *see also* complex; ego-complex
Confessions see Augustine, Saint
consciousness 5, 19, 21, 41, 56, 101, 132, 133, 146, 150, 153, 166, 168–170, 175, 176, 182, 225, 229; analogical 177; contrasted with the unconscious 17, 20, 150, 193–194, 207, 227; coming into 3, 6, 24, 38, 45, 83, 84, 205–206, 223;

For Product Safety Concerns and Information please contact our EU
representative GPSR@taylorandfrancis.com
Taylor & Francis Verlag GmbH, Kaufingerstraße 24, 80331 München, Germany